GIVEN TO THE GODDESS

GIVEN TO THE GODDESS

•

South Indian Devadasis

and the Sexuality *of* Religion

LUCINDA RAMBERG

•

DUKE UNIVERSITY PRESS   *Durham and London* 2014

© 2014 Duke University Press
All rights reserved
Printed in the United States
of America on acid-free paper ∞
Cover design by Natalie Smith
Typeset in Minion Pro by
Tseng Information Systems, Inc.

Library of Congress Cataloging-
in-Publication Data
Ramberg, Lucinda, 1962–
Given to the goddess : South Indian devadasis and
the sexuality of religion / Lucinda Ramberg.
pages cm
Includes bibliographical references and index.
ISBN 978-0-8223-5710-0 (cloth : alk. paper)
ISBN 978-0-8223-5724-7 (pbk. : alk. paper)
1. Devadasis. 2. Yellamma (Hindu deity)
3. Sex—Religious aspects—Hinduism. I. Title.
BL1237.58.D48R3635 2014
294.5′2114—dc23
2014012185

Cover art: Photo by Brett Isis Fisher.

In memory of

two renegade priests

KRISHNABAI KADAPURE

1963–2003

and

JENNY BALLARD RAMBERG

1935–89

CONTENTS

Acknowledgments ix

Introduction: Gods, Gifts, Trouble 1

PART I · GODS

1. Yellamma and Her Sisters:
Kinship among Goddesses and Others 39

2. Yellamma, Her Wives, and
the Question of Religion 71

PART II · GIFTS

3. Tantra, Shakta, Yellamma 113

4. The Giving of Daughters:
Sexual Economy, Sexual Agency,
and the "Traffic" in Women 142

PART III · TROUBLE

5. Kinship Trouble 181

6. Troubling Kinship 213

Notes 223

Glossary 247

Bibliography 251

Index 270

ACKNOWLEDGMENTS

I have spent many a solitary hour bent over notebooks and computers, but I have done none of this writing, or the research leading to it, alone.

Forms of institutional and material support for this project were generously granted by the Magistretti Fellowship at the Center for the Study of Sexual Culture, the Human Rights Center, and the Department of Anthropology at the University of California (UC), Berkeley; the American Institute for Indian Studies; and the National Institutes of Health, Alcohol Research Group (NIAAA predoctoral fellowship grant T32 AA007240); the Andrew Mellon Foundation; the Department of Gender & Women's Studies at the University of Kentucky; the Women's Studies in Religion Program at Harvard Divinity School; and the Department of Anthropology, Program in Feminist, Gender, & Sexuality Studies, and the Society for the Humanities at Cornell University.

Kathryn Poethig introduced me to the reform of the brides of Yellamma by the brides of Christ (Poethig 1992), thereby planting the seed for the project that became my dissertation and resulted in this book. This was but the beginning of the many years of lively intellectual engagement and generous emotional and practical support from teachers, colleagues, and friends in India and the United States that made it possible for me to bring this project to fruition.

My greatest debt is to the women who permitted me to follow them around and met my intrusive and stubborn questions with patience and humor. I owe the deepest pleasures of my fieldwork to them. Listening to their stories, laughing with them, and sharing food in their homes or mine brought me much joy. In particular I am grateful to the woman I call Yamuna, who drew me into her network of kin and appointed her sons to look after my household. They have continued to generously nourish and shelter me on my return trips to the town I call Nandipur in the Belgaum district of Karnataka. Among those who call Nandipur their home, I am most grateful to Jayashree, Laxshmibai, Sharabai, Kasturi, Sangeeta, Satish, Shivaram and Machindra, in addition to all those who participated in my survey of households and granted me interviews.

Across northern Karnataka and southern Maharastra, women who had been given to the goddess Yellamma shared their life stories and vantage on the world with me. Their contributions provided the foundation of this study. In particular, I am thankful to the members of the Veshya AIDS Mukabala Parishad in Sangli, Maharastra, whose HIV peer education program and rights-based organizing provide an extraordinary model for what collectives of sex workers might accomplish. For their provocations, skepticism of research, and generosity of time and conversation, I am grateful. I also want to acknowledge members of the Shakti Collective in Gokak and the staff of the Belgaum Integrated Rural Development Society, who took me on my first trip to meet Yellamma in her main temple at Saundatti.

Ambuja Kowlgi's skills as a fieldworker were indispensable, and her deep intelligence and light spirit continue to inspire me. Jyoti Hiremath's companionship, extraordinary patience, and willing hard work made my research labors in rural South India possible. To both of them I owe gratitude for linguistic and cultural mediation and faithful research assistance through till the end. I thank Jyoti's family for forgoing her presence in deference to her work with me.

I have received valuable guidance from many scholars and teachers within the Indian academy. Amrit Srinivasan's early encouragements emboldened me to undertake this project. Anil Mudbidri's assistance in thinking about problems of political economy and caste mark the book I came to write. K. S. Nair and R. D. Gambhir at Pune University, Hussain Khan at Karnatak University, Jayashree Ramakrishna at the National Institute of Mental Health and Neuro Sciences, and Janaki Abraham and Satendra Kumar at the Delhi School of Economics all graciously invited me to speak and teach in their departments and facilitated various forms of institutional support. I owe my facility in Kannada to Lingadevaru Halemane, Suma Pramod, and A. Murigeppa.

The shape of this work has also been influenced by conversations with researchers and activists working on sexuality rights in Karnataka and Maharastra. Meena Sesho's abundant energy, savvy, and nuanced reflections—not to mention food, drink, and bedding—nourished me. I am grateful to Vijay Thakur, an early provocateur in the formation of my research plans.

I thank Vinay Chandan for sharing his own writing and thinking on sexuality, for innumerable confabs at Koshi's, venturing to Kerala, and tempting me into Cubban Park to discuss *The History of Sexuality*. Sandhya Rao peered over her glasses, asked me wonderful questions, and invited me to her home. For my stay at the Dharni guest house and subtle assistance with translations, I am grateful to Chandra Shekhar Balachandran. For urban respite in Mumbai and endless kitchen table talk about the puzzles of fieldwork and anthropological endeavors in the field of sex and labor, I thank Svati Shah. For companionship in Dharwad and for a model of composure in the field, I acknowledge Treena Orchard. For respite in Goa and always compelling discussions, I am grateful to Cath Sluggett.

Friends in Bangalore sustained me, and thus made this work possible, in innumerable ways. Viva Kermani has kindly opened her home to me on many occasions. Superna Bedi refreshed my sense of irony with her amazement at the folly of my anthropological endeavor. Saras Ganapathy watered my spirit with her effervescent intelligence and warmth; put me up in Bangalore, Bombay, and Dharwar; and introduced me to her husband, Girish Karnad, who delighted me with stories about Brahmanized former devadasis.

At UC Berkeley my early formation as a medical anthropologist and scholar of South Asia took place under the close attention of Lawrence Cohen. His formidable intellectual capacities and spectacular kindness have made possible for me a flourishing of the mind I had not been able to anticipate. Calling the liberal tendencies of feminist theory and politics into question is a project I share with Saba Mahmood, and she continues to be a generous interlocutor who adds conceptual clarity and rigor to my efforts in this vein. Other members of the faculty at Berkeley made critical contributions to my thinking, especially Paola Bacchetta, Philippe Bourgois, Cori Hayden, Trinh T. Minh-ha, Raka Ray, Nancy Scheper-Hughes, and Charis Thompson.

The project took shape as a book under the thoughtful attention of many generous friends and colleagues. Susan Bordo, David Greenberg, Girish Karnad, Ambuja Kowlgi, Anil Mudbidri, Gayatri Reddy, Laurie Schaffner, Karen Tice, and Helen Ulrich all read the whole manuscript at one stage or another, saving me from infelicities and errors and making many useful editorial suggestions. I owe a particular debt to three readers for the Press, two of whom have revealed themselves to be Anupama Rao and Éric Fassin. The generous and thoughtful comments provided by all three readers have helped me hone my prose and elaborate my arguments throughout. Miriam Angress, my editor at Duke University Press, has been unfailingly encouraging and responsive. I am grateful to Sara Leone for her graciousness and expertise in shepherding this book through production and Jeanne Ferris for zealous copyediting.

At UC Berkeley feedback on one or more chapters from Elizabeth Bernstein, Cristiana Giordano, Rebecca Hall, Laura Hubbard, Katherine Lemons, Tahir Naqvi, Anand Pandian, Elizabeth Roberts, Christopher Roebuck, Dar Rudnyckyj, Lisa Stevenson, Fouzieyha Towghi, and Chris Vasantkumar taught what my writing was and was not doing and made it possible for me to add lucidity and nuance to my prose. Comments on the introduction from my colleagues at the Society for the Humanities at Cornell University in 2007–8—especially Brett de Bary, Petrius Liu, Suman Seth, and Micol Siegel—and from members of the Dakshinapatta Group at Duke University—especially Lauren Leve, Sumiti Ramaswamy, Harris Soloman, and Ajanta Subramanian—proved instrumental to the final shape it has taken. Anne Braude, Benjamin Dunning, Susan Crawford Sullivan, Tania Oldenhage, and Solimar Otero at the Women's Studies in Religion Program at Harvard Divinity School helped me clarify the stakes of the book for feminist scholars of religion. Over delicious meals and shared prose in Cambridge, Massachusetts, Sarah Pinto and Jon Anjaria became delightful companions in ethnographic endeavor in India.

I have had the good fortune to work at two excellent universities as an Assistant Professor. I am grateful for the warm welcome and rich intellectual engagement extended to me by my colleagues in the Program in Gender & Women's Studies, the Committee on Social Theory and the Department of Anthropology at the University of Kentucky. In particular, comments on one or two chapters from Cristina Alcade, Erin Koch, and Sarah Lyon clarified the possibilities of this ethnography. Srimati Basu and Emily Burrill, with whom I first began exchanging work in the context of a UK writing group *cum* roving dinner party formation, have become invaluable and cherished interlocutors. I thank my colleagues here at Cornell University in the Department of Anthropology; Feminist, Gender, & Sexuality Studies; the South Asia Program; and the Society for the Humanities for their inspirational thinking and essential support. In particular, Shelley Feldman, Chris Garces, Billie Jean Isbell, Stacey Langwick, Masha Raskolnikov, Camille Robcis, Courtney Roby, Steven Sangren, Neelam Sethi, Rebecca Stolzfus, Sera Young, Amy Villarejo, Sarah Warner, and Andrew Wilford have offered pithy and useful commentary on one or more of the chapters. I am especially grateful to Durba Ghosh, Saida Hoizic, Amy

Villarejo, and Dagmawi Woubshet for superb editorial suggestions and incisive questions.

Over the years of revision and rewriting that have led to this book, earlier versions of portions of it have been published elsewhere, as follows: a part of chapter 2 in "Magical Hair as Dirt: Ecstatic Bodies and Postcolonial Reform in South India," *Culture, Medicine and Psychiatry*, Vol. 33 (4): 501–22; portions of chapter 4 in "When the Devi is Your Husband: Sacred Marriage and Sexual Economy in South India," *Feminist Studies* 37 (1): 28–60; and portions of chapters 4 and 5 as "Troubling Kinship: Sacred Marriage and Gender Configuration in South India," *American Ethnologist* 40 (4): 661–75. I thank the editors of and readers for these journals, their comments and suggestions have helped me to refine my arguments.

Talks about and discussions of my research with colleagues at the following institutions have helped me refine and specify my claims: the University of Pune, Karnatak University, Cornell University, Butler University, Indiana University, Harvard University, Syracuse University, Hamilton College, and Duke University. I thank all of these colleagues and friends for helping me write a better book than I might have done alone. What errors and limitations remain are my own.

Love and friendship have made me and this writing possible. In the San Francisco Bay Area and beyond, through several academic peregrinations I have been buoyed along for over two decades now by Lisa Fiorelli, Nina Haft, and Margaret Thompson. In Lexington I was treated to extraordinary hospitality and delicious cooking in the homes of Suzanne Pucci and John Erickson, Srimati Basu and Tiku Rawat, Karen Tice and Dwight Billings, and Kate Black and Kathi Kern. In addition to the Cornell colleagues I have mentioned above, I have been warmly gathered in to life in Ithaca by Ester Fernández, Arnika Fuhrmann, Andrea Hammer, Billie Jean Isbell, Hope Mandeville, and Lyrae van Clief-Stefanon. Writing retreats with Micol Siegel, Emily Burrill, and Cristiana Giordano have sustained my spirit and spurred on my revisions. I want to thank Amy Huber, who accompanied me on my first research trip and who always knew, even when I did not, that I could see this project through. I am grateful to Brett Fisher for her generous correspondence and beautiful photographs of the denizens of Nandipur. Delightful humor and daily provocations from Susanne Deising saw me through the dissertation phase of the manuscript. Jane O'Connor's grounded and gentle encouragement got me through the first draft of the book. The zany humor and sweet strong presence that Casey Wenz offers helped me finish this book at the writing table she built for me.

Finally, I want to thank my natal family. My sister Julia Ramberg brings both serious determination and playful abandon to life, and she has taught me a great deal about when to buckle down and when to surrender. My sister Jenny Sayre Ramberg models for me the gifts of an unfettered and abundant creativity. I am inspired by this and by her healthy sense of the ridiculous, especially in the conduct of her elder sister. Awareness of my own absurdity has turned out to be invaluable in my endeavors as an anthropologist. My father's vast curiosity about the world and wanderlust laid the ground for my own wide venturing. But last, and first, I am grateful beyond measure to my mother, Jenny Ballard Ramberg. Her passionate commitment to human thriving, skepticism of sentiment, fierce faith, and keen intellectual appetite forged the metal of my mind, filled the well of my spirit, and made the pages that follow possible.

Note on Translation and Transliteration

All transliterations and translations are from Kannada, except where noted, and reflect the spoken character and somewhat distinct vocabulary of the Northern dialect of that language. I have used *Kittel's Dictionary* ([1894] 1994) as the general basis for transliteration of Kannada terms into English orthography and have foregone diacritics in favor of readability, doubling vowels where they are long or consonants where they are stressed. Translated terms and phrases appear in italics. The proper names of deities, castes, individuals and places appear in their most common Anglicized spelling without italics. I have followed the grammatical conventions of English where the plural form of an Indian term was called for, for instance devis rather than devaru, except when directly quoting someone.

The names of most people and some places have been changed in keeping with ethnographic convention and in the effort to protect those people and places from undue scrutiny.

Gods, Gifts, Trouble

DEVADASI RITES

One day the *jogatis* took me to the river for a *puja* (worship, rite). Mahadevi came to our door early in the morning, saying: "Today we are taking the devi [goddess] to the river—will you come along?" As was often the case when they called us to go roaming with them and the two devis, Yellamma and Matangi, we set off with very little information about what might unfold. Usually, my research assistant Jyoti and I followed them from farmhouse to farmhouse, for festivals or for household rites on auspicious occasions such as the birth of a female buffalo calf or the successful drilling of a new bore well. On that spring day, for the festival of the river goddess, we climbed into a flatbed truck that was trailing a big green tractor: the four *jogatis*—Mahadevi, Durgabai, Yamuna, and Kamlabai—assorted children and devotees from the village, Jyoti, and me. The two traveling devis, in the form of faces cast in brass and wrapped in saris sitting in the middle of brightly painted wooden baskets, had been placed in the front of the truck. During our bumpy ride over the pockmarked roads characteristic of this district in northern Karnataka, an area rich in sugarcane but poor in infrastructure, I asked Mahadevi whose tractor we were traveling in. She pointed to the landlord farmer swaying in the tractor seat next to the driver and explained that, even after several years of marriage he and his wife were childless, so he had decided to sponsor the bringing of the devi to the Krishna River.

I recognized in this account the making of a *harake* (vow to a deity) in which devotees seek to secure blessings of fertility and prosperity from the devi through acts of propitiation toward her. Devotees make material or bodily offerings such as parched grain, saris, silver ornaments, pilgrimages, prostrations, renunciations, or ecstatic performances. I came to understand the making and fulfilling of such *harake* as exchange relations between devotees and the devi. These relations are mediated through the bodies of *jogatis* and the rites they perform for devotees. As persons who are given, or who give themselves, to the devi in fulfillment of *harake*, *jogatis* themselves take the form of such offerings. Their dedication to the devi is conducted as a rite of marriage to her. This marriage authorizes them to perform rites in her name, such as the one in which we were brought to participate that day at the river.

Pilgrims from all the surrounding villages thronged the riverbank. Oxen drawn carts were pulled alongside big green tractors into the flowing river, where farmers splashed water on the implements of their labor. Having bathed and finished their *puja*, people sat eating, and children brandished their festival trophies: small plastic toys and candy. After overseeing the carrying of the two devis to a clearing in the crowd and appointing someone to watch them, Mahadevi told me to come with her and the other *jogatis* to bathe, a ritual purification made in preparation for the bathing and ornamentation of the devis. I followed Mahadevi, Durgabai, and Kamlabai to the river's edge, carrying a fresh sari to change into. Stripped down to our petticoats,[1] we immersed ourselves, laughing at the pleasing shock of the chilly water. Meanwhile, the other women in our village party—all *gandullavalu* (women with husbands)[2]—splashed their faces, hands, and feet in a more modest version of the same ritual cleansing. Bathed and clad in fresh saris, we rejoined the rest of the village party, and Durgabai and Kamlabai began to prepare the devis for *puja*. Reaching into the wooden basket where Yellamma sat, Kamlabai unwrapped the sari wound around the devi. Carefully untethering the silver *murti* (a form of the deity) of Yellamma's face from the supporting dowel standing in the middle of the basket, she placed it along with Yellamma's gold and silver ornaments in a large bowl of river water and began the process of bathing the body of the goddess. After repainting and reattaching her face to the dowel, Kamlabai wrapped the devi in her new sari, given by the landlord. Mahadevi, who had just finished the same process with the other devi, Matangi, said to be Yellamma's younger sister, reached inside the basket into the lap or womb (*udi*) of the devi and drew out a fresh coconut. Beckoning to the landlord's wife to follow her, Mahadevi led a small procession, including three musicians playing the instruments of Yellamma, to the water's edge. There she dipped the coconut in the river, anointed it with scarlet *kumkuma*, worshipped it with fire (*aarthi*), and placed it in the curved fold of her silk sari that the woman held outstretched at the level of her abdomen—into her *udi*.

Writing Rites

Rites of devi propitiation are ubiquitous and quotidian in South India. What is noteworthy about this rite, however, is tied to the question of who or what *jogatis* are. The South Indian women this book is about do not marry men; they marry a goddess. *Jogatis* are given, or dedicated, to Yellamma as children by their parents. All those dedicated to Yellamma wrap themselves in saris and embody the devi. That is, whether they were recognized as boys (sexed male) or girls (sexed female) as children, they become women and are called *jogatis*, although male women are more commonly called *jogappas*.[3] *Jogatis* are also called and call themselves devadasis, which is a pan-Indian term usually translated as servant or slave (*dasi*) of the god (*deva*).[4] Dedication is their central initiation rite. They become Yellamma's *pujaris* (priests or caretakers), Dalit[5] women who transact the favor of the goddess outside the walls of her main temple and sex outside the bounds of conjugal matrimony. Their alliance with the goddess, however, is not recognized as a matter of legitimate religion or kinship within the law or by state authorities. Indeed, in the most recent wave of over one hundred years of reform, the practice of dedication, as well as all the rites it authorizes *jogatis* to perform, including the one described above, have been criminalized.

When I began field research in northern Karnataka and southern Maharastra in 2001, I did not expect to encounter devadasis actively performing rites. *Jogatis* are typically defined exclusively through their illicit sexuality. When their rites appear in scholarly or popular accounts, they are marked as something that is not religion. Ethnohistorical accounts of devadasis formerly attached to temples in Orissa and Tamil Nadu detail the significance of their ritual performances in the temple complex (Apffel-Marglin 1985; Kersenboom-Story 1987; Srinivasan 1984), however, ethnographies of devadasis in Karnataka have tended to frame these rites as empty remnants of the past (Shankar 1994; Tarachand 1992) or as once abundant but now effaced (Assayag 1992; Epp 1997).[6] The practice of dedicating daughters is widely represented in newspaper articles and reports by nongovernmental organizations as based in superstition, driven by poverty, and resulting in prostitution. The *Times of India*, a major national English-language daily newspaper, reported: "Every day at dawn [at the time of the annual pilgrimage], poverty-stricken people from neighboring areas gather at the Renuka Yellamma temple, ablaze in a cloud of yellow and red turmeric, to 'marry off' their daughters to the presiding deity. . . . Temple priests persuade the parents, adrift in a sea of superstition, to gift their daughters to the deity, which they do, little realizing that most of the girls will end up as sex workers in the brothels of Mumbai and other cities" (Sehgal 1999).

Schooled by such representations—and no doubt having failed to read them critically enough—I went to the field thinking of *jogati* personhood as wholly defined by illicit sexuality. I was surprised to learn otherwise. One day in 2002 at one of the four minor outlying Yellamma temple complexes near the town of Athani in northern Karnataka, I encountered two dedicated women. They were seated on either side of the dark goddess Matangi, for whom they were receiving offerings and giving blessings. "What do they call you?" I asked. "*Pujaris*," they said, laughing at my ignorance. "What else would they call us? We keep her [the devi]" (*Matten karitarri namna? Naavu akinna itgondeevi*).

What does it mean to "keep the devi"? This question has been answered in different ways. The scene I described above by the Krishna River might be read as (yet another) ethnographic rendering of timeless ritual in the Indian subcontinent, an episode in the story told by the West about the East through an Orientalist lens (Said 1978). Many of the elements of such a story are there: customary enactments of rituals meant to propitiate the gods, hierarchical caste relations, sexualized others, an agrarian scene seemingly unmarked by any significant incursions of modernity (Inden 1990). Alternatively, this story might appear as an account of female religious leadership and ritual balance between cosmic, earthly, and human well-being in a wider record of universal feminine power and ecological value (Shahrukh 1997; Starhawk 1979). From the point of view of Dalit, Christian, and feminist social reformers, the scene by the river displays the degraded position of outcaste women dedicated to a life of superstitious ritual enactments and sexual exploitation (Joint Women's Programme 1989; Rozario 2000; Shankar 1994; Tarachand 1992).

In this ethnography I offer another way to think about what was unfolding at the river that day in 2003, one that I came to by taking the question of who and what *jogatis* are as an open question best pursued by working closely with those whom have come to call themselves *jogati*. This method foregrounds the terms *jogatis* use to describe themselves and the world. As I show, these terms often exceed received categories of social scientific knowledge. As persons who call Yellamma their husband, *jogatis* conform neither to prevailing South Indian patterns of kin making nor to dominant modern definitions of marriage as an alliance between two persons of the opposite sex. The ways that their kin making practices exceed received conceptions of kinship are productive in two ways: they bring another interpretation of devadasi lives into view, and they demonstrate some of the limits of modern forms of knowledge.

I take the practices that *jogatis* enact to be what they and devotees of Yellamma call them, *puja*. Similarly, I take the relationship between *jogatis* and the devi to be what it is called by the people for whom it is an everyday phenomenon: a marriage (*maduve*). Like all marriages, this one has effects. I draw on contemporary debates in anthropology, postcolonial feminism, queer theory, and religious studies, to investigate the effects of kinship with the goddess and to situate devadasis as cultural producers and commentators, rather than as simply objects of moral appraisal. Through the conduct of their rites, including that of marriage to the devi, *jogatis* are "worlding, the world" (Heidegger and Hofstadter [1971] 2013, 179). As they describe it, their goddess is with them and in them, a material presence and force in the world that is not outside social life, but rather part of its making. Thus, *jogatis* inhabit and enact a form of life and mode of being that exceed secular accounts of humanity as ontologically singular.

This delineation of devadasi lifeworlds is not only an invocation of a way of life that is under erasure, but also an occasion to consider what counts as religion, and who and what marriage is for. To ask what counts as religion is to pose a question about forms of knowledge as they intersect with relations of power. Whose ways of talking to gods and spirits are designated as religion, and whose are stigmatized as superstition? To inquire who and what marriage is for is to pose a queer question about whose relations and which desires can receive the mark of legitimacy. It is also to pose a feminist question about the material economies underwriting and animated by sexual and domestic arrangements. These questions matter because religion and marriage are normative categories of knowledge as well as terrains of statecraft. As such, they configure the terms of social, sexual, and political recognition (Povinelli 2002a, 2006) — or of livable life and grievable love (Butler 2000, 2004). The answers to the questions of what can count as religion and who and what marriage is for offer one kind of diagnosis of the wounds of modernity.

Jogatis as Performers of Rites

According to a 2007 government survey, some thirty thousand devadasis[7] are living in Karnataka, across fourteen districts. Every village in the northern part of Karnataka, and many more in western Andhra Pradesh and southern Maharastra, has a small Yellamma temple in it. The *puja* in these temples is virtually always conducted by a *jogati* from the Dalit community. Yellamma is the most popular deity in the region; half a million devotees from all castes throng to her main temple during the pilgrimage season, making her temple by the side of the Malaprabha River the most significant pilgrimage site in northern Karnataka. Until recently, dedications of girls and sometimes boys were performed at this temple. As the result of reformers' pressure on the government to enforce the 1982 law criminalizing these dedications and the significant presence of police and reformers during the pilgrimage time, they are now mostly performed quietly in out-of-the-way places. They are also significantly on the wane—with two exceptions, the hundred or so devadasis I spoke with about the future of the practice said: "This will end with us, we will marry our daughters [to men]."

Dedications are achieved, as conventional Hindu marriages are, by the tying of a string of *muttu* (beads or pearls) around the woman's neck. Once dedicated, devadasis do not otherwise marry. They say, "Yellamma is my husband (*Akine nam gandari*)." As one put it to me, "How many times should I be married? I am already married to her" (Yesht sate madkoludaitri, aki joti agetallri).

As wives of the deity—always married, never widowed—they are auspicious women associated with all forms of fertility and well-being. Trained as ritual specialists through apprenticeship, they enact household, temple, and festival rites and roam throughout their communities giving blessings and taking grain.

Once past puberty, many of these young women begin exchanging sex for means of livelihood—in villages usually through a local system of patronage by a higher caste man and in towns often through brothel-based sex for cash transactions. Between a third and a half of all those who have been dedicated work or have worked in brothels, but many spend their entire lives residing in their natal villages, where they usually take or are given to a patron (or keep—*ittukondaru*).[8] Patrons are typically otherwise endogamously married men of a higher caste with whom devadasis have long-term if not lifelong exclusive sexual relations. The relationship between a devadasi and her patron is a public secret: everyone knows about it, but it is not accorded the recognition granted endogamous marriage. The children born of such unions belong to their mother's patriline. "Good" patrons support the extended household of the woman they keep and see to their children's well-being, education, and marriage. They are not expected to give their name or any of their land, forms of wealth maintained within caste lineages. "Bad" patrons, like bad husbands, "give you children and leave you to fend for them on your own," as the *jogatis* explained to me. "Very bad" patrons, like very bad husbands, "take your money, drink, and beat you." Many *jogatis* transitioned from taking patrons to taking clients in the 1980s. This shift took place in the context of broad economic transitions including land reform, the advent of widespread cash cropping, and general patterns of rural to urban migration for wage labor.[9]

Unlike most village-based devadasis, brothel-based devadasis in towns or cities are not monogamous; they find cash for sex transactions to be more lucrative than patronage relations. Urban-dwelling devadasis are more readily associated with "bad work" (*kettada keilasa*) and more likely to describe themselves as being "in business" (*dhandha*), an expression for sex work used across India. In the context of the HIV pandemic, many have come to situate themselves within a transnational category, that of the sex worker peer educator. All dedicated women, whether based in a village or a brothel, share three key features: marriage to the devi, lack of respectability, and economic responsibility to their natal family.

Jogatis come from landless or small landholding outcaste families eking out a subsistence living in an area prone to drought and largely dependent on dry land agriculture. Often dedicated to ensure the line of descent in the absence of male heirs, *jogatis* are entitled to pass on their name and property to their children and frequently function as the head of the household, supporting extended families. They typically fulfill the obligations and claim some of the privileges of sons, including those of arranging marriages, paying for jobs, purchasing land, and building houses.

In the villages of northern Karnataka and in provincial and urban redlight districts as far away as Mumbai (Bombay), *jogatis* are still very active as *pujaris*. In the village I call Nandipur, in which I lived for nine months in 2002–3, there are four devadasis actively involved in daily ritual work.[10] During the festival of the first harvest season, they make rounds (*phere*) walking from farmer's house to farmer's house. They carry the devi in a large *jaga* (basket or world), singing devotional songs, giving blessings, and asking for grain. They play a central role in the village celebration of all the major festivals and respond to calls from households to bring the devi, perform *puja*, play the *shruti* and *chowdiki*[11] and sing on auspicious occasions such as the successful drilling of a new bore well, a marriage, the completion of a new house, recovery from illness or affliction, and even the successful completion of a research project. Women living in red-light districts are no less active as performers of rites; from Bangalore to Pune, I sat in Yellamma temples and participated in festival celebrations with *jogatis* and

FIGURE I.1 Mahadevi preparing the devi Matangi for *puja*. Photograph by Brett Fisher.

FIGURE I.2 Making rounds. Mahadevi leads, playing the *chowdiki*. Photograph by the author.

other devotees. Nonetheless, after over a hundred years of reform begun in the colonial era, devadasi dedication and devadasi rites are disappearing.

There are a number of regional variations of dedication, generally recognized by distinct terms (*basavi, matangi, jogini, matamma, murali*, and *kalavant*) that imply different relationships to a variety of performing arts, ritual occupations, deities, temples, and social and sexual arrangements.[12] The majority of women I spent time with identified themselves as *jogatis* or *jogammas*, as do most dedicated women in Bombay Karnataka (another name for northern Karnataka). In ethnohistorical terms, the distinctions among patterns of dedication are salient.[13] However, in the context of bureaucratic, journalistic, and policy reports, all of these women are referred to as devadasis, a term they have come, increasingly, to apply to themselves. In this book I use the ethnohistorically specific terms (*jogati* and *jogamma*) and the pan-Indian term (devadasi) as well as my own terms, *dedicated women* and *Yellamma women*. *Jogati, jogamma*, and devadasi are all ethnographically correct in the sense that they are the local terms in contemporary usage. *Dedicated women* and *Yellamma women* are anthropological designations that foreground the most salient features of their category of personhood: the rite defining their mode of being in the world; the devi to whom they are attached; and their gender.[14]

Kinship Matters

Renunciates of ordinary family life, these Dalit religious mendicants may command respect but not respectability. As *pujaris* whose ritual efficacy derives precisely from their alliance with a devi, *jogatis* and *jogappas* are powerful, but not within modern registers of significant personhood. That is, their power and value cannot be reckoned through capital logic or easily accommodated to citizenship. This is a matter of kinship and a consequence of the anomalous configuration of their families.

The goddess Yellamma has her own complicated family history. The universalizing modern family ideal in which men provide, women are protected, and children are innocent goes unrealized in her life, as it does in the lives of those male and female women who wander in her name. According to the history her devotees tell, Yellamma—or Renuka, as she is also called—was married to a great sage, Jamadagni. She was so pure that she was able to perform miracles. Forming a pot from loose sand on the bank of the river and coiling a cobra into a pot rest, each day she brought water to Jamadagni for his morning *puja*. One day as she was walking, bal-

FIGURE I.3 Yellamma is distracted by pleasure. Offprint poster from the bazaar at Yellamma's temple in Saundatti, circa 2001.

FIGURE I.4 A *jogati* carrying Yellamma on a pot of water on her head. Photograph by the author.

ancing this pot on her head, she saw *gandharva* (otherworldly beings; literally, fragrance eaters) playing in the river. She lost her concentration, the pot dissolved, and the snake slipped away. When she returned home, Jamadagni immediately recognized that she had strayed. He became very angry and ordered their three sons to cut off her head. The two eldest refused and were cursed with impotency by their father for this failure of loyalty to him. However, the youngest son, Parashurama, dutifully swung an axe and cut off his mother's head. His father was so pleased with him that he granted him three boons. Parashurama asked for his mother and his brothers to be restored and for his father to forswear anger. Jamadagni granted only the first of the three boons, and Yellamma was restored.

Yellamma failed to maintain the feminine ideals of ritual purity and sexual chastity; she was distracted by pleasure. This turned out to be a capital offense, the punishment for which was ordered by her husband and executed by her youngest son. The failure to comply with the father's injunction to punish the mother's transgression results in the loss of masculinity. The idea, basic to feminist analysis, that the regulation of women's sexual capacity is fundamental to patriarchal social organization and symbolic production is dramatically conveyed through the story of Yellamma. So too is the terrific power of feminine sexual desire, here capable of destroying the calm of a great sage and inspiring matricide.

As a fact of social life and a means of the organization of sexuality, kinship is trouble for Yellamma.[15] It is also trouble for the women who are married to her: their alliance with the goddess sets them outside locally dominant social norms of patrilineal descent and patrilocal residence. Furthermore, their kinship with the goddess exiles them from sexual citizenship, the mode of national inclusion and state protection afforded those whose families conform to the national ideal. As an anthropological category, kinship is troubled by Yellamma and her wives. They enact a form of kin making that exceeds the logic of the kinship chart, the liberal conception of relatedness as a matter of autonomous choice making, and the secular reckoning of alliance as limited to the territory of the human.

How are we to think about this kinship that is not kinship? My approach to this question is shaped by two commitments. The first is methodological: I consider devadasi kin making through the categories used by dedicated women and their families, rather than those supplied by the kinship chart. The second is theoretical and bears the imprint of two major schools of thought within kinship studies: I take kinship to be systematic, as structuralist approaches have (Lévi-Strauss 1969), and inventive, as culturalist accounts do (Schneider 1984).

What kind of kin work are families doing when they dedicate their daughters? The gift of a child to Yellamma produces a distinct mode of intelligible human life. It changes one kind of person, with a particular kin position and reproductive and familial trajectory, into another kind of person. It reconfigures relations between those dedicated and their natal kin, as well as relations among devadasis, the devi, and her devotees. Kin making is practical and innovative; it is also patterned and disciplinary. It is a means of transforming persons that is translated across a field in predictable forms. These forms reiterate techniques of the body (Mauss 1990) such as gender and caste, as well as forms of knowledge about the nature of persons and their place in the world (Strathern 1988). Possibilities of human being and doing are made and unmade through everyday practices such as marriage, adoption, and domiciliation. Innovative kin-making practices open new pathways to forms of social and political recognition and inclusion. For instance, marriage is sometimes pursued as a pathway to legal citizenship, access to health insurance, or other means to and forms of human thriving. As a way of securing the positive regard of the state, however, marriage is not a tool within everyone's grasp. Kin-making practices are thus also constrained: they occur in regulating and normalizing fields of power that shape legitimized forms of relations, recognizable kinds of persons, and possible relations to the state.

In spite of the vast differences among them, evolutionary, structuralist, and symbolic anthropological accounts of kinship have all centered their analyses of human relatedness on the conjugal pair. As feminist and queer appraisals have shown, this focus on human sexual reproduction as the sine qua non of kin making has produced exclusions in the field of kinship studies (Hayden 1995; Rubin 1975; Weston 1997). Modes of relatedness that do not conform to what are presumed to be universal facts of binary sex and sexual reproduction have been excluded, or designated as fictive. These exclusions have circumscribed kinship as a knowledge project, and many anthropologists have failed to describe relatedness where they did not see reproductive heterosexuality replicated over time. In short, they have discursively reproduced the social death that awaits those exiled from kinship (Borneman 1996). Posing relatedness as a question rather than assuming that it has been described by the kinship chart is a way to open up this field and to denaturalize the dominant form of the family, including binary gender and always already sexed bodies that have been carried into the anthropological project through the genealogical imagination and the form of the kinship chart (Borneman 1996; Povinelli 2002b; Strathern 2005). Rather than simply mapping kinship in a field of fixed and inevitable coordinates of biogenetic ties and conjugality, asking about particular and located ways of enacting, conceiving, and valuing relations, as I do here, has been widely endorsed in new kinship studies (Carsten 2000; Hayden 1995; Franklin and McKinnon 2001; Weston 1997). In this ethnography, I elaborate the forms of kinship trouble that devadasi kin making makes and the forms of life and possibilities for an anthropology of relatedness that such trouble opens up.

Modernity, Secularity, Reform

The reform of devadasis is a story about what kind of work the body is made to do to become modern. It is also, and critically for this book, a story about the remaking of forms of life with implications for how modern categories of religion, marriage, and sex can be understood. I take modernity to be an uneven and incomplete project that understands itself to be rationalizing, secularizing, civilizing, and progressive. Those who see themselves as modern subjects (respectable, educated, scientific, and urbane) compare themselves favorably to backward others (superstitious, promiscuous, illiterate, and rural). In other words, the possibilities of social and political recognition and livable life take shape in relation to normalizing designations of personhood taken to be neutral rational forms of knowledge (Asad 2003; Butler 2004; Cohen 1998; Povinelli 2002a). This book contributes to a conversation about how categories of sexual and religious personhood come to specify who does and who does not qualify as secular, modern, and thus admissible to the rights and protections of citizenship in its broad sense as positive state recognition. In everyday conversations with me about caste politics, Dalits frequently captured the terms and stakes of this threshold of admission in a simple and affecting formulation: "We are also human beings, aren't we?"

Devadasi dedication is subject to reform not as a marginal form of kinship or religion but as illicit sex and superstition. This character of reform is a feature of modernity as a normalizing project. Both kinship and religion are normative categories. They do not merely describe, they delimit. The formulation of the devadasi system as prostitution under the false cover of religion is predicated on ideas about what constitutes proper and improper sexual activity as well as true and false religion. The terms of these distinctions—proper from improper and true from false—have taken shape over time as marriage and religion have shifted from terrains of variable if ranked socially recognized and sanctioned practices to fields in which the true can and must be distinguished from the false (Flood 1998; King 1999; Sturman 2012). The rise of a homogenized and purified Hinduism, the normalization of the patrilineal family form, and the advent of sexual purity campaigns are pathways of national assertion and modern subject formation in India that have profoundly transformed the possibilities of devadasis' lives.

As persons whose relationship to a devi cannot qualify as religion, *jogatis* can figure only as a remnant of the past that must be left behind. The eradication of some forms of life in the name of national progress is by now a familiar story, and a feature of what has been called the "postcolonial predicament," in which signs of civilizational lack or backwardness must yield to social improvement (Breckenridge and van der Veer 1993). This imperative clearly shapes governmental and nongovernmental practices of reform. It also constitutes one of the ways modernity is inhabited.[16] Those who perceive their backwardness and participate in projects of improvement become modern. As ex-devadasis—those who have embraced reform and removed the string of beads tied around their neck at their dedication—put it to me: "We have become better" (namage chalo agetri).

Secular projects of governance and liberal modes of reform do not generally see themselves as interfering in religion as such. According to the political doctrine of secularism, religion and secular government each have their own proper domain; neither should impinge on the other's. In India, this doctrine of secularism has been articulated as the state's neutrality toward all religions equally. In Nehru's words: "We talk about a secular state in India. . . . Some people think it means something opposed to religion. That obviously is not correct. . . . It is a state which honours all faiths equally and gives them equal opportunities" (quoted in Madan 1998, 311). This secular principle of neutrality is broadly supported, even championed as the critical safeguard against the atrocities of communal violence. At the same time, secular discourses and practices are reconfiguring what is admissible to that domain as a recognizable form of religion worthy of protection (Asad 2003; Galanter 1971).

In postcolonial India, one of the sites of this reconfiguration has been the effort to purify Hinduism of superstition and to ground it in rationalist conceptions of truth and error (Sen 2010, 86). This reform of Hinduism by the state has been shaped by a dual mandate inscribed in the Indian constitution, which seeks both to protect the freedom of religion (article 26) and to restrict or regulate any secular (defined as economic, financial, or political) activities associated with religious practices (article 25). A boundary between protected religious activity and state-managed secular activity has emerged as a result of these two mandates and through the doctrine of essential practices, which holds that essentially secular practices are a proper domain for state intervention and what is essential to religion stands apart from economics, politics, and sexuality (Sen 2010, 89). For devotees of Yellamma and the women tied to her who perform rites for them, this configuration of the domains of protected religion and secular power has significant consequences. The state finds no impediment to the eradication of a set of practices that offend modern sensibilities about what female sexuality should be for and that do not conform to what can be demonstrated to be essential to Hinduism as a modern form of religion.

I turn here to an elaboration of three features of the chain linking modernity, secularity, and reform, features critical to the conceptual framework of this book about the emancipation of Dalit women from backward practices. These features are the category of religion, the modern formation of the global religion Hinduism, and the emancipatory ambitions of anti-caste and feminist projects of reform.

Only some ways of talking with and relating to gods and spirits qualify as religion, as a modern category of human experience and practice. Enlightened religion is understood to be a matter of theistic belief, rather than embodied practice or mere ritual. This understanding presumes a divide between the territory of the human and the realm of the transcendent and dematerialized divine. The idea that enlightened religion consists of interiorized belief and private devotion to a spiritualized being has a specifically Christian and European genealogy (Asad 1993, 2003; Chakrabarty 2000; King 1999).[17]

This genealogy has had consequences for how Hinduism took shape during the nineteenth and twentieth centuries. Western observers in the eighteenth and nineteenth centuries, many of them Christian missionaries, saw idolatry and orgiastic frenzy in Indian religiosity, but later scholars discovered in Vedic texts[18] evidence of a more evolved religion marked by monotheism, soteriology, and belief in life after death (Dalmia and Von Steitencron 1995b; Viswanathan 2003). Textual Brahmanic religion, predominantly Vaisnava, was produced as the "real religion of the Hindus"

(Dalmia 1995) and the unifying basis for the nation of India. This staging was accomplished through both the purification and the homogenization of Hinduism and the alienation of Islam as the foreign religion of invaders.

The installation of Hinduism as a world religion unifying the citizens of India is, in the language of Michel Foucault (1978), an effect of modern power and its productions of new technologies of the self and forms of governmentality. For instance, as many scholars have argued, colonial courts relied on the interpretations of Brahman pandits when making distinctions between legitimate and illegitimate religious practices. These distinctions resituated practices such as sati (widow immolation) and hook swinging (ecstatic piercing and suspension from hooks) (Dirks 1997; Mani 1998) as repugnant and barbaric customs. Such transformations in turn implied, incited, and sometimes juridically enforced new norms of bodily comportment for relations to gods, spirits, and the state.[19] The shift from marginal religion, in Brahmanical reckoning, to false religion, in the Protestant Christian framework of the British, has had enormous implications for the viability of subaltern religiosity. The folk religion of aboriginal people, members of outcaste communities, and women has been increasingly understood as superstition (Dalmia and Von Steitencron 1995a, 14).

For this ethnography of rites and their reform, this history is critical in two ways. First, it has prompted me, along with other anthropologists of religion, to move away from conceiving of religion as a transhistorical and universal essence and toward an ethnographic invocation of embodied practices occurring in fields of power (Asad 1993; Keane 2002; Mahmood 2005; Ram 2013). Second, it demonstrates that the designation of practices as superstitious is a move of modern power. Such a designation does not simply signal the worship of false gods but rather it points to a mistaken apprehension of the world, a wrongness of reason, or a lack of reason. As such, the designation of superstition cannot be taken for granted.

In his characterization of superstition as a secular and evolutionary version of early modern Christian concepts of idolatry and devil worship, Talal Asad suggests that objects and relations designated as superstitious had to be "constituted as categories of illusion and oppression before people could be liberated from them" (2003, 35). "Liberation" from false religion was a feature of colonial, national, and imperial projects of civilizing mission that sought to eradicate social evils and barbaric customs such as sati, hook swinging, and devadasi dedication. It is also a familiar aspect of any number of more contemporary emancipatory projects, two of which are at issue in this study: anti-casteism and feminism.

In colonial modernity, missionary critiques of Hindu superstition combined with Enlightenment principles of natural rights and freedoms to frame the emergence of anti-caste politics (A. Rao 2009, 31–32). For nationalists, Brahmanical religion (purified of superstition) served as a basis for anticolonial self-assertion. For anti-caste activists, in contrast, politicized identity and rational self-assertion emerged in an antagonistic relationship to Brahmanical religion as well as to superstition.[20] Arguing against the reformed Hinduism espoused by Gandhi and other nationalists, anti-Brahman activist and founder of the Self-Respect movement in South India, Ramasami Periyar, wrote: "It must be said that god and religion are erected on the foundation of the superstitious beliefs of the people. Our daily life is regulated by superstition . . . if anything of old, based on blind faith and superstition, is sought to be retained or tolerated, the result will be the total failure of reform" (2003, 70). Whether all gods and forms of religion were seen to be an obstacle to emancipation, as for Periyar; only Hindu gods and practices, as for B. R. Ambedkar, who called for Dalits to convert to Buddhism; or only Brahmanical religion, as for Jotiba Phule, clear agreement existed among these architects of Dalit emancipation in southern and western India about the relationship between superstitious beliefs and practices and the perpetuation of untouchability. Here, superstition is understood less as a problem of the degradation of Hinduism (which is how it was seen in the context of nationalist reform) and more as a problem of Dalit false consciousness and upper caste hegemony (Vijaisri 2004, 174).

The subject of Dalit emancipation, as Anupama Rao has argued (2009), has taken stigmatized existence as the basis of his or her political assertion. The distinct lifeways, occupations, and modes of cultural production that attach to outcaste *jatis* (subcastes or communities) find no way into this formulation of Dalit distinction as the basis of social exclusion, economic exploitation, and therefore, the ground for politics. They must be left behind in order for the community to progress. However, not all Dalits who perform work designated as polluting seek to escape such labor.[21] Forms of power and possibility can be entangled with stigma in the embodiment of caste-specific labor. Secular humanist visions of Dalit emancipation, such as that articulated by Ambedkar, whose poster adorns most Nandipur homes in the Dalit community, cannot accommodate these forms of power and possibility.[22] In my attention here to the forms of power and possibility that *jogati* lifeways and forms of knowledge manifest in the world, I am pursuing a consideration of Dalit modes of life that exceeds secular reckonings (Abeysekara 2008; Ganguly 2005).

As have Dalit emancipatory projects, feminist programs for liberation in India and elsewhere have tended to conceive of religion as a bond from which one must break free. When we equate freedom with emancipation *from* custom, culture, and religion (Mahmood 2005), we have fenced off these terrains as potential resources for those who find themselves at the margins of social and political life. Furthermore, and of particular concern to me, we have rendered some lives unlivable under the sign of progress. Over a long period of time and through my own efforts as an activist as well as an anthropologist, I have become skeptical of liberal accounts of what constitutes freedom and unfreedom and wary of the unintended effects of efforts to "save" others. I am here in agreement with Saba Mahmood who— in the context of her study of an Egyptian women's piety movement—has asked: "Are we willing to countenance the sometimes violent task of re-making sensibilities, life worlds, and attachments so that women of the kind I worked with may be taught to value the principle of 'freedom'?" (2005, 38).

In the context of the research for and writing of this book, my engagement with the daily lives of dedicated women whose life circumstances can be understood only as difficult has been deeply informed by this skepticism about emancipatory projects conceived in liberal secular terms. For instance, I eschew the terms "exploitation" and "oppression," which rightly characterize the effects of dominating forms of power, but which also assume a liberal subject who can only be either free or unfree. This is not to dismiss the harsh effects of the radically uneven distribution of the resources, forms of recognition, and protection that make life livable. Rather, it is to attend to how difficult lives are lived, and how *jogatis* mobilize and materialize forms of power, possibility, and knowledge, given their difficult life circumstances. It is not my hope to ignore or diminish these difficulties, but to refuse a binary view in which *jogatis* can be seen only as subjects of chosen lives or objects of coerced conditions of survival. I am writing here in between and against the dichotomy of choice and coercion.

As an example of what this representational effort entails, I do not use the term "prostitution" as a descriptive or analytic category in this book. When it appears, it appears as a designation used by others or as an object of analysis itself. As a term of sexual personhood, "prostitution" can imply any number of sexual and economic arrangements and legal, moral, and social statuses. Instead, I use the term "sexual economy," which allows me to include *jogatis* and *gandullavalu* in a single analytic frame and to demonstrate that different sexual economies entail different forms of possibility and difficulty.[23] My method is to specify the terms of these possibilities and difficulties, rather than to assume them. When they are assumed, as when *jogatis* are called prostitutes and conventional marriage is posed as the solution to the difficulties of their lives, normative assumptions about prostitute and wife as categories of sexual personhood are reproduced. We have learned very little, however, about the lives of *jogatis* or the institution of marriage in Dalit communities in South India as a specific disposition of sexuality. By "sexuality" I mean the organization of sexual capacity, not the secret of the modern self, as Foucault has uncovered it (1978). How is sex deployed? What is it for—pleasure, reproduction, earning, intimacy?

I am arguing that the reform of *jogatis*, as people who are understood to embody exploited sexuality and false religion, needs to be considered within a framework that admits prostitution and superstition as objects of analysis. As figures of sexual and religious personhood, the Indian customary prostitute and the idolatrous Indian have been made to constitute the faultline between modernity and backwardness. My effort here is to get beyond the limitations of categories such as prostitution and superstition—indeed, to bring these categories themselves into crisis. Thus I ask not only what kinship with and *puja* for the goddess *mean*, but also what they *do*. What kind of world do *jogatis* world?

WRITING DEVADASIS

The woman question does not travel by itself across borders.
—Susie Tharu, "Problems in Theorizing Feminism"

The Woman Question is, in fact, the hinge or point at which a politics of the nation becomes that of international relations. It is there that absolute freedom and absolute lack of freedom turn on each other. Which is to say, the Woman Question is also always the Eastern Question.
—Rosalind Morris, "Theses on the Questions of War"

Why does the history of the East appear as a history of religions?
—Karl Marx and Friedrich Engels, *On Religion*

Recognizing that "the woman question does not travel by itself across borders" has profound implications for the politics of feminism, theories of gender, and representations and readings of those positioned as women. This recognition has been taken up widely in postcolonial and transnational feminist scholarly writings (Kaplan, Alarcón, and Moallem 1999; Mohanty

1991; M. Sinha 2006), which insist that to pose the woman question is necessarily to pose the nation question. Karl Marx's point that representations
of the East seem always to manifest as problems of religion complicates the
formula.[24] The slippage among these three—woman, East, and religion—
is what makes it possible for photographs of Afghani women throwing off
their burkas to stand for the liberation of a people from oppressive religion and government. Such images circulated widely in the American press
shortly after the United States invaded Afghanistan in 2001. As commentators have noted, these kinds of representations do more work for the identification of the West with freedom than they do for Afghani women, whose
material and political conditions have by many measures been worsened by
the war (Abu-Lughod 2002; Stabile and Kumar 2005). The ways that these
questions—of woman, the East, and religion—have been made to stand
in for each other in discursive and political relations between the putative
East and the West haunt any attempt to think about them. Such specters
can be good to think with, however, and I take the questions of woman, the
East, and religion all to be imbricated in postcolonial modernity. My insistence on this point marks an intervention in studies of devadasis. Before I
elaborate on this intervention, I introduce the history of devadasi dedication and its reform.

Histories of temple women date the practice of dedicating girls to
deities and temples across South India back to the ninth century, based
on epigraphic evidence (Kersenboom-Story 1987; Orr 2000, 5). A specialized class of temple servants, these women were choreographers, dancers,
musicians, and ritual performers whose sexual capacity was harnessed to
their position in the temple as wives of the deity. Their significance in the
wider political life of the deities, temple economies, and the institution of
kingship materialized in the significant usufruct rights in land (*inams*) and
other forms of royal patronage they received (Srinivasan 1988). In other
words, they were public women whose performing arts were dedicated to,
and supported by, the reproduction of kingship—which itself was inseparable from the temple (Dirks 1988).[25] The practice of dedication reached its
height in the tenth and eleventh centuries at the peak of the importance of
the Hindu temple complex as a political institution. As royal patronage diminished, the practice declined, but it continued to be an integral aspect
of temple life up until—and, in some cases, beyond—a period of intensive
reform that began during the colonial period (J. Nair 1994, 2011; Srinivasan
1988; Vijaisri 2004).

The particular ritual duties and performing arts attached to dedicated women varied by region. However, all dedicated women's lives had certain sociostructural features in common, including kinship with a deity and a relationship to a local temple, its economy, and its patronage. In the part of the central Deccan Plateau that currently comprises northern Karnataka, temple inscriptions from the tenth to the thirteenth centuries detail grants of land, as well as sometimes gold, grain, and houses to temple women (Parasher and Naik 1986). In Saivaite temples, dedicated women were referred as *sule, patra, sule patra*, or *bhogam*. *Sule* is generally translated into English as prostitute, *patra* as performer of dance or song, and *bhogam* as pleasure (Parasher and Naik 1986, 68; Vijaisri 2004, 1). Although the term "devadasi" does not appear in this region in early temple inscriptions, it can be found in a twelfth-century Kannada poetic form belonging to a devotional denomination of Shaivism that focused on the worship of the god Shiva.[26] The Kannada term *basavi* is the feminine form of *basava*, bull—especially that bull that is dedicated to Shiva and roams the village (Mahale 1986, 125). The etymological roots of the term *jogati* are less clear, but most scholars point to the Tantric Yoginis, renunciates who embodied the goddess, as precursors (Bhattacharyya 1982, 110; Vijaisri 2004, 81–82). *Jogini* remains the prevalent term for dedicated women in present-day Andra Pradesh. Although some have suggested that temple women were originally chaste, most scholars agree that they were sexually active, as an aspect of their ritual efficacy as well as a feature of their place in the system of temple patronage (Apffel-Marglin 1985; Kersenboom-Story 1987; Parasher and Naik 1986).

Their uncontained sexuality has attracted the attention of generations of reformers. Investments in reform have varied depending on the period, region, and social position of the reformer. That said, the overall effect of reform projects has a discernible pattern, in which the performing arts formerly attached to dedicated women were shifted into newly configured public spaces of aestheticized, secularized, and classicized national arts, and the women were ushered into the privatized domains of domesticated sexuality or personal (rather than royal) patronage.[27] In the colonial period this reform took shape along with the reform of practices of sati and child marriage, in the context of debates between officials of the British Empire and Indian elites who sought to demonstrate their worthiness to rule India. These debates typically focused on women as the bearers of culture and tradition and the embodiment of the future of the nation, as elaborated in the work of Lata Mani, Kumkum Sangari, Mrinalini Sinha, and others.[28]

This civilizational discourse converged with the politics of religion in the colonial-era nationalist rhetoric surrounding devadasis, but in the end it was their lack of chastity that became the basis of their exclusion from temples. The mix of active sexuality and religiosity that they embodied was taken—especially by Christian missionaries—to be a sign of the fallen state of both. The public character of their religious and sexual conduct scandalized Christian observers of Hindu temple rites, and nationalists rushed to cleanse the temple of the stain of scandal.[29] Missionary opinion thus mixed with discourses of social purity and national uplift to incite reform. The pace of reform, however, varied. In accordance with Queen Victoria's 1858 proclamation of religious neutrality, officials of the East India Company initially resisted calls from Christian and Hindu activists in the social purity and temperance movement to refrain from entertaining nautch (dance) performances and to bar further dedications (Presler 1987). In Madras, where South Indian performing arts flourished under the patronage of the Tanjore kings between 1565 and 1856 (when the kingdom of Tanjore was annexed by the British), the reluctance of British officials combined with resistance from devadasi associations and other defenders of temple dance to produce a period of debate over the possibility of abolition that began in 1872 and lasted until 1947 (Soneji 2012, 121–27).

Devadasis' resistance to reform in the princely state of Mysore, in contrast, was quickly dispatched. They opposed efforts by bureaucrats there to ban dancing in Muzrai (government supported) temples by submitting a petition in 1906 calling on the Maharaja of Mysore to protect their right to fulfill their hereditary occupation and be supported though *inams*. The officials looked to the scriptures governing temple conduct (*agamashastras*) for a textual basis for the ban they sought, but pandits affirmed that dancing and ritual conduct by devadasis was authorized by the texts.[30] When pressured for information on the requirements of chastity in such women, however, the pandits produced the desired opinion.[31] In short, the newly illegitimate sexuality of devadasis trumped the religious justification for their temple services found in the texts that were held to define temple rituals, and in 1909 the conduct of and government support for devadasi performances was abolished.[32]

In colonial-era debates over reform, the extended sexuality of the devadasi was repeatedly set against the law and respectable society. Nationalists drew on an idealized Hindu ancient past in order to cast devadasis as formerly chaste, but now degraded, figures in need of rescue (Kannabiran and Kannabiran 2003, 24). British Victorian and textual Brahmanical ideals of exclusive conjugal monogamy converged in a new ideal of respectable womanhood, and temple women were placed in the English-language medicolegal category—prostitute (Parker 1998; Soneji 2012).[33]

The Mysore order of 1909 was the first ban on temple employment of devadasis and became the model for legislation in areas under British rule where British reluctance to interfere in matters of religion slowed the process of removing devadasis from temples. In 1934 the Bombay Devadasi Protection Act was passed. A similar act was passed in Madras in 1947. These acts banned dedications but stopped short of criminalizing any of the ritual or performing arts belonging to devadasis.[34] Once highly sophisticated choreographers, musicians, and ritual performers whose education and wealth was exceeded only by women who were members of royal families, devadasis became illegitimately public women whose exile from the space of the temple was seen to be necessary to the moral uplift of women, religion, and nation. These histories of appropriation and exile exemplify the demands that anticolonial nationalism made on the Indian body.

Histories of anti-caste activism bring other demands into view. Unlike the devadasis who were subject to reform in the colonial era, *jogatis* have never been associated with a highly elaborated dance form or a wealthy urban temple complex.[35] In Bombay Karnataka, *jogatis* emerged as a "blot on the community" in the context of anti-caste radical organizing in the 1920s (Vijaisri 2004, 174). This designation comes from Devaraja Ingle, who was inspired by Phule and Ambedkar. A member of the outcaste Holeyar community, Ingle urged Holeyars to stop eating the carcass meat that they had the right and duty to remove from villages, and to refrain from dedicating their daughters. These practices were understood to establish and reproduce outcaste distinction in the form of untouchability and sexual vulnerability, respectively.

Anti-caste reformers described the rites surrounding Yellamma and performed by outcaste women as invented by caste Hindus and productive of Dalit false consciousness and social abjection. These reformers shared ideals of femininity, purity, and conjugality with nationalist social reformers and situated the resolution of the devadasi problem in marriage and domestication (Epp 1997; A. Rao 2009; Vijaisri 2004, 183).[36] The status of outcaste communities in relation to caste Hindus was at stake for these anti-caste activists. Even as subjects of the British empire, caste Hindus enjoyed forms of social, economic, and political personhood entirely unavailable to Dalits.

Masculinity constitutes the basis of the most significant difference between upper- and middle-caste devadasi reform campaigns and those organized by anti-caste activists in the early part of the twentieth century. The status of the men in the community was far more at stake in anti-caste reform movements than in nationalist debates over the status of devadasis. Their responsibility to be fathers, brothers, and husbands was repeatedly noted, and their vulnerability as men who could not limit sexual access to or the sexual activity of their women was emphasized. Thus, the sexual respectability of Dalit women became a critical site for the emergence of Dalit political subjectivity.

In the postcolonial period, reform efforts have shifted from Nehruvian development projects of economic rehabilitation in the 1970s and 1980s to neoliberal projects of eradication (Pandey 2007). Postindependence campaigns in Karnataka gathered momentum from three social movements in the 1980s: Dalit political parties, the women's movement, and public health HIV prevention initiatives. The interests of these movements converged in the protection of the sexuality of Dalit women from disease and violation. Anti-caste activists sought to withdraw Dalit women from upper-caste patronage. Feminists organizing against sex work and migration for sexual labor as forms of gender violence began framing devadasis as exemplars of child prostitution and sexual slavery (Joint Women's Programme 1989). Interventions in the spread of HIV at that time conflated devadasis with prostitutes and targeted them as vectors of disease (Gilada 1993). Pressure from these three constituencies was effective in prompting the Karnataka State legislature to action. In 1982 it passed the Devadasis (Prohibition of Dedication) Act, which criminalized not only the rite of dedication but all the rites belonging to devadasis and specified fines of 5,000 rupees or prison terms of five years for those who continue to perform them.

Contemporary projects of reform are both continuous with and critically different from colonial-era projects. The debates in the Karnataka legislature repeated many of the themes that had emerged in the colonial period: the threat of contagion, the respectability of women, the distinction between Hindu custom and Hindu religion, and the honor of the nation (Jordan 1993). The legitimacy of governance continues to be at stake in reform projects, but in the context of independent India, the civilizing influence is located in India itself and tied to its ancient past. Thus the aestheticized performer of Indian classical dance represents the sophisticated artistic history and chaste womanhood of India for the new nation, and the devadasi who continues to embody an active mix of religiosity and sexuality stands in need of rescue and reform. Modernist projects of social purification and uplift have combined with a neoliberal logic of eradication in contemporary projects of devadasi reform. According to this logic, productive citizens are distinguished from unworthy populations, which are rendered as "fundamentally without rights" and subjected to discipline (Pandey 2007, 171). In the contemporary period, devadasis have become subjects of state discipline whose protection justifies their abrogation of rights.

At the same time, the logic of purification continues. It helps make sense of why contemporary reform efforts focus intensely on devadasi embodiment, but not on prostitutes generally or female sadhus (mendicant ascetics) at large. Under the national Immoral Traffic (Prevention) Act, 1956, prostitution per se is not illegal, but solicitation is. In the context of an international panic about sex trafficking, some activists have begun to push for the criminalization of prostitution in India (Shah 2008), but for now the secular prostitute is not criminalized or pursued by the state as the devadasi is. Moreover, sex workers in India have been among the most successful in the world in securing human rights and dignity in their communities, whereas devadasis have found no possible ground for collective self-organizing that does not rest on the eradication of the defining rite of their mode of being in the world: their dedication to Yellamma.[37] Recent ethnographies of female renunciates attest to their position in Indian society as marginal but respected figures of religious virtuosity (Denton 2004; Khandelwal 2004). Unconstrained sexuality or female ecstatic embodiment and ritual authority are separately regarded as marginal and circumscribed practices, but they are not subject to erasure in the way that *jogatis*, who incorporate both, are.[38] Religious virtuosity can be made to speak to the spiritual distinction of the modern nation of India, and sexual minority rights to the democratic commitments of the state, but devadasi dedication finds no such translation into modern conceptions of religious and sexual rights. In contemporary national and transnational discourses of reform, the vulnerabilities of caste and gender combine to produce the devadasi as a body of contagion that puts India at risk and to "shame."[39]

Critical histories of devadasi reform in the colonial period have focused on questions of the normalization of conjugal sexuality, the law, and the nationalist movement and have drawn on the legal archives and literatures of reform (Jordan 1993; K. Kannabiran 1995; Nair 1994, 2011; Parker 1998; Vijaisri 2005). That is, they have most closely analyzed the refashioning of devadasis into fit subjects of gender and sex for the new nation and the replacement of a range of family forms recognized in precolonial Hindu law with a single patriarchal model of chaste womanhood informed by Brahmanical and Victorian ideals (Nair 1994; Sreenivas 2008). The reconfiguration of Hinduism through the reform of devadasis has been treated as an aspect of the nationalist dilemma in the face of European appraisals of the presence of active sexuality in temples.[40] In these histories, the problem of religion is subsumed under the question of the woman in the nation—that is, the question of the East and "the colonial rule of difference" (Chatterjee 1993, 33). The religiosity of dedicated women is left to stand as aesthetic performance, an object of secularization or Brahmanization.[41] It is not treated, as I consider it here, as a field of cultural production both shaping and shaped by the woman question and the question of the religion.

Ethnographic work on devadasis has tended to reproduce the representational terms common among missionary and nationalist accounts—those of degraded womanhood and degenerate religiosity (Shankar 1994; Tarachand 1992). Where critical approaches have been taken they have been circumscribed by structuralist and symbolic interpretations of religion (Apffel-Marglin 1985; Assayag 1992; Kersenboom-Story 1987). The vulnerability of devadasis, whose social position and economic viability have been undermined by more than a century of reform, is emphasized by those scholars who see this reform as necessary to progress for women, Dalits, the nation, and Hinduism (Rozario 2000; Shankar 1994; Tarachand 1992). In such accounts, the practice of dedicating daughters to Yellamma is represented as a social evil and a perverted custom exemplifying the exploited status of outcaste women.[42] The structural conditions of the devadasi's existence—hierarchies of caste and gender, exploitive land relations and poverty—are emphasized, and the nonconjugal character of her sexuality is presumed to be coerced. Reformist sociologies frame devadasis as victims and elide the possibility of any sexual or religious agency.

The woman question is always already a question of caste, to be sure. Anti-caste feminist critiques rightly draw attention to the structural vulnerability of Dalit women as a consequence of the poverty and systemic social and political marginalization produced and reproduced through casteism (Kannabiran and Kannabiran 1991; Omvedt 1980; A. Rao 2009, 2003; Rege 1998). They also raise critical questions about caste and gender as entangled forms of embodied personhood, as well as terrains of struggle that can be understood only in relationship to each other. This is true both in the sense that the upper-caste woman was installed as the normative subject of Indian feminism and in terms of the masculine character of the subject of Dalit politics (M. Sinha 2006; A. Rao 2009). These twinned trajectories of politics and representation help make sense of why, in feminist histories, devadasis have most often appeared as exemplary figures of the possibilities of a powerful female and feminine sexuality uncontained by conjugality (Apfell-Marglin 1995; Kersenboom-Story 1987; Nair 1994),[43] whereas in anti-caste and Dalit depictions, they routinely figure as exemplary figures of caste exploitation. Narratives of celebratory recuperation and tragic abjection have overdetermined representations of devadasis.

Here I am working to go beyond the terms of such representations. I am guided in this effort by those scholars who have insisted that caste and gender are materially and conceptually entangled (Kannabiran and Kannabiran 1991; A. Rao 2009; Vijaisri 2004). At the same time, I am departing from the framework of sexuality supplied by most scholarship focusing on the intersection of caste and gender or on the lives of Dalit women. As diagnosed by Foucault (1978), modern forms of power and discourse have installed sexuality as the defining secret of the self, that interior truth that founds identity. In modernity, personhood roots itself in sexual identity and sexual condition. But, as I will show below, modern forms of power and possibility are not the only ones at work on Yellamma's hill (*guddha*). If I were to assume, as many feminist scholars have, that *jogatis* are wholly defined by their illicit sexual identity, I would foreclose these forms of power and possibility. Moreover, a person's structural position in hierarchies of gender and caste constitutes an insufficient measure of the presence or absence of that person's sexual agency or capacity, as close ethnographic considerations of transactional sex have demonstrated (Faier 2009; Kotiswaran 2011; Kulick 1998; Wardlow 2006).

Devadasis are auspicious women. Auspiciousness does not distribute according to social hierarchies; instead, it marks the presence and possibility of life and its renewal. According to Frédérique Apffel-Marglin, "auspiciousness [is] a state which unlike purity does not speak of status or moral uprightness but of well being [*sic*] and health or more generally of all that creates, promotes, and maintains life" (1985, 19). On the basis of her reconstruction of the rituals conducted when devadasis were active at the Jagannath temple at Puri, she demonstrates the salience of the structural opposition between auspiciousness and inauspiciousness in the context of the formal ritual life of a Hindu temple and establishes that devadasis are both auspicious (as wives) and impure (as sexually active but uncontained by conjugality). According to Saskia Kersenboom-Story, devadasis have been situated transhistorically as *nityasumangali* which translates from Sanskrit as always married thus always auspicious. Linking the high ritual and performance arts of temple devadasis with the village rites of the devadasis of Yellamma and Matangi, Kersenboom-Story writes: "At a closer look we see that all *nityasumangalis* and even the devadasi-*nityasumangali* are 'married' first to the goddess or to those objects that can be regarded as her synonyms: the royal staff . . . trident, pot, spear. . . . All these objects can be interpreted as synonyms of the goddess or as the *sakti* of the god. The actual 'marriage' ceremony becomes, due to this symbolism, rather a 'merger' with the goddess" (1987, 78).

In the ethnography that follows, I am building on this recognition of the auspiciousness of the devadasi, but by attending to how and where auspiciousness emerges in concrete and material practices I move beyond the limitations of a symbolic anthropology in which persons appear as signs rather than as actors. For instance, rather than taking the rite of dedication to be a "marriage"—a symbolic version of what is elsewhere real, in my analysis I take it to be a marriage, the thing itself—and ask what the effects of such kin making between humans and deities might be. That is, I am interested not only in what dedication as a rite of marriage might mean, but also, and especially, in what it does as an embodied and material practice undertaken in a field of power. This consideration of devadasi religiosity and sexuality through the lens of practice allows me to situate dedicated women as actors negotiating a variety of constraints and incitements to become more modern, rather than as overdetermined victims of their material conditions or as aestheticized figures of feminine symbolic power.

Worlding the World

The conditions of my admission to the everyday practices of the women who perform rites in the name of Yellamma indicate something about the relations of power structuring the field encounter and the limits of secular social science in the face of a form of sociality that articulates itself in relation to gods and spirits (Chakrabarty 2000; Gupta and Ferguson 1997). Many, even most, of the *jogatis* I encountered in the course of my research for this book were unwilling to talk with me or say much beyond: "The government has stopped all this." *Jogatis* are all too aware that their rites have been set outside the law. Hand-painted murals detailing the banned rites line the walls of bus stations across the region. My efforts to talk with *jogatis* took place between September 2001 and April 2003 and on subsequent trips in December 2005, December 2007, July 2009, and December 2011 in four contexts: (1) at Yellamma temples in Karnataka and southern Maharastra; (2) in a village I call Nandipur (population 5000) in the Belgaum District of Karnataka; (3) among sex worker HIV peer educator communities in Sangli, southern Maharastra, and Gokak, Karnataka, whose members included devadasis and others; and (4) in formal interviews and informal conversations with feminist, sexuality rights, and public health activists in Belgaum, Bangalore, Sangli, Pune, and Bombay. In this book I focus especially on the everyday lives of the four Nandipur *jogatis* who took me to the festival of the river devi in 2002, whom I call Yamuna (then forty-five), Mahadevi (thirty-five), Kamlabai (fifty-three), and Durgabai (thirty-nine). Like most dedicated women in the Belgaum District of Karnataka, they have spent most of their lives in their natal village performing ritual labor, have never contracted a conventional marriage, and have had one or two patrons over the course of their lives.

Nandipur is a medium-size village in the sugar belt, a region in Karnataka just south of Maharastra where Kannada and Marathi are both spoken and frequently mixed. Because of the linguistic complexity of this region and in deference to the conventions of my neighbors, for whom a single unmarried woman constitutes a moral liability, I traveled and worked with research assistants. They were trained anthropologists (Ambuja Kowlgi has a doctorate and Jyoti M. Hiremath a master's degree) and native speakers of both the northern dialect of Kannada and Hindi, a close cognate to Marathi. Kowlgi accompanied me in the temple-based research. Hiremath lived with me in Nandipur, where we were able to create our own household—a space that proved essential for many of the conversations I had with the *jogatis* and others in Nandipur.

As a non-Indian foreigner I was doubly an outsider, and in the rural contexts where I conducted most of my fieldwork, I was widely presumed to take Jesus as my god and to be an agent of the state or central government. In short, I was not to be trusted. These assumptions were well grounded in the history of the presence of white foreigners in rural India as Christian missionaries and agents of the colonial government or, more recently, development workers. My insistence that I was none of these combined with my persistent presence in rural northern Karnataka made me a curiosity. "Why have you come here?" residents of Nandipur frequently asked me. They would have long conversations about the various possibilities: "Is she getting money?" "Maybe from the government?" "How much?" "Did she come to take our names?" "Why is she only talking to *jogatis*?" "Oh, she came to learn about Yellamma, is that it?" There were many theories, some of which found their way back to me. "She came to take you away," some said to the *jogatis*, warning them not to talk to me or at least not to tell me very much. I must have been sent by the government, the denizens of Nandipur decided. The obviousness of this was undermined only by the slow accumulation of evidence to the contrary. I traveled as everyone else did in overflowing jeeps and buses. I lived in the Dalit community. I did not fraternize with officials or socialize with upper-caste householders. Over time, many residents came to believe what I said, that I had come on my own from a university to learn from them and write a book.

Others, I expect, never believed that I was there for any good reason. The self-evident fact of my richness (signified by my American nationality, white skin, store-bought kurtas made of high-quality cotton, camera, and computer) meant I could not possibly be up to anything good. Many of the children, clever, as children are, to discern the best means of disarming adult self-containment, refused to call me by my given name when I passed by, shouting instead, "America, America." At a time when the United States was bombing Afghanistan, I found this substitution of the country of my citizenship for my personal name deeply discomfiting. Whatever it meant for the children, this taunt held a lesson for me in the possibilities of recognition in a geopolitical field of national difference and economic disparity.

In contrast, some people seemed to feel that the privilege I embodied indicated that I could do only good works. One day as I was walking along the road to the next village, a farmer driving an oxcart stopped to say with a broad smile: "Whatever you have come to do here, it is good." For a foolish second I was flattered by this, but then I realized that his praise fit into an overall logic of patron-client exchange relations, in which advance praise of good and generous deeds seeks to secure future patronage. The fraught question of my presence and motivations for information gathering offered some instruction in what anxieties and expectations accompanied the reception of outsiders. One lesson was that among these villagers, little to no distinction was made between government and nongovernmental officials. Both were generally referred to as *sahukar*, a term that can also mean landlord. That a careful calculus of disclosure informed interactions with powerful others—whether landlords, government officials, or Americans with notebooks—seemed an obvious strategy of self-preservation, but sometimes other possibilities of recognition came into play.

One afternoon, I sat and talked with the Yellamma *pujari* in Mandovi, the largest village close to Nandipur, only five kilometers away by a black-top road that cut through fields of green cane. I was a bit drowsy from the heat and a belly full of lunch. She was putting me through the usual queries about my reason for being there, and I said that I had come to learn about

Yellamma. This was my way of dodging the understandable skepticism and defensiveness that saying I had come to learn about devadasis always prompted. She responded with amazement: "But don't they have her in your country?" I explained that some (Hindu) gods had come to America together with many Indians, some of who have built temples to Vishnu, Saraswati, and various other members of the pantheon of Vedic gods, but not Yellamma. "I have only seen her here," I said. The woman sat quietly for a while and then pronounced: "That is why you are here, she has brought you here so you can write this book about her and people in your place can come to know about her."

This *pujari* rendered the seemingly inexplicable presence of an American anthropologist sensible through a theological assertion of the power of the devi in the world. She made a claim not only about Yellamma's power but also about her own knowledge of such power, her ability to speak for it, and, therefore, in some sense to manifest it in the world. This power, I was told, had brought me there to produce knowledge in its name. I was both hailed and positioned, an instrument of the devi's desire to be known.

Such encounters call for something other than ethnography as a signifying practice, an interpretive exercise in "making into an object to be understood" (Spivak 1990, 1). They call on us to be open to the possibility that the world is not as we thought we knew it. My exchange with the Mandovi *pujari* brought to mind Jeanne Favret-Saada's writing about her research on witchcraft in the French Bocage (1980, 1989, 1990). The Bocage peasants refused to "play the game of the great divide" that would have placed her on the side of knowledge, science, and truth and made them exemplars of the backwardness and stupidity of the peasant condition: "They started talking to me only when they thought I was 'caught up in it'" (1990, 191). Being "caught" is to be "affected, malleable, or modified by the experience of fieldwork" (195). It was for me, as for Favret-Saada, the condition of admission to the everyday conduct of a set of highly stigmatized practices. Yellamma, it is said, catches hold (*hididuko*) of those she wants, and the possibility that she had caught me became the ground for my inclusion as a sometimes somewhat insider to the everyday practice of Yellamma *seve* (service, worship) and devadasi rites.

The claim that Yellamma had caught a hold of me was also the way *jogatis* worlded me into their world, a world in which otherwise inexplicable good fortune, hardship, and curiosity are seen as bestowed by the devi, attributable to her play and her power. I use the phrase "worlding the world" to describe the cultural and phenomenal work *jogatis* do in the telling of devotional stories, the singing of devotional songs, the performance of rites, and the conduct of transactions between Yellamma and her devotees. They work on themselves, others, the village, and the world through these practices and enactments. This work, I want to suggest, goes beyond inhabiting a distinct perspective. It is more than simply a view from within a particular symbolic and political order, one not fully encompassed by other, more powerful, orders of knowing and being. *Jogatis* articulate and enact a space, time, and being that centers around Yellamma; they manifest a world. This work is not only about the production and transmission of alternative knowledge; it is also about the manifestation of a cosmological, anthropological, and moral space of being.

Reducing this worlding work to an object to be understood elides the possibility that it is also working on us. In her work on regenerative rituals in Orissa, Apffel-Marglin has written about the epistemic violence such rendering can entail: "Statements [about ritual efficacy] are not meant to be metaphorical, but are literal statements referring to enactments that perform reality" (2008, 17). This critique of anthropological endeavors that conceptually encompass other lifeworlds is consonant with Gayatri Spivak's reminder that modern epistemologies perform the world they pretend to merely describe: "The worlding of a world on a supposedly uninscribed territory [is] the imperialist project which had to assume that the earth that it territorialized was in fact previously uninscribed. . . . Now this worlding is also . . . a making into an object to be understood" (1990, 1).

As a conceptual term, "worlding" refers both to the ritual conjuring that *jogatis* enact and to the refashioning efforts that reformers attempt. Both devadasi rites and reform are world-making projects with epistemological and ontological effects. Multiple ontologies are at play for, and pulling on, *jogatis*. *Jogatis* keep the devi and her rites in order to ward off affliction and regenerate life. They accompany her everywhere she goes in her *jaga*, marking out the paths of her travel across the village, in and around its households, beyond its boundaries for pilgrimages to the main temple, and back again. The forms of power and possibility these paths map out are not legible in anti-caste or secular feminist appraisals of *jogatis'* lives. In order to become recognizably modern, *jogatis* must learn to inhabit the world that reform invites them into and participate in the erasure of the world surrounding their devi. Through ethnography, I invoke the impossible subject position *jogatis* are called into and offer a window onto the violence reform enacts.

The Structure of This Book

Families give their children to the goddess to resolve the *kaadaata* (trouble) she can send. These three terms frame the organization of this book in three parts: gods, gifts, and trouble. The first part takes up the provocation that we do not have to believe in gods and spirits to see that they are alive and well in South Asia (Das 2007; Nandy 2001). Here I am departing from the view that an idolatrous, irrational religiosity is at the root of the practice of dedication. If we no longer wish to map the lifeworld of the peasant on an evolutionary scale as a sign of the past, we cannot continue to relegate the gods and spirits who animate that lifeworld to a time before and space apart (Chakrabarty 2000; Seth 2004, 87).[44] The first two chapters of the book take this postsecular approach to consider what *jogatis* say about the presence of the devi in the world, with them, in them, and through them.

This approach has implications for the organization of the material of the book. Rather than using theory to explain ethnographic description, a method that would place me on the side of knowledge and *jogatis* as objects to be understood, I layer different registers of story and analysis. There are the stories the *jogatis* tell, which incorporate analyses of caste and gender hierarchies; the stories I tell about the *jogatis*—that is, the ethnography; and the stories various other commentators and scholars have told about kinship, religion, and other relevant categories, or the theory. This method makes a point about the politics of knowledge that is germane to the effort of the book as a whole: *jogatis* are not only objects of reform and analysis (knowledge), they are also producers of knowledge. The kind of knowledge they produce is different not in kind, but in register—a point the text makes by tacking back and forth between folkloristic (ethnohistorical), ethnographic, and theoretical modes of writing.

Chapter 1 begins with a devotional story about how Yellamma became sisters with an outcaste devi, Matangi. I put questions of caste politics, land relations, village guardian deities, and sisterhood among goddesses and feminists into play as a means of orienting the reader to a set of overlapping sites of inquiry germane to the book as a whole: material relations, kin relations, and the embodiment of affliction and well-being. The politics of knowledge, authority, gender, and the divine are considered in this account of Dalit female *pujaris* and the Shakta rites they perform.

Chapter 2 counterposes the world that the *jogatis* conjure with the world that projects of reform impose upon *jogatis* and beckon them into. In the first half of the chapter, I describe what it means to keep the devi, to conduct her rites and cultivate oneself in relation to her and to her devotees. I then detail the criminalization of these rites and relations, and the state's injunction to leave the devi. I focus in particular on the medicalization of the matted locks of hair (*jade*) worn by those Yellamma women who enter ecstatic states, act as oracles, and cure afflictions. In a recent government-sponsored campaign, reformers have cut these locks of hair and handed out packets of shampoo as a means of reforming the illicit sexuality of *jogatis*. Associations between sexuality and hair practices have long preoccupied anthropologists interested in the relationship between the body and culture. I draw on this literature to consider the encounter between secular biomedical and Shakta epistemologies of the body that hair reform dramatizes, as well as to situate that reform as a project that seeks to remake not only devadasis but also the goddess herself.

Girls are said to be given to the goddess Yellamma. Both marriage and what is due to the gods take the form of the gift, the focus of the second part of the book. A major theme in social theory, the gift relation has been invoked as a means of critiquing the commodity form (Mauss 1990) as well as of disclosing the social relations undergirding gender as a complementary and unequal relation (Rubin 1975). In this part I consider questions of sacrifice and value in relation to dedication, and dedication as a variation on the form of offerings to deities as well as on the form of marriage.

Are girls sacrificed to Yellamma? Chapter 3 considers the question of the status of devadasi dedication in relation to sacrificial Indian religious practices and its reform more broadly. I describe a practice of naked worship (*bettale seve*) and consider it in relation to Dalit projects of reform as well as scholarly accounts of Tantra in its broadest sense as sacrificial religion. I then consider the configurations of sexuality, gender, and power that relate to sacrificial exchanges, as well as the conception of the human body as an ecstatic medium. This chapter argues that one of the effects of the reform of sacrificial religion is that the mode of bodily commitment (Cohen 2005) that such giving entails has been constrained to secular and familiar ends: kinship.

In chapter 4 I work through theories of the gift and the question of value to challenge the idea that devadasis are sold by their families to the brothels of Bombay. I argue here that we can make sense of the cultural logic of giving daughters only in the context of exchange. Daughters are given, whether to husbands or the devi. When they are given to husbands, they and the wealth they may produce goes with them out of the natal family; in contrast, when they are given to the devi, this wealth remains in the natal family. I suggest, after Claude Lévi-Strauss (1969) and Gayle Rubin (1975), that the devadasi system constitutes a sexual economy that is distinct from the marriage economy and in which the circulation of gifts, women, and gendered obligations implies a different form of value.

The third part of the book considers trouble. Trouble is a discourse about affliction, relatedness, and the devi. Devadasi dedication takes one kind of trouble—*kaadaata*, the affliction Yellamma can send, and converts it into another—kinship trouble. Two kinds of kinship trouble are at stake here: a disturbance in the taken-for-granted form of the family that a marriage between a girl and a goddess implies, and the disruption of the anthropological category of kinship. The third part uses this trouble as an opportunity to consider what kinds of possibilities are opened up when social forms, such as gender and the family, and social scientific categories, such as kinship and religion, are brought into crisis.

In chapter 5, I consider what I call the effects of kinship with Yellamma. In and around the family of Yellamma and in those families said to have Yellamma in them are many forms of kinship trouble. Often dedicated by families that have no male children, devadasis have the economic and social obligations, and some of the privileges, of sons. Like men, they inherit land, pass their name to their children, and roam the village. *Jogappas*, as the male women who are given to Yellamma as boys are called, wrap themselves in saris and sing and dance in her name. Dedication resolves the trouble of Yellamma and produces female-bodied and feminine-appearing sons and fathers and male-bodied daughters, and thus it may be seen to disrupt naturalized gendered divisions of labor and disturb norms of patriarchal arrangement of sexuality—in other words, to trouble kinship.

Chapter 6 considers the implications of this story about the secularization of the marital form and of transactional relationships with deities for anthropological reckonings of kin making and scholarly appraisals of religiosity. Sexuality saturates all religions, I argue, not only those whose illicit nature scandalizes modern sensibilities.

PART I · GODS

CHAPTER 1

Yellamma and Her Sisters

Kinship among Goddesses and Others

"You Will Always Be My Sister"

"Yellamma was hungry," Durgabai began one afternoon over steel tumblers of tea, resting her back against the cool stone wall of my rented house in one of the Dalit lanes of Nandipur. I had asked her to come over and tell me one of the stories she had learned from her uncle, a *jogappa* in Nandipur who was, as she was, dedicated as a child. She was proud of her uncle, whose devotion to Yellamma was renowned and who was a great weaver of tales. He had commissioned the construction of Matangi's multicolored *jaga*, as Durgabai liked to remind people. As a child she accompanied him and the devi to perform rites in the homes of upper-caste landholders. "We used to stay up all night, singing songs and telling stories," she said with evident pleasure. "But now devotion (*bhakti*) has declined among the people and hardly anyone celebrates the devi this way anymore." Wrapping the end of her sari over her head, she eased her way into the devotional tale, displaying the rhetorical grace and skill I had come to expect from her in such telling:

> Yellamma was hungry. She was walking through a farmer's fields and she was hungry. Her stomach was empty and the fields were full. She was walking in the fields and she plucked some green onions and *brinzal* [eggplant] to eat, to fill her stomach. The landlord saw her eating from his fields and became angry. He ran into the fields swinging his scythe and shouting. Shouting and shouting, swinging his arms and that scythe. Yellamma ran and ran to escape him. She ran into the Dalit quarter (*harijan keri*),[1] she was running and running to get away from the landlord. Even into the *harijan keri* she ran to escape him. Yellamma ran into Matangi's[2] house and Matangi said, "Here, hide under these skins," and Yellamma con-

FIGURE 1.1 Durgabai. Photograph by Brett Fisher.

cealed herself in the tanning pits under an elephant hide. The landlord followed Yellamma into Matangi's house. Rushing into Matangi's house he demanded, "Where is she?" "Tell me where she is or I will cut you," he said, holding up his scythe. But Matangi did not say. She did not reveal Yellamma. "Who are you, what are you looking for?" she asked calmly. In anger, he cut off her nose[3] and left. Yellamma came up out of the tanning pits. Seeing what he had done, she restored Matangi's nose, saying: "Because of what you have done, you will always be my sister. When people come to worship on my hill, they will worship you first."[4]

What kind of kinship is this between Yellamma and Matangi? When Yellamma proclaims Matangi her sister, what is she asserting about the nature of the relationship between them? She is not claiming shared parentage or, in the Kannada idiom, of having come from the same stomach (*hotte*). Neither does her tale offer any suggestion of a marriage that would affiliate the two devis through one or the other's husband. This kin making transgresses caste endogamy, according to which affiliation should only occur within one's own community. Matangi—whose tanning pits indicate her membership in the leather-working Madura *jati* (community, subcaste),[5] formerly designated as untouchable—is claimed as kin by Yellamma, whose desperate rush into the Dalit community is evidently into unfamiliar territory. This is an affiliation underwritten by something other than what the father of modern kinship theory, Lewis Henry Morgan ([1870] 1997) identified as the two organizing structures for human kin making: "consanguinity" and "affinity."[6]

I began to wonder about the nature of this tie between two goddesses, and its seeming inextricability from questions of caste, gender, and property, when I first encountered Yellamma and Matangi together on Yellamma's hill at Saundatti. It was during the annual pilgrimage season, the day before a full moon festival, and the hill was thickly carpeted with the encampments of thousands of devotees. Each encampment represented a group of people who had traveled together from a village or town, bringing the Yellamma of that place with them. But she did not come alone. Virtually every encampment had another traveling deity who, like Yellamma, took the shape of a brass or silver face fastened to a dowel set in the center of a *jaga*. In one encampment I watched a woman prepare the devi for *puja*. After polishing the brass *murti*, she wrapped around the dowel a new sari, the ends of which fell in folds in the bottom of the basket. In the basket next to Yellamma was another basket with two *murtis*. I walked from encampment to encampment asking devotees who was in this second basket.

FIGURE 1.2 Yellamma (left) and Matangi. Photograph by the author.

"That's Matangi—Yellamma and Matangi."

"Who are they to each other? Why are they together?"

"They are sisters (*akkatangi*)."

Jogatis told me the story of how Yellamma and Matangi came to be sisters. As I learned, *jogatis* are the keepers of this story and other devotional songs (*bhajans*) and stories about the life of Yellamma and her work in the world. These oral texts constitute a body of knowledge transmitted through a lineage of Dalit male and female women dedicated to Yellamma, and sometimes to Matangi.[7] It is a body of knowledge that falls into a tradition of non-Sanskritic Shakta religion that is widely practiced all over South India. It overlaps and interweaves with the Sanskritic Shaivite tradition that Yellamma is associated with at her main temple, where Lingayat *pujaris* conduct her *puja*. The Dalit body of knowledge transmitted by *jogatis* in the villages and towns where they conduct the *puja*, however, offers a distinct perspective on the life of Yellamma. The particularity of this knowledge and its implications for being and acting in the world are a central preoccupation of this book. What sort of knowledge is this that *jogatis* keep?

I take this body of knowledge and its transmission to be productive of particular ways of conceiving, enacting, and being in the world.[8] That is, this knowledge generates not only a particular perspective or way of seeing, but also a specific world or way of being in it. The oral performances of *jogatis* constitute a mode of creative cultural agency: "Like any art form, [folklore] is a reformulation of the world" (Blackburn and Ramanujan 1986, 30). What kind of world do *jogatis* conjure up in their oral and ritual performances? What sort of knowledge do they produce?[9]

As Durgabai recounted, Yellamma is hungry and, finding herself in the midst of an abundant field, helps herself to the crops. The landlord, apparently more alarmed by this encroachment on his property than concerned about Yellamma's hunger, sets out after her, prepared to do violence. Yellamma finds escape in the untouchable community, in the lane of the lowest among outcaste *jatis*—the Madura (or Matiga), whose hereditary occupation is understood to have been the removal of dead animals and the tanning of hides. Once in Matangi's home, Yellamma conceals herself in the most polluted place possible according to Brahmanical reckoning—the tanning pits—but when she emerges, she has lost none of her powers and is easily able to restore Matangi to wholeness. Her power thus reveals itself to derive from something other than ritual or caste purity. Matangi stands between the violent enforcement of private property rights and

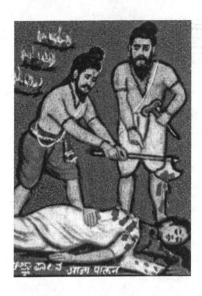

FIGURE 1.3 Parashurama wielding his axe. Offprint poster from the bazaar at Yellamma's temple in Saundatti, circa 2001.

upper-caste entitlement, on the one hand, and Yellamma's access to sustenance and bodily integrity, on the other hand. Matangi's bodily sacrifice becomes the occasion for inclusion in the family of Yellamma, restoration to wholeness and the privilege of being worshipped first.

The kinship between Yellamma and Matangi forges itself in opposition to the violence of gender, caste, and land relations. In addition to being a celebration of the power of Yellamma, Durgabai's story offers a critique of the property relation in which the labor of landless outcastes is extracted in order to produce the surplus wealth of the landholding farmers. This is no abstract matter in a context where most of the arable land is held by upper-caste farmers, and virtually all of the field labor is performed by largely landless Dalits, among whom subsistence living is not uncommon. Hungry men, women, and children from the communities designated as outcaste are surrounded by fields of grain, vegetables, and sugarcane. They might labor in these fields, but they have no right to the harvest except, possibly, as payment for their labor.

In a variation of this tale told about Yellamma, it is not the farmer who chases Yellamma, but Parashurama, her warrior son, who cuts off her head at his father's bidding. In this version, as told by Dalit women *pujaris*, Parashurama pursues but does not kill Yellamma, who escapes into Matangi's home. Parashurama is upset because he doesn't know who or where his father is. Parashurama is angry, running after Yellamma with his axe and demanding, "Who is my father? Why do people call you *randi* [widow/whore]?" The critique of gender relations and the violent regulation of female sexual purity is even stronger in this version of the story. Here sisterhood between Yellamma and Matangi emerges in the face of a son's brutal demand for his patronym.

Jogatis, who tell this story, have no father's name to give their children. Indeed, reformers seize on this lack as a prime indicator of the tragic condition of children of devadasis. In street plays sponsored by a government reform project, young Dalit men dramatize the stigma that children who can claim only *devaru* (god) as a father are made to feel. In one dramatic skit that I observed performed at Saundatti during the high pilgrimage season in 2003, the daughter of a *jogati* was singled out among a classroom of children as the one child unable to provide a patronym. The quiet effort of the child—"My mother is a devadasi"—was drowned out by the teacher's demand: "Who is your father? Who is your father?" The relative advantages or disadvantages of having a father one can claim as such notwithstanding, the stigma of being fatherless is difficult to bear, a fact many of the sons of devadasis I knew made clear to me.[10] But the image of Parashurama chasing after his mother brings another stigma into view: the one attached to the *rande* whose uncontained sexuality is felt to stain family honor. This, then, is also a story in which a kinship between two goddesses emerges in the face of the violent attempt to tether female procreative power to the patrilineal family form. Within living memory it was told regularly, and it is still sometimes told on auspicious occasions in upper-caste landholding households by Dalit female *pujaris* (*jogatis*). This story, and Durgabai through its telling, worlds a world in which dominant constructions of kinship, land, and gender relations are cast in a negative light by and through the devi's manifestation.

Durgabai puts several themes into play in this story about the kinship between Yellamma and Matangi: the political economies of land, caste, and gender in rural northern Karnataka; devi-centered religiosity; and the question of critical consciousness in relation to social position. In this chapter, I offer the reader a set of empirical and analytic orientations to these questions, through which the meanings of Durgabai's devotional tale and the effects of her telling might be considered. In relation to rural economies of gender and caste, Durgabai's position, like that of other dedicated women, is marginal at best. Her relationship to Yellamma, however, complicates this marginality, converting it into possibilities of critique and livelihood that run counter to upper-caste and male-centered conceptions of family. These effects of kinship with Yellamma have implications for feminist appraisals of relationships between goddesses and women, as well as understandings of Dalit women's consciousness. They also speak to the limitations of secular understandings of both kinship and religion.

Gender, Caste, and Land Relations

Rural poverty is centrally a question of land relations. In their analysis of structural inequities in Karnataka, R. S. Deshpande and D. V. Gopalappa write: "Land is a major determinant of access to resources in rural areas . . . [that affects] the intensity and extent of poverty" (2004, 76). Those without access to land lack the means of producing their own sustenance. They must labor on someone else's land or depend on someone who does. Land relations both mediate and are mediated by questions of caste and gender.[11] To put the point somewhat differently, gender and caste are the primary determinants of one's possible relationship to land, whether that relationship is one of ownership, management, or labor. The recent history of land relations in Karnataka, as in South Asia broadly, has been marked by three significant shifts. Under British colonialism, there was a consolidation of systems of land tenure and taxation. After independence, tenancy acts assigned land back to tenant farmers; and more recently there have been changes driven by trade liberalization and corporate globalization.

Under British rule, three types of land administration were stabilized in the subcontinent: the landlord system (*zamindari*), the system of individual cultivators (*ryotwari*), and the village collective system (*mahalwari*).[12] Under all three systems, which aimed to produce greater and more reliable land revenues and worked through bureaucratization and privatization of landholding, women and Dalits tended to lose rights in and access to lands previously held in common and open to foraging.[13] Although the *ryotwari* system prevailed in South India, in some areas landlords were able to maintain their tenure.[14] This was the case in Nandipur, a village in the Belgaum District of Karnataka State, part of the Bombay Presidency during the colonial period. Prior to that, the village was part of the Maratha Empire, which ruled the territory from 1674 until 1818. The medieval Maratha stone gate framing the entrance to the homestead of the once headman of the village stands as evidence of this history. Direct descendants of a Maratha sirdar (feudal landlord), this Brahman family's landholdings included the entire village within living memory.

Under the colonial administration, feudal lords who had been tax collectors over large territories became proprietors, and working farmers—often called peasants—were transformed into tenants. This system disempowered the tillers of the land and produced a whole new class of intermediary managers and moneylenders. Tenancy laws enacted all over India after independence sought, by assigning agricultural lands back to tenant farmers and establishing ceilings on the size of landholdings, to abolish such concentrations of land in the hands of a few and the abuses by intermediaries associated with them. In Karnataka—a state formed in 1956 from territories formerly part of the Bombay and Madras Presidencies, the kingdom of Mysore, and the princely state of Hyderabad—a tenancy act was first passed in 1961. This law remained largely ineffective until landholding ceiling amendments were adopted in 1974 (Appu 1966; Hanstad, Nielsen, and Brown 2004; Rajan 1986).

Across most of northern Karnataka, the greatest beneficiaries of the tenancy act were the Lingayats who had been tenant farmers. Brahmans dispossessed of lands went into industry whenever possible. Partnerships of Brahman men whose landholdings had been radically reduced under the tenancy act owned the two sugar factories closest to Nandipur. This industry was second only to the agricultural sector as a local source of regular paid work. Lingayats are the regionally dominant caste, making up approximately 16 percent of the state population but holding 36 percent of seats in the Karnataka Legislative Assembly (Shastri 2009, 252). In the northern districts of Dharwad, Belgaum, and Bijapur, where they are concentrated and "dominant," they account for 35 percent of the population (McCormack 1963). The concept of a dominant caste was developed by M. N. Srinivas (1955) to convey the social fact that Brahmans are not always or everywhere the most economically and politically powerful caste, although they rank at the top of the Varna system. In his words, "a caste may be said to be 'dominant' when it preponderates numerically over the other castes, and when it also wields preponderant political and economic power" (18). A majority of Yellamma devotees are members of dominant castes, either Lingayats from Bombay Karnataka or Marathas from southern Maharastra.

Although many Dalits were granted lands seized by the government under the tenancy act, these parcels were very small and typically of very poor quality. A Karnataka government report from 2005 describes these lands as "marginal and small holdings which are not viable" (Sudarshan 2006, 215). Moreover, the increase in the Dalits' land did not measurably reduce the percentage among them dependent on other people's land for their livelihood. According to the 1971 census, 47 percent of scheduled tribes and scheduled castes—a bureaucratic category roughly equivalent to the political category Dalit—were landless agricultural workers; in 1991 this percentage was 48 percent (Yadav 2004, 99). The 2005 government report states that 75 percent of scheduled castes were dependent on agricultural labor for subsistence (Sudarshan 2006, 214). In Nandipur the land owned by Dalits was at the tail end of the irrigation distribution system, where water tended to be no more than a trickle. During drought years, owners of these plots often decided against cultivating the land, reasoning that they couldn't count on sufficient water to produce crops enough to cover the expenses of planting. But given rain, or sufficient river water released through the irrigation system, those who farmed these small holdings were able to turn a profit and significantly contribute to the security of their households. In December 2011 Yamuna's son proudly displayed to me the hectare of land he had inherited from his mother, planted with *brinzal*.

Deriving benefits from farming, however, depended on the ability to hold onto one's rights to land, a challenge I watched Durgabai struggle with. She had borrowed against her land, a common practice among the rural poor who need cash to pay medical bills or wedding or death expenses, which frequently far exceed the earning capacity of their household. She did not work the land herself. Her sons were not interested in farming and had gone off to work in textile factories in southern Maharastra. The money she was able to earn by leasing the land to someone else to till was insufficient to pay off her debt, and the exorbitant interest continued to mount. This kind of usury—interest rates can be as high as 50 percent—was common in Nandipur among Dalit families and is cited by analysts as one of the chief causes of the eroding land base among Dalits overall in Karnataka (Deshpande and Gopalappa 2004; R. Rao 2005).

The effects of trade liberalization and the decline in the agricultural sector of the Indian economy broadly are also linked to the declining amount of land owned by Dalits in Karnataka (Yadav 2004). Many young men from Nandipur besides Durgabai's sons have migrated to the towns and cities of Maharastra in search of wage labor in construction, sugar production, or textile factories. But industrial jobs are more and more difficult to come by, and few among these young men are able to acquire the education and payments[15] necessary to gain service-sector or government jobs. State investment in cyber- and biotechnology industries in southern Karnataka have turned Bangalore, often referred to as the Silicon Valley of India, into a global city. These investments have come at the expense of the northern part of the state, where agriculture predominates and where state commitments to industry, transportation, adequate clean water, and regular electricity are lacking.[16] This underdevelopment of Bombay Karnataka comes at a time when practices of monoculture and seed and fertilizer licensing, together with the collapse of agricultural commodity prices, have put farmers in an increasingly untenable position. An epidemic of suicides among farmers has been one of the most dramatic and tragic manifestations of the crisis in the agricultural sector (Menon 2003; R. Rao 2005).[17] The inability of farmers to recover their investments, and therefore to pay off their debts, is partly a result of the deregulation policies attached to structural adjustment packages. For example, as Rahul Rao (2005) describes, beginning in 2001 under the Karnataka Economic Restructuring Loan, the state power utility was privatized, and farmers lost part of the subsidy providing free power to run agricultural water pumps. Some already indebted farmers, when confronted with electricity bills running into thousands of rupees, decided to end their lives (Menon 2003). In the context of international forums, the Central Government of India has been quick to point out the structural inequities built into free trade agreements in agricultural markets and worked with Brazil and China to create protections for small farmers against factory farming (Shiva 2004). At the level of state government, however, debates about farmers' survival have tended to focus on assessments of farmers' characters rather than critiques of free trade. The government of Karnataka report titled "Farmers' Suicide in Karnataka—A Scientific Analysis" concludes that the root causes of farmers' suicides are alcoholism and backwardness, rather than underlying structural changes in the world agricultural economy and domestic policy (Menon 2003; Shiva 2004).

The forms of prosperity produced by the new economy have had little or no positive effect on what opportunity structures (Ong 2003) are available to Dalits or the rural poor generally in terms of access to training, education, salaried work, or loans for entrepreneurial endeavors. Indeed, the conditions of the new economy have intensified the concentration of poverty among Dalits (Desrochers and Veliyannoor 2004). At a time when the promise of the agricultural sector is in decline, the rural poor are increasingly dependent on its possibilities. As we have seen, advocates for Dalits and women of all communities agree on the importance of land rights for the alleviation of poverty and other forms of social and economic marginalization.

Rural women's ability to hold arable land in their own right is arguably the best predictor of well-being for them and their children (Brown,

Ananthpur, and Giovarelli 2002). The economist Bina Agarwal (1994, 1998)—whose extensive research has documented the direct and indirect benefits to women and their children of owning land to which they have unmediated access—cites the direct advantages of the possibility of cultivating crops, growing trees, or keeping livestock as well as the indirect opportunities to gain credit, sell or mortgage an asset, and make claims on and expect support from kin who stand to inherit that asset. This observation held true in the case of Durgabai, who had been able to borrow against her land as well as to use it to win a measure of respect from her brothers, who hoped one day to gain rights to her land.

The fact that Durgabai even held land in her own name was a result of her dedication to Matangi; *jogatis* may inherit land from their fathers or mothers, and most do. Indeed, *jogatis'* ability to continue their lineage by carrying the family land and name into the next generation was frequently cited to me by parents with no sons as the reason for dedicating their daughters.[18] Using a common idiom for lineage, Durgabai put it like this: "I was tied [to Yellamma] so the lamp could continue" (Nanga katyari deepa kayuvadu). Although Hindu women were granted the right to inherit paternal property under the Hindu Code Bill in 1955–56, across India they have mostly forgone this right in favor of maintaining gendered codes of sister's loyalty to brother and self-sacrifice (Basu 1999). According to the Karnataka Household Asset Survey 2010–11, only 13 percent of agricultural land in Karnataka is held by women (Swaminathan, Rahul, and Suchitra 2012, 6). In a survey I conducted in Nandipur among Dalit households, 100 percent of devadasis held land in their own name, compared to 13 percent of *gandullavalu*.

This brings me to a certain irony. Among scholars concerned about the alleviation of poverty among Dalits and women, strong agreement exists that rights in and access to land is critically important. It might seem to follow that the distinctive access to rights in land that devadasis have would be noteworthy in accounts of the status of dedicated women. However, in accounts that seek to specify the economic and social location of devadasis, they are overwhelmingly represented as degraded, lacking rights or agency, and exemplary of the exploited condition of Dalit women generally. Below I offer two representative quotations that exemplify this pattern.

In a predominantly agrarian economy such as India, arable land is the most critical form of property, valued for its economic, political and symbolic importance. It is a productive, wealth creating and livelihood sustaining asset. Traditionally it has been the basis of political power and social status. For many, it also provides a sense of identity and rootedness within a village. However, while the importance of command over landed property is well recognized in household-level analyses, its importance in defining women's situation and gender relations needs elaboration. . . . Independent and effective rights in arable land are important for rural women in general, and for widows in particular, for several reasons, the most critical being the implications for women's welfare. Especially among poor households, land rights can substantially reduce women's risk of poverty and destitution, partly due to the general positive effect of women having access to economic resources independently of men, and partly from the specific advantage associated with rights in arable land. (Agarwal 1998, 2–3)

Dalit women's sexuality has been subjugated to various kinds of interpretations. On the one hand, some have tried to point out that because of their comparative economic independence they enjoy autonomy or control over their sexuality. Whereas the caste-ridden Indian social order has construed and justified them as instruments of upper caste perverted sexual pleasure. The Devadasi system, which legitimizes sexual violence and discrimination against Dalit women, is in fact, an attempt to control and enslave Dalit women's sexuality by giving [it] a religious sanction. (National Center for Advocacy Studies 2001)

Writing about rural women in general, Agarwal argues that rights in land are critically linked to their well-being, especially in the case of women with scarce resources. Focusing on dedicated women, the National Center for Advocacy Studies, in contrast, dismisses the significance of economic independence, arguing that these women's exogamous and extramarital sexual relations constitute sexual violation and situate them as victims of upper-caste sexual perversion. In such accounts, sexual purity is the only kind of positive value that women can embody. It trumps economic autonomy. The loss of sexual respectability is ruinous, and endogamous marriage is quietly placed as the proper container of female sexuality. Religion is a nefarious actor, sanctioning caste violence and sexual slavery.

How might this disjuncture between the facts on the ground and feminist and anti-caste representations be understood? It might be framed as an example of the enduring significance of the woman question, here, as often in colonial and nationalist discourses, a matter of women's status in relation to repugnant custom. It might also be more specifically situated at the complex intersection of anti-caste politics and gender reform. On the

one hand anti-caste radicals critiqued the Brahmanical ban on widows' re-
marriage and advocated for gender equalitarian and intercaste marriages
without Brahmanic priestly officiation. These activists recognized the ways
that endogamous marriage and female sexual constraint were implicated
in the reproduction of the caste hierarchies they sought to dismantle, as
demonstrated by the Satyashok marriages that Jotibai Phule and his wife,
Tarabai Shinde, campaigned for in Maharastra at the end of the nineteenth
century and the self-respect marriage movement led by Periyar, or E.V.
Ramasamy Naiker, in Tamil Nadu in the 1930s (A. Rao 2009, 50–53). On
the other hand, even as they undermined caste ideology by reformulating
marriage and sexuality, as Anupama Rao pithily observes, "they were by
no means immune to the extension of novel patriarchal practices into their
own households" (2009, 53). Late twentieth-century Dalit political ideology embraced sexual purity and respectable womanhood as necessary to
the strength of the Dalit community, the possibilities of Dalit political participation, and the restoration of Dalit masculinity (68). It also conceived
of Hinduism as an impediment to Dalit politicization and conscientiza-
tion (Omvedt 1994; A. Rao 2009). Representations of dedicated women as
totally degraded have taken shape within such conceptions of secular politics, purified sexuality, and encumbering Hindu custom.

The politics and semiotics of gender, property, and personhood are also
critical to understanding why devadasi land rights do not register as an
asset in anti-caste narratives. Whereas feminist materialist accounts focus
on property as an economic resource, anti-caste accounts emphasize the
burden of stigma attached to caste or occupation-specific land grants. Both
Dalits and dedicated women have been alienated from, or have alienated
themselves from, rights to land that were attached to occupational duties.
Two small histories of land alienation are instructive here.

Property regimes generate both forms of sovereignty and personhood.
The advent of modern state formations, privatized (and taxable) land, and
the autonomous (self-possessing) individual are mutually implicated forms
of governance, property, and personhood. In precolonial princely states,
the sovereignty of the king and the *inams* he granted in recognition of extraordinary service were similarly entangled. This was not lost on the new
bureaucrats installed in the princely state of Mysore at the turn of the century. In their bid to alienate devadasis from their lands, according to Janaki
Nair (2011, 209–11), they sought to gain access to land and land revenues
as well as to disturb the role that temple dancing played in reproducing
the sovereignty of the Maharaja. The bureaucrats sought and found—in

the new immorality of the devadasi—grounds for dispossessing dedicated women of their lands as well as a new kind of sovereignty, that of the reformer acting on behalf of the good of the people. As holders of *inams* or *inamdars*, devadasis were allied with the temple and the king; their uncontained sexuality was regularized within this regime of dedicated labor (performance) and property rights. Once dispossessed (either by resumption of lands or claims by others, usually male kin), they became public women who could rely only on private patronage. This, as Nair notes, marked a shift in forms of state sovereignty, from that of temple or king to that of the bureaucratic state, whose functionaries often became the new private patrons of devadasis. The alienation of *inam* lands from devadasis on the ground of their sexual status also paved the way to the establishment of land rights for all women, as chaste wives (within the framework of the patriarchal family) under an amendment to Hindu law in 1933 (Nair 2011, 216). However, as Srimati Basu's (1999) research in the contemporary period demonstrates, female sexual respectability and gendered filial loyalty continue to sit uneasily next to female property holding. Together, Nair's history and Basu's ethnography suggest that in the modern period, land tenure confers sexual illegitimacy and gendered impropriety on women and sexual sovereignty on men.[19] This background helps explain why, as I observed in the contemporary period and as the historians Rachel Sturman (2001) and Anupama Rao (2009) have documented in the colonial period, the Dalit reform of devadasi dedication occurred alongside successful efforts to consolidate land tenure and inheritance practices among Dalits around patrilineality.

B. R. Ambedkar made a bid for land reform among the Mahars in the 1920s. A prominent leader of the anti-caste movement in western India, lawyer, philosopher, and the principal architect of the Indian constitution, Ambedkar is widely revered for his theory of Dalit liberation and skillful political leadership.[20] He was himself from the Mahar community. As boundary keepers and dispute settlers, Mahars were leaders among communities designated untouchable. By the time of Ambedkar's campaign, most of them had left their home villages and traded the military training pursued by their fathers and grandfathers for education and urban life (Fitzgerald 1999). This was Ambedkar's own trajectory: his father had served in the Indian Army and moved the family to Bombay in 1902, where Ambedkar became the first person from a community designated as untouchable to attend Elphinstone High School. His land-reform campaign focused on the *mahar vatan*, a form of untaxed heritable land grant attached to caste-specific labors. Unlike members of other untouchable castes who were associated with a specific trade (for instance, the Madiga with leather tanning) the Mahar Vatandars performed a range of tasks for the village as a whole: delivering mail, rebuilding walls, resolving boundary disputes, and removing animal carcasses. Different from other *inams* granted under the Marathas, the Mahar lands had not been converted into taxable property at the time of Ambedkar's campaign. He framed these holdings as stigmatized because they were attached to the performance of forms of work understood to be impure and to confer untouchability. In an attempt to get the work salaried and to detach the lands from the performance of stigmatized labor, he urged Mahars to give up such lands. Many Mahars resisted, reluctant to forgo their land rights and become, in effect, salaried government servants. Others embraced the possibility of detachment from stigmatized labor and property. The *mahar vatan* was eliminated in 1959 (A. Rao 2009, 107–17).

Ambedkar sought to liberate Mahars from the forms of servility and duty to the village that the *vatans* conferred and to situate them as unencumbered rights-bearing subjects before the state. This implies several shifts: from the sovereignty of the village to that of the state, from obligated to self-possessed personhood, and from rights to land attached to labors performed to the right to own and contract one's labor at will. To restate the overall point of these two histories of land dispossession and reform: property produces forms of personhood as well as political orders.

I was given two different orientations to the everyday life of the nexus of land relations, the politics of caste, and the question of dedication soon after arriving in Nandipur to live among and work with the *jogatis* there. The first came from Dalit activists, young men associated with the Bahujan Samaraj Party (Party of the Majority, BSP).[21] The second came from the *jogatis* themselves.

On hearing a brief description of the study I had come to do in Nandipur, Shantawwa—the woman who presented herself for the job of cooking for Jyoti and me—declared: "No one believes (*nambikke*) in Yellamma in this village any more, only in Ambedkar. In my brother's house, we are not allowed to do *puja* for any of the gods." As we set up rudimentary shelves for dry goods, decanted cooking oil, and boiled water for drinking, I attempted to digest this statement about the fall of the devi and the rise of Ambedkar among Dalits in Nandipur. He renounced Hinduism as irretrievably casteist and, near the end of his life, embraced Buddhism at a mass conversion ceremony. This conversion has been widely emulated among politicized Dalits. In Nandipur twin offprint posters of Ambedkar and Buddha adorn many a household wall.

The next day, as I continued to unpack and attempted to accustom myself to the intense curiosity and early visiting hours of my new neighbors, I received a guest who offered me an erudite and patient lesson on the perspective of young Dalit men and the political project of Dalit mobilization and social reform. I sat down in the middle of my boxes to talk with him and his peers, who began by asking about the nature of my study. I was not the first person to conduct research in this village; my visitor, Rajeev Kamble, had himself conducted research in Nandipur, among other villages, and had completed a PhD at Karnatak University, in Dharwad, with which I was affiliated at the time. It was on the recommendation of his brother, a colleague of mine in the Department of Anthropology there, that I had come to Nandipur in the first place. By the time of this visit, Rajeev was already acquainted with the topic of my study; indeed, that was why he had come.

"You are studying devadasis," he said, making a statement rather than asking a question. "Yes, and broader questions of political economy, religion, and women's lives," I responded somewhat defensively, anxious not to appear entirely naïve regarding the issues that were most important to this mild-mannered but fiercely committed Dalit political organizer. For Rajeev, the practice of dedicating daughters is but another example of the upper-caste exploitation of Dalits, here mixed with their predatory desires and false religion. "They want our beautiful daughters, so they spread this superstition among the people," he said. He drew on Ambedkar to place this practice within a centuries-old struggle between Brahmanism as a hierarchy and Buddhism as egalitarianism. I asked him where Dravidian *amma* (mother) goddesses like Yellamma, deities found all over South India but not in the Vedic pantheon, might fit into this schema. He reiterated the fundamental opposition that Ambedkar posed in his later writings between religion, Brahmanism, and casteism versus rationalism, Buddhism, and democracy. Then Rajeev began teaching me about the history of caste-based reservations as a means of building an egalitarian society. He described the local effects of the tenancy act. Brahmans, who had held most of the land, shifted to industry, and Lingayats, who had been tenant farmers, got a great deal of land. Political representation and economic power continue to be held tightly by Brahmans and Lingayats, who collaborate in the continued marginalization of Dalits.[22] As he described it, the solution for Dalits lies in their conversion to Buddhism, the reservation system, and the political mobilization of Dalits as a voting bloc.

Rajeev framed the devadasi system as a mode of exploitation, based on superstition and caste hierarchy, calling it "just a religious sanction for prostitution." He equated the practice of dedicating daughters and the migration of young women to Bombay to work in brothels. This absolute conflation between devadasis and brothel-based prostitutes was commonly asserted, but not borne out in my research. I questioned his assertion, citing examples of dedicated women who had never left their natal villages, maintained lifelong fidelity to one patron, and did not see themselves as prostitutes. Rajeev then suggested that the illegitimacy of the children of such devadasis renders them prostitutes.[23] The stain of illegitimacy and stigma of loose sexuality cast by devadasi dedication on Dalit families informed the views of Dalit activists like Rajeev, who looked toward a future of social and political equality. The practice of dedicating daughters to Yellamma, in this framework, is just one more impediment to the progress of the Dalit community. I found a general consensus on this point within the Dalit community in Nandipur. However, the horizon the *jogatis* looked to brought other measures of well-being into view.

Later the same day, they called me to come with them to go on *phere* with Yellamma and Matangi. This is a seasonal rite in which the *jogatis* carry the devis from farmhouse to farmhouse, bringing their blessing and taking grain. On that first day when Jyoti and I went on rounds with the *jogatis*, we found them sitting on the ledge of the foundation wall extending beyond the front of the Iyenar Lingayat house. As the priestly—thus the highest subcaste—among Lingayats, Iyenars are considered elders, and this household was referred to as that of a village headman, second in status only to the Brahman household, whose landholdings had once included virtually all the land that now contained the village. As I came to understand, the senior member of this Lingayat household, a widow, was a very important patron and devotee of Yellamma, and the *jogatis* almost always began their rounds at her house.

As we approached the group that had formed a circle around Yellamma and Matangi where they sat in their brightly painted *jagas* on a bare metal bedstead brought out of the house for this purpose, a daughter-in-law from the Lingayat house spread out a blanket for Jyoti and me. This was a gesture of welcome and honor that had not been made for the *jogatis*, a fact made evident by their position on the rough stone ledge. When we reached the second house, I demurred when a call was issued for chairs for us, saying that "otherwise there will be a bigger fuss for us than for the devi." This was an early moment in my attempts to refuse what I was just beginning to recognize as a caste-based reckoning of social status, literalized and spacialized in the relative positioning of bodies.

Interactions between the *jogatis* and the landholding farmers were almost always marked by caste distinction based on the idea of untouchability. When the group of us were offered tea, more often than not the *jogatis* would be asked to produce their own cups. Jyoti, a member of the Iyenar Lingayat community, would be handed a cup from the household, as would I, the white-skinned foreigner—deemed to be rich by all villagers and presumed to be Brahman by those who understood caste to be a universal scheme of social distinction. For their part, the *jogatis* avoided households where, in their judgment, people were too casteist and frequently commented on the superior cleanliness of their own cups. Even they, however, assumed at first that we would not partake in the leftover cooked food (called *mailige* or impure) given by devotees to the *jogatis*, and it took a bit of convincing before they accepted that I wanted to sit with them and eat as they did, even if that meant refusing the hospitality of dominant-caste householders. These were some of my most awkward moments in the field. I often found that I could not both honor my own standard as a foreign visitor to be as gracious a guest as possible and refuse to participate in casteist reckonings of proper seating and eating arrangements. I could be either rude or casteist. The choice was obvious but nonetheless uncomfortable. The morning I arrived to go on rounds with them brandishing cups for Jyoti and me to use in such households, the *jogatis* laughed and laughed.

Since caste distinction was almost ubiquitously marked by members of the dominant caste observing rules of purity and pollution, the fact that most devotees touched the feet of the *jogatis* in order to take their blessing was remarkable. In that act these dominant-caste devotees were touching the feet of persons deemed untouchable, with whom they would not share vessels, food, or a mat to sit on. Yet to touch the feet of whomever is bearing the devi, her instruments, or her turmeric[24] is to touch the devi, to partake in her auspiciousness. The manifestation of this devi is not subject to a Brahmanical logic of purity and pollution: she rises up out of the tanning pits to heal Matangi. She embodies a kind of power that is not encompassed by pollution and the hierarchy of caste it articulates.[25]

"Why do some of the people only touch the *jaga*, but not your feet?" I asked Yamuna, as we roamed through shining green fields. "Some people are casteist," she replied, giving them responsibility for the limits of their devotion. The *jogatis* did not visit every farmhouse; they skipped those they felt did not display proper devotion. Receiving Yellamma and Matangi with some ceremony; putting aside one's work; offering incense, camphor, or a coconut; and giving some grain were expected. The *jogatis* met such a reception with an offering of a pinch of Yellamma's turmeric for the household and the singing of two or three *bhajans*. If they were offered tea, some freshly cooked food for their lunch, or an especially generous share of grain, they would sing more *bhajans*, give more turmeric, and inquire about the well-being of the household members by name. When devotees offered what the *jogatis* judged to be proper devotion, this was taken as a form of respect by the *jogatis*. When devotees did not manifest proper devotion but attempted to call on the *jogatis* to bring the devis to their home for some occasion, they met with resistance of the indirect, foot-dragging sort. "That day is not a good time," the *jogatis* might say, or "we have some other urgent work," "it is difficult to find a male relative to carry the devis, whose heavy wooden baskets are too much for us to carry," "someone else has also called the devi for that day," and so on. In order to overcome this resistance, devotees would have to adjust themselves to the convenience of the *jogatis*, increase the offerings they proposed to give for the rite, and return to the *jogatis'* homes again and again until the terms of the rite were negotiated. In this way, lax devotees were made to assume the comportment of proper devotees.

The sensibility of the *jogatis* about their relationship with upper-caste devotees stood in stark contrast to the feelings of their sons and their sons' peers. When devotees received the devis with proper devotion, the *jogatis* spoke of this as a kind of respect and compared it to the disrespect of inadequate devotion. But most of the young Dalit men in the village saw this differently: "Why must you go on such rounds, 'begging' at the doors of the *vokkaligar* (dominant caste), bringing shame on us?" This perspective, evident in the careful historical and structural analysis Rajeev brings to his thinking about caste relations, is rooted in the idea that the way out of the violence and indignity of caste society is through Dalit self-sufficiency. Forms of caste interdependence can only perpetuate current social inequities, and the ritual mendicancy of *jogatis* can only bring shame on their families.

A different calculus of relations is at work for the *jogatis*. Political equality is not the horizon they are looking toward. As we walked leisurely along the edge of a millet field under the morning sun on our way to the

FIGURE 1.4 Yamuna and Mahadevi on rounds, carrying bundles of millet on their heads. Photograph by the author.

next farmhouse, Yamuna and I talked about the concerns of their sons. "Should we leave all this?" she wondered. "What do you think?" "It's not for me to decide, what do you think?" I responded, attempting to evade the role of arbiter that I was often assigned. "How can we leave her [Yellamma] after all she has given us?" Yamuna responded. "The young men talk like this, but what are they bringing home?" I wondered out loud, thinking about the young Dalit men I saw gathered under the village peepul tree day after day dressed in pants and shirts, too proud to work in someone else's fields and unable to secure either education or salaried jobs, and observing the large sack of grain Yamuna was balancing on her head as we walked. She said softly: "They are eating on us" (*avaru nammyle tinnakttarri*).[26] Yamuna thus quietly framed the obligated character of her personhood. Head of a household consisting of two younger brothers, their wives, and two of her own sons, Yamuna was the most respected Yellamma *pujari* in the village and renowned beyond it for her skill and talent as a musician.

She had been given to the devi, she was providing for her family—she was not free to give this up.

Yamuna's youngest son, Mahesh, who at 18 was still "eating on her," went along with us on rounds one day. It was early in my stay, and he was still very excited about my presence there and his status as an adjunct member of our household—he performed the essential task of bringing water to our house on his bicycle every morning and managed other household matters—such as calling the electrician when I needed another outlet and chasing a big snake out of the kitchen. We were walking out the north road, past newly cut fields of millet. It was the time of the fall harvest. In the midst of our idle and relaxed chatter about how nice lunch had been, how hot the sun was, how wonderful the harvested fields smelled, Mahesh made a sweeping gesture with his hand and said: "My mother has rights in this land." I was perplexed by this assertion; the land his mother held in her name was in a different part of the village. What could he mean? Jyoti was as bewildered as I was. When we went to the next household and observed the teasing, sometimes bawdy, verbal exchanges between the *jogatis* and the householders who held the title to the land Mahesh had gestured to, we learned that Yamuna's grandmother had been kept by the grandfather of that household. By virtue of that past relationship, Yamuna could claim a share in their harvest. This was a claim above and beyond the exchange that took place when she accompanied the devis to their house. She had inherited rights in that land from her grandmother.

As Rajeev rightly pointed out to me, land and caste relations are highly exploitative—a fact that no one who paid the least attention to the everyday conditions of Dalit existence in Nandipur could miss. This social fact is the object of critique in Durgabai's story about Yellamma's hunger and the angry farmer. The fact that she makes this critique does not alter the objective condition of her own struggle to survive, but it does gesture toward other measures of ethical conduct regarding the proper distribution of the fruits of the land. If the village belongs to Yellamma and you are tied to her as kin, this transforms your relationship to that village.

Both *jogatis* and BSP activists are Dalit cultural actors, but they conjure up different worlds: the activists narrate political history from below and project a future of caste equality, economic autonomy, secular freedom, and community respectability based in female sexual purity. Materializing their relationship with the devi in the world, *jogatis* communicate and enact forms of caste critique and hierarchized interdependence among kin, across castes, and between humans and gods. In Durgabai's poetic formulation, "she is our mother, our husband also. After they tie her beads on us, leaving us in her name, from then on whenever someone takes her name, she enters the mind of devotees and they give us grain. We take this grain and live our life. She is our mother, also our only husband." Both *jogatis* and Dalit activists envision and enact relations among property, personhood, and gender, but they do so in different ways. The politics of kinship and sexuality is a critical fault line of this difference. I found it inscribed in the narratives of anti-caste activists as well as in the devotional stories told by *jogatis*. It also marks scholarly accounts of South Indian goddesses.

Shakta Religion

Shakta, the worship of *shakti* (feminine energy or power) in the form of the devi, is practiced all over the Indian subcontinent and in diasporic communities all over the world. Along with the worship of Shiva (Shaivism) and the worship of Vishnu (Vaishnaivism), Shakta is commonly identified by scholars as one of three major strands of Hinduism (Dalmia and Von Steitencron 1995a). *Shakti* devis are typically understood as being either Sanskritic and more or less pan-Indian or vernacular, regional, indigenous, subaltern, and village-based. One of the interesting features of Yellamma is that she transgresses the division many scholars have made between so called big and little traditions. At the same time, she is not the same goddess everywhere. How and why Yellamma differs from place to place has often been framed as a consequence of kinship.

Most scholars place her as one among hundreds of South Indian village goddesses, or *grammadevata*. These *amma devis* are often said to belong to a village or place, but it is probably more accurate to say that the place belongs to them, and stories abound about how a particular goddess came to be in a specific place (Flueckiger 2013; Kinsley 1988, 178–96). They are the source and center of the village, sometimes marked by and worshipped in the form of a stone and at the navel, or center, of the village, other times kept at the boundary as a guardian. Typically worshipped in their villages with greater attention and frequency than the deities of the Vedic pantheon, they are ambivalent, capable of both causing and curing affliction, especially disease (Kinsley 1988, 197–211). They are also independent, often autochthonous. The identification between the village and the *amma* devi is strong; the well-being of each is tied up in that of the other. One of the ways this association is manifested is in the marriage between the goddess and representatives of the village; this ties the goddess to the village and the village to the goddess in a relation of mutual nourishment of the kind Durgabai described above. Yellamma is in many ways this kind of South Indian *amma* devi, propitiated by her devotees in an effort to cultivate fertility and ward off affliction. Like some other *amma* devis,[27] however, her ambit goes beyond any particular village or town locale. She is a deity with influence across the region.

In villages and towns across the central Deccan, Yellamma is invoked both as *Adishakti*, mother of all, original power, and as a spouse deity, married to Jamadagni, who is a version of Shiva. In villages where her *puja* is conducted by *jogatis*, she is mostly called on as an independent goddess. At her main temple at Saundatti, where her worship is performed by Lingayat *pujaris*, she is predominantly portrayed as Renuka Yellamma, wife of Jamadagni. As *Adishakti*, she is the source of everything, subject to no one. A *bhajan* frequently sung by the *jogatis* begins:

> Adishakti Yellamma, our compassionate mother,
> In all the world, your name holds the most sacred power.

In contrast, in her manifestation as a daughter or consort, Yellamma is subject to the parents who begat her. She can be given in marriage to a husband, as the following excerpt from a devotional song narrates:

> Born of the womb, you came, Yellamma,
> In marriage they gave you,
> to Jamadagni they gave you.
>
> King Renu is your father, Bhogavathi, your mother.
> Born from their very womb,
> they rocked you in a cradle.

These two relative kin positions—autochthonous mother, dependent daughter or wife—are identified with different types of goddesses characterized by scholars variously as non-Sanskritic or Sanskritic (Kinsley 1988), village-based or pan-Indian (Foulston 2002), fierce or benign (Hawley and Wulff 1998), hot or cool (Brubaker 1978), autonomous or consort, and tooth mother or breast mother (Ramanujan 1986).[28]

Like all binary forms, these ideal types obscure as much as they seem to reveal, and I am less interested here in any attempt to classify Yellamma through them than I am in tracking some of the symbolic and political work that proceeds through such classifications. To that end, I consider these different manifestations of Renuka or Yellamma and what variously positioned *jogatis*, temple officials, and academics make of them as narratives about the politics of gender and sexuality imbedded in kin relations.

Independent Hindu goddesses are widely understood to be more powerful, and more dangerous, than their married counterparts. Scholarly interpretations of the significance of this pattern, and its relationship to everyday politics of gender and sexuality, differ. Some offer a schema of sexual opposition and complementarity in which the destructive, disease-causing, and bloodthirsty power of the unpaired or ascendant goddess is contained in, restrained by, and balanced through her marriage:

> Within the pantheon a very dangerous force is symbolized, but this is a force that seems to undergo a basic transformation into something almost antisinister, the loving wife—the source of wealth and offspring when placed in the context of an appropriately restraining social relationship, that of marriage. An appetite for conflict and destruction is thus transformed into the most fundamental of social virtues. Underlying this transformation is a dual notion of divinity, a duality that in turn is linked to the opposition between male and female. When the feminine dominates the masculine, the pair is sinister; when male dominates female, the pair is benign." (Babb 1970, 142)

Based on fieldwork conducted in Madhya Pradesh, Lawrence Babb describes the restraint imposed by marriage as a kind of welcome containment of unfettered, and thus malign, feminine power.[29] Other scholars see the devi in her hot and dangerous form as righteously outraged by male violence and neglect, a devi who requires her devotees to face the harshness of everyday life and its forms of gendered violence and who dispenses justice (Brubaker 1978; Kinsley 1988; Ram 2013). Richard Brubaker writes: "The wrath of the goddess is neither capricious nor perfectly impartial and even-handed. As an expression of sacred power it can of course be either protective or destructive. But as the expression of a sacred power that finds itself periodically threatened, it can be not only dangerous but positively fierce. And these subtler forms of ambivalence find highly appropriate expression in the myths which, in a considerable variety of ways, derive the goddess from a female who is both objectively mistreated and personally wronged" (1978, 382). Interpretations of the meaning of the devi's marital status vary not only among scholars, but also among devotees. In her work on a Tamil town, Karin Kapadia emphasizes caste distinctions in how the goddess is understood relative to the symbolism of heat, sexuality, and marital status:

> One of the most striking contrasts between Brahmanical religion and popular lower-caste Non-Brahman religion is the radical difference in their understandings of the nature of Mariyamman, the Great Goddess. Mariyamman is normally understood to be unmarried: in the Brahmanical view, this makes her an "angry," sexually overheated goddess who is unable to "cool" herself because she lacks a divine husband with whom to have sexual intercourse. . . . However contrary to the view, in the Non-Brahman perspective, Mariyamman *does not need a male god to control her*. For Non-Brahmans, Mariyamman is not . . . merely a most powerful consort of Siva. She is entirely "complete," for she is the Supreme Deity herself. (1996, 159–60)

In Durgabai's tale we have seen Yellamma in her independent manifestation. In another story Durgabai tells, called "How the Landlord's Wife (*sahukarti*) Became a Fly," the consequences of offending her are made dramatically apparent. Yellamma comes as a *jogati* to the *sahukarti*'s house and asks for something to eat. The landlord's wife says she is too busy, to come back another day. Yellamma gives her several opportunities, but when the landlord's wife makes it evident that she cannot be bothered with the hunger of this *jogati*, Yellamma begins to express her rage—and her power. She destroys all the crops and the livestock, kills the landlord with a snake bite and their child with a fever, and reappears daily to ask for grain. The *sahukarti* continues to refuse to offer anything and, in the end, Yellamma turns her into a fly. Sometimes the *jogatis* would joke when a fly came hovering over their food: "There's the *sahukarti*." In the village context Yellamma is most likely to be called on as this fertility-bestowing and death-dealing devi, Adishakti, mother of all, subject to none.

The Spouse Devi

At the main temple complex, where she is surrounded by male kin, Renuka Yellamma appears as a different kind of devi. Three members of the Shakti Sangha—a collective of sex worker HIV peer educators working in a small but thriving commercial town in northern Karnataka—took me on my first trip to Yellamma's hill, where her main temple sits beside the Malaprabha River. One of the counselors working at the nongovernmental organization with which they were affiliated drove the company jeep, paid for with funds from a Dutch development agency, and his colleague, a schoolteacher eager to practice his English, came along. I had not yet begun to study Kannada at the time of that preliminary research trip in 1998, and I was grateful for his translations. I struggled to keep up with his questions about America in the open jeep as we hurtled along the pockmarked roads past fields and fields of sugarcane and corn, through herds of goats guided by nomadic shepherds, past village after village toward the temple at Saundatti.

We parked next to a market stall selling devotional paraphernalia that was attended by a smiling young woman and an unsmiling older one, who upon seeing me, pulled the loose end or *pallu* of her sari over the long *jade* hanging down her back. The schoolteacher pointed this *jade* out to me, saying, "Yellamma." Seeing this, I recalled reading reports of government-sponsored *jade*-cutting campaigns held at Saundatti.[30] We bought small packets of camphor, three coconuts, a garland of flowers, and some turmeric and moved toward the temple. After burning camphor at a small shrine housing the *pada* (footprint) of the devi, we descended the steps toward a sacred well, where we washed our feet, hands, and head in cool water, purifying ourselves in preparation for *darshan*.[31] As we greeted the minor gods arrayed just outside the temple, I noticed that the stone temple walls were loud with color: powdered yellow turmeric and red vermillion had been smeared and thrown everywhere. Inside, bare-chested Lingayat priests tended the devi, whom I just managed to glimpse—a beautiful dark goddess wrapped in a brilliant yellow and red sari—before I was pushed forward by the group of devotees pressing in for *darshan* behind us.

My questions about Yellamma were deflected by my fellow pilgrims, who—rather than offering their own versions—led me to the office of the trust administering the temple[32] where a rotund official who was at first reluctant, then increasingly loquacious, began to tell the devi's story:

> In North India there was a king called Renuka Raja, who worshipped fire. His daughter Renuka was born out of this fire, and because she was so pure she was married to the sage Sri Jamadagni. Jamadagni was a short-tempered man. Daily Renuka collected water from the river for Jamadagni's *puja*. She was so pure she could make a pot rest of a coiled cobra and fashion a pot out of sand to carry the water. One day as she was walking back from the river, she saw *gandharva* [otherworldly beings, literally, fragrance eaters] bathing in the river, in a jolly mood. Renuka saw them and thought, "If I had married a rich person I might enjoy that." Renuka had

an ugly feeling, a sexual feeling; she felt desire for a man. The pot fell and the snake slithered away. Her husband came to know what happened and it made him very angry. He cursed her and ordered their sons to cut off their mother's head. All of them refused except their youngest son, Parashurama, who cut off his mother's head with an axe.[33] In his happiness, Jamadagni granted Parashurama three boons. His first wish was that his mother be restored to life, his second that his father be cool-headed, and his third that his brothers be forgiven for their disobedience. Jamadagni granted the first wish, but not the second and third, and Renuka was restored as a devi.

The trust official went on to recount a long story about the battles fought by Parashurama, a tale recorded in the ancient Sanskrit texts known as the Puranas with many versions across South India (Babb 2002). He might have gone on for hours, with me taking notes, but the others began to notice the setting sun and urged our departure. "Never mind," the official reassured me, "it is all written down in the books."

The anthropologist K. G. Gurumurthy (1992) tells the story of Yellamma's acquisition of a family as a tale of the Sanskritization of a Dravidian mother goddess cult. Yellamma (an independent mother goddess) was rendered as Renuka (a consort goddess) through the acquisition of male kin. In this account, the incorporation over time of Yellamma into a family is understood as a means of bringing rogue deities into the Vedic pantheon through the idiom of patriarchal kinship and the textualization of religion.[34]

In the story of Yellamma offered at the temple by trust officials and in published pamphlets, the devi is born from the beheaded body of an errant woman, Renuka, whose failure to maintain her chastity is violently punished. Her sexual desire should be contained and renounced within her marital relation, the story suggests. Her breach of this containment results in bloodshed; the disruption of the patriarchal family; and the birth of a powerful, angry goddess.

Many versions of this origin story incorporate another element. Parashurama chases after his mother, who is running away from his axe. When he catches up to her, he swings the axe so vigorously that he also inadvertently cuts off the head of an outcaste woman walking by. When Jamadagni grants his son's boon, he tells Parashurama to reattach his mother's head in order to restore her. In his haste, Parashurama reverses the heads, making Yellamma a devi with an outcaste head and a Brahman body and Matangi a Brahman-headed devi with an outcaste body.[35]

Yellamma embodies a reversal of the Varna order of caste, and her sexuality manifests itself as an uncontained and potentially abundant fertility. This is the devi in her aroused state, disrupting orders of caste and gender, dangerous and powerful. But what does this mean for the women who become kin with her, who embody her?

Sisterhood, Women, and Goddesses

How might we think about relatedness between women and goddesses? What, if any, is the relationship between the presence of a powerful devi and the social hierarchies structuring the everyday lives of women in whom she manifests herself? A strictly materialist analysis of the status of women in a particular time and place would focus on the conditions of their labor, their access and rights to land, and their other forms of wealth. The presence or absence of goddesses is surely immaterial to such fundamental arbiters of social and economic position. In some sense this is the argument of Dalit reformers, for whom Yellamma is at best irrelevant—and at worst an impediment—to Dalit self-sufficiency broadly and to the liberation of their mothers, sisters, and daughters from the predatory sexuality and economic exploitation of dominant-caste patrons in particular. But as the call for conversion from Hinduism to Buddhist Ambedkarism demonstrates, the symbolic and the material cannot be so neatly divided from each other.[36] This is especially clear in the case of *jogatis*, whose ties to the devi, rights to land, and kin-making practices are inextricable from each other. Is this to say that their relationship to Yellamma is good for them?

Feminist critiques of dominant monotheistic religious traditions organized around a father god have argued that divinized male supremacy naturalizes patriarchal social relations. They suggest, in a Durkheimian formulation, that when the gods are men, the men are gods (see, for example, Daly [1973] 1985; Goldenberg 1979). In search of an antidote to the divine authorization of social relations felt to be inimical to the well-being of women, cultural feminists in the West have reached back in time to goddess cultures in which women, like their divine counterparts, ruled (Gimbutas 1989). Debates among archeologists and historians about whether such a time ever existed miss something about the mythological character of all histories and the power of the imagination to produce new ways of being human.[37] Within scholarship on goddesses in the Indian subcontinent there is a related debate about whether the ubiquitous presence of living and powerful goddesses makes a difference in the everyday lives of women. Do the relations among the gods teach us something about what is possible, imaginable, or manifest among humans? Embedded in this question is another: what is the articulation between the sociological and the theological, between human social relations and the ways of the gods? A common response suggests that the realm of the gods is a mere reflection of the terrain of human social relations. Rather than posing human social relations and symbolic activity as prior to the gods, I want to pursue a question about the articulation between the two domains that presumes the agency of both. We act on the gods, and they act on us, but in what ways and to what effects?

Critiques of the feminist movement to reclaim the goddess abound. Katherine Young (1991), a historian of religion, emphasizes that relations between goddesses and women cannot be universally diagnosed across historical and cultural differences in the way that the cultural feminist vision of the world historical fall of the great goddess, gynocentric sociality, and horticultural production followed by the rise of ruling father gods, divinized kings, warring states, and agricultural production suggests.[38] These relationships must be specified with respect to time and place. At the same time, Young notes that relationships between patterns of kin making (such as patrilineality or matrilineality); forms of social, political, and economic human organization; and the nature of the gods present in a time and place are observable. In her words, "state formation can be correlated with the emergence of patrilineality (where it has not previously existed) and dual-sex or male symbolism, leading eventually to male supreme deities. . . . Some cultural zones witnessed a change from matrilineality and goddess worship to patrilineality and supreme god worship (sometimes through an interim stage of sacred marriage between a god and a goddess)" (1991, 142). The general pattern that Young describes resonates with what historians of religion have documented in India about Shakta devis, a pattern in which over time many goddesses have shifted from playing a central role in the creation of the cosmos and the production of sovereignty to being sidelined as spouse deities and minor handlers of fertility.

Feminists inside and outside of India have looked to fierce Hindu goddesses such as Kali and Durga as icons and exemplars of what feminine power can achieve (McDermott and Kripal 2003). Some scholars are quite positive about the valence of the relationship between goddesses and the women who most closely tend them. For example, Joyce Flueckiger characterizes the relationship between mostly middle- and low-caste women in Andra Pradesh and the fierce goddess Gangamma as "an empowering relationship in which their shared nature as possessors of *shakti* (female power) is asserted and performed" (2013, xi).[39] Others are more ambivalent. Rajeswari Sunder Rajan (2000) speaks to feminist uses of Hindu goddesses in her chapter "Real and Imagined Goddesses" published in a collection called *Is the Goddess a Feminist?* Sunder Rajan considers whether goddesses might be recruited to the feminist project of recovering the agency of women, but in the end she is fundamentally skeptical about the effects of this recuperation. Her concerns focus on the communal politics of the Hindu Right, which has advanced its cause and drawn women into its fold under the sign of the goddess (Bacchetta 2004; Sarkar 2001; Sarkar and Butalia 1995). The bad faith entailed in the deployment of religious symbols for secular gain, whether by the Hindu Right or the feminist Left, worries her, as does the essentialization of widely disparate female life experiences under the category of women. For Sunder Rajan, the only effective ground from which to counter the Hindu Right is secular.

Madhu Kishwar, a longtime social activist and publisher, offers another perspective on this question of the deployment of the gods. She describes a recent campaign to improve the labor conditions of sweepers in a Delhi neighborhood that proceeded in part through the installation of a sweeper devi in the community. With regard to concerns among secular leftists about the embrace of Hinduism being irredeemably tied to religious nationalism, state, and communal violence, Kishwar writes in the magazine *Hinduism Today*:

> If we want people to gracefully yield space for our newly acquired ideologies, we have to learn to be tolerant and respectful of those they already hold. There is no need to treat our traditional Gods and Goddesses as adversaries, especially considering that they are willing to come a long way to support our causes. At the heart of the controversy between these two opposing approaches to social and religious reform is the key question: How do we relate to our cultural heritage and define our relationship to our own people and the values they cherish? (2004)

I share Kishwar's feeling that the desire to distance oneself from the religiosity of others does not sit well with ambitions for social change. Secular feminisms founder at this juncture. In the terms of one review of gender studies in India: "Despite the appropriation of Kali as the name of the most visible feminist press in India, the feminist distance from religion alienates them from the vast majority of Indian women for whom goddesses are a source of strength, meaning and joy" (Purkayastha, Subramaniam, Desai, and Bose 2003, 514). Bridging this distance is one of the objectives of this book.

At the same time, I too worry about risks of gender essentialism and Orientalism implicit in projects of feminist goddess recuperation, and I share Sunder Rajan's concerns about the instrumental deployment of religion as a means of social change (see also Erndl 1993). As any critical history of religion demonstrates, the gods are hardly stable signifiers. But I resist the idea that secularism offers some kind of stable ground outside the slippery terrain of divinely authorized politics. The idea that greater traction might be found in the territory of the secular presumes that it constitutes a discrete domain of values, motivations, and modes of being. This presumption has been challenged on many fronts by scholars who argue that religion and secularism are mutually constituting domains of human activity and discursive production that have a specifically modern history (Asad 2003; Nandy 2001).

But my greatest resistance to the promise of a secular feminism that does not admit female religiosity stems from my desire to be faithful to the women who patiently taught me who Yellamma is to them. The idea that religiosity, especially female religiosity, constitutes a form of unfreedom or false consciousness reiterates a familiar opposition between reason and its imagined other. This opposition is an all too recurrent aspect of the legacy of colonial rule and the forms of knowledge it has produced (Seth 2004). Secular feminist teleologies of emancipation from religion, in short, are just as problematic as cultural feminist invocations of female-centered and goddess-oriented cultures. Although they assign different values to it, both reassert the opposition between reason, masculinity, and secularism and unreason, femininity, and religiosity.[40] Both are inadequate to an account of devadasi lifeworlds within which the challenges and possibilities of reasoned critique, material livelihood, untethered female sexuality, and devi incorporation are mutually produced and enlivened. One day in the course of a long interview, Durgabai put all of these into play:

> We are left in her name, on her life, to do her *seve*. . . . They call us *jogamma*, also *basavi*. We wander and eat, like a bull [given to a temple]. Also lacking a rope, wandering from here to there, eating this and that. Some of these government people say: "Don't ask for grain, don't enter states of possession, don't play *shruti* and *chowdiki* . . . these are all false beliefs." God is false?! God is not untrue! I do not listen to them. Whatever her rules [the practices that surround her] are, those that have come to us from the past,

they have to be done. What is this government that has come in the middle? That brings laws [banning dedication] saying this AIDS comes from *jogatis*. Aaah! But we ask, "Why should it come from *jogatis*? What about *gandullavalu*? They do all these things, why shouldn't it come from them?" . . . These Ghataprabha [the location of the reform project's office] madams say: "Don't dedicate *jogatis*, don't wander like this, don't eat like that." They say all this in a meeting, they organize a meeting and call us. But we say: "You have told us not to dedicate and we have stopped, it will end with us [in our generation]. But those of us who are here now, how shall we live?" "Regarding your living, haven't we given you [loans for] a house?" they said. "Should we wash the house and drink it?" we asked. We said: "Give us two acres of land. Two, two acres [each], a bore well among four [of us], and we will work that land and lead our lives and those of our children." They found it hard to take, but we said it. They didn't call us for the next meeting. When they told us to stop asking *joga* [asking for grain] we stood up with our argument: "Give us two, two acres of land and we will work that and eat, then we will stop roaming."

Durgabai's rich commentary on reform offers a different diagnosis of Dalit affliction than Rajeev's. What she needs has less to do with sexual respectability ("we wander") and more to do with shares in and rights to land. These material resources are inextricable to her relation to the devi; unless and until they are replaced in kind, she cannot leave the goddess. She dismisses the charge of false belief with indignation and portrays the government as a bad patron whose loans for houses fail to match what roaming with the devi provides. She rejects the presumption that *jogatis* are more promiscuous and less sexually responsible than *gandullavalu*—who also "do all these things." Representations of devadasis as persons devoid of religious and sexual agency fail to account for the forms of material, social, and transformative possibility that emerge from dedication, forms of possibility that Durgabai makes evident. For me, taking the world-making activity of devadasis' religiosity seriously and exploring the effects of their kinship with the devi in relation to questions of property as well as personhood becomes a means of documenting something of this possibility.

CHAPTER 2

Yellamma, Her Wives,
and the Question of Religion

Given the mass attendance at [Yellamma's] festival, it is evident that religious considerations continue to play a major role in the lives of common people as against any social considerations. The reluctance to give up an age-old ritual is clear. It is for the government and voluntary bodies to help the masses give up superstitions and beliefs that do not augur well for a progressive society.

—"Persisting Evil," *Deccan Herald*

They are the devadasis, girls from scheduled castes of a Hindu sect who dedicate their lives to the worship of the goddess Yellamma. But over the years, the religious role of these women has diminished. Forbidden to marry and seek any other forms of employment, they rely on sex work, concubinage or begging.

—Vinita D. Singh, "NGO Lobbies for Welfare Scheme of Devadasis"

Religion in Question

What counts as religion? This is a question about the politics of knowledge as well as about the status of any given set of practices and beliefs. In the first of the two commentaries above on the rituals surrounding Yellamma and the women tied to her who perform them, popular religion is cast as an obstacle to social progress. It is superstition, false belief—the sort of religion that secular institutions of government and civil society must work against in order to pursue the social good. In the second commentary, the religiosity of devadasis is consigned to the past. It has degenerated, and they have become degenerate: prostitutes, kept women, or beggars. This narrative of decline and the distinction between true and false religion are both standard features of religion as a modern form.[1] Within this framework, the religion of dedicated women, if they can be said to have religion at all, is both the origin and a sign of their fallen condition. It cannot be knowledge. It is superstition, an incorrect apprehension of the world leading to a mistaken way of being in the world. Eradicate it and you have redeemed them, reformed religion, and advanced society.

In contrast, consider the appraisal of a Dalit public intellectual and historian, Y. Chinna Rao, in an article titled, "Dalits and Tribals Are not Hindu":

> Numerous writings of foreign travellers and works of anthropologists show that before the advent of Christianity in India, Dalits had a religious system of their own. Dalits are concerned with their local village goddesses. The female goddesses appear predominant. Unlike in Hinduism they emerge as independent, unblushing erotic female figures. Be it the Mariamma, Poleramma, Peddamma, or any local deity, they have nothing in common with the goddesses of the Hindu pantheon. Other than the local village goddesses, they worship kuladevata (caste deity) and Inti devata (family deity). Later these traditions were incorporated as "little" traditions by Brahmanical anthropologists and sociologists to protect their tradition as the "great" tradition, on account of its "intellectual," "classical" and "higher" philosophy. (2000, 156)

Rao suggests that the rites and practices belonging to Dalits have been colonized as a historical consequence of Christian missionary activities,[2] as well as a discursive effect of modern anthropological and nationalist conceptions of Hinduism as bifurcated between high textual and philosophical Brahmanical religion and low vernacular practices. Rao's commentary is in keeping with postcolonial critiques of the category of religion as a Christian theological category that operates as a regulating and normalizing force in the variegated fields of rites; rituals; practices; and modes of address for and relationships with gods, spirits, and saints (Asad 1993; King 1999). In this view, the questionable status of the religiosity of dedicated women is the result of historical configurations of power and knowledge between imperial Britain and occupied India, nationalist elites and vernacular folk, Brahmans and Dalits, men and women.

As noted above, when I arrived in the central Deccan Plateau to begin my research, I did not expect to encounter women whose lives were organized around the performance of the rites to which they were dedicated. The scholarly and popular accounts I had consulted before I began my fieldwork suggested either that these rites had been abandoned or that they were negligible, empty in themselves, merely a false cover for prostitution.

As Rao suggests, such accounts constitute colonial modes of knowledge in which the designation of a set of practices as false or empty is a move of power. Before I read Rao, I encountered the dedicated women who reminded me—when I asked them what they were called—of the critical importance of the difference between modernist representations of religion and everyday lifeworlds of practice. "*Pujaris*," they said. "What else would they call us? We keep the devi."

In their world, who they are in relationship to the devi and her devotees is self-evident and unproblematic: "What else would they call us?" These dedicated women are not unaware of the state's position on dedication. But they are standing in and speaking from a different place, a different world. This world centers itself around the devi rather than around the state, or even against the state. This world can produce, and is produced by, ways of knowing that exceed Christian imperial, Brahmanical Hindu, and secular liberal appraisals of nonmodern ways of being in relation to gods and spirits as false or empty. Consider, for instance, what Yamuna had to say about would-be reformers: "People are confident in themselves and don't believe in the goddess, they think what we do is shameful, but we know what we get from her, eat from her, wear from her. They don't know this, those who are saying all this about Yellamma. If we keep her and serve her with devotion then all these things come to us. Our life will flow toward her and we will feel very happy—however much we roam in the world, in her name, belief in her will become strong, so we are not able to believe what people say."

Precisely because reform is constituted outside of faith and devotional practice, she states, it makes no claim on her. She describes her knowledge of Yellamma's presence and force in the world in material terms, as a recognition of what is true about the world. Yamuna foregrounds relationality, rather than rationality, as the ground of this recognition. The presence of those who roam in her name is her presence; as they move across the landscape, her influence is extended through space. The everyday ritual and performative work of and commentary by these Dalit female ritual specialists calls forth a world in which proper devotion toward the goddess is met with prosperity and happiness (*sukha*). In asserting that devadasis stand in an ethical relationship to the devi, who provides for their needs, Yamuna refutes the claims made by reformers about the economic and moral condition of devadasis. Moreover, she criticizes the stance of reformers as based on ignorance and the hubris of self-reliance.

Taking as my starting point the Yellamma *seve* and regard for devadasis that is part of the fabric of everyday life in rural northern Karnataka, I ask what kind of world devadasis are making as they tell and retell the history of their goddess, enact forms of *puja*, devotion, and ecstatic embodiment, and comment on relations among human beings and between humans and deities. I then contrast this world to that of reform as a means of illuminating their respective politics of knowledge and recognition.[3] I do not mean to portray customary rites as more authentic than projects of reform; indeed, this is one of the reasons I use the language of "world making." Both devadasi rites and practices of reform are world-making projects with real effects. However, whereas one project entails a violent remaking of the other, the other project does not.

Keeping the Devi

It was a hot day, and my colleague—a professor of linguistics at Karnatak University—and I were taking a break from our observations and conversations at the main Yellamma temple in the shaded refuge of his car. Curious, or perhaps understandably wary about the presence of a white foreigner, an older *jogati* approached the car to ask why we had come. "To learn about Yellamma," I answered, and I asked her: "Where are you from?" "From here," she said. "I have lived here for over thirty years." I realized as I listened to her that she had witnessed all the changes wrought by the passage of the Karnataka Devadasis (Prohibition of Dedication) Act, 1982: the last time devadasis danced in front of the devi during the annual procession around the temple complex; the last time they processed en masse from the sacred well up the hill to take *darshan* clad only in neem leaves; the violent disruption of dedication rites by police; the arrival of journalists, filmmakers, and researchers; the destruction of the homes they had hereditary rights to on the temple hill, and their relocation several kilometers away; and the ongoing campaigns to cut the matted locks worn by dedicated women capable of entering states of possession and divination and to stop devadasis from playing sacred instruments and singing devotional songs. I asked her what she had seen change over the time she had been at Saundatti. "There is more and more sin (*paapa*) in the world, and fewer and fewer people coming to the festivals. The goddess has become angry, and people are dying of disease and earthquakes," she said, then calmly turned and walked away.

With this speech act she occupied a place of moral authority and theological knowing. This dedicated woman appraised the consequences of reform, the condition of humanity (more sin, less devotion), and described the affective state of the devi. The subject position her speech act performs takes the world, not the nation, as its frame of reference. She invoked a moral economy in which sin varies in direct proportion to devotion and the anger of the devi is legible in the miserable condition of humanity. The authority with which she spoke rests in her relationship to Yellamma, for whom she spoke and who speaks through her during rites of possession and divination. The power of her position was embodied—indeed, it was literally marked on her body by the red and white beads tied at dedication and worn by all *jogatis* as well as by the long matted locks hanging down her back signifying that the devi had come into her body.

Those who keep the devi, who serve as her *pujaris*, world a world that places Yellamma at its center. The word for her vehicle, the *jaga*, translates into English as basket, world. That is, *jaga* means both basket and world at the same time. When *jogatis* carry her from place to place they often say: "We went with the *jaga*" (Naavu jaga hoogidvi). Rather than referring to the devi, they refer to her vehicle, the world: "We went with the world," or "That farmer called us to come and bring the world, he has arranged his daughter's marriage and they want to fill the *udi*" (*Aa raita namna kardana jaga takondu baraka helyanri, magaldu madvi aiti udi tumb bekantari*).

Keeping the devi involves a variety of practices, including washing and dressing the devi in preparation for biweekly *puja*, seasonal festivals, and the celebration of auspicious occasions in the households of devotees. Dedicated women receive offerings that devotees make and give Yellamma's blessings in return. They perform rites of divination and enter states of possession in which the devi speaks, responding to the petitions of devotees. They accompany the devi wherever she goes, play her instruments, sing *bhajans*, and tell devotional stories. When the village makes its annual pilgrimage to the main Yellamma temple, the *pujaris* bring the devi and conduct her rites on the hill there. They assist devotees in the execution of a *harake*.

I witnessed the performance of all of these rites in the course of my observations at Yellamma's main temple at Saundatti and her four regional temples across the central Deccan Plateau. At those temples I spoke with Yellamma women who continue to conduct the rites to which they were dedicated, in spite of—and sometimes in protest against—the state ban. The realization that a significant percentage of devadasis spent much of their lives doing ritual work prompted me to look for a rural location where I might learn more about the everyday lives of these Dalit female *pujaris*

FIGURE 2.1 Durgabai and Mahadevi with a devotee who is performing prostrations in fulfillment of a *harake*. Photograph by the author.

and the *seve* of Yellamma and Matangi that they preside over. A helpful colleague sent me to his father's ancestral village. Off I went with my research assistant, Ambuja Kowlgi, into the northern reaches of the Belgaum District by a public bus with little more than the name of our destination—Nandipur—to guide us. We bumped along the poorly maintained roads in the blue bus, past green fields of sugarcane, millet, and wheat dotted with yellow sunflowers. At the sight of my pale skin, a baby looking over the shoulder of its father burst into tears, offering an affective diagnosis of the disruptive presence of a stranger. His father laughed and patted him on the back.

Arriving in a cloud of dust, we descended from the bus at the center of the village into the shade of an enormous, widespread peepul tree. We asked the men gathered there for directions to the Yellamma temple. Following their indications, we walked down a little lane, past the openly curious faces of villagers washing dishes, repairing bicycles, carrying water, or otherwise occupying themselves with the intense physical labor required to sustain life in a rural village deprived of infrastructure. At the end of the lane and off to our left was a blue, one-room wooden structure on the door of which was painted *Sri Yellamma Devi*. An advance team of children had alerted those inside to our arrival, and we were beckoned inside and invited to sit on a mat.

The *murti* and all the ornaments of the devi and her *jaga* were spread out on cloths on the floor. Yamuna and Durgabai looked up to greet us as they continued to clean and polish these ornaments, preparing the devi as they did each Tuesday and Friday for *puja*. They asked questions about who we were and why we had come, and I answered in my then-halting Kannada or through Ambuja's able translation. I said that I had come from America and wanted to learn about Yellamma. They directed me to scriptures and scholars. I said that I wanted them to teach me: "People say this and that about Yellamma, about devadasis, but I want to hear what you have to say." The older of the two, Yamuna, listened very attentively as she patiently rubbed the tarnish off Yellamma's brass face. When the bustling crowd of curious children pressing into the temple got too thick for her, she shooed them off with the small gesture and the quiet efficacy of a respected elder. At one point she put down her work to come sit beside me and take into her hands the small album of photographs of my family, friends, and home that I introduced myself with. I was struck by the calm deliberation with which she approached everything she undertook, whether it was paging through representations of a life elsewhere or wrapping a fresh sari around Yellamma. As she tucked and pulled at the sari she asked me: "Are you doing this study from the point of view that the gods are there, or the perspective that the gods are not there?" (*Idanna neevu devra adanatheli madakhatteero yen devra illri annu drishti inda madakhattero*). "They are there," I said, amazed by her question and thinking of Ashis Nandy's (2001) observation that one doesn't have to believe in the gods to recognize that they are alive and well in South Asia.

I came to see Yamuna's question for me as a test, the passage of which admitted me to forms of participation in and access to the lifeworld of devadasis not granted to skeptics. Months later, when I traveled with the Nandipur *jogatis* to other villages, they introduced me to other *jogatis* and *jogappas* as a *bhaktaru* (devotee), despite my radically imperfect observances. I came to understand that they were not only making a claim about my relationship to Yellamma, but they were also making a claim about my relationship to them. As a devotee of Yellamma, I was responsible to them. They were entitled to make claims on me and my household, and they did. Those who keep the devi are entitled to make claims on those householders who desire what Yellamma can bestow.

The nature of this exchange was manifest in the performance of devadasi rites and in the interactions between dedicated women and devotees of Yellamma. Within days of my arrival in Nandipur, I took off on foot one morning toward the center of the village from the extension area where Jyoti I had set up house. Under the wide-eyed gaze of our new neighbors, most of whom I had not yet met, I walked down the rough track typical of this region, hoping to find a jeep on its way to the nearest town. If I could get a ride there and find a full-service post office, I might be able to send the permission forms I needed to continue my research by express mail to the United States. These bureaucratic preoccupations scattered as I came over the hill and saw a small but colorful procession of people walking from the center of the village toward me. I recognized the two distinctively painted *jagas* of Yellamma and Matangi, with their flower-printed skirts fluttering and waving around the heads of the two men on which they sat. Kamlabai—a tall, white-haired devadasi with a graceful carriage—led the procession, distributing the brilliant yellow turmeric associated with Yellamma (*bhandara*). When devotees came out of their houses toward her, she stopped, slipped off her sandals, and blessed them by pressing *bhandara* onto their brows as they bent to touch her feet.

As I came to learn over time, the passage of the devi was always an event, prompting villagers to put aside their work and come out into the

FIGURE 2.2 Kamlabai and Durgabai bringing the devi out of the temple into the community. Photograph by Brett Fisher.

road to pay her respect and take her blessing. Some would gather a precious pot of water to pour on the feet of those carrying the deity, playing her instruments, or giving her *bhandara*. On this particular day, the devi and her attendants were on their way to the new house of the Hanuman *pujari* family, where a female buffalo calf had just been born. This auspicious occasion and others like it—the healing of an affliction, arrangement of a marriage, completion of a house, or successful drilling of a bore well— were taken to be signs of the goddess's favor and frequently celebrated by villagers by calling her and her *pujaris* to their home for *udi tumbuwudu* (filling the lap or womb), in which householders put uncooked rice, betel nuts and leaves, money, and new cloth into the laps of Yellamma, Matangi, and their attendants.

A couple of days after I encountered this procession, Jyoti and I were going with the devi ourselves, following the *jogatis* as they made rounds during the festival of Mahawanami *phere*, which begins on the day of the full moon before Navaratri. Navaratri (meaning nine nights) falls in the month of Ashwina in the Hindu calendar, or September or October in the Roman calendar. It celebrates the victory of the goddess, usually in her form as Durga but in this region as Yellamma or Matangi, over the buffalo demon Mahishasura. With his army of demons, Mahishasura has defeated the gods in battle and they cannot fight back having previously granted him protection against any god, animal or demon. Born from the anger of the gods and endowed with their collective powers, the devi is beautiful and fierce. In his arrogance, Mahishsura does not imagine a woman, a devi, could do him any harm and she easily draws him into battle. Cutting off his head, she restores the cosmos to its proper order.[4] On the ninth night of the festival, called Jagrani, when the final battle is fought, the *jogatis* guard the strength of the devi by sitting up all night tending the Navaratri lamp and singing songs. Before I had arrived in Nandipur, I had not known of this seasonal rite.[5] As the *jogatis* explained to me over tea in the cool quiet of the Yellamma temple, "we take the *jagas* from house to house in the village asking for oil for the Navaratri lamp, and people will give us grain." They make rounds like this twice a year at Navaratri (in the fall) and Panchami (in the late summer), and farmers fill the *udi* of the devi with newly harvested corn, millet, or wheat.

When we went on rounds with the devi, we traveled along narrow paths between fields of tall, waving grain ready for harvest, walking from house to house, usually lagging behind the devi, who was carried on the heads of male relatives of the *jogatis*. "We used to carry her ourselves," they told me, "but she has become so heavy with these *jaga*, we ask our brothers to come and give them a share of grain." This distribution of ritual labor in the kin network of Nandipur *jogatis* was not uncommon; it was but one of the ways in which prestations (offerings, payments)[6] made by devotees to the *jogatis* extended beyond individual dedicated women and into their kin networks. By the time we caught up to them, the *jagas* would have been set down in front of the house on a sacred blanket, bedstead, or at least a tarpaulin made from sewn-together fertilizer sacks provided by the household. Untucking the ends of their saris from their waists and draping them over their heads, the women from the household came out with two fans—one for each devi—containing a measure or two of recently harvested grain: corn, millet, or wheat. After offering incense or camphor and applying vermillion and turmeric from their household altar to the devi, the *jogatis*, and often to Jyoti and me, they might touch the feet of the *jogatis* and take their blessing. Taking a rare break from their household and farming labors, they then sat in their doorway or on the outer ledge of the house to listen. After pouring their offering of grain into the *udi* of Yellamma and Matangi, the householders would take back a pinch that had touched the devi's body and return it to the household's fan. Then the *jogatis* sang *bhajans*. Closing

FIGURE 2.3 Singing a final blessing at a farm house. Photograph by the author.

the ritual with a final *harake* for the household, they gathered their instruments, lifted the grain tied up in bundles onto their heads, and set off for the next house.

On one of the days that we went roaming from farmhouse to farmhouse with the *jogatis*, we followed the purple sari of the elegant Matangi *pujari* Mahadevi along the margin of a field of corn edged with bright yellow sunflowers. We moved toward the next house along a narrow track between tall, waving fronds of sugarcane, pilfered bits of which I extended toward children who shyly accepted my humble offering before quickly darting behind the wrap of their mother's sari. The arrival of the devi at a household was an auspicious event that signaled a time to gather and put work aside. Sitting among the farmers gathered around Yellamma and Matangi, I listened to the *jogatis* sing into the slanted afternoon light.

Renukaa, Jagadambaa; Renukaa, Jagadambaa;
Renuka, mother of the world; Renuka, mother of the world;
Your name is very sacred,
Your feet are very sacred [this refrain is repeated after each stanza].

Daily for your *seve*, leaves and flowers are needed;
rose-water for your bath, *pujaris* for your *seve*.

I, thinking they were mine, went about trusting them,
but my people were not for me a refuge.

We gather in devotion, make pilgrimage to you,
Seek boons, seek compassion from you.

Devi, look, on Tuesdays, Fridays,
Devotees smear your sacred turmeric, mother.

Flowers and sacred turmeric they shower on you,
"Hail, hail" they circumambulate you.

Living among seven lakes, born in Nandipur,
Protect us, we pray. I remember you, I sing your praises.

Bowing to people gathered, Laxmana composed this song.
True goddess, Annapurna, he has held your feet.[7]

This song describes a flow of exchange between the compassion of the mother of the world and the devotion of her people. This devotion is expressed through embodied and sensual acts of *seve* and seeks the goodwill and protection of the devi in return. Her pleasure at being well propitiated is manifested in the fecundity of fields, wombs, and all other forms of human thriving. Her displeasure or anger at being neglected is evident in the lack of water or a fruitful harvest or the presence of disease. The terms of this give-and-take run through the songs and stories belonging to the *jogatis*, which they alone can sing or tell. The distinctive position of those who keep the devi vis-à-vis the devi and within their community is enacted through the performance of these songs and stories, which both describe and provide the occasion for the enactment of proper relationship between devotees and the devi, and toward the world. The *jogatis'* position as mediators between the devi and her devotees is materialized through transactions in which the fertility of the devi is dispersed and renewed in the world.

Those who keep the devi also work to ward off, diagnose, and resolve affliction. One morning we found Kamlabai washing the devi's *murti* and her ornaments in the Yellamma temple. She gestured for us to sit on a mat, and we came in and watched her prepare Yellamma for *darshan*. It was Tuesday, one of Yellamma's days, and devotees would be coming to the temple. Kamlabai sat on the floor by the *jaga*, rubbing the silver *murti* with a gray powder, the tarnish from the metal blackening her quick-moving hands. A devotee came in, carrying a small basket covered with a hand-crocheted cloth. From under the cloth the slightly stooped older woman produced a small plate of curd (yogurt) rice and a bowl of *ambli*—buttermilk fortified with millet flour. The *ambli* was delicious—hot and spicy. She gave me a taste when I asked what it was, but not until after she had offered it, along with the rice, to the devi (or at least to the *jaga*, since the *murti* was still being transformed in Kamlabai's hands). After pouring ghee into a lamp in a raised niche in the wall, she lit it. Kamlabai explained that a new buffalo had been born in this devotee's house, and that devotees reserve the first five days' milk for the devi, making ghee and buttermilk and preparing *ambli* to offer her. "My mother does this," Jyoti added, "thinking that the goddess will protect the buffalo."

We sat quietly, and I thought about the flow between the goddess and devotees of blessings and propitiating gifts, transacted in the space of the temple. Kamlabai brought up the terrible scarcity of water and commented on the domestic ill fate of a woman we could hear weeping: "*Paapa* [it is a sin], her husband beats her." The lack of rains and domestic strife were commonly cited examples of the absence of Yellamma's favor. Yamuna came into the temple and sat down, resting her back against the wall. More devotees came to offer *ambli*, rice, camphor, and incense and to touch the feet of Kamlabai and Yamuna. Without interrupting our conversation, Yamuna pressed bright yellow turmeric onto their foreheads in a gesture of blessing, while Kamlabai continued washing and polishing all the devi's things in preparation for *puja*. Mixing water and white powder in the palm of her hand—using that as a palette and her index finger as the brush—she painted long arcs of white over the eyes of the devi. She added a circle of bright red on her brow, making the *tilak*, here an auspicious sign of married status. Using her middle finger to remove errant color, she smoothed the symmetry of the line. Like other *amma* goddesses found all over South India, Yellamma is ambivalent: she has the power to afflict as well as the power to cure. In the words of one of the *bhajans* that *jogatis* sing:

> Adishakti Yellamma, our compassionate mother,
> In all the world, your name is the most transformative[8]
> [this refrain is repeated after each line].
> Devi, you wasted the bad people.
> Devi, you lifted up and protected your devotees,
> Generously granted them boons.[9]

"If we show her proper devotion, she will keep us well," devotees explain. Maintaining a flow of give-and-take with the devi is fundamental to the possibility of any and all kinds of prosperity or fertility—the fecundity of the fields, the fullness of wombs, the procurement of a salaried job, the restoration and maintenance of health and well-being, and all other forms of thriving are generally attributed to her. Affliction in the form of illness or misfortune of any kind is read as a sign of the devi's anger or displeasure and prompts soul-searching about possible failures of devotion. Not all kinds of misfortune and illness are thought to be caused by the devi, only those that have been sent by her. When unsure of the etiology of an affliction, devotees consult a *jogati* or a *jogappa*, usually the one attached to their village, who will conduct a rite of divination to discover if the trouble comes from Yellamma or not. It may be from some other god or spirit, or it may not have been sent by a god at all. Plenty of illness just is, in the logic of devotees, and will be quickly cleared up by a good doctor. The trouble of Yellamma, however, cannot be resolved by doctors or their medicines. Indeed, as devotees explained to me, Yellamma's *kaadaata* can only be aggravated by the ministrations of a doctor, who is applying the wrong medicine.

Regular devotion to Yellamma often aims to secure her favorable regard or to express gratitude after a serious trouble has been resolved. Devotees make *harake* to her as a means of attracting her goodwill: "Devi if you make my daughter well, I will bring you a new sari"; "Our son had lost his hearing; we told the devi we would call her to our house and fill her *udi* if he became well, and since then he has become strong"; and "I am making offerings to the devi for a salaried job." The *murti* of the devi, her *jaga*, her gold and silver ornaments, her extensive collection of saris—everything that belongs to her has been given in fulfillment of a *harake*. Not only material objects of value but acts of bodily self-offering are pledged through *harake*, and at Yellamma's hill it is not unusual to see a muddy devotee making full-length prostrations around the temple. He or she will be accompanied by a *jogati* or *jogappa* who oversees the proper fulfillment of the *harake*. Coming regularly to the village temple is a form of devotion and a means of *harake*. Devotees, especially women, come for *puja* on Tuesdays and Fridays. Having bathed, they bring *navedya* (freshly cooked food offerings) covered with a cloth, or carefully wrapped in a shiny tin box. They wave an open hand over the food, fanning in an arc toward the head of the devi, a gesture of offering to her that transforms the *navedya* into *prasada* (tasted and thus blessed by the deity). They light incense and perhaps pour a little oil in the brass lamps. Sometimes they stay awhile, sitting in the quiet shade of the temple before they begin the long walk home; sometimes they leave quickly in order to get back to their work. Women from all but the highest communities come, and on big festival days—when women are busy with lots of cooking—men and children come to offer *navedya* to the devi, for she should be fed before anyone else eats.[10]

When the festival of Navaratri is celebrated in Nandipur, the lamp is lit for Yellamma, whose fight with the buffalo demon has both cosmic and decidedly local effects. Like other *amma* devis found all over South India in the form of rocks smeared with vermillion and turmeric and wrapped in saris, huddled under trees, or kept in small temples, she is identified with the village itself and thus is appealed to, relied on, and held responsible for not just household concerns but the well-being of the village as a whole.[11] During the Mahawanami *phere*, when Mahadevi, the feistiest of the *jogatis*, felt devotees who could give more were not giving enough money for the Navaratri lamp, she scolded them: "Is this enough to keep the lamp lit? Give some more." "How can we give more when she has sent only this much rain?" devotees replied. "Give more and she will provide," replied Mahadevi, undaunted.

Affliction, whether corporate or individual, is a sign of the presence of Yellamma. "The devi came" (devi bandalu) is a way of saying "I was troubled by the devi." People also describe the resolution of trouble in terms of the devi's departure: "She left us alone (Aki hodalu)." The most common way people recount the resolution of trouble, however, is as the restoration of a relationship. In one of the most dramatic accounts of the *kaadaata* of Yellamma that I ever heard, my neighbor Laxshmi described a series of deaths and dire illnesses in her natal family that took place after her older sister, who had been dedicated to Yellamma, took the beads tied at dedication off her neck and married a man. This decision was in keeping with the wishes of her brother, who was concerned about the respectability of the family. He was the first to fall ill and almost die, Laxshmi told me in hushed tones. As is common in such cases of serious misfortune in a household, the possibility of the presence of Yellamma was considered, and this was confirmed through a rite of divination performed by a *jogati* in her capacity as a *pujari*. Laxshmi's sister attempted a compromise with the devi, which seemed to resolve the trouble in her family. She did not leave her husband or retie the beads around her neck, but she resolved to wear them on her body but hidden from public view, tucked into her blouse. In this way she restored her relationship to the devi, whose anger at her attempt to leave was said to have manifested as affliction in the household. Once she recommenced wearing the devi's beads on her body, the devi's presence in the household cooled and, as Laxshmi put it, "everything became all right" (*ella arama aagetri*).

In South Indian idiom, Yellamma is a hot goddess in her aroused state. In his analysis of the cult of Yellamma as an example of a South Indian system of classification relating color, heat, sexuality, and affliction (Beck 1969), Nicolas Bradford describes some of the possible means of resolving the trouble of Yellamma:

> If the trouble is relatively minor . . . then it is likely that you or your family have been neglecting Yellamma. It may turn out, for instance, that a family icon of Yellamma, carried by an ancestor, has been left unattended in a cupboard. Matters may be put right by paying visits to the Saundatti temple and performing various purificatory rites and acts of humility to the goddess. You may even decide to carry Yellamma yourself, or dedicate the task to one of your children. To some individuals, however, there is no question of choice or of trying to appease the goddess. The persistent growth of matted hair, for instance, would indicate that Yellamma has already caught you, that she fancies you (*devi nanmyele manas aatu*), that she has entered your body (*devi nanmeiga bandaala*). To try to go against such a clear indication of the goddess's desires would be to sign your own death warrant. (1983, 309)

The moral economy of Yellamma's trouble is not a simple calculus of good and bad conduct met, respectively, with reward and punishment. What emerged in my conversations with people about the manifestation and remedy of *kaadaata* is not only that she troubles people who have neglected her, but that she troubles those she desires. As Bradford's account suggests, the resolution of trouble may be as simple as a trip to Saundatti with a new sari for the devi, but her appeasement may require much greater offerings, up to and including the dedication of a member of the family. The establishment of closer ties is a means, perhaps the principal means, of cooling her anger and securing her favor. Yellamma's presence may manifest itself as an affliction or a blessing, and the difference is negotiated though personal and collective acts of propitiation. Just what kind of *harake* she may require is worked out in extended consultation with others about the nature of the trouble and its possible causes. I observed this kind of moral reckoning not only among devotees but also among those who have renounced Hinduism and embraced philosophical Buddhism.

The embrace of Buddhism, inspired by B. R. Ambedkar's conversion in 1956, is widespread among young Dalit men in the region who reject Hindu deities and their worship as implicated in the reproduction of caste hierarchies and incompatible with Dalit self-respect. This does not mean that they do not also perform Yellamma *seve* and make *harake*. The idea that conversion should mark a total break from the past is itself a modern, and arguably Protestant, notion (Vishwanathan 1998; Kent 2004). Mahesh, for instance, told us that he would go to Yellamma when he was in trouble but would abuse her when things were fine. His older brother, Ishwara, struggled for days over whether or not to celebrate Laxshmi *puja* in his new phone shop, the license for which his mother, Yamuna, had helped him secure. His Ambedkarite friends discouraged him. Still, he felt his mother—who in her characteristic wisdom expressed no opinion on the matter—would want him to honor the devi for bringing prosperity into their lives. In the end, he celebrated Laxshmi *puja* by setting up an altar featuring Yellamma (as Laxshmi) directly underneath twin portraits of the Buddha and Ambedkar. He made offerings of fire and food to this unusual trinity.

Jogatis world a world in which all forms of renewal and prosperity depend on the ongoing cultivation of exchange relations with the devi. A farmer who has an especially bountiful crop is expected to enact his gratitude for this manifestation of Yellamma's favor by filling her *udi*. If he does not, he is considered to be vulnerable to her trouble. Should someone in his household be troubled, those who perform rites of divination will not hesitate to offer a diagnosis: he has not served the devi well, so she is troubling him. The failure to share one's good fortune is a moral liability, one that those who keep the devi turn to their advantage. They depend for their livelihood on the flows of offerings from devotees to the devi and to them. They, in turn, must cultivate their ties to the devi by embodying her in various ways and performing the rites to which they are dedicated. In particular, they see to the regular bathing and feeding of the devi, for which they must rise early, bathe, open the temple, wash the *murti* and all the ornaments of the devi, play her instruments, sing her songs, and stay with her to receive the offerings of devotees and to give her blessing in the form of turmeric and *prasada*. They take the devi to the homes of devotees and wherever she might travel outside the village for a *jatra* (festival or pilgrimage). They are dedicated to perform these forms of labor and care for the body of the devi, which they learn over time in apprenticeship relationships. They wear her beads around their necks and, if they get them, her matted locks of hair down their backs. To carry the devi on your body is to be responsible for her and to make her devotees responsible to you; it is to cool her wrath, to transform her troubling presence into an auspicious one. To keep the devi is to cultivate her presence in your body and through your body, in the body of the place and people you keep her for. Her presence in the fields, the livestock, the home, the womb, and the world ensures the renewal and preservation of life. *Jogatis* world a world that is centered around Yellamma and situates them favorably within the predominant moral and material economies of everyday rural life. These, however, are not the only moral and material economies circulating, especially in the places and among persons striving to become modern.

Leaving the Devi

The reform movement that led to the criminalization of the rites *jogatis* conduct began in the 1980s and resulted in the passage in 1982 of the Karnataka Devadasis (Prohibition of Dedication) Act.[12] The stage was set by regional intra- and interstate politics, in which politicians in Maharastra depicted Karnataka as a sending state, filling the brothels of Bombay with dedicated women. At the same time, politicians in southern Karnataka— where the capital city, Bangalore, is—portrayed northern Karnataka as a backward region based on the ongoing occurrence of dedications. Legislators directly addressed the concern that this law might be seen to deny religious freedom. For example, K. H. Srinivas "affirmed the right of the state to discriminate between appropriate and inappropriate religious expressions [and] asserted that the government could not protect the downtrodden from exploitation if it did not reject the dogmatic superstitions that were often intertwined with religion," according to the historian Kay Jordan (2003, 153–54). Like modern forms of religion everywhere, Hinduism is understood here to be entangled with, but separable from superstition. "Superstition" is defined as that form of nonreligion that the government may eradicate in order to fulfill its dual duty to protect its vulnerable citizens, without trespassing on their rights to religious freedom.

The interests of three social movements converged to produce this recent wave of devadasi reform. Christian feminists, concerned about the sexual exploitation of Hindu women under the cover of false religion; public health workers, for whom devadasis were metonymically and inextricably linked to prostitution and the spread of HIV; and Dalit activists, who were opposed to sexual liaisons between upper-caste men and Dalit women, together created sufficient publicity and public pressure to generate the passage of the antidedication act.

A key actor in the generation of feminist concern, Jyotsna Chatterjee, described how she came to be concerned about devadasi dedication in an interview with me in 2003 in her Delhi office. She was then the national director of the Joint Women's Programme, a Christian women's nongovernmental organization (NGO) with regional offices all over India. Chatterjee had come from Delhi to serve a four-year stint in the Bangalore offices of the Joint Women's Programme in 1979:

> I was organizing a meeting of tribal women in Bellary District. I got down [off the train] at Bellary station, and I saw a woman with a basket with mango leaves and a *lota* [pot] of water. I asked my local guide, "Who is she?" "Don't go near her, she is a devadasi," he said. So I said in Bengali— because I am a Bengali, I am not a Kannadiga—"In Bengali the word 'devadasi' means a woman who worships in the temple." But he said, "They worship in the temple, but they are also prostitutes, they are dedicated as little girls." This upset me very much because I have always been a human-rights person. My concern was the religious sanction, even though I was attacked: "Who are you to take the support of this Christian organization to attack a Hindu practice?"

Chatterjee's anxieties about the specter of Christian imperialism were close to the surface, and she acknowledged her Christian family background in our interview. But she stressed the principles of humanism this background had instilled in her, especially the universal principle that no religion should sanction the violation of human rights. In short, for her, this was not a contest between religions. Rather, it was a matter of humanist religion (whether Christian or Hindu) versus a repugnant custom. Her motivation and commitment were inspired; she was determined and effective.

Chatterjee organized a public meeting of concerned women on the issue in Bangalore in 1981, commissioned a study, and called a press conference. The study, first published in the agency's journal *Banhi* in 1981, represented the practice of dedication as one that had been legitimately a matter of religion in the past but that was currently "nothing but prostitution practices under the garb of religion" (Joint Women's Programme 1989, 30). A draft of the recommended antidedication bill was included in the journal, along with the demand that the Joint Women's Programme was making of the government: to take immediate economic, educational, and social measures of reform. This report and Chatterjee's skillful exercises in lobbying and publicity played a primary role in making the devadasi problem a matter of public concern in Karnataka and in the passage of the antidedication law in 1982.[13] The law was implemented in 1984.

The passage of the law, however, made for very few changes on the ground. As J. S. Gilada described to me, when he went to the temple at the height of the festival season in 1983, dedication ceremonies were taking place in the temple and the police were not registering cases.[14] A medical doctor and an indefatigable public health activist and organizer, Gilada promoted sexual health and the prevention of sexually transmitted diseases among sex workers, their children, and their clients for decades. Gilada is also the founder of the Indian Health Organization, a health and social welfare NGO working in Kamathipura, Mumbai's largest brothel district. In 1983 he went to the temple with a team of doctors and social workers to set up medical camps as well as to protest against and publicize the ongoing dedications. In an interview with me in 1998, Gilada described ending dedications as a means of fighting against "child prostitution, forced prostitution, and HIV." He went to the temple every year for several years and was very successful at generating publicity and pressuring the government to enforce the ban. His trip in February 1987 generated articles in virtually all the Karnataka newspapers as well as a couple of national ones (Shankar 1994, 131).[15]

Each of these movements, as well as the Dalit movement I describe in more detail in the next chapter, conceived of their aims in liberal terms, as efforts toward emancipation from exploitative and harmful practices. The terms of emancipation were more black and white for outsider activists like Gilada and Chatterjee than for local observers. Those familiar with the practices surrounding Yellamma sought to defend the region against charges of backwardness. They also worked to separate good religion from bad superstition, a distinction that the oft-invoked idea of prostitution with religious sanction (Joint Women's Programme, 1989) fails to capture. The district commissioner in Belgaum, for instance, was quoted in the *Hindu* as saying: "Dr. Gilada and many others like him fail to appreciate myths and legend connected with the goddess . . . even decent women also don beads. It is only to fulfill their religious vows" (as quoted in Epp 1997, 230). Reform projects were sometimes developed in conversation with, and in deference to, devotional attachments to Yellamma. In the context of a traveling antidedication public drama, Laxshmi—a Dalit social organizer—simulated a possession state and spoke as the devi's oracle:

Here this pujari is sitting in my temple and doing all this to people. This is very bad. I have not told him to do all these things. You come to me and tell me. I'll see how the pujari is handled. You stop giving money! You stop giving gold and silver! You stop giving a girl or boy to this pujari! . . . There are hospitals. Medicine has progressed so much. In my name you should take all the facilities which are available to you and get all these things cured. . . . Jogula bhavi [the sacred pool at Saundatti] is so dirty. These priests are not getting it cleaned, you go and take a dip in that [water tank] and get all kinds of disease. . . . You think goddess Yellamma likes this stinking smell? I want you to be in good health, have a clean atmosphere. (quoted in Epp 1997, 253)

The anthropologist Linda Epp, who interviewed Laxshmi, notes that her oracular performance lent the authority of a possession event to a modern agenda for social uplift and health. It also introduced a distinction between a corrupt and filthy priesthood and a benevolent devi interested in hygiene and health.

The idea that Yellamma might be such a benevolent devi was not necessarily readily embraced by devotees. In 2011 I interviewed a playwright in Belgaum who staged a reformist drama in 2000. A Brahman homemaker and mother, she had put her own acting ambitions aside upon marriage but continued to write poetry and dramas. She described the actors' reluctance to rebel against Yellamma: "We did this drama. And then I prayed. Nobody was willing to play the role of Renuka. Nobody was ready to play the role of the devadasi Renuka, who rebels. What to do? Everybody said: 'We are worried. If we play that rebellious role, what will happen?'" After describing the plot of the drama—in which a girl is dedicated, falls in love, comes to a tragic and murderous end as she avenges the killing of her beloved, and decides to renounce the devi, who has not taken care of her— the playwright continued:

Saying "I don't want this devi," she throws the whole devi in the river. "She is not there, if she were there, [my lover] would not have died. I committed a murder, and for what? I didn't commit any sin. What kind of fate has she given me? She is not mother [amma—a name for the devi]." She threw the jaga, all of it. . . . This is my drama. But nobody was ready to throw it. Instead of cowrie shells, we used popcorn. From a distance they look the same. Instead of a stone [murti], we placed a picture. We said, "Just lift it as a symbol [of throwing]. I will do penance, fasting for five weeks. No harm will come to you people." It took so much convincing.

In the experience of this reformer, separating the *real* benevolent devi who responds to fasting and prayer from the *false* dangerous devi who punishes those who fail to recognize and embrace her presence was an arduous, if worthwhile, task.

The good intentions of reformers notwithstanding, the means of reform have often been repressive. Initial government reform efforts focused on enforcing the 1984 ban on dedications. According to the police inspector stationed at the main temple complex in the late 1980s, this often involved violence. At the height of the main pilgrimage season, at the time of the full moon, his teams of officers would patrol the far reaches of the temple complex and break up camps of devotees conducting dedication rites with billy clubs and shouting. In my conversation with him in 2003, he regretted beating up poor farmers but described this force as necessary by invoking a pedagogy of coercive transformation for the ignorant and unreasonable: "This is the only way they will learn, through violence—otherwise they won't understand!"[16] This sometimes violent enforcement of the ban was accompanied by rehabilitation schemes promoting tailoring, animal husbandry, basket making, and so forth as alternatives to ritual and/or sex work. Widely acknowledged to be ineffective, these economic rehabilitation schemes have mostly been abandoned in favor of an approach that more directly beckons devadasis to inhabit a new subject position, that of the ex-devadasi (*maji devadasi*).

In the early 1990s, the Karnataka Women's Development Corporation subcontracted with an NGO, Myrada, to start a new kind of campaign. The architects of this campaign, whom I interviewed in their Bangalore offices, determined that in order for the devadasi system to be eradicated, the auspicious status and income-generating power of these ritual specialists would have to be undermined. The activists mounted a major education campaign and recruited young Dalit men, many of whom were sons or brothers of devadasis, to paint posters in bus stations and put on skits dramatizing the social evil of devadasi dedication and the criminal penalties that might be imposed for practicing any of the devadasi rites. They created mechanisms of surveillance and reporting that extended into the smallest village community. The primary agents of these mechanisms are ex-devadasis, women who have refashioned themselves though renunciation of their dedication and participation in reform. They are warned and, in turn, warn others to break the beads tied at dedication and throw them in the river; to stop roaming with the devi, singing devotional songs, and asking for grain; to stop playing Yellamma's instruments, the *shruti* and

FIGURE 2.4 A mural at Saundatti warns: "Don't give *joga* [alms]."
Photograph by the author.

chowdiki; to cut their *jade* and groom their hair as respectable women do; to stop practices of divination and possession—in short, to leave all devadasi practices behind or face the possibility of fine or imprisonment. In 1997 a cooperative organization of ex-devadasis was formed under the supervision of Myrada; it was called Mahila Abhivruddhi Matthu Samrakshana Samsthe (MASS), which translates as the Women's Welfare and Protection Association.

This second phase of the reform campaign is taking a distinctly different approach than the first phase. In the first phase, the logic was that if you managed to stop the flow of girls into the practice and offered women who were already dedicated alternative means of livelihood, the devadasi institution would die out. In the second phase, necessitated by the failure of the first, the criminalization of the devadasi rites aims to transform the embodied subjectivity of the dedicated woman. She is called on to renounce her unique tie to the devi and join the campaign against the devadasi tradition. What becomes apparent in the context of the production of the ex-devadasis' subjectivity is that one must become either an object or a subject of reform in order to be modern. The discourses and practices of postcolonial modernity produce two possible positions: reforming selves and reformed selves. Especially for Dalits and others framed and produced as backward, survival can depend on figuring out how to produce oneself as a reforming body. My thinking here is in part informed by the politics of recognition I was subjected to. As a self-evidently white and seemingly respectable woman, I presented what was consistently read as a reforming body. This fact was confirmed by the strong reluctance and, in many cases, refusal by devadasis and their allies to talk to me based on the suspicion that I was taking names for the government. It was also evident in the strong presumption made by every reformer and virtually every middle-class person I met in the region that I had come to stop the practice of dedication.

This developmental form of subjection, in which the backward peasant stands in need of uplift and improvement, has an obvious colonial history in the formation of social reform as a demonstration of the worthiness of self-rule. It also helps explain the intensity of investment in devadasi reform. Protecting society against the danger of sexually undomesticated Dalit female *pujaris* is not the only aim of reformers. Those who become reformers are invested in their own projects of self-fashioning, in which the stakes are their own relationship to modernity. To direct one's self toward the reform of backward practices is to be modern.

Increasingly, the rehabilitation of devadasis is being carried out by the objects of reform themselves, remade over into the agents of reform. Ex-devadasis now throng the temple at the height of pilgrimage season, dressed in uniformly navy saris and sporting visored caps befitting the policing function they now serve. They pass out fliers detailing the banned rites and threaten those who would dare play the sacred instruments of Yellamma with arrest, imprisonment, and fines. One of the condemned practices is the wearing of locks of matted hair.

If the goddess Yellamma wants a person, devotees explain, there are several ways she might call them to her, all of which manifest in the body of the one she desires. One of the most common signs of Yellamma's vocation is the appearance of a lock of matted hair. This hair is taken to be an indication of the presence of the devi in the body. To ignore it, devotees say, is to risk the wrath of the devi, whose ability to afflict is as well known as her ability to cure. At her temples across the central Deccan Plateau, Yellamma women can be seen wearing heavy locks of matted hair anointed with brilliant yellow turmeric. To see one of them is to take *darshan* of the devi, to enact a Hindu practice of visual encounter with the deity, to see the god and for the god to see you (Eck 1996). Devotees worship this hair as the devi herself and perceive the women wearing it as especially capable of entering states of possession and giving oracles. Called *jade*, these matted

FIGURE 2.5 A *jogamma* holding her *jade*. Photograph by Aroon Thaewchatturat.

locks of hair mark the bodies of those chosen by the goddess to manifest her presence in the world. In the words of one Yellamma woman whose *jade* reached to her knees, "not everyone gets matted hair. Only if the Goddess wants you to be her dasi does she give you matted hair" (Seethalakshmi 1998).

Between April 2001 and March 2002, one thousand *jade* were cut from the heads of Yellamma women, according to the report of the NGO that organized the cutting (MASS 2002).[17] This is but one year in a campaign that began over twenty-five years ago. The primary rationale for this cutting is that *jade* are manifestations not of the devi but of dirt and disease. *Jade*-cutting campaigns have been an abiding feature of governmental and nongovernmental efforts to rehabilitate devadasis.

I quote at length from a flier distributed at the main Yellamma temple complex during the height of the pilgrimage season in 2003:

> Clean hair makes for a wise head and greater beauty. Wise people, have you seen people worshipping hair that is unclean, knotted, dull, smelly, and full of dust, dirt, and lice being worshipped as the Goddess's *jade* with turmeric and oil? Join in the meritorious work of social change and raise the awareness of people. When hair is not properly combed, oiled, and washed clean, it knots and a microorganism called "fungus" [English word] gets into the hair, causing a disease called *plica neuropathica*. This disease can easily be cured. [A lengthy description of hair cleansing and grooming is omitted here.] It is a misconception that the Goddess troubles those who clean knotted hair. Some grow such hair, tell people it is god, and frighten them as a means of earning and acquiring position. Such fake practices push society in the wrong direction. Devotees should not be misled, they should clean such tangled hair. Thousands of people have gotten their knotted, dirty hair cleaned and are living a healthy life. This is evidence that the appearance of *jade* or knotted hair is not due to the Goddess.[18]

The flier is addressed to an audience of would-be reformers, who are enjoined to bring an enlightened perspective to the matter of hair and religion. *Jade*, it states, are not a manifestation of the devi but simply matter out of place: dirt (Douglas 2002). Dirt can be disentangled from the hair through a careful process of grooming, and disease and superstition can thus be averted. Yellamma has nothing to do with such hair; she is clean, purified. The implication here is that those who persist in wearing *jade*, whose diseased and dirty state can no longer be attributed to ignorance, are nefarious actors promoting "fake practices" and inspiring fear in people as a means of advancing themselves. In this view, *jade* mark not the dangerous or auspicious power of Yellamma's presence but a threat to social progress. Within the discourse of reform, *jogatis'* embodiment is said to pose a danger not only to themselves, but also to society at large.

The medical rhetoric of contagion linking diseased bodies, ignorance, and social decline draws on unstated but widely held beliefs that associate *jogatis*, illicit sexuality, and communicable disease. This rhetoric has been successful in raising doubts about the provenance of *jade*. In my conversations with devotees and other observers of reform, I was asked over and over again: "Is it really from the devi or is it disease?" Anxious to dispel the notion that I was somehow especially capable of this discernment, I tended to respond to this binary choice between divinity and pathology by introducing a third option: fashion. "In the United States, some people go to the beauty parlor to get such hair," I would offer. According to his research assistant, another anthropologist working at the temple complex in the early 1980s sent a sample of a *jade* to a laboratory in England for analysis. The idea that the presence or absence of a fungus in matted hair could prove or disprove the presence or absence of the devi is consistent with a biomedical logic of single etiology, but not with Shakta epistemologies of the body, in which some forms of affliction are understood as the effect of the heating and troubling presence of the devi in the body. The belief that American or British anthropologists might have a particularly reliable grip on biomedical logic and its presumed powers of discernment is not particularly surprising. Nor is the fact that the state government would draw on such logic to better discipline, police, and manage unruly bodies for their so-called own good. This rationality, however, is not the only one at work on Yellamma's hill.

On the walls of the main temple complex, painted posters illustrate proper and improper modes of bodily comportment. One such poster features a woman with long *jade* next to another with carefully groomed hair bound together at the back of her head. A big black *X* marks the woman wearing *jade*, while a check mark endorses the properly groomed woman. On one of my trips to this temple I encountered two Yellamma women with long locks sitting under this poster. I asked them what they made of the poster and the *jade*-cutting campaigns. "Who is the government to cut our hair?" one of them demanded. "We have been living here for several years and we know the tradition and customs. If it was unhygienic, we would have cut it ourselves. They cannot force us to cut it." In the face of the government's desire to refashion her as a proper subject of bourgeois femininity and bodily constraint, this Yellamma woman was defiant. She claimed superior knowledge of "tradition" and the right to judge her own cleanliness.

In fact, many Yellamma women have had their *jade* forcibly cut. In the context of a discussion about the reform efforts of MASS and the government, one devadasi offered the following account of an incident at a *jade*-cutting campaign she had witnessed:

> There was a great *pativrata* [celibate ecstatic][19] and she had *jade*. These people [members of MASS] cut her *jade* against her will—she was screaming. There were old women, and they were made to bend over and their *jade* were cut. . . . Even though they said we are old and we are not like "that" [not prostitutes], they beat them and forcibly cut the *jade*. . . . The police and the *sangha* [MASS] people were here together.

More than packets of shampoo and lessons in hygiene are being dispensed in this violent enforcement of a hairstyle. According to the architects of the campaign, the elimination of this superstitious practice, along with all the rites and bodily practices specific to Yellamma women, is necessary to undermine a system that results in the prostitution of Dalit girls. But it is not only the extended sexuality of the devadasi that is being rehabilitated, it is also her religiosity. Indeed, as the reformers recognize, the two are inextricable and bound up together in her hair.

How have *jade* come to be such powerful representations of everything that is wrong with devadasi dedication? Anthropological reflections on hair practices offer some helpful, not to say provocative, ways to think about the potency of hair and its sexual implications. In 1958 Edmund Leach wrote a delightful article titled "Magical Hair," in which he considers the general problem of the interpretation of symbols through readings of hair behavior. Leach disparages the use by psychoanalysts of ethnographic material about hair symbolism from primitive societies to extend clinical observations of individual patients into universal features of the human unconscious. Along the way, he concedes that the ethnographic record offers many cases of sexually significant hair rituals. Examples from the South Asian context include the imposition of celibacy on the Hindu widow symbolized by the shaving of her head, the tonsured Brahmanical tuft as an indication of sexual restraint, and the wearing of matted locks by ascetics as a sign of bodily detachment from the phenomenal world. Leach offers a general formula: "long hair = unrestrained sexuality; short hair or partially shaved or tightly bound = restricted sexuality; close shaven hair = celibacy" (1958, 154).

Both the meaning and the efficacy of symbols are at stake here. Symbols, like words (Fortune and Malinowski 1932), don't merely say something, they also do something. Hair rituals are not just communicative symbols but also pragmatic tools for making things happen in the world.[20] For Leach, hair is not powerful because it represents the phallus; it is powerful, phallic, and divine or sacred. Hair relics, he suggests, are magical materials, "thing[s] of power in [themselves]" (1958, 158). When the locks of Yellamma women fall, they are often kept by devotees with other sacred objects in their household shrine along with their *mane devaru* (family deity); when they are cut off by reformers, they are discarded as so much meaningless dirt. But this is not to say that reformers do not grasp the efficacy of hair cutting in shifting the sexual status of Yellamma women.

Within both Hindu conceptions of purity and pollution and biomedical categories of hygiene and pathology, in Mary Douglas's formulation, dirt is "matter out of place." Understood in this way, dirt implies both the presence and the transgression of a "set of ordered relations": "Where there is dirt there is a system. Dirt is the by-product of a systematic ordering and classification of matter, in so far as ordering involves rejecting inappropriate elements" (Douglas 2002, 36). The dirty hair or matted locks of Shaivite or Shakta ecstatics, such as Yellamma women, mark their rejection of and by the ordinary organization of social and sexual life. Their bodies have been seized by, or given over to, another order—Yellamma's—and this is what makes them powerful. The power, dirtiness, and sexual status of these ecstatics are all aspects of the same thing: the presence of Yellamma in their bodies. *Jade*, then, are not simply either personal or cultural symbols, but the thing of power in itself, Yellamma.

Within the logic of reform, the power of dirty matted locks can only be negative and must be neutralized, cleansed, and purified in order to restore Yellamma women to their proper place in the gendered social order. Following Leach, one might say that whereas the appearance of a lock of matted hair marks the sacred/powerful/phallic/dirty status of a Yellamma woman, the *jade*-cutting campaigns render them profane/weak/castrated/purified. In other words, when reformers cut *jade* from the heads of Yellamma women, they effectively strip the women of their ecstatic knowledge and unruly sexuality in order to render them proper subjects of reason and middle-class femininity who groom, bind, and oil their hair.

Many devadasis I spoke with who had been given locks were afraid to cut them, an act that for them amounted to refusing to embody Yellamma, rejecting her call to serve her. Some whose locks had been cut had renounced the possibility of such a vocation and proclaimed the truth of the reformer's claim that *jade* were nothing but dirt and disease: "Look," one said to me, pulling her wavy, untangled hair around her shoulder to show me. "They cut them and nothing has happened to me, the devi has not troubled me." Others told stories about intensifying affliction and loss of divinatory and healing powers associated with failing to embrace, and thus please, Yellamma. For all of the women, associations among cutting locks, ceasing ecstatic practices, marrying in the conventional way and rejecting Yellamma's call were explicit.

This suggests that *jade*-cutting campaigns might be framed as projects of sexual conversion. Conversion here is not a matter of sex acts (who does what to whom), but rather a question of the disposition of sexuality, the uses to which it is put. Ganneth Obeyesekere (1981) has described the trajectory of Saivite female renunciates in Sri Lanka as moving from one phallocentric economy to another (husband to god). Yellamma women have been implicated in a different sexual order, one in which generalized and abundant fertility is cultivated and distributed. In this sexual order, rather than circulating around the phallus, Yellamma women with *jade* might be understood as having incorporated the phallus as a part of their own bodies. I am drawing here on a point that Veena Das makes in a critique of the phallocentric readings of female asceticism as the substitution of one form of male domination for another. She writes: "The material on female ascetics described by Obeyesekere would point to a different direction—asceticism as a means of transforming the oppressive demands of heterosexuality into the power to heal" (1989, 323).[21] Furthermore, as Judith Butler has argued in "The Lesbian Phallus and the Morphological Imaginary" (1993), it is not necessary to have a penis to incorporate the phallus. The *jade* of Yellamma women might be seen to point to the lingam of Yellamma, the phallic power of a devi who manifests herself most often as an autochthonous devi. Marry her to a god, or her dasi to a man, and you will have tamed her *shakti* (Gatwood 1985; Kapadia 1996; Kinsley 1988). Left unconstrained, this fierce feminine energy may become too hot; autochthonous goddesses are known for their ability to trouble and destroy as well as their ability to heal and create.

Magical hair marks the bodies of some Yellamma women, called by the devi away from family life and endowed with the capacity to heal afflictions and disperse the blessings of fertility and well-being in their communities. These capacities and powers are locked up in their hair as a sign of their renunciation of conjugal sexuality and their primary attachment to this hot devi. But this hair is not merely a communicative sign: it constitutes their incorporation of the devi. Thus to have their *jade* cut is to have their body severed from the body of the devi.

A radical and violent refashioning of the sexuality and religiosity of the body is at stake in these campaigns, as well as the very nature of the body itself. The body figured in *jade*-cutting campaigns is whole in itself, atomistic, and self-contained, and matted hair is a matter of unwanted intrusion of dirt and disease. In contrast, the ecstatic body is open to incursion, which can manifest itself as affliction but may be cultivated as a form of power. One may renounce this possibility of ecstatic embodiment and undertake this refashioning voluntarily, as a modern subject of reform, or be forcibly subjected to it, as an object of reform. Subjects of reform get access to state-sponsored micro-lending programs and new forms of respectability; objects of reform are disciplined by state power and threatened with fines and punishment. Reform campaigns resignify *jade* as a problem of dirt and disease within the logics of hygiene and biomedicine, thereby seizing on a potent symbol of social, sexual, and religious distinction but redirecting its efficacy toward the production of citizens.

Within the rhetoric of reform, the cutting of *jade* from the bodies of devadasis represents the surgical removal of superstition and disease from the social body as a whole.[22] *Jade*-cutting campaigns serve as an especially dramatic example of the reification of a social problem as a medical one that can be neatly excised from the body. I am drawing here on the idea of surgical logic and the concept of operability developed by Lawrence Cohen in his work on state campaigns for sterilization and kidney selling as modes of biological citizenship. He writes: "To be operable is to be assimilated to norms of modern citizenship and its constitutive will—despite oneself—through a radical, here surgical act of subsumption" (2004, 167). Cutting reorients the sexuality of dedicated women, turning it from the generalized cultivation of auspiciousness and the devi to the reproduction of the heteronormative patrilineal family form and the state.

To submit one's *jade* to the scissors of the state is a means of becoming assimilable as a citizen subject, to become embraced, rather than censored, by the law. The effect of this cutting is not simply the redemption of individual outcaste women from vice, dirt, and disease, but the collective uplifting of Dalit men and women who, as participants in reform, become admissible as rights-bearing citizens worthy of protections and eligible for loans. The biomedical language of isolable disease and the modernist distinction between superstitious practices and authentic religion produce reasonable bodies shorn of magic, backwardness, and contagion, and thus eligible for inclusion in the national body.

The medicalization of *jade* as a manifestation not of the devi but of disease resignifies the body as secular, a biological system vulnerable to infection, virus, or fungus but not to divine incursion. In this way, the medicalization of *jade* also shifts the truth value of religion toward the status of the body, especially its sexual orientation. Ecstatic embodiment characterized by possession, oracular powers, and renunciation of procreative marital sexuality (*janma*, family life) is thus cast as superstitious, and the milder devotional bodily practices consistent with Brahmanical Hinduism and Virashivism are upheld as true religion. Dalit female *pujaris* are displaced from the main temple and dispossessed of their rites.

Reform campaigns seek not only to rehabilitate Yellamma women—to introduce and enforce new modes of bodily comportment among them, modes that correspond to norms of femininity and domesticated (contained) sexuality—but also to rehabilitate Yellamma. Within discourses of reform she is figured as a goddess who neither claims nor enters the bodies of those she desires, nor becomes angry if she is thwarted, but rather as a devi who merely requires a devotional and chaste orientation of the heart. Such a goddess is not involved in the messy substance of fertility and its renewal. She has no *udi*. She has no sex. More precisely, her *udi* is not open to the world for filling, and her sex is only for her consort, Jamadagni—who, it turns out, as the pamphlets widely distributed at the main temple complex describe, has secured from her a vow of chastity.

Devadasis, Ex-Devadasis, and Faux Devadasis

In the summer of 2002 I went with Jyoti and Ambuja to the annual business meeting of MASS, held in one of the great halls built on Yellamma's main temple grounds. This construction was part of a long-term project run by the temple trust to improve the facilities at the site. One of the first improvements was the destruction of dwellings built around the outer wall of the main temple that were occupied by and passed down through a lineage of devadasis dedicated to service on the temple grounds. When I interviewed temple trust officials, they emphasized the need for clean water and toilet facilities for pilgrims, and outlined a master plan including destruction of all the dwellings belonging to hereditary Lingayat *pujaris* and Dalit devadasis as a necessary prelude to the construction of large plazas and market halls allowing for the easy passage of thousands of pilgrims. The spatial remaking of the temple complex entailed shifts in the organization of the care of Yellamma and the material economy circulating through her. Hereditary *pujaris* were being replaced with ones licensed by the temple trust, and devadasi *pujaris* were exiled entirely.[23] There was, then, a certain irony in the fact that MASS held its annual meeting of ex-devadasis on the temple grounds, inviting the women there to participate in their own re-form.

We entered the hall and walked into a sea of women arrayed in their best saris, feet tucked under them, sitting on the vast floor for hours awaiting the commencement of the program. As it began, we sat among a thousand ex-devadasis, listening to the annual report being read out loud. The secretary of the organization, herself an ex-devadasi, told us how many new members had joined, how many educational tracts had been distributed, how many *jade* cut. None of the women there, that I was able to observe, wore *jade*. However, many, perhaps a third of the women there, especially the older women, still wore their *muttu*, tied at dedication. Visible as flashes of red and white when they adjusted their saris, these beads suggested that a less than complete remaking of devadasi embodiment had been accomplished. An especially beautiful woman sitting near us kept coming in and out of the hours-long meeting. On her return from one of these excursions, she sat back down among her friends, leaned forward with a radiant smile and said, "I just took my third *darshan* of her." The women evidently took pleasure in taking *darshan*, singing *bhajans* on stage, and being with each other. Apparently there were motivations to attend besides hearing the annual report or avoiding the fine the NGO threatened to impose on all members of MASS *sanghas* who did not attend the meeting. As one woman on the bus we traveled on said, explaining her excitement at arriving, "How often do we get the chance to be among so many of our people?"

Others exhibited no such mixed motives and described a clear break from a past and mistaken way of being:

I don't feel bad for removing the beads. We are also human beings like you [deserving of respect], now I go to the temple simply to take *darshan*, and nothing has happened to me [the devi has not troubled me]. I noticed a case of *muttu* being tied to a twelve-year-old girl in my village, so I contacted the [MASS] officers by phone and told them what was happening. I also helped the girl. The devi has not asked us to tie beads, but our parents may have tied them because of tradition (*paddati*).

I learned that it is not good to have *jade* when they found maggots [in my *jade*]. The devi does not ask us to wear these *jade*, it is a disease. Devotion is sufficient.

The narratives of ex-devadasis emphasized a break with bad (degraded, exploitative, or unhealthy) practices mistakenly thought to be called for by the devi and a continuation of devotion as an internal orientation of the self toward the goddess. This devotion was described as the relationship any devotee might cultivate with the goddess, rather than as an attachment enacted through a set of embodied practices specific to a particular relationship with her. Respect was a common theme, much evident in the speeches of the NGO staffers and in the rhetoric of ex-devadasis generally. From the stage came the message that their newfound respectability was more important than any material benefits they might or might not gain from the government. After explaining the importance of participating actively in the MASS *sanghas*, taking independence from the NGO Myrada, and "standing on their own two feet," the representative from the Myrada, the NGO most closely involved in setting up the membership organization MASS, said:

> So you should pay back your [government] loans, and attend meetings properly. You are not all directors [of MASS], [but] even being a member entails a great deal of responsibility. Everyone may not have gotten a loan or a house or a buffalo, and you may not all get them in your lifetime, but your children may and will definitely get the benefits, and your membership itself means you get a lot of respect, you are respected. People have come to see how you conduct your meeting—would they come if you were not doing something worthwhile? So what do you want a buffalo, or respect?

As she hit this question, a voice rang out from the crowd of gathered women, "A buffalo!" and the hall erupted in laughter.

That buffaloes might turn out to be more valuable than respect is a possibility I will return to, but first I want to consider the relationship to reform cultivated by two dedicated women I came to know through a series of life-history interviews. Both of these women lived in villages neighboring Nandipur. Pratima was the secretary of the MASS *sangha* in her village. She was a lively, alert woman who simultaneously tended her grandson, cooked us lunch, and patiently responded to my questions. She was dedicated as a very young girl, when she contracted a bad case of boils taken to be a sign of Yellamma's presence in her body. As she described it, she stopped performing the rites she was dedicated to when she met her husband, a Maratha (dominant caste) man who was not content to be her patron but wanted to take her parents' permission and get married in court. After six months of clandestine meetings, they went to the court for a registered marriage. He also wanted her to stop roaming with the devi. She was willing to stop performing rites and was very proud of their sixteen-year marriage, which had cost him his place among his natal kin. Pratima described a shift in the attitudes of devotees who had in the past received dedicated women with respect, giving grain and blouse pieces for the devi. As the reform campaign begun in the 1980s intensified, devotees began to accuse dedicated women of doing bad work (*kettada keilasa*—a common euphemism for prostitution) and turned them away when they came with the devi, saying, "what is she, nothing but a *jogati*, a *veshya* (prostitute)." Although Pratima had some complaints about how little Myrada had delivered on its promises of loans for small businesses and houses, she described the life she and other former devadasis had chosen, in the wake of this shift, as full of happiness:

> When a devadasi goes asking for *joga*, men look at her badly. "Come back tomorrow," they say, insulting her. There was no happiness in it for us; we used to cry to be spoken to like this. Now we have left this. There was no value for us as human beings [worthy of respect]. No human being derives value from being a devadasi. Now we cover our heads with the end of our sari and work into the evening in the fields, earning twenty rupees. There is value in that. We are beautiful and the people call out to us, *amma* [mother], *tangi* [little sister], they regard us with respect.

Anusha, another rurally based former ex-devadasi I met with many times, felt the heaviness of the burden of supporting her children more acutely than Pratima did. She spoke at length about the difficulty of providing for her two children's schooling and maintaining their household of three. She had had a good patron who paid for the delivery expenses of both her children and regularly gave money to help support them. He died, however, leaving his wife and Anusha with nothing. In her role as an elected member of the *gram panchayat* (village council), she had helped her former patron's widow obtain a pension. Anusha was entitled to a share in the family land, but her brothers, who oversaw its cultivation, gave her only a small amount of the yield. They lived in the same small lane, at the end of which was a small Matangi shrine. Anusha's brother's relative prosperity was evident in the respective condition of their homes, which faced each other across the lane. On one of the many occasions when Jyoti and I rode our scooter over to the village of Mandovi where Anusha lived, she greeted us at the door, her head wrapped in a towel, fresh from washing her hair. She combed and braided her daughter's hair, talking about how worried she was about finding the money to pay for the daughter's marriage. Anusha earned a little money working for Myrada. She traveled from village to village in the district, gathering devadasis to encourage them to begin *sanghas* in their communities and to leave all the devadasi rites behind. During previous conversations we had spoken about the work she did with MASS, so I was surprised on that day when a woman came in and touched her feet while we were talking. Anusha let go of her daughter's hair to press turmeric into this devotee's brow and asked, "Has he become well?" "Yes," the woman replied with evident relief.

Dedicated women cultivate different kinds of relationships with devadasi identity and embodiment. Both Pratima and Anusha identified themselves as ex-devadasis and were involved in the reform and policing of other devadasis. Anusha was also continuing to act as a *pujari* in her community. In other words, she was conducting the very rites that she was encouraging others to renounce, citing economic necessity as the reason for her seemingly paradoxical position. This explanation offers an interesting perspective on the investments of dedicated women in reform as a means of access to state benefits, as well as on the new forms of respectable identity and community status articulated by Pratima.

I return to a consideration of one of these state benefits, loans for dairy buffaloes. Virtually all of the forty village-based devadasis I surveyed mentioned the loan for a buffalo as a benefit that they had received. At a certain point in my fieldwork, however, I noticed that these buffaloes were nowhere to be seen. Where had they gone? When I began asking, I heard many stories about sick and dying buffaloes, and some tales about the difficulty of paying for their fodder and the decision to sell them. These stories did not emerge readily; indeed, in Yamuna's case, it was months before she told me about her buffaloes. In a room full of devadasis telling their stories, good and bad, about their experiences of reform, she began laughing. She had given a farmer some money, got his two buffaloes branded, had her photograph taken with them (the necessary proof of purchase), collected her money from the government plan, and then returned the buffaloes to their owner. Many women took advantage of the loans for buffaloes to acquire badly needed funds to service debts and pay medical bills, but turning buffaloes into cash didn't necessarily serve them well: the debt for the animals remained, and without the income from milk that the plan was calculated to produce, they were simply saddled with a new form of debt.

The fact that the buffalo scheme was not working the way it was intended to was obvious to me, to every devadasi I spoke to about it, and even to evaluators sympathetic to the goals of reform.[24] Consider the following critique of the buffalo scheme as a figure for reform in general:

> Since you are on rehabilitation, I must tell you about myself, as I was also a subject of rehabilitation. They gave me a buffalo. Well, I had this small room, which I now found myself sharing with the buffalo. You see the buffalo eats a lot, and as I was expected to stop sex work after rehabilitation, there was not much money. I didn't mind for myself, but I couldn't bear to see the buffalo wasting before my eyes. So soon I found myself doing twice the sex work to feed the buffalo and me. Well, now the buffalo was in heat, and I had to get her crossed [mated]. I was told that it would cost 100 Rupees per attempt. So there I was now being forced to do sex work to pay for the buffalo to have sex! That was enough. I decided I had enough with rehabilitation. (Sampada Gramin Mahila Sanstha, Point of View, and Veshya Anyay Mukti Parishad 2002, 18)[25]

This commentary was offered by someone who is neither a devadasi nor an ex-devadasi, but who nonetheless assumed the latter position in order to authenticate her critique of government policy. Revathi is a *hijra* ["neither man nor woman"],[26] an activist on issues of sexuality rights generally, and, like many *hijras* in Karnataka and Maharastra, a devotee of Yellamma. Her remarks, made in the context of a Karnataka State Women's Development Corporation meeting evaluating rehabilitation schemes, use both humor and irony to demonstrate that reform often works to worsen, rather than better, the economic position of devadasis.

State loans to buy dairy buffaloes are meant to provide a means of economic rehabilitation. Supplied with a buffalo to milk, devadasis need no longer be dependent on the support of patrons and devotees. Deprived of its material basis, the practice of dedication will wither away, or so the logic goes. However, as Revathi deftly notes, the buffalo is just another mouth to feed, another member of the household for whom a mate must be found, and the *jogati*'s obligations to others are increased. She may exchange indebtedness to the devi for indebtedness to the state and thereby acquire a kind of social capital in the currency of respect, as Pratima did. She may, like Anusha and others who sold their buffaloes, cultivate both kinds of obligation in an effort to maximize the possibility of return and maintain her ties to Yellamma.

The reform of devadasis produces new kinds of subjects with new kinds of relations to the state, including indebtedness. The effort to eradicate modes of being seen to be backward may seem to constitute a loss, but reform campaigns have also made new kinds of mobility, respectability, and identity available to dedicated women. The ways that women position themselves in relation to these new modes of life does not necessarily entail a renunciation of their ties to the devi. The ongoing cultivation of devadasi embodiment may be combined with the adoption of modes of being and relating befitting the norms promoted through reform. This possibility of the incorporation of both is, in the end, not surprising given the episte-mology of Shakta religion, but it is clearly not what the reformers had in mind. My aim here is not to gloss the forms of violation inherent in reform campaigns, but rather to emphasize the agency of dedicated women in mo-bilizing all possible means of livelihood and thriving. Reform projects are remaking forms of life; however, these lives are at the same time remaking themselves and not necessarily toward the same end.

As I have argued in this chapter, the reform of devadasis is not only elid-ing a distinct form of life, it is also reformulating religion. More precisely, in this case, it is reformulating what among the embodied practices per-formed in the name of Yellamma might count as religion, setting others aside as superstition. The designation of practices as superstitious in the Indian context has a long history, both in the presence of Christian mis-sionaries on the subcontinent and in native reformers of Hinduism. For instance, Vivekananda, widely credited for situating Hinduism as a world religion in the late nineteenth century, had this to say about place of super-stition in the national body: "The fact is that we have many superstitions, many bad spots and sores on our body—these have to be excised, cut off, and destroyed—but these do not destroy our religion, our national life, our spirituality. Every principle of religion is safe, and the sooner those black spots are purged away, the better the principles will shine, the more glori-ously" (quoted in Sen 2010, 99).

As we have seen, superstition is that religion which is not religion, which cannot be accommodated to modern social mores or find its justi-fication in the *shastras*, and which therefore may be excluded by the law. This distinction has its historical roots in the first-century Roman designa-tion of foreign cults, especially that of the Egyptian goddess Isis, which at the time was becoming very popular among Romans. Roman authorities applied the term to the early Christians, who eventually turned it back on the Romans: in Europe, superstition became the term Christians applied to pagan religion, as the worship of false gods (Bailey 2007, 20). This distinction was planted in Indian soil by Christian missionaries and propagated through the colonial courts when they were called on to arbitrate disputes over religious matters. In the postcolonial Indian state, it has come to be codified as a matter of constitutional law and state legislation. As "superstition," devadasi rites are festering sores on the national body; they must be excised in order to safeguard the health and longevity of that body. The unique modes of life that these rites animate; the worlds they world; and the ties they bind between the devi, her women, and their communities are all subject to erasure. The devi herself is being exiled from her autochthonous manifestation, her power to destroy as well as to create. She herself has not been exiled from the temple, as her wives have been, but through the discourses and practices of devadasi reform, she has been reformulated as a spouse devi and resituated within devotional religion. She is barred from materializing herself in the bodies of *jogatis*, from disseminating and renewing fertility through the rites they conduct, and from displaying her dissatisfaction in affliction. The devi, reform discourses and practices insist, does not manifest herself in these ways, nor does she matter in these ways in the bodies of Dalit women. The devi does not work in the world in the ways *jogatis* world it, according to reform.

However, as I was reminded again and again by the *jogatis,* more than one world is being made in the name of Yellamma. One day, somewhat sorrowfully, I asked the *jogatis* as we roamed: "What will happen to the devi when all this stops? When there is no one to keep filling the *udi,* to do her *puja?*" "Oh," responded Mahadevi, quickly and in her usual defiant manner, "I am not worried about *her,* she can take care of herself." My worry that the devi herself was somehow fragile was thus dismissed by one of her wives. Indeed, it is not evident that the eradication of the rites by which she is most evidently made manifest across the Deccan Plateau will somehow diminish or easily domesticate her. This was most eloquently suggested to me by a temple trust official at Saundatti who kindly granted me an interview in 2002. He was a very gentle man, whose tremendous devotion to the devi was quietly manifested in the mindful quality of the full-bodied prostrations he made when he took us for a special *darshan.* He had been working at the temple for fifteen years at the time of the interview. His attitude toward reform was that of a diplomatic bureaucrat. "The government has made these changes, so we comply with them," he said. At the end of our conversation, I asked him what he thought of the fact that dedications and rites were continuing despite reform, of the presence of the police and reformers at the temple, and of the murals illustrating improper and proper forms of *seve* that were painted all over the temple hill. He responded: "The rites, the reform — it is all due to her play (*aata*)."[27] In this formulation, reform is not a matter of cleansing superstition from the bodies of the ignorant and vulnerable, it is yet another sign of the playful and troubling presence of Yellamma in the world.

PART II · GIFTS

CHAPTER 3

Tantra, Shakta, Yellamma

Without thousands of pots of liquor, without hundreds of heaps of meat, and without the nectar of the vulva and penis, O Beautiful-Hipped One, I will not be pleased.
—Kularnava Tantra 8107, quoted in Hugh Urban, *Tantra*

[Popular traditions] are less concerned with asceticism than with ensuring that crops grow, that illness keeps away from the children, and that one is not haunted or possessed by ghosts. Such popular traditions are low-caste and need to appease "hot" deities, particularly goddesses, who demand offerings of blood and alcohol.
—Gavin Flood, *An Introduction to Hinduism*

Simply put, blood offerings are ends in themselves. They are pragmatic, material transactions and one cannot substitute a goat with thought or intention. As one villager told me, substituting intentions in place of goats would be like repaying a loan with smiles.
—Mark Elmore, *Bloody Boundaries*

"When my parents left me like this [to Yellamma], they cut my throat. I am just like a sacrificed cow (*aakalu*)," Durgabai said to me one morning, gesturing with her hand across her throat, in the midst of a worried soliloquy about her son's demand for money, the fate of her blind daughter, her mounting debts, and the lack of a husband to "take care" of her. "If they had not left me like this, I would have a husband and my life would be good." When I pressed her for examples of husbands who "took care" of their wives, she admitted they were rare enough. She could be as fierce about the freedom she had as "an untethered cow," as she could be bitter about her condition as a *dasi* (servant). Like the sacred cows dedicated to deities and allowed to wander the village, eating from any field, she was free to roam wherever and whenever she pleased. In this sense, she compared herself favorably to *gandullavalu*, who, in her words, have to ask for permission to "move an inch" from the house.

How are we to understand Durgabai's sense of herself as both sacrificed and liberated? Given by her parents to the devi, her sexual capacity is harnessed to her priestly function but available for patronage. Given by their parents to husbands, the sexual capacity of *gandullavalu* is delimited to the monogamous and reproductive imperatives of endogamy and conjugality. Both categories of women are committed, but to different ends. I am drawing here on Lawrence Cohen's work on commitment as a form. Organ donation, marriage, labor, adoption, and sacrifice, he suggests, are all instances of the body's being given over "to or for another, in a way that remakes the limit of that body's existence or horizon" (2005, 1). In his research on organ transplantation, he observed that people often try to make moral sense of one kind of bodily commitment by juxtaposing it to another. "Dad, if I had to choose between becoming a prostitute and selling my kidney which would you want *me* to do?" the daughter of a transplant surgeon asks her father over dinner with Cohen (2005, 6). "My parents should have given me to a husband instead of to this devi—my life would be better," Durgabai says. She also observes: "Those *gandullavalu*, they are always under the thumb of some man, father, husband, son. Nobody tells me where to go, what to do." Durgabai compares herself to *gandullavalu*, invoking the relative stakes of these two modes of commitment: conventional marriage and devi dedication.

Within discourses of reform, one of these trajectories of bodily commitment is placed under the sign of ethics, the other under the sign of terror (Cohen 2005).[1] In the next chapter, I consider how these two categories of sociosexual personhood—the ethical wife and the terrorized prostitute—have come to be defined in opposition to each other. Here, in an effort to disrupt this binary moral calculus as well as to attend to Durgabai's lament, I open up some ways of thinking of dedication as an ethical practice. I mean ethics here as "a work on the self and the world that cannot be reduced to a response to coercive norms" (Cohen 2005, 10). In other words, how might we think about dedication as something both more and less than an annihilation of personhood? What anthropology of the body is animated and reproduced through the movement of *jogatis* toward Yellamma in a relationship of dedication? To use Cohen's language, to or for what is the *jogati* body given over?

Durgabai's analogy between herself and a "sacrificed cow" brings our attention to three aspects of sacrifice: violence, value, and relatedness to God. When her life as a devadasi felt full of hardship, it was the violence of being dedicated to the goddess that Durgabai emphasized. In this reckoning, to be given was to be left, abandoned. Yet being left, being given, is also to be of value. One does not make offerings to the gods that are not valuable. Indeed, as devotees pointed out to me, the most valuable offering one can make to Yellamma is a daughter or a son. But this value does not simply inhere in the *dasi* or belong to her as an autonomous person—rather, it indexes relatedness. Once given, she becomes a conduit between the one making the offering and the deity receiving it. In this sense, her value is inseparable from the relationships that are made through and in her. She is valuable in her community, to devotees, and to her natal family as one who belongs to Yellamma. This belonging, and the value it produces, is what she has been given to. Such value, however, cannot be reckoned according to either a secular calculus or within the modern form of religion generally referred to as classical Hinduism.

In the rhetoric of reform, sacrificial idioms of dedication throw the light of scandal on the practice of giving daughters.[2] Horror at the rite of dedication is usefully considered against the background of the reform of blood ritual and related ecstatic practices—all features of a sacrificial religiosity. The reform of sacrificial religion on the subcontinent intertwined ideals of nonviolence and ascetic renunciation in the emergence of Buddhism and Jainism in the seventh century and what has been called the Brahmanical synthesis or Vaishnaivism between the tenth and sixteenth centuries. In the modern era, this reform of sacrificial religion took on a new vitality through political nationalism (Fuller 1992, 99). One of the chief architects of this reform, often referred to as the Father of Modern India, was Ram Mohun Roy who, in the nineteenth century, drew on Protestant Christian conceptions of religion to condemn idolatry and superstition and to envision a rational, monotheistic Hinduism based on a reading of the Vedas and Upanishads. Within popular religion, however, ecstatic practices and animal and other forms of sacrifice continued, as they do today. They continue as the practices of marginalized people; fierce goddesses who eat meat, drink alcohol, and are associated with low castes are ranked low, if not dismissed altogether in favor of vegetarian Sanskritic gods and goddesses attended by Brahman priests. Increasingly, this complementary relationship between high and low (because polluting) is displaced by the distinction between true and false, and "popular 'superstitious' practices . . . are now condemned as wrong and not even part of authentic Hinduism" (Flood 1998, 99–100).

Modern presumptions about what sex is for saturate reformist understandings of dedication. The status and limit of the body in relationship to personhood is at stake here, as well as the question of the purpose or aim of sexual activity. As a means of unsettling some of these presumptions, I take the question of sacrifice through a discussion of a set of sacrificial practices generally framed as Tantric. I am especially interested here in those sacrifices—forms of bodily offering, or modes of commitment—that are associated with sex and fertility. My aim here is to derive some materials for thinking differently about the sexual capacity of devadasis as sacrificed; materials from a specifically Indian and Hindu archive rather than from the universalizing and mostly Christian set of meanings and sense of horror that undergird reform. Although today this horror finds expression across Indian publics, its most virulent antecedents and futures are Christian and colonial.[3]

Methodologically, my effort here is better understood as an anthropological inquiry into questions of symbolization and form, as well as their politics, than as a project of ethnohistorical documentation. I do not seek to make a claim about the Tantric origins of devadasi dedication, or the essentially Indian character of dedication. The heterodox practices and literatures that I turn to in this chapter allow me to provincialize the horror that dedication elicits. The repugnance of certain customs cannot be taken for granted. Discerning when and where forms of bodily commitment elicit horror, as well as to what uses this horror is put, is a means of diagnosing the possible ethical ends of the body. For Durgabai, this question of ethics leads to a paradox. She is both more and less free than *gandullavalu* are. For reformers, the answer is clear: Neither ecstatic embodiment nor public sexuality is compatible with the ethical disposition of female bodies. They should be conjugally committed.

Bettale Seve, the Naked Worship of Yellamma

In July 2002 I made off in a southwestward direction, leaving the dry plains of the Deccan Plateau for the lush Malnad region of Karnataka. Ambuja accompanied me. Our progress was somewhat impeded by urban unrest, which had been provoked by the desecration of a statue of B. R. Ambedkar in another district. The statue had been fitted with a green cap, festooned with a green flag, and decorated with bangles. Thus was Ambedkar draped in symbols of both Pakistani nationalism and femininity. This kind of vandalism, which was then occurring every couple of months or so, was generally attributed to Muslim youth by the mainstream press. Skeptics suggested that those attempting to advance the Hindu Right in Karnataka orchestrated the desecration of the Dalit hero themselves in an effort to produce tensions between Dalits and Muslims. In either case, the efficacy of a demand for dignity and political recognition from a burgeoning Dalit public was apparent in the response to the desecration, the publicity surrounding it, everyday talk among Dalits, and the government's response.[4] On that particular occasion, the ensuing protest in Hubli, the town where we were to transfer from one bus to another, involved throwing stones at public buses and threatening bus drivers who declined to observe the strike called for by the protestors. The city government responded by calling a halt to all buses in and out of the central bus depot on the following day. This was the day we had chosen to begin our journey to another site of the formation and assertion of a Dalit public: the reform of *bettale seve*, a form of naked worship conducted in Yellamma's name. Thanks to Ambuja's determination, we managed to get off by cramming ourselves onto a bus headed in the general direction of our destination. Four transfers later and without further incident, we reached our journey's end: the Renukamba temple at Chandragutti.

Renukamba is one of Yellamma's names, and this beautiful temple is one of the four significant minor regional temples where *puja* is performed for her.[5] The temple is famous for a controversy that erupted in 1986 over *bettale seve*, which was—and according to some, still sometimes is—practiced there by her devotees. *Bettale seve* is one of the practices devotees vow to perform for Yellamma in return for her help in some matter or with the resolution of some affliction. *Joguli̇s* and *jogappas* assist devotees in the performance of the rite of procession, as they do the fulfillment of other *harake*, generally during the pilgrimage season and not only at Chandragutti.

In the early 1980s Dalit activists began trying to discourage the naked procession. They came at festival time and offered clothes to the participants, urging them to dress and not appear undressed in front of other persons. These tactics of persuasion, however, were not especially successful. In 1986 the activists solicited the help of the police. A young woman had come with her family to perform *bettale seve*. She had bathed in the temple spring and received *aarthi*. Just at the moment she was about to go up the hill, an activist grabbed her and started trying to force clothes on her. Her family and the *jogamma* who accompanied them struggled back against the activist. Soon other *jogammas* and *jogappas* joined in, throwing turmeric up in the air and saying "the devi has been outraged." In the melee that ensued, several police officers and journalists were stripped, smeared with vermillion and turmeric and forced to make their own procession. Police came from all over the state and shut the temple complex down. *Jogammas* and *jogappas* were barred from entering the temple complex, and all forms of *puja* were placed under a ban.

In 2002, when we arrived in Chandragutti, we were received with tremendous hospitality by some relatives of a friend. Our host began to speak of the *gellate* (commotion, riot) over *bettale seve* without any prompting from us and virtually as soon as we entered his house and sat at his table to enjoy fresh chapatis, spicy vegetables, and rice. He took particular pleasure in describing how *jogammas* and *jogappas* stripped the policemen trying to stop the naked procession and made them march. He said that even though he lived just fifteen kilometers from the temple, he had not known of this practice until the *gellate*, when some of the police officers involved came to eat at his restaurant. His narration was marked by anxiety, as if he could not be sure what we might think of such things, and he rehearsed the conventional condemnation of this practice as wrong, exploitative, and based in ignorance. He and his son had big plans for us to talk to the *tahsildar* (subdistrict officer), a temple official, and an archeologist, but we begged off, explaining that we preferred to simply go to the temple ourselves, take *darshan*, and talk to whomever we might find there.

The following morning—a Friday, one of Yellamma's days—we set off on another bumpy bus ride, fortified with tea and in awe of the spreading green fields of paddy flecked with white waterbirds that stretched out from the road in all directions. We proceeded toward the temple from where the bus dropped us just outside the temple grounds. As we walked we passed buffaloes ambling across the street; dogs stretching and circling into naps on the warm pavement; and a woman wearing a printed and ruffled housedress, who watched us from the doorway of her house. We were greeted by the curious glances of children and open stares of young men. As we approached the temple hill, a few small shops selling coconuts, green blouse pieces, oil, camphor, *kumkuma*, and *bhandara* came into view. After walking through an enormous arched gate and passing a police substation and a big water tank (where we duly washed our feet, hands, and faces), we came to the bottom of a set of stone steps reaching way up the hill and into the trees.

Leaving our sandals at the foot of the steps, we began to climb, passing several small temples along the way. An array of *nagas* (Shaivate snake gods), cut into tablets of stone and anointed with *kumkuma* and adorned with flowers, sheltered under a boulder, where an old man wrapped in a white dhoti attended to them. As we hesitated at one small temple another man passed us, dressed as a *pujari*, bare-chested with a *lungi* around his waist reaching to the ground and a linen towel draped over one shoulder. He carried a bowl full of bright red hibiscus flowers and a full pot of water balanced on his shoulder. Soon we were at the top talking to him as he washed—with splashes of water and his bare hands—the gods he tended in a small temple facing the front entrance to Renukamba's temple. The view from the top of the hill was extraordinary, extending for kilometers around and across an expanse of green valley broken by a few rolling hills.

It began to rain, so we took refuge in a triangular opening in the huge rock face backing the temple. In this opening was a small Matangi temple attended by a woman who had invited us in out of the wet. She talked with us as she worshipped the devi with the flame of lit camphor when devotees approached for *darshan*, to leave offerings, and to take *prasada*. Earlier we had seen her applying *kumkuma* and *bhandara* and flowers to stone carvings of deities facing Matangi, but we didn't realize she was a *pujari* until we saw her receiving devotees. She said: "Because I worship *amma*, they call me *jogamma* (*Na devige seve maadtivallari adakka nanga jogamma antari*)." She began to talk about the controversy over *bettale seve*, indicating a pond a short distance down the hill, in which during the *jatra* (festival) people used to bathe and then come naked to the devi. "The police have stopped it," she said. "Now it's a police *jatra*, and fewer devotees are coming" (*Policeru band maadidare. Eegenri adu polisara jatrene, bhaktru barodu kadimene*). When we asked her what she thought about *bettale seve*, she hid her smiling face in the *pallu* of her sari and shyly declared: "The devi herself has made this happen" (Idanna akine maadyalri).

This was not the feeling of the Dalit activists who sought to stop the practice in 1986. "Why would the devi call only women in our community to go like this? Why not women from other communities?" they asked, framing the practice as a social evil perpetrated on their community by prurient upper-caste men.[6] The historical accuracy of such an origin tale cannot be determined, but it found a certain contemporary resonance in the then-growing presence of Indian and foreign photographers who began coming in the 1980s to capture devotees performing *bettale seve* on film. Several of the people we spoke to, including government officers, a politician, and a man running a courier business felt that these foreign journalists (they did not speak of the Indian ones) started the whole trouble. "Before they came, nobody was concerned about this, there was no problem, but then they wanted photos of this thing to put in their papers and make more money," one government officer told us, when he came to share his neatly compiled collection of newspaper clippings, including many such photos. One featured a group of foreign, white, and male journalists handling telephoto lenses attached to expensive cameras. This documentarian suggested that perhaps, very early in the morning and not during festival time, the practice of coming before the goddess naked continues.

After the *gellate*, many police were stationed at the temple grounds, especially at the time of the *jatra*. For four years no *jogammas* or *jogappas* were allowed on the temple grounds at all. Since then they have resumed coming from the plains, as had we, but in lesser numbers. Those who were local are all but gone. Indeed the *jogamma* we spoke to at the Matangi temple was the only one of her kind we saw in three days. Since we couldn't talk to *jogammas* and *jogappas*, which is usually how we spent our time at these outlying Yellamma temples, we decided to talk to the archeologist and the *tahsildar*.

The archeologist was more interested in symbolic than political analysis. He was from the area and had been studying the temple complex for over twenty years. He dated the main temple to the Vijayanagara period (thirteenth to fourteenth centuries), but he had found material evidence of a much more ancient history of worship at the site, including bricks dating to the fifth century and sculptural remnants of Yakshi, aboriginal and/or early Jain feminine spirits or magical beings. He drew our attention to the *linga-yoni* (a phallic materialization of Shiva's generative power set in a round stone with a groove and spout, or *yoni*—the seat of *shakti*) at one temple on the way up the hill. He indicated the stone carvings along the lintel at the Renukamba temple of female figures with prominent vulvas and widespread legs, and couples in what he described as "erotic embrace." According to his analysis, these carvings represented material evidence that this was the site of a Tantric cult, whose followers often sought such settings with caves for their rituals. He described the red hibiscus flower as symbolic of the bleeding *yoni*, and I noticed that the *pujari* in the Renukamba temple had draped fresh garlands of red hibiscus across the fold in the rock

FIGURE 3.1 Stone carving at Chandragutti. Photograph by the author.

that suggested the meeting thighs of a supine female body. At the top of this fold, lit up in the back reaches of the cave by an oil lamp, I could just make out a silver *murti* of Renukamba's face.

Why do devotees go naked before Renuka Yellamma? What kind of bodily commitment is this? Devotees explain that Renuka was startled while bathing in the pool down the hill by some bad men who chased her as she ran into the cave, where she prayed to Shiva to save her, which he did by uniting her to himself. In this origin story, the complementarity of the sexes is raised to cosmic and heroic dimension—Shiva saves Renuka from being sexually outraged by other, bad, men. This is the version offered by the Brahman priest attending the temple. Matangi's *jogamma* had a different version to tell us: Renuka was fleeing her son Parashurama—who had been ordered to kill his mother by his father, who felt she had dishonored him by allowing herself to be distracted (that is, sexually tempted) by a god playing in the water. Saying that the world could not continue without Renuka, Matangi took Renuka's sari from her and wrapped it around herself, successfully misleading Parashurma, who cut off her head instead. Here the hero is the Dalit goddess, said to be Renuka's younger sister, who sacrifices herself to protect Renuka from masculine and familial violence. Devotees from all castes come to the temple as Renuka herself did, naked, having made a *harake* promising to undertake this bodily offering if she would restore their health, give them a child, or provide a good harvest. As we have seen, she is widely felt to be very powerful and capable of bestowing such blessings.

How do local observers understand this rite? One woman, a resident of the town of Chandragutti, represented it as an encounter with the devi. A wonderful and animated storyteller, she recounted her experience of the *jatra* as a child:

> At festival time we used to count the bullock carts as they arrived. There were so many, they would go on and on, and we would be very excited. The whole family would go with a picnic in a bullock cart and stay overnight. Those doing the *bettale seve* would come with their families and the *jogammas* and *jogappas* from their village. They would bathe in the pool, then the *jogamma* or *jogappa* would perform *aarthi* to them and put flowers on them and they would run up to the temple. You didn't feel like laughing. If you see a person without clothes you might feel like laughing, but you didn't feel like that at all. People stepped aside to let them pass and did *namaskara* [a salutation]. You felt the devi herself was in them.

Another way it is seen is as a caste-specific religious rite. This is how a Brahman Congress Party politician and a former Renukamba temple trustee framed it. Lean, handsome, and dressed all in white, he manifested the self-possession of one enjoying the security of a prominent social position. He talked for a long time about the legal struggle he had led to regain permission for the performance of certain *pujas*, such as the rite of marriage and house blessings. These ceremonies had been banned by the state along with *bettale seve* after the *gellate*.

The politician was sympathetic to the efforts of the Dalit activists and had himself supported police involvement, citing the increasing presence of photojournalists and male onlookers. He felt, however, that the activists had gone too far when they took hold of devotees in order to force clothes on them. He regarded Yellamma's outcaste *pujaris* with respect, as efficacious religious figures, and he rejected the popular notion that they were duping the devotees, convincing them to do this *bettale seve* for their own financial gain. In other words, he refused a secular reading of the rite as really, always, and essentially about profit or titillation, if not both. For the Brahman politician and Renukamba devotee, the question of religious freedom was the most salient issue at stake in the controversy. He treated caste distinction as an unproblematic feature of social life.

In contrast, for Dalit observers caste distinction was the most salient feature of the practice. Toward the end of my interview with the politician, my friend's brother-in-law showed up with a friend of his, Satish. We sat for a while, talking about the success of family planning in India, why I had come to study devadasis, what we all thought of George W. Bush being elected president, and the *gellate* over *bettale seve*. The politics of nationalism, gender, and sexuality hovered around this amiable conversation. What kind of progress could India, or the United States, lay claim to? What possible good could come of a foreign scholar's study of a backward custom that signified a lack of civilization in India? What kinds of social, religious, and political practices make for civilization? As we were driving back to our lodging, Satish offered an anti-caste critique of the politician's defense of the rite: "Those upper-caste people say this practice is good, that practice is good, but they don't observe these practices." His appraisal was marked by the secular and egalitarian orientation of Dalit activists, in which freedom from religion as a coercive, caste-specific custom was the critical issue.

The Dalit movement's focus on the abolition of *bettale seve* was based on the success of one of the activists in stopping the practice in Gulburga District. A leader in the Dalit Sangha Samiti (DSS), or Committee for the Struggle of the Oppressed, B. Krishnappa described his motivations to Linda Epp in 1991:

> Any democratic government must see that the people behave in a civilized manner. In a democracy wherein we have got equality, liberty, fraternity . . . in such a civilized society a barbarous thing is going on. Taking the women in the nude is really uncultured and barbarous. This type of procession going on in Karnataka is shameful on the part of the people's representatives to the government. Shameful to the government itself allowing such processions in the name of the deity, arranging the buses for that fair. So, we have attacked the government, [saying, "You] must stop it or we will fight against the government." In this way we converted a social issue into a political issue. (quoted in 1997, 332)

In this view, civilized society and democratic government should not accommodate public displays of female nakedness. *Bettale seve* is framed as a barbaric custom and as antipolitics. The fact that it had endured called the moral legitimacy of the government into question, a question the DSS pressed to its advantage as a way to gain political recognition. The secular liberal project for Dalit emancipation, inspired by the vision and writing of Ambedkar among others, calls on the state to produce and safeguard social equity. This strategy has been key in the formation of Dalit publics across the subcontinent in the past century:

> The fact of stigmatized existence secures the ground of political struggle even while politics anticipates its disappearance. This supplementing of the Dalits' political body with something outside politics and history—the natural body, religion, culture—suggests why Dalit and state efforts at political commensuration consistently reengage the social degradation and nonrecognition Dalits experience at the edge of the Hindu social order. (A. Rao 2009, 25)

Within political modernity, Dalit publics take shape as necessarily secular formations that define themselves in relation to the state. As such, they can accommodate religious practices in which modern protocols for proper bodily constraint and gendered comportment are violated only as a form of caste degradation. Within Dalit publics, *bettale seve* cannot appear as a mode of religious self-assertion or bodily commitment with positive effects. It can appear only as a wound, a cut inflicted by another that requires redress.

Krishnappa's powerful statement takes as settled a question I want to raise: what aesthetics and politics of the body undergird this demand for the end of *bettale seve*? As Philippa Levine, a historian of the British Empire (2000), points out, states of undress can have different meanings. The naked body does not stand outside either politics or history. On the one hand, the unclothed body is recruited by science and medicine as a source of knowledge and power, as a specimen of the human animal to be measured, examined, and mapped. Wrapped in the embrace of medicine, the unclothed body displays the reach of scientific knowledge, with its amoral mastery of the human body as a natural, biological object. On the other hand, within histories of colonial representation—whether ethnological, missionary, anthropometric, or expositional—the nakedness of the native indicates his savagery and wildness. Indeed, Christian missionaries in South India measured their success by the newly clothed state of converts, enacting what is by now a familiar trilogy: Christianity, civilization, and clothing.[7] The standards of comportment signifying sexual restraint have been reformulated in the context of anti-caste politics, and Dalit women have long been exhorted to conform to them. In a meeting with women from the devadasi and *jogini* communities in 1936 in Bombay, Ambedkar challenged them to "give up this degrading life" if they wanted to join the movement. A changing room was set up in order to teach them how to properly wrap their saris (A. Rao 2009, 66 and 310, note 139).

In short, the state of nakedness as a shameful lack of clothing has to be produced in a particular place and time. As concerns *bettale seve* in Karnataka, it was first produced as a shameful scene through mass publicity, specifically in the form of photographs of the processing devotees, clad only in garlands of flowers. This was a pornographic and colonial scene, in which the processing naked Indian was visually consumed by metropolitan Western and Indian audiences. The shame of *bettale seve* was later produced through Dalit protests that framed the practice as one that was specific to the Dalit community and could only reflect badly on its condition. In this view, the political and social progress of Dalits is visible in the raiment of cloth forced on the processing devotee.

The fact that the Dalit activists themselves produced these scenes was not lost on *jogatis*. At the *gellate* they reportedly asked the activists: "Why do you take photographs? If you don't want us naked, then give us clothes. Why do you not take action again the *jaina digambara* [Jain monks]? Why do you not stop cabaret dance? Catch first those Goa beach hippies" (quoted in Epp 1997, 344). By naming three other sites of relatively unproblematic unclothed or semiclothed comportment in the Indian context—the "sky clad" followers of a Jain sect; Mumbai professional entertainers; and bikini-clad New Age *bhaktas* [devotees]—they called the attribution of shame to the naked *seve* of Yellamma into question.[8]

Within the rhetoric of reform, the practice is described as specific to dedicated women, or Dalit women. It is framed as a caste-specific custom. What I found in my own research and what other scholarly writing (Epp 1997; Murthy 1988) indicates, however, is something different: Renukamba devotees—men, women, and children—from a variety of caste communities, including Brahmans, Lingayats, and Marathas—the dominant caste in Southern Maharastra—participated in *bettale seve*. Thus was a devotional practice undertaken by members of various castes reconfigured as an outcaste- and gender-specific coercive custom whose eradication would signal a triumph for liberal governance and Dalit progress.[9]

In her analysis of the "Chandragutti Incident," Epp suggests that the female body became a site for rationalist reform that "violated the sacred," casting religious rites as superstitious and exploitative, and eliding the religious subjectivity of Dalits (1992, 1997). The reformers have done what even Jamadagni could not, she argues: they have made it impossible to escape from patriarchal surveillance and control of the female body, and thus they have aroused the anger of the goddess. This anger was cited by some devotees to Epp as the reason for the bringing down of every chief minister who supported the government ban on naked worship. These devotees offered political commentary in the form of a theological assertion: Yellamma acts in the world; she brings down powerful others when they fail to receive her or her women. Recall the fate of the *sahukarti* (see chapter 1). When *jogammas* and *jogappas* throw *bhandara* up in the air, they are committing themselves to and calling on this power and the forms of healing and critique of social domination it enables.

Genealogies of Tantra

What kind of bodily commitment is under erasure here? Does the naked body necessarily bear sexual significance? If so, for whom and in what contexts? How might we think about the relationships among the forms of *seve* Yellamma is said to demand, the Tantric history of Chandragutti, and the sexuality of *jogatis?*

A strain of religious practice and philosophy present in Hindu, Buddhist, and Jain traditions since the seventh century, Tantra continues to constitute a major strand of Hinduism. Some scholars have argued there is no Hindu practice that has not been influenced by Tantra (Sanderson 1988; White 2003). Yet Tantra may be best known in the West for its most antinomian and transgressive aspects, in which substances considered prohibited and highly polluting in orthodox Brahmanical religion—including alcohol, blood, and sexual emissions—are used ritually as a means of offering to or communion with the deity (I. Sinha 2000, 16; Urban 2003, 40). These antinomian practices fit within Tantra as a broader body of powerful techniques, especially mantras, possession, and sacrificial offering. Bodily self-offering, the religious studies scholar and Sanskritist David Gordon White writes, compels the deity toward the practitioner: "Human practitioners make the supreme sacrifice of their own person, moving the Tantric deity to reciprocate with untold powers and supernatural enjoyments" (2003, 3). Here, I consider some of this Tantric material in relation to the problematic and possibility of bodily commitment. This sort of inquiry is perhaps hobbled by the indeterminacy of Tantra as an object of historical knowl-edge.[10] Its promise lies elsewhere, in elucidating a conception of the human body's sexual capacities beyond the aims of reproduction and pleasure, including its potential intoxication, its ability to consume and transform substances, and its symbolization.

For early European scholars of Sanskrit texts, or Indologists, Tantra rep-resented the antithesis of the rational philosophical Hinduism that they sought to reconstruct (M. Elmore 2007, 753). They wrote against Tantra and its horrors. Celebrations of Tantra, in contrast, attribute it to the original inhabitants of the Indus Valley and pose links between it and matriarchal culture, goddess worship, and fertility cults.[11] This account originated in nineteenth-century Orientalist literature, was popularized by Mircea Eliade and other historians of religion, and was most recently taken up in neo-Tantric discourses. In this narrative, the migration of Aryans into the subcontinent (approximately 1700 BCE) effected the repression of devi wor-ship and associated sexual practices, including "sacred prostitution." They nonetheless survived, as a part of what Eliade has called the "autochtho-nous substratum" of what came to be called Hinduism and were codified in the textual record a millennium later. In the *Padma Purana*, *vaidika* is associated with Brahmans and other twice born castes and *tantrika* with "lowly" *sudras* (Urban 2003, 27).[12] Scholars point to this substratum, espe-cially within Shaivism and Shakta, as the space of aboriginal or outcaste religiosity (Bhattacharyya 1982; Vijaisri 2004).

Tantric readings of Yellamma and the practices that surround her have been suggested by several scholars (I. Sinha 2000; Vijaisri 2004; White 2003). I engage this set of literatures here as a way to approach the question of the status and symbolization of the devadasi body, its movement toward Yellamma, and its movement toward her devotees. These literatures sug-gest an alternate story line to that unfolding from ethnohistorical accounts emphasizing property, performance, kingship, and caste as the essential attributes of devadasi embodiment. Rather than situate these story lines as mutually exclusive, as some scholars have (Soneji 2012), I layer them, thereby accumulating interpretive possibilities. *Jogatis* have been described as "living Yoginis" "heiresses of the former south Indian *devadasi* tradition as well as of Yaksi (female Dryad) mythology" (White 2003, 270).[13] Yaksis, who appear in the Buddhist *Jatakas* and Hindu *Matsya Purnn*, are fierce female avengers who use their sexual powers to subdue the men they then feed on. In the *Valahassa Jataka*, dryads inhabit the forest, lie in wait for passing men, and "seduce them with the charm of their wanton beauty. But, having excited their lust, they have intercourse with them and then they kill them and eat them while the blood flows" (quoted in White 2003, 72). In present-day Kerala women who die tragically are said to become Yaksis, ghosts who haunt the men who abused them in their past lives. Women, the anthropologist Sarah Caldwell asserts, "never have such problems with Yaksis" (1999, 182). In Tantric cosmology, *yoginis* are variously Tantric aspirants, priestesses possessed by the goddess, goddesses, and condensations of feminine power in the female body (Vijaisri 2004, 82). To situate *jogatis* as heir to these Tantric figures is to place them in a symbolic tradition linking the cultivation and communication of fertility with a rapacious female sexuality.

The temple at Saundatti—built in the tenth century, when medieval Tantra was spreading across South India—is described as one of the central *saktistahanas*, or centers of Tantric *shakti* worship in the text *Devibhagavata* (I. Sinha 2000, 79). Within the complex of Tantra, Shakta, and Shaivism that characterizes many of the practices and stories surrounding Yellamma to this day, she is Adishakti and her consort is Shiva. Their pairing is the cosmic union of the male principal with the female principal symbolized by the *linga-yoni* carved in stone as I encountered it at Chandragutti. In 2010 I asked one of the Lingayat *pujaris* attending Yellamma at Saundatti about the place of Jamadagni in Yellamma's shrine. "He is brought in every night," he explained to me, "just before the temple is closed, and taken away again in the morning."

Connections between fertility cults and sacred prostitution have been made by scholars who compare Yellamma with other mother goddesses across the present-day Middle Eastern and Mediterranean worlds whose consorts were killed and reborn (Vijaisri 2004, 33–34; I. Sinha 2000). Goddesses such as Astarte and Cybele were also served by castrated men and prostituting women.[14] Here a fertility cult of sacrifice centers on a goddess whose consort must die. This cycle of sacrifice and renewal—in which Jamadagni must die, Yellamma becomes a widow, Jamadagni is restored to life and Yellamma to her *muttaide* (auspicious fertile status as a married woman)—is mourned and celebrated in solidarity with Yellamma by devadasis and *jogappas*. Those dedicated to the *seve* of Yellamma also embody and enact this cycle of sacrifice and renewal. In this view, sacred prostitution is understood as the sacrifice of female sexuality, and castration as the sacrifice of male sexuality.

Scholars who place the rite of dedication within symbolic histories associating fierce female sexuality, autochthonous goddesses, and the renewal of fertility invariably invoke a narrative of decline, in which fierceness has been displaced over time by the coercions of caste and economy (Vijaisri 2004), Brahmanical hegemony (Gurumurty 1996), and licentious and dominating secular masculinity (I. Sinha 2000). Nonetheless, these histories offer glimpses of an ecstatic body, moving toward the devi and committed to the renewal of life. They also offer a way of thinking about sexual symbolism and sex rites as a medium of exchange between devotees and deities. Drawing on unspecified archeological evidence, the anthropologist K. G. Gurumurthy describes transactional sexual rites as a part of the history at Saundatti:

> At one stage in the religious history of the temple in the name of ritual activation, the mother goddess was worshipped in the form of [the] Great Clitoris (*Bruhat Yoni*). Huge female vaginal symbols made in stone were installed at the shrine. When the devotees came with their mundane problems they were made to insert a male phallic form of stone into the female symbol and rotate it to symbolize the activation of the deity. When the tradition totally got Sanskritized the priestesses, who were the personified forms of the goddess, were made to have sex in the temple enclosure itself, with the devotees who came with problems. By indulging in "divine sex" with the priestesses it was propagated [made known] that the deity who received the seminal fluid from the devotees through the devadasi will free them of their problems. (1996, 136)

If Yellamma is one among angry, hungry goddesses, is semen one of the foods she demands?

Participating in the Body of God

In order to consider this question, I turn to provocative readings of Tantric texts describing the role of *yoginis* and the consumption of sexual emissions in a ritual context. First, I want to specify how I find this narrative of Tantra useful, albeit problematic in its claims to authenticity.[15] First of all, this story of Tantra is consonant with long-standing South Asian accounts of personhood and kin making as transactional. But this account introduces something that is useful to my analysis of devadasi kin making—namely, the idea that transactions between persons and deities constitute a form of kin making. Finally, reconstructions of *yogini* rites challenge accounts of substance exchange, kin making, and reproduction that naturalize the heterosexual reproductive domestic unit as the family.

The Sanskritist Alexis Sanderson (1988) situates his consideration of *yoginis* within a discussion of Shaivism and Tantra. He follows the experience of the *tantrika*, as written in the earliest surviving texts (400–800 CE). In Sanderson's description, the initiate ascends progressively through levels of esoteric practice and revelation. Beginning with the worship of a form of Shiva and his subordinate consort, the Saiva initiate may proceed toward the final stage of liberation from self into the realm of Kali, the destroyer who obliterates the self and reveals the void at the heart of consciousness, thereby supplying release (*moksa*):

> The Cult of the Yoginis appears in the middle of five levels of revelation: When the initiate passed into [the cosmic level governed by Rudras] he found that this masculine hierarchy was replaced by ranks of wild blood-drinking, skull decked Yoginis. Radiating out from the heart of the Deity as an all-pervasive network of power (*yogini-jala*), they re-populated this vertical order of the S'aiva cosmos, appropriated the cycle of time ruling as incarnations in each of the four world-ages (*yuga*), and irradiated sacred space by sending forth emanations enshrined and worshipped in power-seats (*pitha*) connected with cremation grounds throughout the sub-continent.
>
> The goal of the initiate was to force or entice these Yoginis to gather before him and receive him into their band (*yoginigana*), sharing with him their miraculous powers and esoteric knowledge.... [Siva is] not "married" to the Goddess as in the cults of entry, he is rather the wild ascetic who leads the Yogini hordes (*yoginiganayaka*).
>
> The ... Yoginis ... were believed also to possess women and thereby to enter into the most intimate contact with their devotees. (1998, 675)

All Yoginis belong to the family (*kula*) or lineage (*gotra*) of one or [an]other of a number of higher "maternal" powers, and in any instance this parentage is ascribed on the evidence of certain physical and behavioral characteristics. An adept in the cult of Yoginis can identify members of as many as sixty-three of those occult sisterhoods, but is most vitally concerned with the eight major families of the Mothers (*matr*) Brhmi, Mahesvari, Kaumari, Vaisnavi, Indrani, Varahi, Camunda, and Mahalaksmi. For at the time of consecration he entered a trance in which the possessing power of the deity caused his hand to cast a flower into the *mandala* enthroning these Mothers. The segment into which the flower fell revealed that Mother with whom he had an innate affinity. This established a link between him and the incarnate Yoginis, for these families of the eight Mothers were also theirs. On days of the lunar fortnight sacred to his Mother the initiate was to seek out a Yogini of his family. By worshipping her he aspired to attain supernatural powers and occult knowledge. (671–72)

A sisterhood of *yoginis* stands as the gateway to the families of the mother goddesses. Entrance to these families and the power that flows through them is accomplished through the bodies of women possessed by *yoginis*.

Shakta has been the term applied to the practices and scripture associated with the worship of the goddess as Shakti since the eleventh century. Prior to this, the name for such religiosity was Kula or Kaula, which translates as matrilineal clan. Kaula practice was counternormative: "The *Kaulas* . . . practiced sexual rituals . . . sexual yoga, breath control and meditation, they broke taboos and defied prejudices . . . admitting outcastes and prostitutes to their rites and flouting Hindu caste law by accepting as their most sacred sacrament the panchamakara, or five-fold communion, of meat, fish, grain, liquor and sexual intercourse" (I. Sinha 2000, 23). In a book titled *Kiss of the Yogini* (2003), White reconstructs the medieval ritual practice of the Kaula by drawing on textual, material, cultural, and ethnographic sources. White defines Kaula as a body of ritualized sexual practices that first appeared in seventh-century Hindu and Buddhist texts and continues in popular form to today. He departs from the dominant scholarly practice by reading these textual descriptions of sex acts literally rather than symbolically (2003, 8).[16] At the heart of White's reconstruction of the original rites of Tantra is a ritual transaction of substances that effects initiation into the *kaula* or clan. Practitioners of Kaula sought these worldly powers (*siddhis*) and bodily immortality (*jivanmukti*), rather than liberation from the cycle of birth of death sought by practitioners of more esoteric forms of Tantra. These powers were acquired by transacting with the *yoginis*, who possessed the human consorts of male initiates. On the darkest night of the lunar calendar, members of the *kaula* gathered at particular sites of power: clan mounds, seats, or fields. At these minglings (*melakas, melanas*) *yoginis* would be called down from the sky with offerings of alcohol, meat, and/or "a more subtle and powerful energy source" (White, 2003 10–11), the semen of the initiates. Tamed by these offerings, the *yoginis*, rather than devouring the initiates, offered counterprestations of their own generative fluid. This fluid, which White suggests is not only the milk shed by the aroused female body but also the blood of menses, is the clan essence:

According to the *Kaula* world-view, the godhead—the source of all being and power in the world—[is] externalized . . . in the form of a series of female hypostases, a cluster of (often eight) great Goddesses, who in turn proliferated into the multiple circles of feminine energies (often sixty-four) that were their Yogini entourage. These semi divine Yoginis and the human women who embodied them therefore carried in their bodies the germ plasm of the godhead, called the "clan-fluid" (*kuladravyam*), "clan nectar" (*kulamrta*), "vulval essence" (*yonitattva*) . . . or the clan (*kula*). While this fluid essence of the godhead flowed naturally through these female beings, it was absent in males. Therefore, the sole means by which a male could access the flow of the supreme godhead at the elevated center of the mandala, the clan "flow chart," was through the Yoginis. . . . It was therefore necessary that male practitioners be "inseminated," or more properly speaking "insanguinated," with the sexual or menstrual discharge of the Yoginis—rendering the "mouth" of the Yogini their sole conduit to membership in the clan and all its perquisites. (2003, 11)

Here it is the male initiate who is being fed. Consumption of the clan essence, coded feminine, connects him bodily to the devi. Sex acts here accomplish a transaction in powerful substances. In other words, the sexual aim here is not the reproduction of children or the cultivation of affective intimacy that moderns pursue, but rather the exchange of bodily substances that establish relatedness.

Theories of the person as an effect of transactions in substances have been elaborated on through ethnographies across South Asia (Daniel 1984; Lamb 2000; Marriot 1968, 1976; Marriot and Inden 1977; Raheja 1988) and in Melanesia (Strathern 1990). The idea that persons are fluid and open; may be transformed through transfers with others of food, bodily substances, and forms of contact or touch; and are thus composite by nature was captured by McKim Marriot with the term "dividual." Marriot (1976, 111) argues that the South Asian "dividual" concept of the person stands in contrast to Euro-American ideas about the "individual" as a bounded, discrete, and solid person. In the work of Val Daniel (1984) among Vellalar Tamils, all things are fluid and have the capacity to mix and separate; thus persons create relations with others through sexual encounters and the sharing of food, and by proximity in a household or village. According to Francis Zimmermann, the Ayurvedic body is fluid, "composed of a network of channels and fluids, which flow not only within the body but also among persons and their environments" (quoted in Lamb 2000, 31).

Most scholarly considerations have focused on asymmetrical exchanges and the production of hierarchies of caste, as Sarah Lamb (2000, 35) notes in her discussion of persons as open to substantial exchanges. Setting the stage for generations of scholarly debate, Louis Dumont (1970) argued that relations of giving and receiving pure and impure substances reflected a fixed hierarchy of caste (*jati*), whereas others have focused more on the production and reproduction of ranked orders of relations through transactional exchanges (Marriot 1968; Raheja 1988). Studies of auspiciousness, also focusing on the capacity of transactions to produce kinds of people and relations, have displaced the axis of purity/impurity as the sole meaningful significance of substances (Apffel-Marglin 1985; Raheja 1988). Building on this horizontal dimension of "mixing," Lamb describes Bengali efforts to seek out, cultivate, and intensify "mixings with kin, loved ones, friends, neighbors, things and places" (2000, 35). She elaborates on the ways that the social relations of kinship and family, as well as of *jati*, in Bengal are understood to be "created and sustained though various kinds of bodily and other mixings, sharings, and exchanges" (36). These theories have been critiqued for framing Indian personhood in culturalist terms, as somehow essentially or fundamentally different from others — "dividuals" instead of individuals. By framing my discussion of dedication though Cohen's concept of bodily commitment, I seek to draw on this rich literature on substantial personhood without reproducing its limitations. All bodies are committed, not just Indian ones. Like other bodies elsewhere, Indian bodies are committed, or commit themselves, in different ways. Transactional exchange constitutes one possible mode of commitment, one way of "being given over" (Cohen 2013, 319).

White's reconstruction of the *Kaula* rites posits a similar process of transactional personhood in which initiates seek out "mixings" between their own bodily substances and those of the *yoginis* as a means of acquiring esoteric powers and knowledge. These "mixings" or minglings produce membership — through transactions of intoxicants, food, and bodily substances — in the clan, the *Kaula*, the family of the goddess. White's reading of the *Kaula* rites suggest that kin making, as the intimate exchange of substances, occurs not only between persons but among persons and deities. The fact that *jogatis*, like human women who embodied *yoginis*, mediate these transactions is something I will elaborate on in the following two chapters. What I want to emphasize here is that the *Kaula* rites enact a practice of kin making and sexual congress that is limited neither to the territory of humans nor to the aim of reproduction.

Furthermore, the fact that *yoginis* carry the clan essence, which the initiates can access only through them, reverses the logic of patrilineal clan continuity.[17] In a patrilineal regime, the continuity of the clan is carried through the substance coded male, semen. Women participate by contributing the nourishment of blood and food to the lives of sons, but they have no clan of their own. Their clan substance is said to change from the father's to the husband's on marriage (and through sexual intercourse). This spermatogenic model of sexual reproduction underlies the formulation of patriliny in ancient Hindu laws regarding inheritance. Family wealth should follow the flow of family substance through the bodies of men.

Consider, in contrast: "The great Goddess or multiple goddesses of the Tantric clans were neither human nor married. Independent sources of life and energy, they defined clan continuity, in a reversal of the fate of human daughters and wives. . . . Whereas the Tantric *kula* flowed naturally through the wombs of these goddesses and their human counterparts or incarnations, the Yoginis, the most that a male could hope for was to become a *kulaputra*, a son of the (female) clan through initiation" (White 2003, 20–21). In White's account of *Kaula* rites, a matriline is established between the godhead and the cult initiates though the bodies of the women possessed by *yoginis*. This transmission occurs though the sacrificial offerings and consumption of sexual fluids and other intoxicants. The aim of sexual congress here is the reproduction of the body of god. These transactions in substance and kin challenge the theories of reproduction and gender that take sexual difference, the aim of sex acts, and reproductive heterosexuality for granted (see, for instance, Busby 2000). Instead, we are invited to envision the clan essence flowing through the bodies of women possessed by spirit deities. Male initiates who want to participate in the power and presence of the supreme godhead must consume this essence. Access to this family of god is through the bodies of women, whose reproductive aim is not to birth children but to multiply male initiates.

Bodily Ecstasy and Intoxication

As we have seen, in the context of *Kaula* rites, alcohol was ingested as a sacred or sacramental substance—that is, a substance dedicated to the deity. The properties and/or essence of liquor, imbibed in particular ways, in particular contexts, and at particular times, are understood to enhance or intensify the encounter between the deity and persons. Commentators on Tantra emphasize different aspects of the ritualized use of alcohol and its effects. Some emphasize the intoxicating effects of alcohol, which disrupts habitual modes of perception and promote transgressions of everyday norms of comportment (I. Sinha 2000). In this view, the consumption of alcohol is one of the techniques for the achievement of an altered state of consciousness (23). For others, intoxication is a means of opening the body up to the possibility of possession by a deity, of making it more porous (Flood 1998, 161). Along with meat and semen, as situated by White, alcohol is a substance that pleases and tames *yoginis*, tempting them to fly down to earth, enter the bodies of human women, and consort with (rather than devour) the initiates who desire their favor. Still other commentators focus on the communal nature of the consumption of the alcohol as part of what establishes a corporate body of persons acting together on behalf of a collective aim: the enhancement of the fertility of the soil (Hardiman 1985). In her work on contemporary Tantric practices associated with the worship of Bhagavati, a form of Kali in Kerala, Caldwell emphasizes the symbolic valence of toddy in relationship to sexuality and fertility:

> Toddy is produced from the fermented sap of the coconut palm. The chotta, or bud (used in the female puberty ritual) is tied tightly with a thread or dinew, and the tip is sliced off. . . . Every few days the sap is collected and drunk as an alcoholic beverage. . . . Its taste is musty and sweet. The action of toddy-tapping has obvious parallels to human sexuality. Toddy drains the essential fluid from the tree through its flower bud, which is metaphorically associated with the female genitals in the puberty ritual discussed above. The phallic appearance of the bud and obvious symbolic parallel between the tapping action to the production of semen from the penis, by heating and stimulating the exterior surface in order to draw the clear, milky fluid from the rounded tip, is hard to miss but was not consciously admitted by anyone I interviewed. . . . This symbolic correspondence reinforces the parallel between the processes of human procreation and agricultural fertility. Toddy is in a sense the bijam, the essential blood-seed of the coconut tree itself. It is not surprising that certain very fierce goddesses and demonic spirits in village shrines demand the offering of toddy, as well as blood sacrifice and meat, to satiate their thirst. (1999, 110)

What might the use of alcohol in the context of Tantric rites and Shakta *seve* suggest about the understanding of the body that is being enacted in the rites surrounding Yellamma? Yellamma no longer receives offerings of alcohol or meat, though there is some evidence that she did in the past (Assayag 1992; Gurumurthy 1996). The vegetarian habits of Sanskritized

FIGURE 3.2 A portrait of Chandrawwataayi with mother and sister.
Photograph by the author.

deities are well known (Fuller 1992, 103). Yellamma is directly propitiated
with offerings of coconuts, raw and cooked food, cloth, incense, and *ambli*. However, at large festivals in Nandipur, goats are still killed and shared
among the Yellamma and Matangi *pujaris* and the one offering the goat (the
sacrificer). At such times, alcohol flows throughout the village.

I was once taken by the *jogatis* to an all-night singing program on a
full moon night for a saint. Chandrawwataayi demands alcohol, I was told
when I was instructed to purchase some to offer. I duly brought a pint of
"foreign liquor," as all distilled spirits are called in India, wherever they are
produced, and placed it on the altar in front of a large framed photograph
of the garlanded saint. Chandrawwataayi was taken to be an ordinary girl
at birth, but was revealed through a series of miracles to be a saint who
embodied both Shiva and Parvati. Widely revered and seen as very powerful, this saint draws tens of thousands to an annual festival. In the temple
built for Chandrawwataayi, a life-size portrait presents the saint wearing a
dhoti and turban in the manner of local masculine attire. Everyone who
had known Chandrawwataayi spoke of the saint's love of alcohol. After the
bottle I had brought had been offered to Chandrawwataayi—that is, after it
had sat on the saint's altar for about half an hour—it was brought out and

shared among the *jogatis* and *jogappas* who had gathered to sing. With a sidelong glance at Jyoti—whose standards of comportment were perhaps more challenged in that moment under the moon among drinking men and women than at any other point in our work together—the Nandipur *jogatis* declined to partake.

A great deal of alcohol is consumed during the festivals of Yellamma at Saundatti. Indeed, of the two most common types of market stalls on the grounds of her main temple, one sells ritual offerings and the other alcohol, sold somewhat clandestinely out of sight behind rows of brightly colored bottles of soda pop. But the smell is unmistakable, and it wafts out of these shops and off groups of devotees dancing in front of the devi they have brought from their village as they take her around the temple. Sometimes those dancing will be caught by Yellamma, as happened when I was performing such circumambulations with the Nandipur *jogatis* and devotees at Saundatti in 2002. Kamlabai began to jerk and start, and two strong young men from the village quickly stepped close to her, each taking an arm. It seemed to take all their strength to contain her flailing about, but soon she grew still and began to speak in another voice. Yellamma had come, everyone agreed.[18]

Associations between drinking and dancing, dancing and possession, the time and space of the festival, and illicit sexual congress are strong. These might all be described as ecstatic states, in which devotees cultivate heat. Alcohol, meat, and sexual activity are all considered to be heating activities, and Yellamma, as we have seen, is a hot goddess whose presence manifests as heat, whether as fertility or as affliction.

When Yellamma's head was cut off, pilgrims at Chandragutti say, her body fell there. The temple there is constructed around an open cave, which resembles the meeting thighs of a reclining figure. Devotees who come to take *darshan* look into the cave and see the *yoni* of the devi adorned with bloodred hibiscus blooms. Homologies between the landscape and body of the devi are legion in India (Dube 1997; Kinsley 1988). Cultural constructions of and about the body sustain particular views of society and social relations (Douglas 2002, 65; Scheper-Hughes and Lock 1987, 19). The cultivation of the fertility of the soil and the well-being of its inhabitants requires tending to the body of the devi as well as consuming substances and enacting bodily practices that open one's body to her. Through these practices, devotees symbolize and materialize the power and danger of *shakti* in the world.

Secularity, Sexuality, and Sacrifice

What makes an offering a sacrifice? What does it mean to put oneself forth as a body, as an offering, through transgressive or physically demanding practices? Do such offerings entail harm? Do they constitute violations of one's self or another? In other words, on what grounds are forms of bodily commitment to be deemed ethical and distinguished from those understood to constitute violence?

Anthropological theories of sacrifice have emphasized the communicative effect of sacrificial rites as either a matter of transactional exchange with the gods or of the giving of death for life, if not both. For Edward Tylor (1874), blood sacrifices were simply gifts of food to feed the gods. William Robertson Smith's ([1889] 2002) analysis, based on the sacrifices performed in totemic cults, focused on the effect of a blood covenant between devotees: "establishing a commonality of flesh and blood, guarantee[ing] the common life that animates them and the association that binds them" (quoted in Hubert and Mauss [1964] 1981, 2). According to this theory, the purpose of the sacrifice is the kinship it produces. In contrast, Henri Hubert and Marcel Mauss offer a theory of sacrifice based on a study of Vedic and Hebrew texts. The unity of sacrifice, they argue, consists in the sameness of its operation: "This procedure consists in establishing a means of communication between the sacred and the profane worlds through the mediation of a victim, that is, of a thing that in the course of the ceremony is destroyed" (97). This destruction need not be total, as in death, but it must at least be partial. Sacrifice is a means of communication through the sacrificial victim; the victim is a conduit between the sacrificer and the deity. Hubert and Mauss distinguish this from a blood covenant, "in which by the exchange of blood a direct fusion of human and divine life is brought about" (4) by offering one's hair, or a part of one's person. For Hubert and Mauss, sacrifice entails destruction or harm, generally not for the sacrificer but for the victim. For them the crucial point is that the Christian paradigm of sacrificial death and resurrection has its basis in ancient sacrificial rites.[19] The victim is male.

This kind of anthropological thinking about sacrifice is both Christocentric and masculinist. When assumptions about the nature of humanity, society, and God derived from the Abrahamic religions appear in anthropological theories as universals, we are up against what Fenella Cannell (2005) has called "The Christianity of Anthropology." Veena Das offers an amendment to this kind of anthropological thinking about sacrifice based on an exegetical reading of the Mimamsa school's interpretation of Vedic sacrifice. Das notes the idea that the sacrificer "is a bearer of pollution, sin or guilt," from which he and the social body are cleansed by means of the sacrifice, is not, in fact, universal. She distinguishes this theory of sacrifice from the one articulated in the Vedic sacrifice, that the sacrificer is the bearer of desire (for heaven). The aim of the sacrifice is to obey the Vedic command "for the desire of heaven [or to fulfill more worldly desires], perform sacrifice" (Das 1983, 447). Her aim is not so much to put forth a general theory of Hindu sacrifice as it is to provincialize an anthropological theory based in Christian conceptions of sacrifice and redemption. Two aspects of this argument are useful here. First, the sacrificer is a bearer of desire whose aim is to achieve a state of pure pleasure (*prith*). Second, material offerings of libations and food are included in the ambit of sacrifice. Hubert and Mauss exclude such offerings from their theory of sacrifice, I am suggesting, because the mundane materiality of such things place a drag on the transcendentalism they seek to ascribe to sacrifice generally.

The transcendental logic of most anthropological theories of sacrifice obscures the force of material transactions and offerings. The logic of sacrifice in the range of Tantric practices under discussion here, however, is more material than transcendental. Both Yellamma and Jesus were killed, but the transformations that followed their sacrificial deaths are different. Resurrection is transcendental; recombination is material. The body of the devi Yellamma came together when Parashurama mixed up the heads of the two women he had struck: Renuka and a Mang woman passing by, according to *jogatis*. Yellamma is a devi with the body of Brahman woman and the head of an outcaste woman. Matangi mirrors her: she combines the head of a Brahman with the body of an outcaste. As material and bodily offerings that compel the gods to relate to human beings, the range of Tantric practices under discussion here might all be considered forms of sacrifice that aim to mix in order to transform. Bodies so committed are not self-contained and may be seen as violated.

In his work on the reform of hook swinging in the Tamil country, Nicholas Dirks (1997) writes about the reform of sacrificial religion in a similar vein. In the practice of hook swinging, versions of which persist (Harman 2012; Kapadia 1996), hooks are placed in the deep muscles of the back of a devotee, who is then suspended from a pole and swung at the head of a festival procession for the goddess. Missionary horror over blood ritual combined with anxieties among colonial officials about the moral legitimacy of a government that allowed the public conduct of such a ritual, and eventually the practice was banned. As Dirks notes, the problem of the agency of the devotee was of central concern (198), a preoccupation that informed debates over sati as well (Mani 1998). Within humanist conceptions of the person, such as those that informed these debates over the reform of so-called barbaric customs, the voluntary submission of the self to such practices is inconceivable. This focus on agency has also deeply informed debates over devadasi reform, in which *jogatis* are widely framed as either duped or coerced. One of the ways this question of agency has been decided is through the rhetoric of sacrifice. Devadasis, it is said, are sacrificed—in particular, their sexuality is sacrificed. This kind of assertion rests on a prior negative moral appraisal of sacrifice, which, I am suggesting, must be seen within the history of the reform of sacrificial religion.

As a false practice, *bettale seve* can no longer be a rite, a means of offering oneself to the devi and compelling her favor. Neither can it continue to reproduce Dalit female religious authority in the persons designated *jogatis* and *jogammas*, who used to officiate at it. If it continues, it does so in secret; it cannot be performed in public without provoking scandal and inciting policing. Its publicity has been appropriated in the formation of a Dalit public whose secular humanist project of emancipation addresses itself to the state as the guarantor of life.

The sexualization of *bettale seve* as pornographic, achieved through the concerned attention of Dalit reformers and the licentious gaze of foreign journalists, brought about its ban. In her writing about the politicization of performative female sexuality, Mary John considers a controversy over the publication of a photograph of a "Dancing Girl" from Mohenjo Daro in a Delhi tourism brochure, and the objections made by Bharatiya Janata Party legislators in the Central Government. She writes: "These instances are indicative of the twin processes of production and disavowal, whereby images are first sexualized as pornographic in order to then be disowned or banned from representing 'Indian Culture'" (2000, 373). Reconstructions of *Kaula* rites may offer glimpses of another way to view the naked female body before the gods as well as to consider acts of sexual congress in and around Shakta temples such as Yellamma's. Through transactions in bodily and intoxicating substances and states of possession in which gods enter the bodies of devotees, forms of relatedness are produced between humans and gods. In their modern formulations, sexuality and religiosity are interiorized as the secrets of the self, those which render one proper to oneself (Asad 1993; Foucault 1978). Sacrificial modes of embodiment operate according to a different anthropology, or understanding of the human, one in which one is given or gives oneself over as a mode of relatedness. In modernity, this kind of embodiment is constrained to kinship, in its narrow sense of affinal and lineal kin (Cohen 2005).

To elaborate on this point, I will return to the question of the gender of sacrifice. It is evident that the sense of horror driving reform is underwritten by a politics of gender, but reform is also gendered. The male women surrounding Yellamma are not subjected to reform campaigns. They continue to perform on Yellamma's hill under the eyes of police without being troubled by them. Why? The assumption undergirding the gendered character of reform is this: the men chose the disposition of their sexuality. It might be illicit, but it belongs to them. "Why is it always women who are sacrificed?" a Brahman woman reformer from Belgaum asked me in 2011. She explicitly linked human sacrifice, sati, and devadasi dedication as effectively the same, all forms of female sacrifice. For her the absence of sexual agency, loss of respectability, and the threat of contagion congealed in the dedicated woman. "She is simply sacrificed," she said to me over and over again, in a soft tone of compassion and concern. For the Dalit reformers, there are two cuts. One is on the sexual body of the dedicated Dalit woman, the other is to their manhood. Both the Brahman woman and the Dalit reformers see the resolution to the devadasi problem in conventional marriage. Durgabai sees the terrain of gendered sacrifice differently. "They burned my blood," she said to me, speaking of her own children. "Why did I burn my blood, giving birth to children, bleeding my blood away? Your blood has not gone. It's there, strong. My blood bled away, but my children don't see me [take care of me], patrons also don't see me. My condition is bad, isn't it? Right? Many experiences come, what can I do?" She was no more sanguine about conventional marriage, however. "They cut that girl's throat," she said, describing the fate of one of her daughters. She was married off to her brother's wife's brother, a man Durgabai found cruel and disrespectful. For Durgabai, dedication, motherhood, and marriage all make women bleed. Their lifeblood drained away, women are left to see to themselves.

The reform of sacrificial religion and projects of Dalit emancipation undoubtedly constitute forms of progress. They answer Durgabai's lament: "When my parents left me like this, they cut my throat." Yet they also sever ties between humans and gods and eradicate the modes of life they produce. One kind of abandonment has been exchanged for another, or one kind of belonging for another kind of belonging.

CHAPTER 4

The Giving of Daughters

Sexual Economy, Sexual Agency, and the "Traffic" in Women

I thought: "Who will they give me to? I am still young and I don't want to get married this early." But my father said, "[Your aunt, to whose son you have been promised] has come asking. You have to go." I got married and came here.

—Sushila, married to her father's sister's son

I didn't understand then. My mother and father tied *darshan*, tied beads on me. They made me sit in a temple and performed my marriage. They put the devi on one side and me on the other, tied the *tali* [marriage necklace] and put toe rings on.

—Pratima, given to the goddess Yellamma

Tying Beads

Why do families give their daughters to Yellamma? The relationship between Yellamma and the women who are given to her as children is described in two idioms: gift and trouble. In this discussion I take my hermeneutic from the everyday language of dedicated women and their families. Daughters are said to be given (*kodu*), left (*bittu*), or tied (*kattu*) to Yellamma as a means of resolving the trouble she can send. Affliction and hardship of all kinds are said to be Yellamma's trouble, and prosperity and fertility of all kinds are her gifts, the result of her generosity. To marry a daughter to Yellamma is to turn her trouble into her favor. This transformation occurs within the body of that daughter and within her family where Yellamma is to be found as an inhabiting presence.

When devadasis describe how they came to be tied to Yellamma, they report terrible skin ailments, fever, persistent and inexplicable illness worsened by medical treatments, deaths in the family, loss of livestock, failure of crops, serious quarrels within the family, and stubborn and terrible poverty. This is the trouble (*kaadaata*) of Yellamma, her play (*aata*), and it is often articulated as a form of divine possession (Bradford 1983). She is said to have come "onto the body" (*maiaage mele bandalu*), to be "in the family" or "with us." Like other South Indian goddesses, Yellamma is hot in her aroused state and, as we have seen, must be propitiated (cooled) with offerings of devotion and gifts of *ambli*, turmeric, grain, new cloth, silver, and cattle (Kinsley 1988, 205). The highest-stakes version of this type of gift is a daughter.

The following narrative is drawn from a life-history interview with a village-based devadasi in her forties, Pratima. On the day I conducted this interview, Jyoti and I sat for hours talking with Pratima, her grandson, and her mother in their home. This is her description of how she came to be dedicated to Yellamma:

> Still no one has understood [Yellamma's] power, how much power is there. Still no one has understood her play (*aata*). As for me, listen, I will tell you. When I was small, as small as my grandson, I got blisters on my head, all over my body, filled with blood and pus, I could not be held, could not nurse properly, blood and pus used to drip down, even now scars are there [leaning forward to show me her arms]. They used to drip and smell bad, only my mother would touch me, no one would touch me, some knowledgeable person said: "It's from god (*devardinda*), ask god [perform a rite of divination], then see what happens. And then [if it's from god] apply Yellamma's turmeric (*bhandara*) saying her name, leave her as a *jogamma*." Then my parents took her turmeric and applied it to my head. After three days the sores were all dried up. When they dried up, they left me as a devadasi.

Pratima's mother added: "We threw turmeric on her, taking the devi's name and it [her illness] lessened. After it lessened, we took her to Yellamma's hill, tied beads, and brought her back."

Some kinds of trouble are less bodily than this, and more familial and material. Durgabai described the trouble that befell her family when her grandfather arranged marriages for her aunts, because his mother had made a *harake* that one of them would be given to the devi instead:

> My father's sisters were married, but my grandfather's mother was tied. She had told them she would leave one of them in the name of *devaru*, but both were married to Bodiyal [a village]. When my grandfather's mother threw turmeric, my grandfather said, let it end with you. He didn't listen,

he married both of them. But because her grandmother had thrown turmeric, when one of them went to marry, listen to what happened. Everyone went to the husband's house for the marriage. Nine buffalos were there; all of them ate stones or needles and died. The decorations for the marriage went up in flames, and a snake was roaming on the roof. These are all signs of her trouble. At the marriage, when they tried to beat the snake and kill it, it disappeared. They put out the fire, and threw rice and came back. Yellamma started showing her play (*aata*), which is not simple—no one has understood it yet. She caught my grandmother, who stopped being able to nurse her baby or eat food. It was all her trouble. When my grandmother sat down to eat rotis, she would see a big snake wrapped around the tray in which rotis are pounded. It was her vision. When she sat to eat roti, she would find beads in place of rotis, like the beads we have around our neck. When she was thirsty and wanted to drink water, she would find cowrie shells. It was all Yellamma's play, because they had said they would give one of them [to Yellamma] but they married her instead.

Once Durgabai's grandmother vowed to dedicate one of her sons, her trouble ceased.

Dedication, like a Hindu marriage, is achieved through the tying of a necklace. In lieu of a groom, devadasis carry the goddess as a *murti* in a basket. The beads tied are distinctive red and white glass, worn only by those dedicated and taken off only in the rare case that they need to be purified from death pollution.[1] The natal family typically bears the expenses of the dedication, which is generally conducted by an elder devadasi acting in her priestly capacity.[2] The following account of the tying of beads was given to me by a brothel-based devadasi in Pune, herself a guru or elder among the community of *jogammas* and *jogappas* gathered there in the name of Yellamma. This extract is drawn from my field notes:

I am sitting in an urban clinic specializing in the treatment of sexually transmitted diseases talking with a devadasi in her midfifties and the medical doctor who runs the clinic when there is sufficient funding to open it, which there is not at the moment. In a break in the interview, they begin discussing how to come up with the funds to have free government condoms transported to the area. It is dusty and quiet in the empty clinic, but our conversation is animated. Kamala is a leader in her community, highly respected for her work as an HIV peer educator. She has lived and worked in the same lane in the market area of this city her entire life. In that lane, she built her own house and a temple to Yellamma. She is very proud of her daughter, a properly married paralegal. We have been talking about the relationships between gurus and disciples (*chelas*) among devadasis and *jogappas* and the ritual cycle that orders the household and public rites they conduct in the name of Yellamma. I ask who ties the beads. "The guru," she replies, adding: "If you want to get into this family you must tie *muttu* [beads] for the devi. If someone comes to me and asks, I will tie beads on the disciples. It is a marriage." "Who do disciples marry?" I ask. She responds: "The devi. Jamadagni is not the father of the disciple, he is only the husband of Yellamma."

Kamala makes several assertions of interest to this discussion of the effects of sacred marriage. Those dedicated to Yellamma constitute a family, entrance to which is negotiated through alliance with the goddess. This marriage does not follow the heterosexual norms governing conventional marriages: the disciple (whether sexed male or female) marries the goddess. Moreover, the normative pattern of kin relations does not obtain: Jamadagni may be the husband of Yellamma, but he is not the father of the *chelas*. Yellamma is both husband and mother.

The trouble of Yellamma is resolved through sacred marriage, an alliance that transforms the valence of her presence from affliction to fecundity; disrupts normative and naturalized correspondences between sexed bodies, gendered persons, and kin positions; and troubles kinship. This sacred marriage resolves one kind of trouble and produces another. It ties a knot between trouble and alliance, a knot tied in beads. The most common way for those dedicated to inquire after each other's dedication is with the question: "When were you tied?" To tie is to join, to connect, to tether. Beads are sometimes called *darshan*, which refers to the Hindu devotional practice of encountering the devi through sight—to see the god and for the god to see you (Eck 1996). As Pratima suggests above, to tie beads is to carry the devi's *darshan* on your body; devotees may encounter her through your auspicious presence.

In this chapter I explore what it means to be given to Yellamma, to be tied to her and the economy of auspiciousness transacted through her. I consider how the modern dichotomy between the wife and the prostitute has been produced in part through the recasting of devadasis as merely prostitutes, sexual commodities in an alienating and exploitative market. In contrast to this reformist framing of dedicated women, I describe how *jogatis* explain what it means to be given to Yellamma. In particular, I turn to theories of the gift to think about what forms of value the dedication of daughters as *jogatis* produces. Building on the insights of feminist anthropology (Rubin 1975; Strathern 1988), I pose marriage as a means of producing value in and through gendered persons and argue that the contemporary practice of sacred marriage is a means for Dalits of increasing the value of daughters. It is also, and not incidentally, a way to produce daughters as sons entitled to inherit land and obligated to support their families. Specifically, I propose that the devadasi system constitutes a sexual economy distinct from the sexual economy that underwrites conventional marriage. Daughters are given, whether to mortal husbands or to the devi, to form productive alliances. When they are given to men, the wealth they produce through productive, reproductive, or sexual labor flows out of the natal family. In contrast, when they are given to the devi, these forms of wealth accrue to the natal family.

Randi Hunnime: The Full Moon of the Untethered Woman

Each winter, the festival of *randi hunnime* marks the widowhood of Yellamma. The term *randi* refers to both widows and prostitutes. Ferdinand Kittel's dictionary offers the following: "a widow; a slut; a whore; an adulteress" ([1894] 1994, 167). I translate *randi* as "untethered woman" because the structural feature that widows and whores share is that they are not contained by marriage; as a result, their sexual propriety is subject to question. According to devotees, Yellamma became a *randi* when her husband, Jamadagni, got into a fight with a king over a boon-bestowing cow, Kamadenu. Jamadagni lost the battle and was killed. The widowhood of Yellamma is observed every year during the full moon (*hunnime*) in the winter month of Pousha, which falls in December or January of the Roman calendar. This full moon marks the beginning of the pilgrimage season, during which tens of thousands of devotees travel hundreds of miles by foot, oxcart, or bus to visit the temple hill of Yellamma at Saundatti. This season ends three months later, at the beginning of spring, with the celebration of *muttaide hunnime*, the restoration of Yellamma's auspicious marital status or *muttaide*. On the night of *randi hunnime*, Yellamma's green bangles are broken, the vermillion is wiped from her brow, and her gold is taken off: all signs of her auspicious, fertile status are removed. The rite is performed to this day, both at the main and regional temples, where it is conducted by Lingayat (dominant caste) *pujaris* in the sanctum sancto-

FIGURE 4.1 Durgabai bringing Yellamma out of her temple in Nandipur. Photograph by Brett Fisher.

rum, and at village temples throughout the central Deccan Plateau, where it is conducted by *jogatis*.

On *randi hunimme* in 2002 in Nandipur, the excitement in the air was palpable. Children ran around, laughing and squealing; women cooked festival sweets over smoky open fires; young girls swished by in their mother's overly long saris. A contagious sense of elation and heightened animation focused on the preparations. The *jogatis* assembled in Yellamma's temple: Yamuna took up the *chowdiki* and Mahadevi the *shruti*, and Durgabai lit some camphor, while the rest of us sounded the bells tied to the overhead beams. As Durgabai circled the burning camphor in front of Yellamma, performing *aarthi*, the *jogatis* began singing the invocation (*harake*): "Behold, behold, mother of the seven lakes, mother of Shiva's pond, mother of the snow-covered hills, performer of magic, gracious god, behold" (*Udho yelukkolladavva, taalakolladavva, shivakolladavva, siddarakolladavva, manjinaguddadavva, maayakariati, prassannadevara, udho*). Yellamma was carried out of the temple, and a young man beating a frame drum led the small procession into the center of the village, where she was set down under the peepul tree on lengths of old saris spread evenly over the ground. After being offered *aarthi* and *harake*, Matangi was brought out of her temple and placed beside Yellamma. The *pujaris* sat in front of their respective devis. I settled myself off to the side, where I could still see but, I hoped, be out of the way. I was, of course, never really out of the way, obtrusive onlooker that I was. Nor could my seeing, and relating here, be but colored by the nostalgic invocations of village festivals favored by moderns everywhere.

As darkness fell, villagers began to arrive, at first in a trickle and then in a flood, until there was a crush of people pressing to get close to the devis and leave their offerings. They brought *holige* (a fried pastry made with flour and jaggery), cooked rice and vegetables, *ambli*, money, oil, and coconuts. A couple of boys crouched over rocks against which they energetically smacked the coconuts, sending up arcs of sticky sweet water as they broke them open. Anointed with spots of vermillion, the cleaved white flesh of the nut was placed among the other offerings: a vegetarian sacrifice to the goddess. The offerings piled up into a mound one meter high, and prestations of oil, brought to light the temple lamps, overflowed the buckets put out to receive them. After putting the *navedya* (offerings) in front of the devis, the *pujaris* pressed turmeric onto the brows of devotees and pushed generous pinches of the yellow powder onto the homeward bound tin vessels, now emptied of *navedya* and filled with auspicious substance. Devotees came from every community in the village to bring offerings to and take blessings from Yellamma and Matangi.

When the bringing of *navedya* had tapered off, the *jogatis* walked off the side of the peepul tree together, away from what remained of the crowd. They beckoned me to follow them, and I saw they were gathering around a small pit dug into the ground. Mahadevi was marking the rim of the pit with vermillion and turmeric. Durgabai tossed in some camphor and lit a fire, and they circumambulated the pit, joking and singing. When they crouched down around the fire, I saw that Yamuna was holding the tiny green bangles that were usually on Yellamma's wrist. Across the subcontinent bangles, especially green ones, are signifiers of fertility and auspicious married status. Virtually all Hindu women in rural South India wear bangles, and a bare wrist, as I was frequently admonished, is very inauspicious. According to symbolic conventions of auspiciousness and female embodiment, widows should not wear bangles. Indeed, the widows are expected to wipe the vermillion from their brow and break their bangles at the news of their husband's death. As Yamuna began to break Yellamma's bangles with a stone, married women turned their heads away, urging me to do the same and covering up the eyes of their children. After these bangles had been broken over the fire, the *jogatis* began to break their own bangles—carefully, so as not to cut themselves, and close to their bodies and out of the light, so as not to be too easily observed. Sitting back from where they were gathered around the fire, I watched, an ambivalent witness to this criminalized rite.

Thousands of devadasis used to converge annually on the Yellamma hill for *randi hunnime* to break their green bangles, wipe the vermillion from their brows, remove their *mangalasutras* and dance before the devi on the night of her widowhood. Through the efforts of reformers, who see the eradication of all the rites belonging to devadasis as necessary to end the practice of dedication, this ritual enactment of widowhood has been all but abolished. Public commemoration of *randi hunnime* by devadasis at Saundatti has ceased, but any pilgrim traveling there today will notice bits of green glass lodged everywhere between the stone steps leading to her temple. "We do it late in the night," a *jogappa* at Saundatti confided to me.

In villages and towns across the central Deccan Plateau, the festival of *randi hunnime* continues to be celebrated, though not without awareness of the state's view of things. I was invited to and then subsequently warned away from the celebration of this festival in one village, where doubts about the presence of an outsider at a banned rite ban prevailed. According to my friends, concerns about the perceived impropriety of dancing and drinking—still a central feature of the celebration of *randi hunnime* in that village and many others—was also involved in the decision to disinvite me. At a Yellamma temple in one of the brothel communities in Sangli, Maharashtra, dancing, drinking, the sacrifice of a cock, and fire walking in states of possession were all part of the celebration of *randi hunnime* that I took part in 2004. In Nandipur the *jogatis* no longer dance, and that night in 2002 several politicized young Dalit men told them not to break the bangles either. "If dancing is good," they said to me, "let the upper-caste women do it." The *jogatis'* own ambivalence about carrying out the rite and my documentation of it was clear to me. Indeed, their ambivalence was more evident at that time, than at any other point in my work with them. But as I saw in 2007 and 2011, celebration of the feast, as well as the rite of possession and oracle telling, is ongoing.

What is at stake in the celebration of the devi's widowhood? Why does this rite continue, despite its criminalization? In the days following the 2002 *randi hunnime* rites in Nandipur, I had several conversations with the devadasis about the festival. I turn here to an exegesis of the rite by Yamuna in order to approach these questions and to specify the value of *jogatis* within their families and communities. As Yamuna's description outlines, their marriage to the devi situates them in a symbolic and material economy of auspiciousness.

Sitting outside Yamuna's house eating *prasada*—in this case a piece of dried *holige*—I asked her who had brought all these offerings.[3]

> *Yamuna*: They come from all the communities, Samaghar, Harijan, Wada, Holeyar, and other *jatis* also—even if they are not able to prepare *holige*, they bring this much rice [gestures to show a small handful], two coconuts, *ambli*, incense, camphor . . . that is why so much is there. Since everyone comes, you get loads and loads—Sahukar, Inamdar, Gowda, Jain, Vokkaligar, Lingayat, Maratha, Koruba.[4]
>
> *Me*: Would you say that more people come from one community or another?
>
> *Yamuna*: Everyone comes. Even if they are three or four kilometers away, they will come. Only birth or death pollution in their house prevents them from coming.
>
> *Me*: Why is it so important to come?
>
> *Yamuna*: They generally won't miss. It has been there since the root time, it is a form of devotion to Yellamma, and if they miss, she generally manifests [her presence] in their house.
>
> *Me*: How?
>
> *Yamuna*: Some way or the other. Children may fall ill, cattle may become sick—it will show in the household.

Trying to understand the implications of failing to propitiate the devi, I asked:

> *Me*: If they come, the devi will not trouble them?
>
> *Yamuna*: They will not be troubled. Those who come regularly, every Tuesday, and those who do not, will and must come to this *hunnime* and the one after we come back from *jatra* [pilgrimage, here to the main temple for the *muttaide hunnime*].
>
> *Me*: If I am a devotee and I come those two times, can I expect favor, or just no trouble?
>
> *Yamuna*: She will not trouble [you] and things will go smoothly in the house. There will be *shanti* [peace] in the house. If there is no *shanti* in the house, a week's worth of flour gets used up in two days. Whatever you bring into the house, it goes quickly, it wastes away, turns to lack.

People start wondering why this is happening and say, "we missed the *hunnime*," and then again they will come and give *navedya* and break coconuts.

Yamuna articulates a moral economy of prosperity and affliction in relation to Yellamma *seve*. The proper expression of devotion in the care and feeding of the devi and the keeping of her festivals is rewarded by peace and fertility in the household and the body of the village. To neglect her is to risk her trouble and to court lack, waste, and illness. What emerges in Yamuna's account of the *randi hunnime* festival are the ties between this moral economy and the symbolic redistribution of wealth in the village. This redistribution is not to be confused with redistributive justice. As a transactional economy of food, this ritual occasion and others like it do nothing to fundamentally reorganize hierarchies of caste and exploitative land relations. Nonetheless, the Yellamma *pujaris* in Nandipur commanded forms of respect generally unavailable to other Dalits and were prosperous, compared to their neighbors who survived on waged seasonal agricultural labor. This redistribution is mediated through the *jogatis*, who receive the offerings of the whole village, give Yellamma's blessing in return, and share out the foodstuffs within their *jati*. I asked Yamuna to explain about the *navedya*. She said: "Giving *navedya* brings satisfaction to both the devi and the devotee. It is returned as *prasada*. Some people take it home and eat it, and some tie it in a piece of cloth and hang it from the ceiling. It will bring peace in the house, and rice will not become scarce." After discussing the effects of eating *prasada*, and how it produces well-being and protection from the malign intentions of others, I asked about the distribution of the *prasada* after the festival. She answered:

All year we [herself and the members of her household], eat *prasada*, but when do the people in the *jati* get it? [At this festival] we call them into the house and give them [*prasada*]. The *navedya* is collected. First [it is given] to the deity, then some is reserved in the *udi* of the devi, then it is distributed to the *jogatis* as individuals, and another share goes to their households. Then people are sent a message to come and collect the *prasada*, and if there are a hundred houses they may not all receive on the *hunnime*— fifty may get it for this *hunnime* and fifty for next year's *hunnime*.

The exchange relations between householders, Yellamma, and the women tied to her articulate and reproduce an economy of value. As I observed and Yamuna describes, devadasis are transacters in this economy. They produce

FIGURE 4.2 Kamlabai
blessing a farmer with
Yellamma's turmeric.
Photograph by the author.

value and are produced as valuable. They give turmeric and *prasada*, providing auspicious substances to both dominant devotees and *jati* brothers and sisters. Indeed, it is as women given to the devi that they are able to serve in this village economy as givers of substance and not only receivers of substance, the role Dalits are usually constrained to. My point here is not that *jogatis* transcend caste as a hierarchy of social positioning or upper-caste reckonings of purity and pollution—with which, in any case, Dalits are not much concerned. It is that their marriage to the devi situates them as persons who may perform transactions across castes, "up" as well as "down."[5]

The place of devadasis in this transactional economy of auspiciousness is reenacted and renewed every year at the festival of *randi hunnime*. Yamuna described the relationship that sacred marriage establishes between *jogatis* and the devi in this process of renewal when I asked her why they break Yellamma's bangles at *randi hunnime*.

Yamuna: Because Yellamma's husband died, he was killed.

Me: What about your bangles?

Yamuna: We are devotees (*bhaktaru*) of the devi. Whatever happens to her should also be done to us.

Thinking of all the female devotees living in the village with intact bangles, I pressed her for a further explanation. She said:

> Those who are tied with beads and who have become *jogatis*, they must break [their bangles]. As it has happened to Yellamma, so it must happen to us also. When we are tied beads, her *bhandara* is applied to us, so we are like Yellamma. . . . If a devotee is not able to bring the *jaga* to his house, he invites five of us because we are regarded as Yellamma.

Yellamma becomes a widow. With her, as her, every year at winter the *jogatis* undergo the rites of widowhood. They remove the markings of *muttaide* and enter a state of ritual mourning, during which they do not attend any auspicious occasions or conduct any rites. Strictly speaking, this period lasts three months, until the festival of *muttaide hunnime*, when the restoration of Yellamma's auspicious status is celebrated. In practice this period lasts only a few days. All the *jogatis* in Nandipur wore new bangles within days, saying that it was not good for the married women in their homes to see their bare arms. Over time the tolerance for the inhabitation and witness of inauspiciousness, a fallow state, has diminished.

The symbolism of *randi hunnime* in the context of everyday agricultural life is unmistakable: fertility is gone from life. The fields lie fallow, the cattle are loosed, the women untethered. This is an inauspicious but necessary time in the seasonal cycle of life: a loss that heralds renewal, a death that foretells new life. On the occasion of her widowhood, Yellamma is propitiated with abundant offerings. The *jogatis* receive these offerings and bestow her blessings, redistributing the favor of the devi in their own communities.

Devadasis are *randis*, untethered women. They wander. "We are as free as the birds," Radha told me, comparing her position to that of *gandullavalu*:

> How many children do I want? I am a devadasi, true, but I will have a tubectomy after I have the number of children I want. I don't have to ask my husband. But that's not the case with a married woman, only after the husband gives permission can she undergo the operation. We are independent. Are they independent like us? No. [Points to Jyoti.] The difference be-

FIGURE 4.3 Durgabai and Mahadevi sitting. Photograph by Brett Fisher.

tween her and me is as big as the sky. She has to listen to her husband, but no one speaks to us like that, we don't have to listen to anyone.

Laughing about the difference between herself and *gandullavalu*, Durgabai put it to me like this: "I go wherever I please. I never take anyone's permission like *gandullavalu* have to every time they want to move an inch from the house. I am like the cow whose rope has been cut." In central Karnataka, women dedicated to Yellamma and other similar goddesses are called *basavi* (literally, female bull). This name communicates a play on gender: she is a bull, her sexuality is masculine, she roams the village. A bull that has been dedicated to a deity is not tethered; he is allowed to wander the village and take what he likes from the fields. *Jogatis* claim this right for themselves, gathering fresh vegetables from the fields they wander through on their way to ask for grain and give blessings. As we have seen, not all landholding farmers appreciate this incursion by sacred cows and women into their private domain. According to the *jogatis*, this stinginess will be met in kind by the devi.

Marriage for the Dalit women I went to South India to learn from is not to men, but to a goddess. When they are given, or married, by their families to the goddess, they become her wives. Just as *gandullavalu* are expected to perform *seve* to their husbands, *jogatis* are responsible for Yellamma's *seve*. In turn, the goddess takes care of them. As her wives, they are entitled to give blessings and ask for grain in her name. For a devotee of Yellamma to fail to give respect and some offering to a *jogati* who comes to her or his house, passes her or him on the street, or assists her or him in carrying out a ritual is to risk the wrath of the goddess, whose power is renowned in the region. In order for the flow of auspiciousness to proceed in such a household, the devotee would have to resume the proper worship of Yellamma by making offerings, which the devadasis receive on behalf of Yellamma as her wives. In short, devotees depend on what devadasis can give, and devadasis can give because they are bound in marriage to Yellamma but unbound by conventional marriage.

Marriage or Prostitution

Are devadasis given in sacred marriage or sold into prostitution? Recall what Kamala had to say on the subject: "If you want to get into this family you must tie *muttu* for the devi. If someone comes to me and asks, I will tie beads on the disciples. It is a marriage." She says that the rite of dedication is a marriage, a way of making kin with the devi and others tied to her. In contrast, in a survey conducted by the Joint Women's Programme, a retired teacher, echoing the view of many reformers, is quoted: "The Devadasi system is pure prostitution and nothing else" (1989, 28). This charge rests on the idea that the difference between prostitution and marriage is self-evident and morally decisive: married women are good, and prostitutes are bad. The nature of the underlying exchange—gift or sale—determines the moral and legal status of the woman.

Neither what constitutes prostitution nor what counts as marriage, however, has been easy for social scientists to delimit. On this difficulty, Philippa Levine writes: "But whether in domestic or colonial settings one arena in which legal thinkers were spectacularly unsuccessful was in deriving a satisfactory definition of what was meant by, and what could be defined under the rubric of prostitution" (2000, 6). Marriage has proved no more easy to fix. As Kathleen Gough puts it, "the problem of a satisfactory definition of marriage has vexed anthropologists for decades" (1959, 23). Consider that in at least three respects, the lives of village-based *jogatis* and village-based *gandullavalu* are virtually indistinguishable. Both generally maintain lifelong exclusive relations with one man, both look to that man for means of economic survival, and neither takes cash payments for sexual acts.

However vexed the empirical delineation of sexual economies such as marriage or prostitution remains, as discursive categories of modern sexuality and personhood, wife and prostitute have become increasingly distinct. In the late modern period of the British-occupied Indian subcontinent, stigmatizing discourses about sexual commerce as immorality, vice, and exploitation secured intimacy and legitimacy to the marital form (K. Kannabiran 1995; Tambe 2009). The wife became increasingly what the prostitute could not be: the legitimate bearer of her husband's children and the embodiment of chaste womanhood for the new nation.

Jogatis consider themselves to be married, but they are aware that this is not necessarily how they are seen. In discourses of social reform, they are framed as prostitutes regardless of the actual circumstances of their sexual activity and sources of livelihood—the two usual arbiters of women's status in this area. As I have shown, although many *jogatis* work or have worked in brothels, many others spend their entire lives residing in their natal villages, where they may take a patron—usually an otherwise properly married man—with whom they have long-term if not lifelong exclusive sexual relations. Still others are single and celibate. Means of *jogati* livelihood vary across the span of life and come from among a variety of sources, including gifts from patrons, ritual prestations, vegetable marketing, and agricultural labor.

Reformers familiar with local custom admitted knowledge of this range of sexual practices and economic means to me in interviews. This variation, however, did not prevent them from equating the devadasi system with prostitution. This was an equation that *jogatis* did not appreciate. In an essay about devadasis written in 2002, K. Santhaa Reddy, then a member of the National Commission for Women, recounts attending a series of six public hearings across Andhra Pradesh, Karnataka, and Maharashtra. At each event women demanded that they should not be branded as prostitutes. For Reddy, this call signaled their ongoing struggle for dignity, an interpretation that reveals the foreclosure in public discourse on the moral condition of the prostitute as a figure who does not already have, but might struggle for, dignity. Yamuna's own self-representation sometimes fell within this paradigm. For example, one day during a discussion of a trip

I had recently taken to Mumbai, she invoked the distinction in decidedly moral terms: "Those women who do bad work, they are not like us who do the *seve* of Yellamma" (*Avaru, a hengsuru yaaru ketta kelasa maadtaralri avru namgate alri, naavu yellammana seve maadteevri*).[6]

The conflation of the devadasi with the prostitute has a history in the colonial-era standardization of marriage and emergence of the common prostitute. Multiple nonwife categories such as *veshya, besya sule, kanki, basavi, bandi, murli, jogini*, concubine, and courtesan, were socially and legally recognized in precolonial contexts across the Indian subcontinent (S. Banerjee 2000; Oldenburg 1990; Vijaisri 2004). These terms referred to persons associated with a wide variety of domiciling and labor practices, sexual arrangements, and performative arts. The categories both overlapped with and differed from that of devadasis, who were distinguished by their connection to temples and elaborate performing arts. In the context of reform, these distinctions began to collapse into the figure of the prostitute. The common prostitute emerged in the context of colonial legal discourses and state practices that sought to regulate sexual commerce as a matter of public health and racial order (Levine 2000; Walkowitz 1980). As Ashwini Tambe (2009) describes in her history of the regulation of prostitution in late colonial Bombay, the colonial state sought to meet the naturalized needs of British soldiers for sexual release without risking either their health or the threat that conjugal relations between native women and British men to imperial order implied. The authorities did this by creating a brothel district inhabited by common prostitutes, whose conduct and persons were regulated by the state. This new spatial delineation and the state practices that produced it served to animate a new distinction, that between sanctioned and criminalized forms of extramarital sexual transactions. Thus, a range of regionally and caste-specific categories of personhood attached to a variety of performing, ritual, and labor practices and sexual economies were collapsed into one, and the common prostitute became a person whose status was defined in relation to the medical and legal apparatuses of the colonial state.

At the same time as a range of customary nonmarital sexual transactions were being consolidated under the rubric of common prostitution, a variety of marital forms and transactions were becoming increasingly standardized into one. For instance, as Uma Chakravarti (1989) describes, women from the Teli or Abheer communities who, according to customary law, could remarry if their husband took a second wife or contracted leprosy were charged with bigamy by the colonial state if they did so. Pre-

colonial patterns of matrilineality among the Nayars of Kerala were undermined by court decisions that favored male inheritance and reframed
Nayar *sambandham*[7] alliances as concubinage rather than marriage (Kodoth 2001). Through readings of the colonial legal archive of the Bombay
courts, Rachel Sturman (2001) describes the codification of Brahmanical
marital practices in Hindu family law as the norm for all communities. Mytheli Sreenivas (2008) argues on the basis of court decisions about disputes
in Tamil *zamindari* households over property and inheritance that legal
institutions distinguished concubines from wives. This distinction was not
made in terms of sexual relations, reproductive issue, or affective proximi-
ties, but by recourse to the form of the marriage ceremony, the place of the
woman's residence, and her caste identity. Sons of wives were designated
legitimate heirs to *zamindari* estate property; sons of concubines were not.
Women's relationships to property, as well as to the state, were determined
by their sociosexual status (Ghosh 2006). As Sreenivas (2008, 5) points out,
the courts were not just adjudicating the question of women's status, they
were at the same time defining the possible meanings of, and criteria for,
the positions of wife, widow, and concubine.

Almost invariably, these colonial court decisions sought to resolve disputes within families over property and inheritance. The meanings of and
relationships among gender, property, and personhood were at stake: "If
marriage was about creating bonds through people and goods, the meanings of personhood and of property themselves were undergoing transformation in this period" (Sturman 2001, 205). In her reading of court decisions, Sturman finds, as does Srinivas, that property claims were often
adjudicated according to courts' determination of what type of marriage
had transpired. Based on the courts' reading of *shastras*, the Brahmanical *kanyadan* (gift of a virgin) form of marriage, in which the bride comes
laden with jewels, was read as a gift transaction and "approved," whereas
the *asura* form of marriage, in which "the bride is given after the bridegroom gives largely (a large quantity) of money," was "unapproved" (as
quoted in Sturman 2001, 237). The nature and direction of the material
transactions taking place at the time of marriage occupied the court. Were
these gifts (nonreciprocal) or payments (wealth in exchange for a bride)?
The distinction was more ideological than practical: in practice, patterns
of material flow were discernible (toward the groom's family in *kanyadan*,
toward the bride's family in *asura* marriages), and both reciprocity and
material exchanges were commonplace, as Sturman points out (238–39).
The normative instantiation of the Brahmanical dowry form of marriage

was also taking place in relation to broader public concerns about sexual slavery. Sturman argues:

> At issue here is a blurring between brideprice marriages, explicit buying and selling of girls in marriage, and buying and selling girls as slaves (who could also have been used for sexual services). [This conflation] stems from a larger similarity that shadowed this entire debate, between marriage in general and slavery. In other words, [public] anguish over the need to root out the evils of slavery whose source is rural desperation and explicit trafficking "out there," in order to refuse the possibility that marriage in general, even marriage in an "approved form" constituted a form of slavery. (2001, 244)

In short, colonial efforts to define what might constitute legitimate marriage had several effects. The Brahmanical form of marriage and its attendant specification of patrilineal descent became the legal norm for all alliances between men and women. The normalization of this form served to establish a clearer distinction between marriage as a form in which women (and the sexual access to them that marriage confers) are given, and slavery as a form in which women (and sexual access to them) are sold.

The question of female sexual purity and its ties to the status of the nation were also central to the production of the wife and the prostitute as mutually exclusive categories of sexual personhood and status. Modern conceptions of sexual personhood and the new science of sexuality combined with the nationalist quest for sexual respectability to establish the wife as the body of honor for the new nation. The prostitute became a distinct kind of person, defined by her perverse sexuality. Judith Walkowitz, a historian of sexuality, describes the emergence of this conception of sexual personhood: "By ferreting out new areas of illicit sexual activity, a new 'technology' of power and 'science of sexuality' were created that facilitated control of an ever-widening circle of human activity. The new 'science of sexuality' identified sex as a public issue; rigidly differentiated male from female sexuality; focused attention on extramarital sexuality as the primary area of dangerous sexual activity; and 'incorporated' perversions in individuals who, like the homosexual, were now accorded an exclusive and distinct sexual identity" (1980, 4). This perverse implantation (Foucault 1978) combined with the politics of sexuality in anticolonial nationalism to situate the resolution of the problem of dedicated women in the framework of marriage. This was something elite reform projects such as that led by Muthulakshmi Reddy in Madras as well as Dalit campaigns agreed on (J. Nair

2000, 99; A. Rao 2009, 63–66). Both sought respectability—Dalits for their community, elites for the nation.

Reform campaigns recast dedicated women as prostitutes, sent them out of the temple, aestheticized their dance form, and appropriated it for the nationalist project (Srinivasan 1988). Among the effects of this refiguring of the devadasi—her exile from the temple and her placement outside the law—was the shift of the fulfillment of affective and sensual desires out of the territory of the devadasi into the bounds of marriage, and the consolidation of female sexuality around the binary of wife and prostitute. The recasting of devadasis as nothing but prostitutes in the colonial era was a site for the articulation of an emerging protocol of modern sexuality. It was also the locus of shifting alignments between female artistic and erotic power, the state and the temple, in which sex, religion, and economics were being established as mutually incompatible spheres of activity that might, and should, be delimited from each other (S. Banerjee 2000; Srinivasan 1988). These distinctions were produced, maintained, and enforced—and their incommensurability legally and socially marked—though the resignification of the devadasi as nothing but a prostitute. In the context of colonial Madras, this transformation took over fifty years to accomplish. In rural northern Karnataka, it is ongoing.

Within the symbolic and material economy surrounding Yellamma, devadasis are both *muttaide* (wife) and *randi* (prostitute, widow). Indeed, this double valence is precisely what makes them, and the devi they embody, powerful and valuable. As wives of the devi, devadasis can and must transition from *muttaide* to *randi* and back again. Their religiosity and their sexuality are inextricably tied to each other. They embody the transformative relationship between sterility (inauspiciousness) and fecundity (auspiciousness). Devadasis thus incorporate the status of both the wife and the nonwife, and threaten the distinction between them. But insofar as the ability to make and enforce this distinction was and is crucial to the production of female respectability, whether for community or nation, devadasis must be rendered as either wives or as nonwives—they cannot be both.

By the time the current ban in Karnataka was drafted, the equation between the devadasi and the prostitute was complete. The opening language of the Karnataka Devadasis (Prohibition of Dedication) Bill, 1982 reads:

A Bill to prevent dedication of women as devadasis in the State of Karnataka;

Whereas the practice of dedicating women as devadasis to deities, idols, objects of worship, temples and other religious institutions, or places of worship exist in certain parts of the State of Karnataka;

And whereas such practice, leads women so dedicated to a life of prostitution . . . (quoted in Joint Women's Programme 1989, 45)

This bill nullified the dedication of any woman to any deity and specified that dedication should not be an obstacle to what it called "valid marriage" (46). It conferred legal status on any existing conventional marriages entered into by dedicated women and legitimacy on any children born from such newly legalized unions. It prescribed penalties of imprisonment for up to five years and fines of up to five thousand rupees for violating the law. It provided funds for economic rehabilitation schemes, such as loans for the purchase of sewing machines or dairy cows, and payments of five thousand rupees to men who married devadasis (Jordan 2003, 153; Joint Women's Programme 1989, 47).

This law rewrites marriage to the deity as a crime against the state and marriage to men as rewardable by the state, which has set itself up *in loco paternis*, arranging marriages and paying dowries. This bill established as law the identification of devadasis with prostitution and codified conventional marriage as the only legitimate form for reproductive sexuality. Patterns of relatedness between Dalit families and the goddess were criminalized, and normative and naturalized patterns of kin making were privileged in relation to the state. This is, among other things, a modernizing process in which the state seeks to shift the allegiance of Dalit families from the goddess to itself through a resignification and transformation of the subjectivity of the devadasi: from *randi and muttaide* to nothing but a prostitute.

Sacred Marriage and Histories of Exchange and Alliance

In my writing here about why parents give their daughters to the devi, I attend to the interrelatedness between kin making and strategies for material sustenance, an interrelatedness that is obscured by the dichotomy between wife and prostitute. Social scientists have thought about the knot between material and sexual relations in terms of three analytic models: hostile worlds; nothing but; and differentiated ties, to draw on Viviana Zelizer's (2005) typology. In the hostile worlds model, material transactions and intimate sexual relations belong to separate domains of human relating. Because money contaminates intimacy and intimacy corrupts the market, this separation preserves the purity of both. Zelizer delineates three variations of the "nothing-but" model: nothing but economy, nothing but culture, and nothing but power (29–32). Nothing-but models are common in representations of devadasis, as we have seen: it is nothing but superstition, nothing but poverty, and nothing but exploitation. Such characterizations of dedication, like much social theory, understand economy, religion, and kinship as separate domains of human activity. Within the act of devadasi dedication, however, economy, religion, and kinship are inextricably bound together.

The intertwining of material and intimate relations might be thought about in terms of the differentiated ties that they signify and negotiate, Zelizer suggests. A gift between lovers works symbolically and materially differently than a payment does. A struggle over what kind of material transaction is taking place is always also defining what kind of relation is at stake. Thus, the question: Are *jogatis* given in marriage or sold into prostitution? It depends who you ask. Within discourses of reform, daughters are said to be sold. Within the narratives of devadasis and their families, devadasis are said to be given to the goddess.

How are we to think about this gift? Anthropologists have worked though the force of the gift in social life in three ways relevant to this question. First, as *reciprocity*: Marcel Mauss (1990) has proposed that there is no such thing as a disinterested gift and that gift economies operate through three obligations, to give, to return the gift, and to receive. Second, as *gender*: Gayle Rubin has drawn on Claude Lévi-Strauss to argue that the exchange of "that most precious of goods, women" (Lévi-Strauss (1969, 61) is constitutive of a sexual economy that bestows on men rights in women that women do not have in themselves. Third, as *value*: Marilyn Strathern (1988) and ethnographers working in South Asia have theorized that exchange relations produce distinctive forms of value in persons such as caste or gender (Lamb 2000; Marriot 1976; Raheja 1988). These formulations suggest ways to think about why dedication has persisted.

What distinguishes a gift from a payment? In her introduction to the 1990 edition of *The Gift*, Mary Douglas reminds us that Mauss was responding to Malinowski's distinction between commerce and gift exchange in relation to the question of motive. In his work on prestations in the Trobriand Islands, Malinowski (1922) concluded that perhaps only the small gifts offered by husbands to their wives could count as given freely, without expectation of return. "'Pure gift?' Nonsense!" declares Mauss. "The Trobriand husband is actually recompensing his wife for sexual services" (1990, viii). Mauss collapses the distinction between marriage (as a relationship uncontaminated by material interest) and prostitution (as the exchange of sex for a means of livelihood).

Interested or not, gift exchange has a social function. It achieves human solidarity through the creation of a network of material and moral obligations. Transactions and the obligations they engender have implications not just for relations among persons, but for persons themselves. Consider the circulation of offerings at *randi hunnime* in light of Mauss' formulation: "The circulation of foods follows that of men, women, and children, of feasts, ritual ceremonies, dances and even that of jokes and insults. All in all, it is one and the same. If one gives things and returns them, it is because one is giving and returning 'respects.' . . . Yet it is also because by giving one is giving *oneself*, and if one gives *oneself*, it is because one 'owes' *oneself*— one's person and one's goods to others" (1990, 46). Building on Mauss's theory of the gift, Lévi-Strauss constructed a model of kinship as a form of exchange: men transact in women in order to produce alliances between clans; men give wives and receive wives in return. For Lévi-Strauss, the exchange of women is part of a total system of exchange that includes both material and symbolic transactions: "Exchange, as a total phenomenon, is from the first a total exchange, comprising food, manufactured objects, and that most precious of goods, women" (1969, 60–61). Although some feminists have criticized Lévi-Strauss for producing a theory of culture based on the subjection and commoditization of women as objects of exchange between men (Irigaray 1985), others have drawn on his work to argue that gender hierarchy is not inevitable.

Thinking through exchange reveals the systematic and relational aspects of personhood and the disposition of sexuality, as Rubin has shown. In her essay "The Traffic in Women," she looks to the organization of sexuality through kinship for the roots of the oppression of women. Reading Mauss and Lévi-Strauss against the grain, she locates the exchange of women as the cultural basis of a system that produces gender as complementarity: "[Gender] is the product of the social relations of sexuality. Kinship systems rest upon marriage. They therefore transform males and females into 'men' and 'women,' each an incomplete half which can only find wholeness when united with the other" (1975, 179).[8] This "obligatory" heterosexuality, as Rubin has termed it, combines with the principle of endogamy to reproduce caste purity over generations. In Anupama Rao's formulation, "caste is the effect of sexual regulation" (2009, 235).[9] Sexual economies organize material and symbolic transactions: marriage is a technology for producing particular kinds of persons and specific forms of relations.

However, thinking about relations of gender and sexuality through the lens of exchange raises feminist as well as anti-caste radical concerns about the commodification of women as well as their agency. Strathern examines readings of Lévi-Strauss that locate the domination of women by men in the marital exchange and warns against any easy equation between circulation as an object and loss of agency. Based on material from Melanesia, Strathern offers a different model of personhood than that of the proprietary individual that emerges from Western metaphysics and commodity logic. A person may be the form that relationships take or a composite of relations, but not a proprietary individual. Strathern shifts our attention from the properties of persons to the question of relations: "What commodity logic promotes is a perceived diversity of and complexity not in relationships but in the attribute of persons as selves and agents" (1990, 312). She quotes Rubin: "If it is women who are being transacted, then it is the men who give and take them who are linked, the woman being a conduit of a relationship rather than a partner to it. The exchange of women does not necessarily imply that women are objectified, in the modern sense, since objects . . . are imbued with highly personal qualities. But it does imply a distinction between gift and giver" (Rubin 1975, 174). Strathern continues:

> I do not further labor [Rubin's] point that women are not being objectified "in the modern sense," that is, being rendered as things alienable *from* persons. Women's value as wealth, so evident in Hagen [society] for instance, does not denigrate their subjectivity. . . . In other words, it would be an error to see certain people as always the objects of others' transactions and equally an error to assume their natural, "free" form is as subjects or agents. One might put it that people do not exist in a permanent state of either subjectivity or objectivity. The agent is a conduit. (1990, 331)

The fact that women circulate as gifts within sexual economies does not imply that they are alienated from themselves as persons, or without agency. Assumptions that, as Dalit women, *jogatis* are de facto alienated, exploited, and without agency are common within anti-caste radical and feminist characterizations. Shifting our sights from the question of agency to that of value, I am arguing, disturbs these assumptions. The question remains: what sort of value, as gender or as the form of relations, is being produced in persons through specific patterns of circulation?

This sort of thinking about persons—as the form of relations or the effect of transactions—has been elaborated especially in the South Asian context (Daniel 1984; Inden and Nicholas 1977; Lamb 2000; Marriot 1976; Raheja 1988). As "dividuals," persons are always implicated in relations with others and are more open to being transformed through transactions than are people understood as bounded autonomous individuals (Marriot 1976). Sarah Lamb's work in Bengal has specified transactional relations in familial households as "entailing long term-term bonds of reciprocal indebtedness" (2000, 46). The bodily care and feeding that parents provide for young children is returned to them in kind in their later years. Daughters married out of the natal family ritually repay their debt to their parents as they leave, thus loosening the ties that bind them. They enter their husband's household as a *dasi* and, in time, move along with their husband into the center of the household. Those at the center of the household are responsible for giving food to, imparting knowledge to, and making decisions for, those at the periphery: elders, children, beggars, guests, servants, and ancestors (Lamb 2000, 57–59). In the Bengali households Lamb describes, relations of gender and age are produced in persons through transactions. Those on the periphery depend on the deferral of the indebtedness that obtains between parents and children for their place in the system of household transactions.

Whereas Lamb's work focuses on transactions within households, Gloria Raheja's (1988, 251) semiotic analysis of giving and receiving (*len-den*) in a North Indian village concentrates on exchanges between households. Raheja argues that the logic of giving (*dan*) is driven by the need to dispel sin and promote auspiciousness. The distributions made by the village cultivator are made for the well-being of the household and the village as a whole; they establish the centrality of the cultivator in the flow of auspiciousness. Transactional economies, in which women may circulate, are economies of value that articulate hierarchies of gender and caste. This is Rubin's point, but as Lamb and Raheja document, substantial exchanges can also work to produce lateral relations of centrality and marginality in households and villages, of givers and receivers. Devadasis are dedicated to a position of centrality in their natal households through their marriage to Yellamma, who herself occupies a position of centrality in the village economy of auspiciousness.

To be a conduit of value in a transactional economy is not necessarily to be rendered as a thing, a passive object of others' actions, to restate Strathern's point. To be given, whether to a mortal husband or to the devi, is not to be discarded or to be objectified. It is to be implicated in a transactional economy of debt and value as a conduit. *Gandullavalu* and devadasis bear different forms of value in distinct ways. Both are conduits of auspiciousness, which they embody and transmit through their presence, but in different ways that are precisely articulated with the nature of their marital relation. Devadasis cannot be permanently widowed, in contrast to conventionally married women, whose auspiciousness is contingent on their active fertility and the survival of their husband. Marriage is a means of producing value through women, and women as conduits of value. Both sacred marriage and conventional marriage animate sexual economies in which the potential for pleasure, reproduction, and auspiciousness embodied by women is put to work for the family. In this sense, sexuality for both is marital, not marital for conventionally married women and prostituted for devadasis. In Rubin's sense of the term, both devadasis and *gandullavalu* are trafficked.

A Question of Value

What kinds of value do these two kinds of traffic in women mobilize and produce? How are these gifts and these marriages different? In the context of the patrilocal and patrilineal kin arrangements dominant in the region, *gandullavalu* move out of their natal homes and into their husbands' households. Sometimes, as was the case of Laxshmi, my friend and neighbor in Nandipur, this shift is made before a girl reaches maturity, after which point conjugal relations begin. Through this early change in residence, her natal family is relieved of the burden of sustaining her, and the husband's family gains her domestic labor. The position of the youngest daughter-in-law in a household is not enviable; typically the most physically demanding forms of domestic labor fall to her. If she works in the fields, weeding sugarcane or picking vegetables, her earnings come to the household. Her children belong to their father's lineage, and if the marriage fails, she will be expected to leave them behind. Returning to the natal home in the late stages of pregnancy for delivery is expected, but returning to stay after marriage is very difficult. As in the case of another neighbor who fled a violent marriage, daughters can be made to feel very unwelcome by daughters-in-law who have married into the household. This neighbor's sisters-in-law felt that her husband and her husband's family should be taking care of her, and they were not shy about expressing this. Laxshmi described this pattern to me, comparing the situation of *gandullavalu* to that of *jogatis*:

But for a *jogamma*, if he [the patron, or *ittikondaru*] is good, she spends her life with him. If he is not good, she will take another one. But it not like this for us. Once we are married to a husband, without thinking [whether] he is good or bad, we should spend our life with him . . . if we fight and go to our natal place we still have to come back. . . . In the natal place they will scold: "Where you have been married—go there and stay." If some problem comes and we go to the natal place to stay, they can feed us food, give us clothes, everything, but they can't replace a husband. Mother and father can take care, giving food, clothes, but they can't replace a husband. They say whatever the problem is, we have to stay with the husband. Brothers will be harsh if some problem arises. It's good being with a husband, and if we do something and go and stay in the natal place, father, mother, brothers will lose respect. If we stay in the husband's house with all the difficulties, then they get respect. So we have to live in the husband's house, whatever problems come.

From the point of view of the natal family, in the short term little is gained by giving a daughter to a son-in-law, though some relief from the burden of caring for her is shifted to his family—which has gained rights in her reproductive and productive labor and an interest in her respectability. In the longer term, over generations, through the principle of reciprocity and the pattern of mother's brother and cross-cousin marriage,[10] the gift comes back to the bride givers in the form of a daughter-in-law, who will bear children for the patriline and perform domestic labor. But for our purposes here, and in the context of subsistence living, the short term is where the difference lies.

In order to spell out something of the difference in the circulation of debt, gendered obligation, and forms of care that obtain when daughters are given to Yellamma, I draw on an extended exchange between myself and a brothel-based devadasi, Shantamma. She had migrated as a young woman from rural northern Karnataka to Mumbai (Bombay); later she moved to Sangli, in southern Maharashtra, where I interviewed her and where she is an active member of a collective of sex worker HIV peer educators.

> *Shantamma*: When my mother died, my uncles thought: "She is the only child." If I were married someone would take my mother's property [meaning it would go out of the lineage]. But, if I am left like this, if I am tied, I can continue [to own] my mother's land. Her property will come to me. They tied [me]. I was tied when I grew up [reached matu-

rity].... In the beginning I didn't understand.... When I came [home] from working in the fields, sitting in front of the house, I used to watch those women who had gone to Bombay to work. They used to come visit their relatives. I saw them and thought, if I go to Bombay, I can also earn like them, I can also wear good clothes like them. Maybe my life would become good, because at that time our condition was very bad. We didn't have enough food to eat or clothes. I decided to come here and work.... I used to send money to my uncles. Then my uncles said: "It's enough, you have done lots for us, now you come to Manrad, take a house for yourself and stay happily on whatever you earn." In the beginning when I came to Manrad, my condition improved, I took a house. Business (*dhandha*) was good in Manrad.

Me: How much did you give to your uncles?

Shantamma: Five thousand, six thousand [rupees].

Me: Monthly you gave this much?

Shantamma: Not monthly. Monthly I used to give one thousand, two thousand. Sometimes I brought clothes for everyone.

Me: Do you have any debt?

Shantamma: One lakh [100,000 rupees]. We took land to cultivate, but it lost money, the interest increased; we fixed a pipeline [for irrigation] in our field—like this we have some debt.

Me: Is this your debt? Your uncles' (*cakkas*) debt?

Shantamma: It's their debt, it's our debt. I should help pay it back because they are depending on my life, I have taken the responsibility of running the family, I must help them in their hard times.

Later in the interview, she explained her decision to dedicate her own daughter.

Shantamma: I don't have any male children, with that in mind I left my daughter, she will come to leave water before I die.

Me: What about your *cakkas*' sons?

Shantamma: How can I tell about the future? You are seeing how the days are now. If they marry and get wives, who knows how they will treat me? Because my mother was adopted and I was tied to take care of her property, and to continue her light (*deepa*), I was tied—like this to take care of me and mine I tied my daughter.

Shantamma describes deciding to dedicate her daughter for reasons similar to those of her mother's brothers—to continue her lineage, because she has no sons. But she is not talking just about property: she emphasizes the continuation of forms of care secured through the dedication of her daughter. As a devadasi, her daughter can perform death rites for her mother: "she will come to leave water before I die." Forms of care, and movable and immovable wealth, circulate between dedicated women and their natal families. More precisely, they circulate through devadasis as conduits and producers of wealth, whose value in the natal family is enhanced through an alliance with the goddess.

This value is both material and symbolic, at the same time a matter of earning and a question of auspiciousness. In conversations with me, brothel-based devadasis emphasized the material contributions they were able to make to their natal families through sex work; village-based devadasis focused on the livelihood they derived through ritual work. Sex work and kin work were tied together for both. Gangawwa's account of tying beads and doing business (*dhandha maaduvudu*—a common expression for sex work) illustrates the general pattern for brothel-based women. A large and imposing woman with a ready smile and a keen eye, Gangawwa described to me the exchange that took place at the first customer ceremony, called *hennu maaduvudu* (making a woman).[11]

> *Gangawwa*: You are asking about *hennu maaduvudu*, aren't you? It is like this: the first customer who comes should bring a *tali*, toe rings, and a sari.
>
> *Me*: He gave these things for you, toe rings, a sari . . . did he give money?
>
> *Gangawwa*: Two thousand [rupees].
>
> *Me*: Whom did this money go to?
>
> *Gangawwa*: It came to me. I also gave some to my sister—she has a house here, so it came to us.
>
> *Me*: To you yourself or to you both?
>
> *Gangawwa*: To us, because my brothers in the village were poor, and as we continued doing business, things got better for them, also we fixed both my brothers' marriages. We helped them get jobs, [by] paying bribes. . . . I have been sending money for twenty-five years.

Payments from first customers, some of whom continue as patrons, are typically made directly to parents. In Gangawwa's case, it was her elder sister, also a *dhandewali* (literally, a woman in business), who arranged for Gangawwa's dedication, so the payment went to her. But as Gangawwa's narrative suggests, in any case, the flow of money is from the first customer through the dedicated woman to the natal family. This does not mean that brothel-based devadasis do not also have their own wealth. In Gangawwa's case, in addition to arranging marriages and jobs for her brothers, she had seen to the education of their children as well as that of her own children and grandchildren. She had constructed two houses in her natal village, one for herself and her children and one for her extended kin network. In the course of our interview, she made an explicit connection between her work as a *dhandewali*, her sense of obligation to her kin, and her dedication. After describing to me the sense of pride and feelings of happiness she derived from working as a sex worker peer educator against the spread of HIV and for the dignity of women in the community, I asked her what, if anything, she found had been hard or bad about her work. She said:

> Not bad, but the men who used to come, one will be like this, one will be like that, we have to tolerate and convince them [to wear condoms], which was sometimes difficult, which was bad. Business itself was not bad, once we fall into this business we cannot say it is good or bad, we should accept it as it is, because our family is depending on us. It is like a job for us. People who have gone to school get jobs and earn; *dhandha* is like a job for us. The responsibility of running the family is on us. Being devadasis we support our families, including parents, brothers, children. We run the family, marrying brothers, marrying children, getting them educated.

Another rendering of the effects of alliance with a goddess was offered by Yamuna, who has supported her extended household by acting in her priestly capacity. As we have seen, for this ritual work and the auspiciousness of her presence in their households and village, landholding upper-caste devotees give grain, saris, and money. Let us return to Yamuna's comments on the efforts of reformers:

> People are confident in themselves and don't believe in the goddess, they think what we do is shameful, but we know what we get from her, eat from her, wear from her. They don't know this, those who are saying all this about Yellamma. If we keep her and serve her with devotion (*bhakti*), then all these things come to us. Our life will flow toward her and we will feel very happy—the more we roam in the world, in her name, the stronger Yellamma *bhakti* becomes, so we are not able to believe what people say.

In her account, the reformist reckoning of devadasis' status in terms of respectability is trumped by a moral economy in which devotion to the goddess is met with blessings of prosperity. The flow of their lives toward

Yellamma brings in return not only forms of material sustenance, but also happiness (*sukha*) and a part in the increase of the devi's strength. In the account of this *pujari*, the relationship, the flow of exchange between devadasis and Yellamma, constitutes a basis for counter-reformist knowledge and well-being in life.

Recall what Durgabai said about the link between devadasis' unique relationship with Yellamma and the flow of grain from the households of upper-caste devotees into *jogati* families: "She is both husband and mother for us. Look, after they leave us, tying us with her beads, when we take her name she comes into devotees' minds and they give us grain. On that grain we live our lives, meaning she is both our mother, only mother, and she is our husband. She is everything." On the occasions when I went on rounds with the *jogatis* from farmhouse to farmhouse, asking for grain and giving blessings, I frequently witnessed them ask for more when they felt that the flow of return was insufficient. This bid for more often came in the form of a quiet, ironic comment: "Is this enough?" I never heard this in a household evidently struggling for its own survival, but they were not shy before the prosperous. Mahadevi, the youngest and most spirited of the *jogatis*, would tease and joke with people, reminding them how they had been blessed with the devi's favor, and usually, as in the case of the exchange with my landlord[12] below, more was given. He gave ten rupees at first, which she took in her hand, gesturing.

Mahadevi: Is this enough? There are four of us, it is not enough, whatever devotees give, it is not much.

Landlord: If you get ten—ten rupees at each house roaming from morning till evening it will be enough. You should not ask for money.

Mahadevi: It's our *dharma* [duty or right] to ask, we are asking. You didn't even call us for your son's marriage, and he has a job—you didn't give money for bangles then. We didn't come for Mahawanami *phere* to your house.

Landlord: Keep an account of it, I will give [what is due] at my younger son's marriage.

Mahadevi: You fixed the older one's marriage at twelve in the night and you escaped from the expenses [of bringing us]. And for your younger son, you may have it early in the morning at 3 AM. So we don't want to rely on your saying you will give money then.

Landlord: You are saying don't marry my younger son. If we don't, he will take a girl and run away with her.

FIGURE 4.4 Mahadevi smiling. Photograph by Brett Fisher.

Mahadevi: If he takes a girl, her family will come and beat you, saying your
son has done this.

Mahadevi finished by raising her hand in pantomime of the outraged
girl's family's raised fist, and they ended in laughter as the landlord gave
ten more rupees. In her provocative and playful way, Mahadevi explicitly
linked the household's generosity with the well-being of the family lineage,
its continuity into the next generation through the proper marriage of sons.

Consider the status of the dedicated woman. She is by no means a
simple object of exchange. On the one hand, she is given, she is the gift. On
the other hand, she is the countergift; she comes back to the family transformed by her marriage to the goddess, whom she now embodies, whose
blessings she is empowered to bestow, and—in possession states—whose
wisdom she can communicate. Through an alliance with the goddess, she

is empowered to make claims on the resources of dominant-caste devo-tees, patrons, and customers, whose offerings in turn provide the means of livelihood for her family. Also by virtue of this alliance, she is able to draw on her sexuality as a resource for her natal family, whether by producing children for the patriline, gathering patronage from higher-caste men, or earning in a brothel economy. Both material and symbolic forms of value are produced through this alliance, and this value is not only the property of the one given but also hers to bestow. She is both gift and giver.

Sexual Economy and Sexual Agency

Among feminist scholars, the relationship between sexual agency and sexual economy remains vexed. Attention to caste can only complicate this formula. My premise here is that this relationship cannot be stated in a general way, with meaningful universal application. Instead, careful inves-tigation of specific material and symbolic economies, and the ways women produce them and are produced through them, can be a fruitful means of considering the question of sexual capacity and personal will. Holly Ward-low's work on "passenger women" in Papua New Guinea demonstrates this. These women, who exchange sex for money or other goods, are "appropri-ating their own sexuality as an individual capacity rather than a resource for the clan" (2004, 1035). When they seek out sexual encounters with men other than those designated for them in the marital economy, they are "eat-ing their own bride wealth," spoiling themselves in order to deprive male kin of their sexuality as a resource. Wardlow frames female sexuality as a form of wealth, a resource for the clan, as well as a signifying practice that produces new configurations of gender and new sexual practices. Drawing on Rubin, Wardlow suggests that when passenger women refuse to cooper-ate in their exchange, they are "disrupting the kinship-based trafficking in women by abandoning or refusing marriage, appropriating their own sexuality, selling it, and keeping the resources for themselves" (2004, 1037).

Within legal and policy discourses on sexual labor and sex trafficking in India, it is commonly asserted that although Western women might be able to choose to sell sex, Asian women are surely coerced by poverty. Such as-sertions reiterate essentializing and Orientalist representations of Western women as full of agency and Asian women as powerless and victimized, as Ratna Kapur (2001) has pointed out. Equations between choice and wealth, or coercion and poverty, leave no space for the recognition of the choices women make in contexts of economic constraint and hardship.[13]

The conventional distinction between the sexuality of a prostitute and that of a married woman is that the former is available on the market. The idea that there is a pure realm of intimacy entirely distinct from the zone of marketized sex is a feature of modernity, in which companionate marriage based on romantic love is the conjugal norm. However, the notion that marriage has ever been uncontaminated by material interests has been challenged in the work of social scientists who have documented a range of forms of material transactions accompanying nuptial rites including bride wealth, dowry, and bridegroom wealth (see especially Comaroff and Comaroff 1980; Collier and Yanagisako 1987; 2005). Drawing on Henry Lewis Morgan's work, Friedrich Engels linked the emergence of bourgeois marriage in its monogamous, patriarchal form with the institution of private property and the transformation of "all things (including love) into commodities" (1985, 96). The implication here is that social analysis must attend to the everyday materiality of sex, wherever it is found. Conjugality is no more a guarantor of intimacy, equality, and the absence of coercion than the selling of sex is de facto devoid of affection, mutual regard, and willing participation. The presence of material interests in the context of sexual activity is not a necessary or sufficient indicator of coercion.

For *jogatis*, material and sexual relations are tied together. This was evident in the ways they spoke about the difference between a good patron ("He gave money for schooling") and a bad one ("He gives nothing!"), but it was made clearest to me in the context of a conversation about my own failure to marry. We had been out all morning roaming with the devi and asking for grain, and we were sitting under the welcome shade of a neem tree on a tarpaulin of sewn-together chemical fertilizer bags. Durgabai picked up the thread of an argument she had been relentlessly pursuing with me for days about marriage. "Why haven't you gotten yourself married?" she demanded. Thus far I had pleaded work, specifically the task of the research they were observing me attempt, and the writing of a book. She said: "When you get back, finish this work, then you can find a husband." "But I don't want a husband," I responded honestly. "But how will you get children? It's good to have children," she insisted. "I will write a book; that will be my child," I said, without much hope that this would seem an adequate substitute to her. Finally, in great frustration at my stubborn ignorance, she burst out "But who will be there to take care of you when you are old if you have no husband, and no children?" In this framing, the failure to marry and to reproduce is not simply a failure of gender, of proper and fulfilled femininity, but an economic failure, a failure to produce one's future possibility of material survival.

To return to Zelizer's point, struggles over what kind of material transaction is taking place are also always defining what kind of relation is at stake: are *jogatis* given in marriage or sold into prostitution? Reformers say they are sold, commoditized, discarded. But as I have argued, following the logic of the gift reveals the *jogatis'* value in the system. In the context of rural South India, all daughters are given or trafficked, whether in conventional marriage or sacred marriage. Although the two forms of marriage have distinct effects, they cannot be said to simply produce one set of valued, cared-for women full of agency (*gandullavalu*) and another set of valueless, discarded victims (*jogatis*).

Gender, Traffic, and Violence

The sexual economy in which *jogatis* circulate is bound up with economies of caste, gender, kinship, and rural survival. The inextricability of these material and symbolic relations—which produces certain kinds of persons and forms of value—has implications for theories of gender, traffic, and violence. I conclude this chapter with comments on transacting gender, the traffic in women, the questions of value and agency, and the violence of kinship.

I have argued that gender is the effect of marriage, of circulating and transacting in particular ways (Rubin 1975; Strathern 1988). Within this rubric, gender emerges more as an activity—an effect of acting in particular ways—than as an essence. This activity is apparent not only in the performative sense, as the reiteration of norms enacting a bodily identity that successfully signifies a sex (Butler 1990), but also in the sense of transaction. Among *jogatis*, gender is the effect of exchanging and being exchanged according to the norms of such transactions.

I have written here against narratives that attempt to situate devadasis as exemplary victims of trafficking, defined as "the buying and selling of women and children for sexual and non-sexual purposes" (P. M. Nair and Sen 2005, 1). My account of *jogatis* suggests a very different kind of traffic in women than the one anti-trafficking discourses offer. What such narratives elide is the question of value. The assumptions embedded in such discourses about the singularity and universality of the commodity form demonstrate something about tendencies in feminist thinking about prostitution, as well as about marriage. Perhaps, as Gayatri Spivak has suggested, devadasi modes of life exceed the logic of capital (1996, 251).

If the value of the devadasi cannot be written in the logic of capital, what is its coin? Devadasis circulate in and mobilize a marital economy in which not only the exchange of material goods, forms of and rights to labor, and care must be reckoned, but also the favor and fecundity of the devi. Working through the social force of the gift suggests that rather than selling off daughters, families increase their value in the family and community by marrying them to the devi.

Auspiciousness, however, cannot be converted into citizenship or positive state recognition and modes of address. As we know, marriage delimits the terms of sexual citizenship within contemporary nation-states. It not only arranges households, reproduction, labor, and sexuality in particular ways, but it also produces exclusions or forms of social death (Borneman 1996; Povinelli 2002b). Those kept outside of socially sanctioned and legally legitimated forms of alliance are exiled from the protections and rights that positive recognition from the state can afford. Increasingly, to remain a devadasi is to suffer this form of social death, to be excluded from the possibility of sexual citizenship. On the other hand, to remove one's beads and renounce one's union with Yellamma is to be alienated from the forms of recognition, material survival, and value that are possible for those tied to her.

Debates on the status of women in prostitution have focused on the nature of the exchange of sex for money. Activists for sex workers' rights frame this transaction as a form of contract labor and press for decriminalization and the enforcement of appropriate labor laws as a means of mitigating the exploitative and violent conditions under which this work takes place (Kempadoo and Doezema 1998). Feminists arguing for abolition refuse the possibility of such a transaction. The conditions of possibility for entering such a contract freely do not exist anywhere: sex can only be given freely or stolen, it cannot be freely sold (Barry 1995). These debates tend to circulate around the question of agency and its presence or absence in the prostitute.

In my discussion of the dedication of daughters, I am suggesting two things. First, that marriage, like prostitution, is a transactional form that produces forms of value in persons and in relations. This suggests that within feminist debates about the status of women in prostitution, as well as in marriage, pursuing the question of value may be more fruitful than attempting to measure the absence or presence of agency as the property of a person.

One of the implications of this story about the giving of daughters is that kinship entails violence, or—to use Lawrence Cohen's evocative phrase— "it is a mode of bodily commitment that often involves a wounding" (2003, 3). Whether they are sent to work in brothels or not, daughters given to Yellamma by their families as a means of ensuring the continued flow of all forms of prosperity into the household are exploited in the sense that their human resources are appropriated for the good of the family. The same must be said about any family member whose reproductive and productive labor is channeled back into the family. The obligation to return is a burden, which can entail forms of injury.

This serves as a reminder to us that many women in prostitution are escaping what they found to be worse conditions in their families, a fact which belies the oft-invoked notion that it is always better to be returned home (Oldenburg 1990). Equally dubious is the idea that returning women from the metropolis to the village constitutes a form of rescue (Agustín 2005). This notion is ridiculous to many of the world's rurally located people who are grappling with the difficult conditions of rural survival produced by an increasingly globalized postindustrial economy. Attending to the materiality of devadasi lives, I have found, makes it more difficult to think of the exploitation and violence that women (and men, for that matter) suffer in prostitution as radically different from the violence and exploitation of home and family. As figures of sexual personhood, however, the prostitute and the wife invoke wholly different associations. The prostitute bears the stigma of sexual violation and ruin. The wife bears the honor of sexual respectability and domestic companionability. This draws our attention to the costs of maintaining the domesticated position as protected, good, sanctioned, and safe: insisting on the honor of the wife produces the abjection of the nonwife.

PART III · TROUBLE

CHAPTER 5

Kinship Trouble

When the beads are tied, they throw rice and turmeric on us as in a marriage. The *pujari* ties the *mangalasutra* and beads. A *kailasha* [pot] is put beside us [as] the groom, as the devi. Then rice and turmeric is thrown in her name and she becomes our father, mother, husband, everything.

—Yamuna

I don't have any male children, with this in mind I left my daughter, she will come to leave water before I die. I was tied to take care of my mother's property, and to continue her light [*deepa*], in the same way, in order to take care of me and mine I tied my daughter.

—Shantamma

Transformations in Gender and the Power of the Devi

"So," she said, gesturing for me to sit down across from her in the afternoon light, "you have come to learn about Yellamma."

"Yes," I said, nodding at the *pujari*, who was studying me as she considered my standard self-introduction in such contexts. We sat—Jyoti and I, the *pujari*, members of her family, and a small collection of neighbors and curious passersby—on the stone platform in front of the Mandovi Yellamma temple. Jyoti's and my brows were marked heavily with the turmeric of the *pujari*'s blessing.

"She is not simple," she began deliberately. "She makes men into women" (*Aki saralillri. Aki gandsarna hengur maadtalri*). The complex and generative power of the devi is manifest in gender transformation: "she makes men into women."[1] I was, by then, familiar with this kind of story about the troubling and playful power of Yellamma. Saying "she came to me in a dream and called me to her temple," women withdraw from sexual relations with their husbands and leave untenable marriages.[2] They take the path of divine service out of gendered kin obligations, which are otherwise extremely difficult to escape in this rural context, where kinship practices remain one of the most powerful—if not the most powerful—arbiter of social belonging.

Other women exchange saris for dhotis and turbans, renounce the kin obligations conventionally assigned to women, and take up men's work in Yellamma's name. Called *ganda udigi* (literally, dressed as a man), such a masculine woman is said to embody the god Shiva. Devotees explained Chandrawwataayi's change in gendered embodiment in terms of divine presence or possession. "Shiva is very strong in *avaru*,"[3] a gentle devotee said to me about the saint one day as we sat under the spreading branches of peepul, banyan, and neem trees that had grown together. This was a place where devotees came to bring offerings and prostrate themselves before the *udaya* (the miraculous self-manifestation of a god in the physical landscape; literally, spontaneous stone) of Durga. The devotee continued: "In the beginning when Chandrawwataayi was a young girl, *avaru* wore dresses, then as *avaru* became older, *avaru* began to wear a sari, until *avaru* realized Shiva's form (*rupa*) was in *avaru's* body. [Then] *avaru* began wearing a dhoti, kurta, and turban." At Yellamma's festivals, *jogappas*—male women in whom the goddess is very strong—wrap saris, play sacred instruments, dance, and sing in her name. They say: "all women are our mothers, we do not go [have sex] with them," suggesting a link between their kinship with the goddess, embodiment of gender, and sexual orientation.

One of the first devadasis I ever spoke with was a brothel-based woman introduced to me as someone who had been given to the devi as a girl. As an adult, Devaki had renounced her ties to Yellamma and become very active in the collectivization of sex workers and HIV prevention education work. In answer to my question about who the devi was to her now, she launched into a story about Yellamma's transformation of a rich Jain landlord. My nervous excitement about our conversation contrasted with her calm and confident demeanor; she was evidently more experienced in talking to foreigners than I was in talking to devadasis at that point. "Look, I will tell you how she [Yellamma] is. There was a very rich landlord," Devaki began:

Yellamma came to him in a dream and called him to her temple. She would not let him rest. Finally he went to his mother and said, "Yellamma has called me to the [temple] *guddha* [hill], I will leave everything and go." "But

FIGURE 5.1 A *ganda udigi* at Saundatti. Photograph by the author.

FIGURE 5.2 A *ganda udigi* preparing the *murti* of Yellama at Saundatti. Photograph by the author.

what about your wife and children, your property, your family?" she protested. Saying he would see that they were provided for, he left, traveled to the temple, wrapped a sari [around himself], and began to sing and dance for the devi."

"When you go there, you can see him dance," Devaki said, "that is how great her power is." Yellamma, as Devaki taught me, can break the ties between a man and his wife, his children, and his property. She can cause an upper-caste landlord to wrap a sari and dance at her feet. This is a power that disrupts orders of caste, sex or gender, and sexuality, orders produced through the human technology of kinship. Marriage organizes forms of social and sexual reproduction in human life. It also produces gendered divisions of labor and household organization that are basic to notions of sex or gender difference, and it works to delineate legitimate sexual relations from illegitimate ones. The taboo against intercaste marriage maintains and signifies the purity of caste as a substance inhering in the body and transmissible through sexual contact and sexual reproduction.[4] Lineage— including the legitimacy of children and the propriety of the parents whose sexual relations produced them—is also marked by and marks out regulative orders of caste, gender, and sexuality. To disrupt these orders, as the devi does, is to disturb normative patterns of kin making. Indeed, as theorists of kinship have taught us to see, it is to disrupt social order itself (Barrett and McIntosh 1982; Butler 2000; Rubin 1975). This is Yellamma's power.

In this chapter I further explore what I call the effects of kinship with the devi. How might we think about transformations in gendered embodiment as effects of ties with the devi? Is this a disorder of affiliation or a different order of affiliation? As persons whose productive and reproductive labor, sexuality, and kin ties are organized though sacred marriage, devadasis do not conform to dominant Dravidian patterns of kin making. Dominant human practices of kin making tend to take on the status of the natural facts of life within a society (Collier and Yanagisako 1987; Uberoi 1993). They stand as given and beyond question. Anomalous patterns of kin making call the given, natural status of dominant patterns of kin making— and the orders of caste, gender, and sexuality they produce—into question.

What might attending to the effects of kinship with the goddess teach us about relatedness in general? I am interested here, in particular, in the articulations among kin positions (mother, daughter, father, son, wife, husband, and so on), the embodiment of gender as masculinity or femininity and the achievement of social recognition as a woman or a man, and the disposition of sexuality. I am drawing here on one of the key contributions of kinship studies: the idea that persons are not simply born, but are made, through the human technology of kinship. I am also drawing on the insistence within queer theory that the articulation between the sex of a body (phenotypic and anatomical) and the embodiment of gender (femininity or masculinity) is neither natural nor inevitable. Working through the logic of the gift, I have argued that sacred marriage serves for families as a means to increase the value of their daughters within their families. It is also, and not incidentally, a way of producing female-sexed offspring as sons. Here I consider more closely the gendered effects of kinship with the goddess and their implications for the disposition of sexuality.

Upsetting the Vocabulary of Kinship

What happens when kinship goes awry? To recapitulate, in "The Traffic in Women," Gayle Rubin argues that gender is the effect of marriage as the exchange of women between men. In a published conversation between Judith Butler and Rubin about this essay, Butler makes the point in these terms: "You then speculated that it might be possible to get beyond gender . . . if one could do something like overthrow kinship" (Rubin with Butler 1997, 72). In her own writing, Butler explores this question of an "overthrown" order of kinship. Through the figure of Antigone, she suggests that destabilizations in normative kinship can produce disruptions in gender: Oedipus's sons have become like daughters, his daughters like sons, "and so we have arrived at something like kinship trouble at the heart of Sophocles" (2000, 62).

In the Greek tragedy, Antigone is the daughter of Oedipus, who is also her half-brother; they share a mother in Jocasta. Antigone's mother, then, is also her grandmother, and her brothers are also her nephews. As Butler points out, the terms of kinship have become "irreversibly equivocal" in the case of Antigone: "Antigone is caught in a web of relations that produce no coherent position within kinship" (2000, 58). Yet, even as an inappropriate subject of kinship, she acts in defiance of her uncle, the king, by performing burial rites for her brother. He died in a bid for the throne and was declared a traitor and condemned to remain uninterred and unmourned. For Butler, Antigone's action is more than a transgression of the law that reiterates the force of the law, as many readers of Sophocles have argued. Antigone's acts have their own effects; they inaugurate something new. Butler writes:

Prohibited from action, [Antigone] nonetheless acts, and her act is hardly a simple assimilation to an existing norm. And in acting, as one who has no right to act, she upsets the vocabulary of kinship that is a precondition of the human, implicitly raising the question for us of what those preconditions really must be. . . . If kinship is the precondition of the human, then Antigone is the occasion for a new field of the human, achieved through political catachresis, the one that happens when the less than human speaks as human, when gender is displaced, and kinship founders on its own founding laws. (2000, 82)

Antigone is Oedipus's sister and daughter, but her actions are manly. This disruption of the founding laws of kinship, correlations that have been naturalized and are felt to be necessary between sexually dimorphic bodies, gendered divisions of labor (such as the conduct of burial rites), and patrilineal arrangements of sexuality threatens social and political order and produces new and dangerous ways of being human. Like Butler, I am interested in what unanticipated field of the human is opened up when kinship is troubled.

As we have seen, trouble is something devotees of Yellamma are very familiar with. That afternoon in Mandovi, the *pujari* continued elaborating on the power of Yellamma to transform gendered embodiment and to disrupt kin ties: "She will make a man wrap a sari within one hour; it is not easy to understand her. The *jades*, which they [the reformers from Ghataprabha] say have been made intentionally, do not come like that. It's all her *mahima* [miraculous power]. She even has the power to make people's hair fall out. For example, in our village, there was a girl who woke up the night after her engagement to find that all her hair had fallen on the bed. It was that very night, still her fiance's family was in the house. We have witnessed this." "Why would Yellamma do this?" I asked. "She wanted that girl, because she had lots of devotion toward the devi. The family came running to this temple asking what they should do. We told them to wait for some time, but they brought a wig and she was married. She is still living in Nippani, and lots of trouble has been given to her husband's family."

The kinship trouble in Antigone's family seems to be the effect of a transgression of the taboo against incest. In the families of Yellamma devotees, it is an effect of the presence of the devi and a sign of her power. As Nicholas Bradford (1983) has noted in his work on Saundatti, Yellamma plays with people in ways that are troubling. Her play (*aata*) and trouble (*kaadaata*) may be manifest in failed crops, persistent drought, illness, infertility, or even death. In short, affliction of any kind might be attributed to her, especially that which is not easily explained or resolved through other means. As we have seen in the accounts of *jogatis*, her trouble is taken to be a sign of her anger. It is also a sign of her desire: "she wanted that girl." She troubles those that she wants, and she manifests this desire through possession. The presence of Yellamma in the body of an afflicted person may be evident in any number of ways, but it is most commonly marked by the spontaneous matting of hair, skin diseases, and gender trouble.[5] As I have described, the matting of hair signifies Yellamma's call and presence, and *jades* are anointed with vermillion and turmeric and worshipped as the devi herself. Skin afflictions, especially boils or other eruptions of the skin attributed to an excess of heat, are frequently cited forms of *kaadaata*. Yellamma's presence in the bodies of those she is calling may produce a change in *rupa* that has consequences for normative sex or gender expression and family life. In a conversation with a devotee in Nandipur about how her mother-in-law came to wear pants and a shirt, the woman told me: "The devi gave her lots of trouble. First she had four children, and then the devi said: 'I will not give you a family life (*janma*), I need you.' Her children died. She left home and began living alone, and the devi made her wear white clothes and bells (*geje*). Yellamma is so powerful she gave her a different *rupa*."

The loss of "family life" and a change in form is a sign of the devi's trouble and her power. Becoming kin with the devi, getting tied to her, is the best way to resolve this trouble and channel her power toward one's own well-being and that of one's kin and community. As Durgabai put it to me when I asked if she felt she had been troubled by the devi, "Why would she trouble us? We are her bulls" (*Namgyak aki traas maadtala? Naavu aki guligolu*). Yet, as I explore in this chapter, becoming kin with the devi has its own troubling effects. In and around the family of Yellamma, and in those families said to have Yellamma in them, there are many forms of kinship trouble.

The Beheaded Devi

Yellamma's own troubled relationship to kinship is at the center of the stories that devotees recount of her life. Her fall from chaste wife with miraculous powers to beheaded victim of matricide is represented in clay dioramas along the pilgrimage route to her main temple and in the borders of the iconic poster art worshipped by devotees with incense in their

FIGURE 5.3 Yellamma's story. Offprint poster from the
bazaar at Yellamma's temple in Saundatti, circa 2001.

FIGURE 5.4 A clay diorama of the beheading and restoration of Yellamma made on her hill at the time of the annual pilgrimage. Photograph by the author.

homes. In a typical version, the image at the center is of Yellamma. Surrounding her radiant head are scenes from her life story: her marriage to the sage, Jamadagni; her daily trip to the river to fetch water for his *puja*; balancing on her head a pot of sand on a coiled cobra; the tumbling snake, pot, and water at her sight of erotic play in the river; Jamadagni's recognition of her loss of chastity and his immediate curse of disease and banishment; her mendicant wandering and cure by two forest sages, who transfer their powers to her; her bold return to Jamadagni; his outraged command that their sons kill her; the execution of this order by their youngest son, Parashurama; and, finally, Jamadagni's granting of a boon to his obedient son—the restoration of his mother.[6]

For K. G. Gurumurthy (1996), who has conducted many years of research at Yellamma's main temple complex, this story mirrors the historical decline of an autonomous devi and the women given to her in sacred marriage, as I have mentioned. When I met with him, he detailed a process over time, through Sanskritization, in which the goddess and her wives were progressively subjugated to male gods and their priests. The valorization of textual histories over oral traditions and the incorporation of the devi into a patriarchal familial structure degraded the status and lessened the power of the devi and her women. Gurumurthy's rich narrative of decline tacked back and forth between the patriarchal conquest of agricultural societies centered on mother goddesses, British imperialism in India, American imperialism in Thailand and Vietnam, and the incorporation of rogue Dravidian deities into a Vedic pantheon through the idiom of patriarchal kinship. Setting up parallels between the colonization of the global South by the North, the East by the West, the oppression of the goddess by her patriarchal kin, and the sexual and economic exploitation of devadasis by corrupt priests and landlords, Gurumurthy figured the patriarchal family as analogous to imperial or colonial powers: violent and appropriative. The colonization of the devi's potent fertility and auspicious power—and that of her women—was accomplished through the slow attribution to the devi of male kin and the regulation of her sexuality.

The Sanskritization of this vernacular tradition has several interrelated effects. First, the autochthonous mother goddess falls to the subordinated position of wife or daughter of a presiding male Vedic deity. As either the consequence or the cause of this fall, the sexuality of the devi comes into question. She is no longer identified as a generative force, as fertility itself, but as housing something threatening or spoilable that must be contained or protected. This is the story of Renuka Yellamma, wife of Jamadagni, as published in pamphlets sold by the temple trust and illustrated on posters for sale in every town in the region. As the chaste wife of a sage, she has miraculous powers. As a woman capable of being distracted by desire, she is condemned first to disease and banishment, and finally to death. In this tale the fate of female desire uncontained by patrilineal kinship is clear, as are the virtues of chastity and wifely and filial obedience.

But perhaps this is not the simple story of patriarchal ascendance that it might seem to be. There are other ways of understanding Yellamma's family drama, which are evident in the lives of the men and women who are given to her. Bradford (1983) suggests that the heroes of the story of Renuka Yellamma's beheading are not the manly men, upholders of father's rights and enforcers of female chastity, but rather the elder sons who refused to obey their father's command to kill their mother and were thus cursed by him with impotence. These sons are claimed as ancestors by jogappas, who today partake of Yellamma's power by renouncing masculinity and becoming sacred women.

To the *pujari* at Mandovi, Yellamma's story demonstrates the ascendancy of her devi and the ethical failure of Jamadagni. In response to my comment that "the devi did not have very good luck with her husband," the *pujari* replied: "She is the daughter of a king, but her husband was cruel. Now luck is with her, she is ruling the world." A similar interpretation was offered to me by a devotee who heard I had come to learn about Yellamma and sought me out to ask: "Do you know about her third avatar?" Standing in the doorway of my neighbor's mother's house, where this devotee had found me drinking tea, he explained:

> In her first avatar Jamadagni cursed her with leprosy for being late for the *puja*. In the second, after being healed [by the forest saints Ekkayya and Jogba], she returned and he ordered Parashurama to cut off her head. Her third came after she was restored through Parashurama's boon. She said: "In my first avatar I came to you, you rejected me. In my second avatar, I returned to you, but again you sent me away. In this third life I will not stay with you. I will go into the forest and save the world, and I will live forever, but your life will be destroyed."

In this account Renuka Yellamma begins as a dutifully chaste wife and ends as a renunciate who has cursed and left her husband. She rejects him and the role of a wife, goes into the woods, and becomes a *sanyasini* (renunciate) whose care extends to the whole world. This version follows the reverse trajectory of Gurumurthy's narrative, in which Yellamma begins as a powerful autonomous devi and ends as a diminished consort devi, whose women have been sexually exploited. In a psychoanalytic reading of ambivalent South Indian *amma* devis' origin stories, including Yellamma's, Richard Brubaker (1978) has suggested that female outrage and violation (often sexual) by men is vindicated in the figure of the devi. In this reading, the violence of the patriarchal family is displayed and transformed into a feminine power, an outraged creator or destroyer goddess whose pacification is achieved through forms of human devotion.

There is kinship trouble in Yellamma's life, whether we read it as a lesson in the consequences of transgressing patriarchal law or as an indictment of the violence that law requires for its own maintenance. This trouble calls the patriarchal family form into question, displays its cruelty, and disallows its naturalization as the happy outcome of the biology of reproductive sexuality. Relatedness is fraught in the life of the devi; it does not follow the norms of patriarchal protection, feminine chastity, and filial obedience. These disturbances show up in the lives of those who are dedicated to her, as if they are tied in the knot of beads that *jogatis* and *jogappas* wear around their necks.

Genealogies of Kinship

Before I elaborate on the kinship trouble in the lives of those given to Yellamma, I want to locate my thinking about the politics of the family in the field of kinship studies. In particular, I want to situate the form of the family as both systematic (orderly, regulating, and patterned) and innovative (historical, changing, and contested). Like many anthropologists conducting research in South Asia, I am interested in the ways that marriage produces forms of mutuality (obligation) as well as hierarchies of gender and caste through endogamy. At the same time, my analysis of relatedness departs from those constrained to reproductive heterosexuality replicated over time. Over and over again in conversations with me, *jogatis* told me that they are married to the goddess and that this has consequences for the disposition of their sexuality. In order to attend analytically to this claim, I have found that I had to work in between what has become a bifurcation in the literature on kinship. On the one hand, feminist appraisals of kinship have foregrounded gender as a critical axis of analysis but have subsumed sexuality within gender (Collier and Yanagisako 1987; Uberoi 1993). On the other hand, queer critiques have foregrounded the forms of social death produced by heteronormative kinship structures but have neglected gender (Borneman 1996; Warner 2000). I am drawing on and departing from both of these trajectories to think about a form of same-sex marriage (between girls and a goddess) that organizes opposite-sex relations (between *jogatis* and their patrons or customers). I begin by recalling some early conversations among anthropologists about the marital form.

Gurumurthy's account of the displacement of an ancient matriarchal order by a patriarchal one has its place in the history of anthropology (Bachofen 1861; Morgan 1877).[7] In Lewis Henry Morgan's hands, the family form offers an index of social evolution: "The principal institutions of mankind originated in savagery, were developed in barbarism, and are maturing in civilization. In like manner, the family has progressed . . . advancing from the consanguine, through the intermediate forms, to the monogamian" (1877, vi). From promiscuous horde to monogamian patriarchal family, humanity has progressed through stages of savagery and barbarism along the way to civilization. Morgan suggests that the shift from matrilineal to patrilineal reckoning of decent occurred during the barbaric stage and was inspired by the advent of the institutionalization of private property.[8] In this evolutionary model, the patriarchal overthrow of matriarchal or matrilineal kin systems is a sign of social progress. Monogamy, private property, and the tracing of descent through the patriline mark the achievement of civilization.

The legacies of such evolutionary thinking persist. In the United States, it makes an appearance in the pessimistic evaluations of the fate of children in female-headed households or those raised by same-sex couples.[9] In India it shapes public concern focused on the sons and daughters of devadasis, whose lack of a father through whom to trace descent is so self-evidently tragic it needs no explanation. The afterlife of Morgan's evolutionary kinship represents a way of thinking about kin making that I am writing against here. His idea that the form of the family is a human achievement (rather than a natural fact), however, is a significant and enduring one in kinship studies and an important one for my argument. As anthropologists have shown, the considerable variation of the form of the family across the ethnographic and historical record demonstrates that the norms and patterns governing kin making are neither natural nor given.

Whereas for Morgan the form of the family was an expression of social evolution, for theorists of kinship influenced by structural linguistics, it was a symbolic field demonstrating principles of social and cognitive organization. The structural approach to the study of kinship was extended in the South Indian context by the French sociologist Louis Dumont. Based on his research on Dravidians, Dumont declared alliance to be "the fundamental principle of South Indian kinship" (1983, 103), complementary to the principle of descent thought to be found in the African context by British social anthropologists (Uberoi 1993). Dravidian kinship has played a special role in the history of kinship as a field of knowledge. First described by Morgan, who argued for the Asiatic origin of American Indians on the basis of similarities between Dravidian and Iroquios kinship terminologies, Dravidian kinship inspired not only this comparative methodology but also the work of alliance theorists. The ethnographic record in South India served as key data for Claude Lévi-Strauss in his development of a structuralist method for the analysis of family systems and marriage practices. By tracing the prohibitions and norms established by incest taboos, he sought to articulate "the elementary structures" of marital exchange (1969). The Dravidian case—in particular, its rule of cross-cousin marriage—was taken by Lévi-Strauss to reveal the principle of reciprocity underlying marriage (Trautmann 1995, 2).[10] This principle of alliance, along with the shastric ideal of the gift of a virgin, which established norms of sexual purity for women, shaped structuralist and functionalist inquiries into norms and practices of exchange, alliance and debt in family, and kinship and marriage in India (Trautmann 1995; Uberoi 1993).

In addition to the idea that the family is an artifact of human achievement produced within a regulative field of structured possibilities, I am drawing here on developments in kinship studies since World War II. Principally as a result of the work of David Schneider, the empirical presumption underlying the concept of kinship as a universal domain of human social organization saw its demise. In *A Critique of the Study of Kinship* (1984), Schneider suggests that there is no such thing as kinship out there, to be discovered and described—instead, kinship is a doing rather than a being. Schneider's cultural approach to kinship drew the anthropological gaze to concrete practices and local articulations of the patterning and meaning of relationships.

Feminist anthropology emerging in the 1960s and 1970s shifted the discussion from considerations of kinship as structure to questions of social change, stratification, and female agency. These feminist scholars began analyzing the political economy of the household; gendered divisions of labor; sociology of the family; socialization of children; and the family as a site of violence and exploitation, as well as for the reproduction of gender, class, and sexuality. The shift from preconceived structures of kin relations to locally articulated representations ushered in another change: women anthropologists began asking their women informants how they conceived of their kin relations (Collier and Yanagisako 1987; Reiter 1975; Rosaldo and Lamphere 1974; Uberoi 1993).

In an ethnography titled *Siva and Her Sisters: Gender, Caste and Class in Rural South India* (1996), Karin Kapadia demonstrates feminist innovations in kinship studies. Like Dumont, she notes the importance of alliance among the non-Brahman Tamil villagers she studies, who uphold matrilateral cross-cousin marriage as ideal. Unlike Dumont, Kapadia foregrounds the experience of women in such a system, for whom the debt of kinship frequently seems to outweigh the gain. Critiques of kin relations are rarely spoken by women, and it was not until the very end of Kapadia's research that she was taught the expression "kinship burns."[11] This expression refers primarily to women's negative experience of marriage and is especially evident in the lives of women in upwardly mobile, low-caste families, in which the adoption of Brahmanical norms means women are increasingly secluded in the home and men's interests hold sway more and more.

Although they consider women's particular experiences and representations of kinship, feminist studies of kinship in India have rarely focused on relatedness or patterns of caring in the lives of women exiled from normative family structures.[12] Sexual norms and alliance practices among the unmarried in the Indian context have received some attention in the literature on courtesans, devadasis, prostitutes, *hijras*, and renunciates.[13] Scholarship on devadasis has noted the ill effect of state policies outlawing adoptions of daughters by devadasis and banning their dance, which brought economic ruin to whole kin networks (Apffel-Marglin 1985; J. Nair 1994; Srinivasan 1988). In "Lifestyle as Resistance: The Case of the Courtesans of Lucknow, India" (1990), Veena Oldenburg takes up the notion of marriage resistance and troubles the kidnapping narrative popularized by the novel *Umrao Jan Ada* by Mirza Muhammad Hadi Ruswa. In her research among the members of a household (*kotha*) of courtesans in Lucknow, she uncovered stories of "self-consciously elaborated, subtle and covert forms of resistance against patriarchal culture" (Oldenburg 1990, 23).[14] They were establishing a "female lineage" (48). Twelve of the thirty women she interviewed had escaped sexual or domestic violence; another four had been widowed in their early teens. Borrowing an expression from the Tamil non-Brahman village women Karin Kapadia wrote about, one might say these courtesans were fleeing the "burn" of kinship. Serena Nanda (1990) briefly describes the division of *hijras* into houses, or symbolic descent groups. As one *hijra* described the community, "there is only one caste of hijras all over India, all over the world. But for convenience, like in one family there are six brothers, it's like that, we have kept these houses also" (40). These are families, however, that do not count as such before the state.

Patterns of affiliation formed outside and against the law have also been considered in studies of kinship in queer contexts. As Kath Weston points out, anthropologists have not been the only ones to "subject the genealogical grid to new scrutiny" (1997, 34); lesbians and gay men have been constructing critical discourses of kinship for some time. In a critique of feminist privileging of marriage systems in the study of gender and kinship, John Borneman (1996, 1997) has suggested that the presumed universal principles of descent and alliance produce exclusions, and he calls instead for the study of patterns of caring and being cared for.

Posing relatedness as a question, or asking about indigenous ways of enacting and conceiving relations, is a means of inquiring into the nature of people and how they become subjects endowed with gender or intelligible sexuality. It is a way of interrogating the effects of kinship. Within normative configurations of kin, for instance, marriage bestows intelligibility on sexual activity. Sexual relations outside marriage are intelligible only as violence or perversity, violations of the laws governing the proper configuration of the family form. I am interested here not only in the positive effects of kinship — or, more specifically, alliance — but also in the forms of social death that marriage produces. What kinds of lives, forms of desire, and modes of embodiment are enabled, and what kinds are disallowed through the grammar of kinship at work in a particular place and time? What are the consequences and possibilities of falling outside the grammar of dominant kin-making practices?

Devadasis as Sons, Fathers, and *Mamas*

As is often noted in the literature on Karnataka devadasis, one of the most common local explanations for their dedication is the absence of sons in a family (Joint Women's Programme 1989; Mahale 1986).[15] This production of so called honorary sons through sacred marriage is seen by some scholars as simply a strategy of placeholding that seeks to maintain the continuity of the patriline through hoped-for male children of the dedicated woman (Epp 1997). My conversations with devadasis and their families suggest, however, that dedication has more to do with the work that gender is made to do under conditions of hardship than simply with the continuation of the patriline. Within dominant constructions of gender, labor, and kinship, sons are produced as economic actors who earn for their families, whereas daughters and the reproductive and productive wealth they create belongs to their husband's family. Moreover, even in families with male children designated as sons — in which the patriline is secure — daughters are given to the devi. Sometimes, as was the case in Yamuna's family, they become head of the household instead of their male brothers by virtue of their ability to better earn and sustain the kin network — that is, to successfully fulfill the obligations of sons. This suggests that not only may daughters be produced as sons, but also that the presence of *jogatis* in a kin network may disrupt the articulation between male sexed offspring and the designation of persons as sons.

Another way in which the status of devadasis as sons is marked is in their right to inherit land. This is a customary right that female-sexed women positioned as daughters do not have. This right is increasingly contested, as is evident in what the brother of one devadasi said to me: "Why should we share our land with them? Let this practice end." In the course of my conversations with people, I learned of two cases of murder over disputed land involving devadasi claims and many other cases of family acrimony. There is some evidence, then, that support for ending the practice of dedicating girls has been building among young Dalit men who are eager not to have to share their usually fairly meager property inheritance.[16]

As well as having implications for the gendered entailments of property, the recognition of devadasis as sons in a kinship system is linguistically marked. The children of devadasis do not call their genetrix's male-sexed sibling *mama* (mother's brother), they call him *cakka*, the term in Kannada for father's brother. These terms mark a distinction between matrilateral and patrilateral kin that is essential in a society in which cross-cousin marriage is ideal and parallel-cousin marriage is taboo.[17] When the children of a devadasi call their mother's brothers *cakka*, they are indexing her position as father to them and brother to her male siblings. This is a recognition that governs decision making about the marriage of the children of devadasis. Although the ideal marriage partner in this region for a daughter is the mother's younger brother,[18] this person would be taboo for the daughter of a devadasi.

This was first brought to my attention by Meena Sesho, who has worked with devadasi and nondevadasi sex workers for many years building a model program for HIV prevention and rights-based community organizing in Sangli, Maharastra. In listening to a conversation among devadasis about the marriage of Devaki's daughter to one of their sons, Meena gathered that they were trying to sort out whether the prospective groom was kin to the bride: "What does it matter if you are in the same *gotra* [patrilineal clan]? Mother's brother's marriage is there." In response Devaki exclaimed: "But as a devadasi I am as a son, he would be *cakka* [father's brother], not *mama* [mother's brother]!" All the other devadasis exclaimed in spirited agreement. Over the course of my research I came to understand that this effect of kinship with the devi was taken for granted and explicit among devadasi families and those familiar with them.

Meena told me this story about the marriage of Devaki's daughter with a great sense of amazement that she had not known of this kinship effect of dedication and its gendered implications. She said: "I had not realized the extent to which they are a man in the family. If I could have the status my brother has in my family, I would choose it in a minute. To think, all the years I have been with them and I didn't even realize this. It is not just that they are *like* the man, they *are* the man." The distinction Meena made raises some interesting questions: What is the difference between being a man and being like a man? Why do we make this distinction? What is at stake, and for whom, in how the gender of embodiment is parsed from the gender of kin position?

If devadasis are like sons, if they are honorary sons, this is not the same as their being sons. The former is an analogical or indexical position, the latter an ontological status. The use of the term "honorary" in reference to the cultural transformation of persons recognized as female into persons with the obligations, responsibilities, and privileges of sons seems to insist on the limit of culture in the face of nature. Sex (maleness or femaleness) is situated as natural—understood as essential, perpetual, and real—while a gendered kinship position (son or daughter), designated honorary, is cultural—ascribed, adopted, and fictive. In other words, the logic would seem to be that devadasis cannot actually be sons but only like sons, because they are not persons recognized as male or masculine, and a person who is a son is necessarily a male or masculine person.

If, however, we untether kin position from the logics of sexual dimorphism and binary gender assignment and follow, instead, the logic of dedicated women and their families, other forms of gendered personhood and anthropological recognition come into view. Devadasis are described, recognized, and related to as persons who are both women and sons. They are not either women or men, either daughters or sons. They are both women and sons. I learned more about how to think about this question on a follow-up research trip in the winter of 2004 when I met with a group of brothel-based devadasis, many of whom I had conducted life history interviews with in 2003. I asked them more about the kinship effects of their dedication: "As devadasis many of you have fixed marriages, bought land, and made payments for education or jobs for your sister's children." "Yes, yes," they chorused, seemingly unmoved by this banal line of questioning.

> Me: "This is the work of *mamas* [mother's brothers], these are the things that *mamas* do for their sister's children."
> Them: "Yes, yes."
> Me: "Because you are a devadasi, your brother is a *cakka* [father's brother] to your children. Are you like a *mama* to your sister's children?"

To my great surprise, the circle erupted with retorts: "We are not *mamas!*"; "No one would say we are men (*gandisu*)!"; "No, we are not like that, you have not understood."

We went back and forth in a very spirited conversation, in which I attempted to clarify that I was not suggesting that anyone saw them as male persons or men. Meena added that she did not see them as men (as her earlier comments to me might suggest) but as having the actual status of men in the family. I clarified that I was trying to learn if they occupied the structural position and fulfilled the material and affective responsibilities that *mamas* have toward their sister's children: "Do you do the work of *mamas*?" This was not the sticking point; they quickly agreed that they were expected to and did fulfill these obligations. What seemed to upset them was the possibility that I had misrecognized them as men. Finally one of the most vocal contributors to the exchange said in a suddenly quiet voice: "The children of two sisters cannot marry, but because I am a devadasi, my [married] sister's children can marry my children. In this way we are *mamas*."

This was another surprise, one which clarified two things. The first is the fact that the devadasis' position as sons in their natal families does not affect their embodiment of sex or gender or their recognition as women. They act in their kin network as sons, but this poses no threat to their social recognition as women, persons whose bodily comportment successfully signifies womanhood. The second is that the kinship effects of dedication are not limited to the dedicated person. They ripple across the whole extended kinship network in terms of patterns of care and obligation, as well as inheritance rights and marriage rules. Devadasis' status as sons is incorporated in and across the kin network and, through time, across generations. They are not men, but they are sons. As a matter of bodily comportment or perceived essence, they are not men. As a matter of structural position, affective orientation, and transactional obligation, they are sons. This seemingly paradoxical social fact of gendered personhood puts what is often taken to be the ontological foundation of the category "son" into question. I return to this point below. For now, I pose it in the form of two questions: What role does bodily masculinity or male sex assignment play in constituting who is or can become a son? How might devadasis trouble this?

The masculinity of devadasis in the grammar of kinship is not limited to their recognition as sons. Sometimes they are also seen as fathers. In the course of a series of life-history interviews, part of a larger comparative project between brothel-based devadasis, village-based devadasis, and village-based women with husbands (*gandullavalu*), I had the following exchange with Margawwa, a brothel-based devadasi:

Me: What was it like in your family when you were young?
Margawwa: My father and mother were working hard and filling their

stomach. They left me to Yellamma; from this I started filling my stomach. I have two children. Our situation was very bad. I have brothers, but they are [only] taking care of themselves. My father died, my mother is still there. I came here to this town ten years back. One year back my father died, my brothers separated from the family. I have two children, one is in school. I am working and earning my food, taking care of them.

Me: Before coming here, where were you?

Margawwa: I was in the village, working hard and eating.

Me: How did you come here?

Margawwa: I came here to earn in the name of Yellamma.

Me: How did you decide to come to this town?

Margawwa: I came here to fill the stomach on my own.

Me: Your children's father?

Margawwa: Father? I am the father.

In her terms, as the one who provides for her children and sees to their education, she is their father. She fulfills the obligations of a father and claims for herself that kinship position, marked by gender and generation. In the course of my conversations with devadasis, this claim was rarely made so directly. The conviction it captured, however, was not unusual among devadasis, almost all of whom have children and almost all of whom provide for their children, if not also their extended family networks, through ritual and sexual labor. It was a claim that was also sometimes corroborated by children. As Yamuna's son Ishwara said to me over tea one day on the subject of the man who contributed biological material but not material sustenance to his making, "he is not my father, I have no father. My mother is my father, she is everything to me." When this young man married, he brought his bride home to his mother's house, in keeping with the dictates of patrilocality and the place of his genetrix as father. This pattern was observed by all the sons of devadasis living in Nandipur.

Jogappas: Male Women and Their Families

Yellamma's ability to transform people sexed as male into sacred women is evident everywhere she is worshipped. At her temples and festivals, *jogappas* dance and sing at the head of processions, help devotees fulfill *harake*, and perform rites of divination and blessing. Most of the ones I encountered at Yellamma temples and festivals traveled and lived in groups, headed by a guru or teacher they call *amma*, often the one who tied their beads. Some of them also maintained connections with their natal families; a rare few were said to have wives and even children. Most were said to have *malaks* (patrons or husbands) or be doing *dhandha* as well as ritual work. Only one, whom I met five or six times over a period of three years, openly discussed his sexual relations with other men with me. But the fact that most *jogappas* went with men was commonly recognized, as much among those living in the villages of northern Karnataka as among those running HIV prevention programs in Bangalore or Pune, for whom the public health category of men who have sex with men (MSM's) included *hijra*s, *kothis*, *panthis*, and *jogappas*.

I know a great deal less about the everyday lives of *jogappas*[19] than I do about those of devadasis, with whom I spent much more time and found an easier rapport. The exception to this was in the cases where I was able to make my own queerness more readily legible, something I found virtually impossible in the rural context where the possibilities of sexual recognition were delimited to my unmarried status and well-beyond-marriageable age. In the cities, largely through my associations with other queer people, and because of the growing salience of metropolitan queer culture and identities, I was read as queer by *jogappas* and *hijra*s, who spoke with ease about their lovers and involvement in sex work. The difference between urban and rural settings seemed salient not only in shaping the possibilities of queer recognition, but also in how feminine men, or male women, represented themselves.

In the villages and towns of northern Karnataka, southern Maharastra, and western Andhra Pradesh, where Yellamma is especially powerful and widely followed, *jogappas* are sacred women tied to her as boys. They identify her eldest sons as their ancestors. These are the sons who risked and earned their father's curse of impotence by remaining loyal to their mother and refusing to cut off her head. *Jogappas* identify themselves primarily with their ritual work, as people dedicated to the *seve* of Yellamma, and they distinguish themselves from those running after worldly pleasures. I quote at some length the response of a *jogappa*, Kallappa, to a brothel-based woman who was encouraging *avaru* to do *dhandha*, saying: "Now you are young, this is the time you can earn." First, a brief note about gender and grammar: In the contexts I encountered them, *jogappas* were referred to and referred to each other with the respectful form of the third person pronoun, *avaru*. This pronoun is not marked by gender. The most literal translation would be "they," but this usage in English makes for ungrammatical prose. Thus, I retain the Kannada *avaru*. Kallappa spoke with conviction: "I am happy with my way of life, I don't want to get involved in all this. We are doing the *puja* of the devi; devotees give grain, saris. Performing her *seve* gives peace of mind. Why run behind all these things? I want to keep my body as it is. Being a *jogappa* is better than becoming a *hijra*. They have taken off their organ (*anga*) to do *dhandha*." I asked: "Jo-gappas don't cut [self-castrate]?" The gentle *pujari* continued:

> Sometimes, but their lives are not very good if they cut. They are kept outside the village, nobody will come forward to give their daughters for their brothers, no one will speak with them. They will have to pay a penalty if they want to come into the community, to pay money and to feed all the people. *Hijras* have their own guru; if a *hijra* dies, only *hijras* go to their funeral. If no *hijra* comes, their body will rot. No one will go to cremate them. If a *jogappa* dies, all the *jogappas* will come; they are cremated by the village people. [As for devadasis] the government gives schemes and helps them build houses, but they are also going behind this *dhandha*, running after money. I want to keep my body as it is: I won't marry, I won't keep anyone [take a patron].

In practice, I found the distinctions between those who conduct ritual labor and participate in sex work, and between rural and urban dwelling patterns, to be less fixed than Kallappa suggests. In Bangalore I spoke with a *hijra* who knew three or four *hijras* who had tied beads. These *hijras* were *nirvan*—that is, they had castrated themselves—but when they traveled home to their natal villages, they called themselves *jogappas*. Another described how some deployed their identity as *jogappas* strategically. When they got stopped by the police for suspected solicitation, they would say, "I am a *jogappa*, I just came here to see my friend." That such a strategy works suggests that *jogappas* are perceived primarily as ritual specialists associated with Yellamma. But what is especially interesting to me in the context of this discussion of kin ties is the set of associations that Kallappa makes in outlining a morality of conduct and an ethics of kin and community ties. In his account, there are worse fates than the trouble of Yellamma: to be exiled from community and kin, refused death rites, and left to rot in the open.

In addition to associating themselves with an ethic of renunciation and a practice of Yellamma *seve*, *jogappas* are also seen as especially powerful *pujaris*. Indeed, although—as is the case with devadasis—not all *jogappas* act as *pujaris*, those who do frequently head particularly large and prosperous temples. In Mandovi, the largest of the villages bordering Nandipur, there were three Yellamma temples. Mihir, a *jogappa* who was well known all over the district, presided at the biggest of these temples. When Jyoti and I first went to meet him, we found him sitting on the floor in the middle of a circle of people. Directly behind them was the devi, whose *murti* was made of gold. She was decked out in multiple gold chains, wrapped in a fancy sari with a border threaded with gold, and garlanded with a chain of dark red hibiscus buds for *ammawase*, the day of the new moon. Next to Yellamma stood a portrait of another *jogappa*, garlanded, wrapped in a sari, and hung with a *mangalsutra* and a gold chain in a manner befitting an honored ancestor. As I later learned, this *jogappa* had previously kept the Yellamma he was now worshipped next to.

Mihir was splendid, wearing—according to Jyoti's expert estimate—seven *tolas*[20] worth of gold chains and a simple white and pink sari, with a matching blouse. Mihir meticulously folded tiny newspaper packets of Yellamma's turmeric while interviewing me; issuing orders for tea and snacks; and introducing his elder sister, mother, and *cakka*'s wife as they came in. Mihir asserted *avaru*'s lack of involvement in any *lafdas* (shady business); and began to tell *avaru*'s life story. Yellamma was not a deity in Mihir's religion, which was Jainism. When she began to trouble Mihir, Mihir was working as a bank manager. After two years of "lots of her trouble," colleagues at the bank insisted Mihir had to choose: Yellamma or the bank. Deciding to keep the devi, Mihir resigned the job: "Whatever I do is all for the devi."

At Mihir's invitation, we stayed that day for the special *ammawase puja*. Off Mihir went on the back of a motorcycle to take a ritual bath in the river. Upon return to the house, Mihir began slowly circling *avaru*'s head and dancing or jerking before the fifty or so devotees who had gathered. Mihir's attendants performed *aarthi* to the arriving devi as Mihir entered a state of possession and sat on a special chair reserved for the *helikke* (oracle; literally, speaking or telling) of Yellamma. Through the body of this *jogappa*, Yellamma spoke to the mostly upper- and middle-caste women devotees gathered there. She counseled them about family matters and admonished them to be more devoted to her. The speaking voice began: "Anger, suffering, desire, resentment, husband, wife, children, back and forth, restless minds, whatever is there in your mind, tell me, daughter. What is the nature of the play or trouble?" (*Koopa, taapa, kaama, kroda, ganda, hendati, makkalu, goongniag, tikkaata manasinaga. eenua aiti helu magale. Aadata, aadata, kashta danga eena aiti?*). After an initial brief petition from a devotee, the following exchange ensued:

> *Mihir/Yellamma*: You are worrying about your son's job. I know how much devotion you have toward me: you come weekly, but still I am not satisfied with your devotion. That's why I have given you only half of a full roti.
>
> *Devotee*: When will you give me the other half? What mistake am I making? You have not given anything to me.
>
> *Mihir/Yellamma*: Do not speak like this, daughter. I have given you half a roti, whatever you have taken, admit it.
>
> *Devotee*: Yes, you have given a half roti, but it is not enough.
>
> *Mihir/Yellamma*: I will give the other half, but I will test you. Just before or after *randi hunnime*, I will come to you and give you another half roti. Apply *bhandara* to your son, ask him to come and take my blessings. Daughter, I know your husband is not feeling well. I will not harm him. Give him my *bhandara* with water. He will be all right. I promise you I will not take your *kumkuma*, that much I can tell you, don't worry.

Two weeks after this exchange, before I had the opportunity to ask Mihir about the devi's trouble in Mihir's own life and in those of the devotees who came to the temple, Mihir fell ill and died. Among devotees, *jogappas*, and *jogatis* in the area, with whom I traveled to Mihir's natal village for the death rites, there was much speculation about what had taken Mihir. Five doctors had been consulted, and all said there was nothing wrong. Most theories involved a jealous ghost (*gale*) or the evil eye (*nedaru*) and focused on how beautiful and prosperous Mihir was. On our way to pay our respects, some twenty of us crammed into a hired jeep, we learned that the death rites were already over from other mourners coming back. Mihir's natal family had cremated Mihir in the manner befitting a Jain. This news was very upsetting to the *jogatis* and *jogappas* I was traveling with. As we bumped along the rough and dusty road, they began to describe how death rites should be conducted for *jogappas*. "The procession should be grand and go throughout the village." "Yellamma's turmeric should be thrown, not *gulal* [pink ritual powder]." "*Jogatis* should lead, playing *shruti* and *chowdiki*, and the palanquin should be carried by *jogappas*." "They should have waited for us. None of us was there."

One woman said she had gone to Mihir's natal village with Mihir for *udi tumbuwudu* and had asked to go to Mihir's family's house, but Mihir had refused, saying: "They don't value me there, so I don't want to take you there." Back in Nandipur, we reported to the *jogatis* that we had been to Mihir's family's house, where the death arrangements had been managed by the family without input from or participation by the *jogatis* or *jogappas* who had surrounded Mihir's daily life. Durgabai commented: "And *avaru* always said *avaru* had no family other than *jogatis* and *jogappas*, that we were *avaru*'s family." I was shown once more that the ties Mihir had to the family of Yellamma were trumped by natal ties at the time of Mihir's death. Several weeks after his death, Jyoti and I met the woman in the Mandovi market whom we had first met at Mihir's home. We stopped our comparison of vegetables to talk with her. She had been a *chela* and companion to Mihir for fourteen years, leaving her family in order to cook and keep house and serve as a ritual assistant. She told us: "*Avaru* was like a child to me. Mihir used to say, 'I will take care of you, if you die, I will make all the arrangements.' *Avaru* was a good person, *avaru* should have left something for me." That day in the market, she told us in great distress that his house had been locked up by the *pancharu* (village headmen), and no provisions had been made for her. None of her appeals to the *pancharu* or to the man who was Mihir's patron and lover (*malak*), a married Maratha man, had had any effect, and she was forced to return to her son's home. She was unsure whether he would take her in, since she had left fourteen years earlier.

To answer Yellamma's call, Mihir left *avaru*'s natal family and renounced the obligations assigned to *avaru* as a son to marry and produce the next generation. Becoming a sacred woman in the name of Yellamma, by means of being tied to her, had several effects: a transformation in embodiment of gender, from masculine to feminine; multiple new ties to others with whom ritual, household, and affective life was bound up; and tacit community acceptance of Mihir's taking a man as a lover. But the fragility of Mihir's kinship ties to Yellamma were revealed at *avaru*'s death. Mihir was reclaimed by *avaru*'s natal family and buried according to *avaru*'s status as a Jain man rather than as a Yellamma woman. I was unable to learn definitively whether Mihir was cremated sitting up—as befits married people, including those who have undergone sacred marriage—or lying down, as is the custom for the unmarried. One of the things that clearly contributed to the vulnerability of the ties between Mihir and *avaru*'s Yellamma kin was the structure of patronage supporting the temple *avaru* served. The financial control was held by a Maratha man, a member of a sugar baron's family, whose political influence in the village was unmatched. His patronage of Yellamma and of her popular *pujari*, Mihir, did not include any sense of obligation toward the wider network of Yellamma kin, the *jogappas* and *jo-gammas* whom Mihir called family.

I encountered another *jogappa* who is an extraordinary dancer. Kishar can balance a full pot of water on *avaru*'s head and splash you with a flick of the hip. With donations from devotees—many of them brothel keepers, and one of them Kishar's rich *malak*—Kishar has built a Yellamma temple in southern Maharastra, where *avaru* presides as *pujari*. When Jyoti and I went for a festival at Kishar's invitation, we were greeted by *avaru*'s mother and sister-in-law and introduced to *avaru*'s brother, who does much of the daily *puja* work. Kishar's nieces and nephews were running around, playing and going in and out of the temple, where their mother sat, and the house next door, where the whole joint family lived. Kishar appeared to be fulfilling all *avaru*'s responsibilities as the oldest son in this joint family household, short of producing heirs. The festival brought carloads of *hijras*, *kothis*, and *jogappas* from all over Maharastra and northern Karnataka, as well as women from local red-light districts. After a joyous ritual procession through the neighborhood, people danced and sang late into the night. The ritual work completed, Kishar held court, exchanged bawdy jokes with women, and quizzed me about my love life, while a young man rubbed *avaru*'s feet. Like Mihir, Kishar had renounced *avaru*'s obligations as a son to marry and produce children for the lineage, and *avaru*'s marriage to the *devi* had placed *avaru* within another network of Yellamma kin. But *avaru* still feels and answers the pull of natal ties, and the result is an unconventional overlapping of families. As the result of the resignification of the practice of dedication by reformers, the pull of conjugal responsibilities appears to be growing stronger. In short, the possibility—and desirability—of eluding them and transforming oneself through sacred marriage is on the wane. Risking the trouble of Yellamma is becoming preferable to risking kinship and gender trouble.

One indication of this change was that fact that not all *jogappas* wrapped saris and adopted the habitus of women. A few wore pants and a shirt and told stories about how they had negotiated with Yellamma, declining to wrap a sari in her name and substituting some other form of commitment. Kallappa, the Nandipur *jogappa*, wore pants and a shirt, refusing to wear a sari for Yellamma. However, he played the *chowdiki* and accompanied the *jogatis* whenever they were called to perform *udi tumbuwudu*. He did not conduct rites, and I never witnessed anyone fill his *udi*, something I saw devotees do many times in the case of sari-clad *jogappas*. He had tied

FIGURE 5.5 A *jogappa* at Yellamma's temple in Near Manvi.
Photograph by the author.

FIGURE 5.6 Kishar dancing, carrying Yellamma on *avaru*'s head. Photograph by the author.

muttu for Yellamma, but he had not become a sacred woman for her; he had married and fathered two children. He suffered from a partial muteness, a loss of speech that was many times described to me as the consequence of his failing to fully answer Yellamma's call—he displeased her and so she troubled him.

On my second visit to Nandipur, I met a man dressed in conventional rural masculine attire for that region: a short kurta, long pajamas, and a cap, all in white. He was sitting in the Yellamma temple talking with Yamuna, whom he had come to ask to participate in a singing program. She introduced him to me as someone who plays the *chowdiki*. When I asked him if he were a *jogappa*, he said no, but when I asked him if he had tied beads, he said that he had, and offered a typology of *muttu* indicating a status different from that of a *jogappa*. His *muttu*, he explained were *sattipatti* (wife-husband) *muttu*. Perhaps in response to my perplexed expression—I had never heard of this type of *muttu*—Yamuna offered a more nuanced elucidation. "We just call it that now," she said:

The wife has nothing to do with that *muttu*, if he ties *muttu* he should wear a sari and ask for *joga*, but this *sattipatti* means he only plays the *chowdiki* and sings. They have made it like this, in his family only men are tying and playing *chowdiki* now. In this generation we have stopped, women tied in my family for four generations, and I am the last, now we have stopped tying *muttu*. My son and daughter-in-law will do the *puja*. Before only those who have tied *muttu* could do it, but now that is ending. As long as I am alive I will do the *puja*, but after I die I don't know what will happen. Who knows. It is left to *devaru*.

In Yamuna's account of what *sattipatti muttu* means, she describes an innovation in kin-making practices. The normative effects of marriage to the devi—"if he ties *muttu* he should wear a sari" and "only those who have tied *the muttu* could do [*puja*]"—are under revision. The gender or kinship trouble and ritual authority that tying *muttu* inaugurates retain the status of the norm, or what should happen. But this is changing, she explained. We are changing it, she asserted. When asked directly if the nature of Yellamma's trouble has changed, *jogatis* quickly insist, "She is the devi, she does not change." However, I found that narratives of trouble indicate a shift over time from an emphasis on problems of lineage, life, and death to difficulties of family poverty and individual illness.

In the summer of 2003 Yamuna died, after a long struggle with cancer. Durga and Kamlabai led her death procession, and she was buried sitting up, as a married person. A crow came quickly to taste the food offerings left at the time of burial. Ishwara, her eldest son, who was quite broken up by his mother's death, explained to me with great relief that the quick arrival of the crow indicated that all her desires in life had been satisfied. After her death, Yamuna's family contracted with Kamlabai to do the *puja* when it was with them in the rotation of responsibility for *puja* among families with dedicated women in them. After some time, Kamlabai demurred. Now, Yamuna's son Mahesh prepares Yellamma on Tuesdays and Fridays, washing her and dressing her in preparation to receive devotees who will come for *darshan*. It has happened as Yamuna said. Yamuna did not give any of her daughters to Yellamma; they were all married in the conventional way. Responsibility for Yellamma has fallen to her youngest son, whose most eager ambition is to start a small business, and most ardent devotion is to his young daughters. His devotion to Yellamma may not be deep, as was his mother's, but that is not to say that he is willing to abandon her altogether and risk being troubled.

Transactions in Kin and Trouble

Devadasi practice disrupts a fixed logic of relatedness and the correspondences between sexed bodies, the embodiment of gender, and the occupation of kin positions presumed within normative kinship arrangements. These normative correspondences are troubled: devadasis are wives to Yellamma, sons in their family, fathers to their children, mother's brothers to their sister's children. In some cases these anomalous positions are linguistically marked: devadasi are sometimes hailed as *Yellammana hendati* (Yellamma's wife), and their children call their mother's brother *cakka*, the Kannada term for father's brother, indexing the kin position their mother holds in the family as son and father. In other cases these anomalous positions are evident in terms of everyday practice of devadasis, the way they fulfill the obligations and claim the privileges of sons, fathers, and mother's brothers. This suggests the productive and enabling possibilities of kinship trouble. Devadasi dedication produces female-bodied forms of personhood not available to domesticated women; *jogatis* are economically productive lineage bearers (as sons and fathers are) and conduits of auspiciousness (as married women can be). Further, they are not only conduits of auspiciousness, they are also transactors of it, reproducing children for the next generation as well as fertility in the households of devotees and the agricultural body of the village. The value of men in a patrilineal society—as economic actors, property holders, and lineage bearers—and the value of women according to Hindu conceptions of life and the conditions for its renewal—as auspicious persons—is consolidated in the person of the *jogati* or the *jogappa*. This consolidation is achieved through a kin-making practice, the marriage of a child to a goddess.

I would like to make two points about the implications of this cultural practice, in which people are made and unmade through kin relations with a goddess, for how anthropologists have thought about relatedness, gender, and the body. The first is that disarticulations between the sexed body, the embodiment of gender, and the assignment of kin position that occur among Yellamma's kin demonstrate that an alignment between sex, gender, and kin position is not inevitable. The devadasi in a sari is a son, not a daughter, in the house. The *jogappa* in a sari is a daughter and a son. Thus, kin making with the goddess denaturalizes kinship as a system of fixed positions.

Second, the social masculinity of devadasis suggests that gender cannot be understood only as the property of a person, as in accounts that naturalize gender through recourse to the sex of the body (Busby 2000). Kin positions are maintained by transacting with kin in specific and gendered ways: a father is a father because he fulfills the obligations of fathers. A man who does not fulfill these is insulted: "he is not my father." A devadasi who does claims the position: "I am the father." This suggests that gender can function as the property of transactions, rather than simply as the property of particularly sexed bodies or a person's successful performative iteration of normative femininity or masculinity. Thus a *jogati* is a son, although her body is sexed female and her embodiment is unambiguously feminine. She is a son because she is given the structural position and the social obligations of a son in the natal family, and she fulfills them. Gender, as I argued in the previous chapter, is not only performative but also transactional. It is also necessarily tied to strategies of and for relatedness. The transactional aspect of gender emerges when we are attentive to the operations of the gift and if we take kin making to be a technology of the human, a tool for producing certain kinds of humans endowed with particular obligations to and claims on others, social functions, and forms of value.[21]

CHAPTER 6

Troubling Kinship

We live, more or less implicitly, with received notions of reality, implicit accounts of ontology, which determine what kinds of bodies and sexualities will be considered real and true, which kind will not. . . . The question of who and what is considered real and true is apparently a question of knowledge. But it is also, as Foucault makes plain, a question of power. Having or bearing "truth" and "reality" is an enormously powerful prerogative within the social world, one way in which power dissimulates as ontology.

—Judith Butler, *Precarious Life*

The normative conception of religion internal to liberalism assumes the truth of such distinctions [between inanimate objects, humans, and divinity] and the form of the subject that can make them.

—Saba Mahmood, "Religious Reason and Secular Affect"

Who and what is marriage for? What is happening when a girl is married to a goddess? What kind of human and what sort of deity are produced through this alliance? What kind of relatedness is this, and how might its existence in the world as a practice disrupt heterosexual and biogenetic terrains as the natural and inevitable grounds of kinship? How might we specify the grounds and effects of such a practice of kin making, one that ties a knot between the realm of the divine and the territory of the human?

For Dalit families, the marriage between Yellamma and her wives is a means of producing gender and value in the bodies of their children, a way of securing some access to the wealth and favor of the goddess and her landholding devotees, and a mode of self-perpetuation over generations. Making gender, securing wealth, reproduction over time—these effects of marriage have long been recognized by feminist anthropologists.

The making and unmaking of persons through kin relations with gods and spirits, however, is not easily admitted into the house of anthropology. Like other social-scientific modes of inquiry, anthropology tends to position the social as prior to the gods. People might make cultural meanings *through* gods, as products of human activity, symbolization, and consciousness. They do not, however, make culture (kin or worlds) *with* the gods, according to secular conceptions of religion and the human being.[1] Moreover, and more critically for Dalit families and dedicated women, anthropological recognition falls in a different register than state legitimation.

Marriage to the goddess has been recast as a crime against the state, encoded in the law as a punishable act. Stripping this marriage of its historical and customary social legitimacy and force, the state has rendered the children of dedicated women illegitimate in order to make their mothers available for conventional marriages. Such marriages have been identified as the only sanctioned site of reproductive sexuality, and devadasis have been defined as prostitutes in the antidedication legislation. Kin making between Dalit families and the goddess has been set outside the law, and the dominant form of the family has been upheld by the state and for the future. This law and the reform projects it has led, shift the allegiance of Dalit families from the goddess to the state. Among other things, marriage serves here as a technology for sexual conversion, from prostitute to wife. In this instance, marriage is for making citizens and normalizing their sexuality. It establishes the secularity of sex and secures the state by displacing the devi.

The research for and writing of this book has taken place in the context of broad cultural and political struggles in India and the United States over what constitutes the proper family and its members. These struggles are powerfully shaped by—and, in turn, shape—forms of governance and religion in India and the United States. The stakes are high. The recognition of people as endowed with rights and entitled to make claims is inextricably tied to the politics of the family and effects what kinds of love are legitimate, what kinds of lives are livable. In closing, I consider what we might make of kinship trouble in terms of its implications for the politics of the family in modernity, as well as for the study of kin making and religiosity.

Trouble in the System

Talk about trouble (*kaadaata*) constitutes a discourse on affliction, power, and the body. The trouble that Yellamma can send implies suffering at the level of the body, whether individual or corporate, and whether found in the family, the village, or the world. It is also a discourse about power, the power of the devi in the world to upset people, to disturb healthy living systems: human bodies, animal bodies, and agricultural ecologies. In addition to referring to affliction and the body, talk of trouble refers to relatedness. If Yellamma is troubling you, this is an indication that your relationship with her has gone awry. You have turned away from her, and she is calling you back to her. She manifests herself in your body as a means of calling you to her. She is present to you and in you. To resolve the trouble of Yellamma, her affliction, devotees make vows and give gifts. They commit themselves to her, usually as or through their bodies. Forms of bodily commitment to Yellamma resolve the trouble she can send. Bodily affliction is converted through commitment into auspiciousness, authority, and obligation. But, as Lawrence Cohen has suggested, forms of bodily commitment such as marriage, labor, or organ donation often entail a wounding. That is, one kind of trouble might be changed into another kind of trouble by "giving oneself over" (2005, 5; 2013), but trouble remains in the system. It has not been banished from the body, the family, the village.

For whom is kinship trouble troubling? The kinship trouble that marriage to the goddess produces makes for two kinds of difficulty for dedicated women and their families. When families lack a son, they can turn a girl child into an economic actor and lineage bearer by marrying her to the devi. Having solved the question of material and generational survival, they face a disturbance in patterns of patrilineal and patrilocal patterns of kin making and those forms of sexual respectability that such patterns ensure for women. The second kind of trouble that devadasi families face is in relation to the state. Devadasis lack sexual citizenship. The first kind of trouble is like the *kaadaata* of the devi — indeed, that is how it is referred to. This is trouble in the system. As persons, *jogatis* may not conform to normative patterns of gender and kinship, but they are fully members of their families. Indeed, as I have argued, dedication is a means of strengthening kin ties, tethering daughters to their natal kin, and obligating them to support their natal household. The second kind of trouble is an effect of being placed outside the system, exiled from national belonging and state recognition. This kind of trouble cannot be converted within the body; it must be cut out, excised as a disreputable former self. Vis-à-vis the devi, affliction is resolved through *transformation*; one kind of trouble is turned into another. Before the state, lack of citizenship is resolved through *purification*; the bad is separated from the good.

What kind of trouble does the marriage between Yellamma and her wives pose for the anthropological analysis of kinship? In my early field-work, I attempted kinship charting as part of a survey of devadasi and non-devadasi households in Nandipur. I was equipped with the rudimentary tools of formalist mappings of kin: circles, triangles, horizontal lines of alliance, and vertical lines of lineage. My efforts in the territory of what Malinowski called "the bastard algebra of kinship" (1930, 19) came up against a certain kind of productive failure. The kind of people whom *joga-tis* become by virtue of their marriage to the devi Yellamma—women who are also sons—cannot be situated in a formalist mapping of kin relations, in which every position is always already gendered.

Even after I had devised a system for marking liaisons with patrons by whom many devadasis bear children, I remained unable to map the kinds of transformations and anomalous articulations of kin position (father), gen-dered embodiment (feminine), and sexed body (female) that are combined in devadasi personhood. They are socially recognized women, therefore 'O.' They are also sons whose children's relationship to the wider network of kin in terms of inheritance and marriageability is reckoned through their mother's kin position as a father, so 'Δ.' The system cannot admit a per-son who is both 'O' and 'Δ.' This impasse is not only produced by gender as a binary system, in which one must be 'O' or 'Δ,' but cannot possibly be both. In a region where cross-cousin marriage is ideal and parallel-cousin marriage is taboo, the distinction between matrilateral and patrilateral kin is critical. Indeed, as I have described, kin making among families with de-vadasis in them also follow this pattern of cross-cousin marriage. They fol-low it by situating devadasis in the patrilateral position, producing an un-mappable grammar of kin that is nonetheless working within the system. As the devadasi in Sangli explained it to me, "the children of two sisters cannot marry, but because I am a devadasi, my [married] sister's children can marry my children. In this way we [devadasis] are *mamas* [mother's brothers]." Devadasi kin making troubles kinship as a system of fixed and always already gendered positions. It troubles this system even as it inhab-its it. In short, it troubles it from within.

One of the things this impasse within the system makes clear is that the kinship chart is performing what it purports to merely describe.[2] It natu-ralizes correspondences between the sex of the body, the gender of a per-son, and that person's kin position—a male-sexed person Δ, is a man Δ, is a father Δ, brother Δ, son Δ—that do not occur everywhere. The sex of the body, the gender of presentation, and the assignment of kin position do not align so easily among Yellamma's kin.

Dalit families grasp the tool of marriage, turning a daughter into a son and making the devi into her husband. They deploy the logic and effects of marriage as a transactional system that transforms nonkin into kin. This effect of marriage is widely recognized. Yet scholarly treatments have tended to render this marriage as a merely symbolic act—a "marriage"—that does not have the same force as a "real" marriage in organizing social and material relations and forms of value in and among people, such as instance, gender (Orchard 2007; Orr 2000; Soneji 2012). This appraisal of sacred marriage as fictive sits uneasily next to the fact that the state has found it necessary to legally annul this marriage between devadasis and the devi in order to make dedicated women available for conventional marriage. If it is not real, why does it need to be abolished? Kinship with the devi troubles the limit of the social by reaching into the territory of the gods to gather forms of value. Its abolition confirms the divisions between true marriage and "marriage," sons and honorary sons, and religion and superstition.

Familiar as forms of knowledge, these divisions also constitute moves of modern power, as Judith Butler (2004) suggests in her writing about gender and realness. Accomplishing recognition as a rational subject depends on one's being able to demonstrate one's ability to make these distinctions and to incorporate them as aspects of one's personhood. This is true for the liberal subject of religion, as well as the properly gendered person, as Saba Mahmood points out. Writing about liberal responses to Muslim protests over blasphemous cartoons, she notes that for protesting Muslims, the images in question were not inert objects or mere representations, they were "animated beings that exert a certain force in the world" (2009, 842). This is evidence not of a lack of rationality but of a different rationality, one that does not make the division between subjects and objects that modern epistemologies presume. This is where power comes in. Those who do not recognize the truth of the distinction between subjects and objects are not seen as thinking differently but as unthinking. When devotees of Yellamma say "she is in the family," they are not making a symbolic statement. They are pointing to the material presence of the devi among them, in the body of a girl, in her *jade*, on her skin—present as an affliction that will not be resolved until Yellamma is made kin, truly kin. The truth of this kinship, however, is inadmissible. The linking of property and personhood that marriage accomplishes has been limited in modernity to the privatized sphere of the family. Families might legitimately give their daughters to sons-in-law, but not to a goddess. Belonging to a family is coded as a moral good, but belonging to a deity framed as a "social evil," as reformers frequently refer to dedication (see for instance Srinivasa and Shivasharanappa, 2012, 2).

How does this account of kinship trouble speak to theorizations of trouble? Sacred marriage produces forms of life that trouble the form of the family upheld by the state. This is counternormative trouble. It produces people who disturb the assumptions about sex, gender, and relatedness that have been smuggled into the anthropological project as kinship. Devadasis put the kinship chart as a universal representation of human relatedness into crisis. This is category trouble. The trouble that families with Yellamma in them encounter, her *kaadaata*, is a disturbance in the field that opens up new spaces for life in the field. Yellamma plays with people in ways that are troubling, it is said. Her power, or her trouble, is transformational. The power of reform is purifying. "We have become better," ex-devadasis say.

The Secularity of Sex and the Sexuality of Religion

I have taken both kin making and religiosity to be technologies of the human, ethical practices of self-cultivation that occur within regulating and normalizing fields. Understood as a system of orthodox beliefs, religion forecloses questions of historical agency, power, and the uneven purchase of modernity in the lifeworlds of South Indian peasants. I have shown what is distinctive about the modes of self-cultivation and world making at work in the performance of devadasi rites. This study of the marginalization and persistence of religious practices and the forms of subjectivity they enable contributes to the deconstruction of the notion of the Indian self as static, captive to unthinking religiosity. It also disturbs the liberal presumption that intense forms of religiosity are incompatible with meaningful agency among women.[3] As women who persist in ritual and kin-making practices that cannot count as religion, devadasis are unable to achieve full recognition as subjects or persons. They must be remade, reformed. My effort here has been to turn this equation on its head by situating their ritual and kin-making activity as epistemologically and ontologically significant. In other words, if they are worlding worlds and we have failed to see this, then perhaps it is our categories, rather than their lives, that need to be remade.

When the social is positioned prior to the gods, the gods are left to stand as some kind of reflection or effect of human social and symbolic activity. This kind of epistemology reaches a limit in an encounter with a person caught between the human realm and the territory of the gods. In a disenchanted world, such a person can only be alone. As a way of unfolding secular conceptions of the human as ontologically singular, I have taken seriously the possibility that the gods and spirits are with us, that devadasis really become kin to the devi, and she to them.

In terms of the question of what can count as religion, one thing seems clear from this story about devadasi lifeworlds and their eradication. Sex cannot count as religion, at least not modern religion. What I have hoped to show is that the very idea that these domains of human activity are discreet is itself a feature of modern epistemologies and projects. For over a hundred years, devadasis have been seen as persons who made sex present in the temple; indeed, this is precisely why they must be exiled from it. Sending devadasis out of the temples, however, does not rid Hinduism of sex. Instead, it entangles the two differently. Religion and sex have always been tangled up in each other. But this is not how these domains are understood in modernity. For moderns, sex is secular—a matter of reproduction, perhaps of pleasure, and of the risk of contagion and population to be managed by the clinic and the state. Religion, in contrast, has no sex. It is asexual, or at least it should be. Sex in the house of religion can only be violence or scandal. Once cloaked in marriage and aimed at reproduction, sex is civilized. White mommy-daddy-baby-families never seem to be saturated with sex in the way that gay bishops, headscarved women, or dedicated women do. The reproductive sexuality of proper families does not offend modern sensibilities about what is proper to religion or sexuality. This, again, is a matter of the secular dispensation of the body and its capacities and powers.

As a mode of statecraft, a political philosophy, and a sensibility, secularism would seem to have disavowed the body. It would seem to be indifferent to it. We know of course that this is not the case: the secular body is no less saturated with meaning, caressed by power, and cultivated as an inhabitation of the ethical. The point is that secularism does not declare its desire for the body as a body in the way that dissident sexuality or non-Protestant forms of religion do. In Talal Asad's (2003, 16) terms, the secular is conceptually prior to the doctrine of political secularism. As a habitus or sensibility, it precedes self-conscious projects of secularization. In other words, political secularism takes the secularity of the body for granted: "The secular is the water we swim in" (Hirschkind 2011, 4).

There is nonetheless a contest over the body; its possible meanings; and its capacity to make meaning, to world a world, to constitute a territory for the enactment of ethics, as state-sponsored projects of devadasi reform demonstrate. The character of this contest comes across clearly in a very different context in an essay written by the literary critic and queer theorist Michael Warner. In "Tongues Untied" (1993), he writes that although being a literary critic is nice, it cannot compare to what either Pentecostalism or homosexual acts can offer: the intensely felt sense that what you do with your body matters; that modes of bodily comportment and sex acts have powerful effects, saturate a life, world a world.

In secularism's story about itself, the body does not matter in this way. It is a mere biological system, genetic code, dirty or hygienic object, vector of disease. However, as medical anthropologists and scholars of science and technology have argued, medicine, psychiatry, criminology, sexology, and public health are not neutral discourses. They are moral and moralizing discourses that perform neutrality and inhabit indifference as an aspect of their authority, power, and modernity. Secularism's story about itself is that it is indifferent to sex qua sex, as indeed it is to religion. It acts only to regulate or contain sexuality or religion as a matter of crime or public health, to protect the population which secures its sovereignty from harm, and to safeguard the domains it has delimited for the sanctioned enactment of sexuality or religiosity.

We may have been taught to doubt this story, but yet, it seduces us. We want the freedoms that such promised indifference suggest will be ours: for example, that what we do behind closed doors, privately, is safe from state incursion; and that Christian nationalism will not be embraced by the US government. In India the seduction of this story is evident in the widespread confidence that a more robust and extended secularism will safeguard against the dangers of excessive religion, as communal violence is often conceived. It is also evident in the common assumption that political secularism guarantees equity for women, and that its advance will correspond to greater freedom for women from the strictures of patriarchal religion.

Many remain persuaded by the equation between secularism, the free expression of sexuality, the end of the oppression of women, and the triumph of individual liberties and rights (Scott 2009b, 1). This thinking is evident in feminist calls to restrict the wearing of headscarves or veils in public spaces, as Joan Scott's (2009a) work in France has shown (see also Fernando 2010), as well as in feminist critiques of devadasi dedication as a tyrannical patriarchal Hindu custom imposed on Dalit women. This account of secularism entails several assumptions: sexuality should be proper to the individual, freely chosen, and freely expressed; and personhood should be self-possessed and unencumbered by custom, community, or religion.

Jade-cutting campaigns serve as an example of the work the body is made to do to become modern. These campaigns do not frame themselves as projects that seek to remake the sexuality and religiosity of dedicated women. They frame themselves as projects of hygiene and social uplift, projects that seek to liberate women from false belief. The point is this: they do not see themselves as remaking sex as sex, the body as a body; they cut *jade* to prove that *jade* don't matter. Recall the language of the flier handed out at the main temple during the pilgrimage season: "Thousands of people have gotten their knotted, dirty hair cleaned and are now living a healthy life. This is evidence that the appearance of *jade* or knotted hair is not due to the Goddess." Hair, according to the campaigns, does not world a world. *Jade* are just dirt. Reformers act on hair not as a materialization of the extended sexuality and ecstatic religiosity of Yellamma women but as dirt, a matter of hygiene and health, proper objects of secular concern.

The fact that the campaigns do not declare their desire for the bodies of devadasis—even as they intensively, even violently, work on and through those bodies—may offer us a clue about why the secularity of sex is so elusive as an analytic object. In its story about itself, by which we may be seduced, secularism doesn't take sex as its proper object. Indeed, this is how our sexuality seems to belong to us rather than to the state, just as our religion should be a matter of free affiliation, neither constrained nor advanced by properly secular governments. According to the logic and practice of reform campaigns, a religiosity organized around the cultivation of all forms of fertility and prosperity and the warding off of affliction is characterized as false, and the milder devotional practices consistent with Brahmanical Hinduism are upheld as true. Reform campaigns enforce and incite new modes of bodily comportment for *jogatis*, modes that correspond to norms of domesticated and secularized sexuality.

But there is another point to be made here. Secularism, self-authorized sexuality, and women's liberation from oppressive custom are equated in a particular way in postcolonial India. It is no accident that (otherwise ubiquitous and unproblematic) ecstatic embodiment and outcaste personhood come together as a social problem in need of government intervention in the bodies of women. The public religiosity and sexuality of these women must be eradicated, so they might emerge as proper subjects of privatized sex, personal devotion, and respectable religion—for the sake of the progress of the Dalit community and the legitimate sovereignty of the postcolonial state. Once again, women are made to bear honor, whether for the nation or the community. But also, as in other postcolonial contexts where dual systems of family law and civil law operate, the question of the disposition of women's sexual capacity constitutes the fault line between their rights as individuals before the state and their rights as members of their community to keep the customs regarding marriage and property that are particular to that community (Mahmood 2012). This means that both secular state governance and the authority of religious communities are bound up in the question of women's sexual conduct and status.

Finally, what do I mean by invoking the sexuality of religion? In what sense can religion be said to have sexuality? In the case of the religiosity under description here, it not only has sexuality, but this is precisely the problem with it. Its sexuality constitutes the ground for its eradication. Sex has no place in religion. In fact, as we have seen in the case of devadasi reform, if sex is mixed up in that religion, then it must not be religion. All of this is familiar and consistent with modern and secular presumptions about the domains of human existence as discrete from each other (politics and religion) as well as the privatization and interiorization of both sex and religion. This logic, in my experience, is also manifest in the operations of academic fields and modes of inquiry, in which sex and religion rarely come into the same conversation. Yet they are always wrapped up together, implicating each other. As the reformers of Yellamma women found, they were unable to change devadasi sexuality until they began to undermine their ritual practices, their religiosity. Their interventions are not only eradicating the bad sexuality dedication is seen to produce, they are also inciting good conjugal sexuality and devotional religiosity. My point here is that not only the ecstatic rites surrounding a South Indian devi, but all rites and religions have sexuality:[4] they mobilize and organize sexual economies, distributions of fertility, the limits and possibilities of public pleasures, and the shape of our desires. Forms of secularity and religiosity both invest themselves in bodies and pleasure; they shape the possibilities we are given over, or give ourselves, to.

NOTES

Introduction. Gods, Gifts, Trouble

1 The English word is often used among speakers of the Dravadian language Kannada for this ankle-length cotton undergarment. Kannada is the official language of the state of Karnataka.

2 I use this term—generally used in the region of my fieldwork to refer to women married in the conventional sense—throughout the book. This usage allows me to avoid calling such women married women, a term that fails to distinguish between them and devadasis, who are also married but who are not *gandullavalu*. I did encounter a few ex-devadasis (*maji devadasis*) who had registered conventional marriages, a fact I specify when I discuss these women.

3 *Jogappas* are *pujaris* (priests, caretakers) performers and mendicants who wrap themselves in saris, adopt the habitus of women, and perform all the same rites as devadasis. In this book, I focus on devadasis, by far the largest number of these wandering mendicants, who as illicit female women are the focus of social reform in a way that the male women are not.

4 There is some effort in the ethnographic literature (see, for instance, Assayag 1992; Tarachand 1992) to distinguish devadasis (meaning prostitutes) from *jogatis* (meaning religious mendicants and ritual specialists). This split between ritual performance and sexual economy was not borne out in my research. Throughout the book I use both *jogati* and devadasi to refer to dedicated women whose sexuality and religiosity are bound up in their relationship with the devi.

5 Dalit (meaning crushed or broken, in Sanskrit) is the self-designation of politicized members of communities formerly labeled untouchable. In the context of contemporary party politics, the term "Dalit" is often used to refer to all non-Brahmans. My usage here and throughout the book is specific to members of those communities formerly designated as untouchable. According to Vedic reckoning, these communities are outside the caste system that is comprised of the four varnas (classes or types)—Brahman (priests), Ksatriya (warriors), Vaisya (merchants), and Sudra (agriculturalists, laborers)—thus the designation "outcaste," a term I also use. For a brief history of the term "Dalit," see Guru 2001. For a compelling history of Dalit identity and political formation, see A. Rao 2009.

6 For instance, the sociologist Jogan Shankar asserts: "The functional relation of devadasis of the village with the local Yellamma temple deity is very insignificant and symbolic only" (1994, 7). An article by Chaya Datar offers the only exception to the overall representation of the women given to Yellamma as superstitious and exploited by false religion. Datar suggests that they may be considered as members of a priestly caste and questions the neglect of this aspect of the practice by reformers: "The main feature of this tradition seems to be that it offers a place of some kind of priesthood to women, which is a rare phenomenon within the Hindu culture. . . . It is interesting that their role as priestesses within the 'little' tradition has been neglected by the reformers and only the sexual life of the ritual person is highlighted as an oppressive aspect of the custom" (1992, 84–85).

7 See Shiva Kumar (2009). In the 1990s the government of Karnataka reported 22,941 identified devadasis to the National Commission on Women, while Andhra Pradesh reported 16,624, and the government of Maharastra—which has repeatedly accused Karnataka of being the source of devadasis working in the brothels of Bombay and Pune—reported only those numbers of devadasis receiving government pensions and other forms of support (Joint Women's Programme 2001–2).

8 Estimates of the percentage of dedicated women working in brothels vary widely, from 80 percent, a figure cited in public health contexts (Gilada 1993; Shreedhar 1995) to 40 percent (Shankar 1994, 107). In Shankar's survey of eighty-five devadasis in a village he calls Yellampura (population 5,700) in the Belgaum District of Karnataka, 40 percent reported "indulging in prostitution" in urban brothels and 6 percent in "prostitution" in the village proper. By "prostitution" in the village proper, he seems to be referring to patronage relationships. Thirty percent of the dedicated women he surveyed were working as agricultural laborers.

9 "With the loss of feudal estates owing to enactment of tenancy laws, the devadasi women failed to find suitable partners in their own villages. So they went to cities and town to earn their living in red light districts" (Gurumurthy 1996, 144).

10 I made subsequent research trips to Nandipur in 2004, 2007, 2009 and 2011.

11 The *shruti* and *chowdiki* are stringed instruments, usually given by devotees to Yellamma and always kept with her. Typically, they are played only by those dedicated to her.

12 For a recent account of *matammas* in Andhra Pradesh, see Flueckiger 2013. For sociological accounts of *basavis* in Karnataka, see Mahale 1986; Assayag 1992. For an account of the *kalavant* tradition in Goa and Maharastra, see Arondekar 2012. For a detailed history of "patterns of scared prostitution" in the central Deccan plateau, see Vijaisri 2004.

13 See especially Vijaisri 2004, for a distinction between a *sule* or *sani* pattern associated with Mizrai temples and a *jogati* or *basavi* pattern associated with more rural and less well funded temples in Kannada-speaking areas.

14 Here my usage differs from that of the religious scholar Davesh Soneji (2012, 10), a scholar of religion, who sets *jogatis* apart from devadasis based on caste distinctions.

15 Trouble (*kaadaata*) is an everyday category for those attached to Yellamma, as I will show. At the same time, I am here drawing, and playing, on Judith Butler's work on what she calls "kinship trouble" in Sophocles's play *Antigone* (2000, 62).

16 The anthropologist Talal Asad describes how forms of knowledge shape the inhabitation of modernity: "Modernity is not primarily a matter of cognizing the real but of living-in-the-world. Since this is true of every epoch, what is distinctive about modernity *as a historical epoch* includes modernity as a political-economic project. What interests me particularly is the attempt to construct categories of the secular and the religious in terms of which modern living is required to take place, and nonmodern peoples are invited to assess their adequacy. For representations of 'the secular' and 'the religious' in modern and modernizing states mediate people's identities, help shape their sensibilities, and guarantee their experiences" (2003, 14).

17 Richard King puts this point in strong terms: "We should be aware, therefore, that the central explanatory category of religious studies, namely the notion of 'religion' itself, is a Christian theological category" (1999, 40). The term "religion" comes from the Latin *religio*, which King, drawing on Cicero's etymology, renders as "the retracing of the 'lore of the ritual' of one's ancestor's" (36) or, in effect, tradition (*traditio* in Latin). At the time of the Roman Empire, this meant that Christians were often referred to as atheists, because they did not acknowledge the (ancestral) gods of others. Roman Christians themselves could not be said to belong to any *traditio*, having no shared ancestors or established body of traditional practices. In his genealogy of the category religion, King notes that the early Christian transformation of *religio* had a number of effects: it worked to consolidate the authority of Christians in Roman society; to delineate between them and followers of false gods; and, ultimately, to establish the monotheism of Christianity as paradigmatic to the concept of religion itself.

18 The Vedas are a body of texts (written between 1500 BCE and 500 BCE) that are considered to be revelatory by many and are taken as the basic texts of Hinduism. There are four Vedas: the Rig Veda, Sama Veda, Yajur Veda, and Atharva Veda. They contain hymns, mantras, and rituals and have had a vast influence on Buddhism, Jainism, and Sikhism, as well as Hinduism.

19 Nicholas Dirks (1997) considers the complicity of anthropology in the colonial project of social reform, here focused on the practice of hook swinging and its construction as not merely backward but also physically dangerous and morally polluting. Dirks notes that contrary to the aims of reformers, their campaign produced an opportunity for peasants to assert their presence and identity in a process that ensured the continuation of the practice.

20 In an essay titled "Why I Am Not a Hindu" (2006), the scholar, political scientist, and Dalit activist Kancha Ilaiah departs from this formula for Dalit assertion by arguing that the practices surrounding and deities worshipped by Dalitbahujans are radically distinct from caste Hindu religion.

21 Sarah Pinto (2008) has made this point in her study of women designated as untouchable who do postpartum work.

22 An ironic example of the limit posed by secular conceptions of the politics of caste is offered in an essay titled "Paraiyars Ellaiyamman as an Iconic Symbol of Collective Resistance and Emancipatory Mythography," by the Dalit liberation theologian and Episcopal priest Sathianathan Clarke (1998). Clarke draws on the story of Yellamma (Ellaiyamman), as told by Dalits, to argue that Dalit religion and consciousness is distinct from Hinduism and Brahmanism. Through the lens of liberation theology, Dalit forms of knowledge offer both a sign of and resource for Dalit lifeways as more than exploited and abjectified existence. This is a possibility that cannot emerge in a framework that insists on the rejection of anything of old—those forms of knowledge and practice that have been constituted as superstition.

23 I concur here with the feminist theorists Mary John and Janaki Nair (2000a) that "sexual economies" is a preferable term in the Indian context, since that term allows us to insist that all sexualities have a material basis that can and should be specified. My use of "sexual economy" is also in keeping with the queer theoretical insistence that the study of sex not be subsumed under an analysis of gender (Rubin 1984).

24 Rosalind Morris cites Marx's response to Engels' claim that "Mohammed's religious revolution, like every religious movement, was formerly a reaction, an alleged return to the old, the simple" (2002, 157).

25 The Hindu temple complex was a political, economic, and religious institution that revolved around the sovereignty of the king (Dirks 1988; Stein 1978). The importance of devadasis to the symbolic and political life of temples has been most closely examined in Kersenboom-Story 1987; Apffel-Marglin 1985.

26 This sect of Shavism, called Virashaivism, began as a movement of radical reform in twelfth-century Karnataka and was led by Basava, a poet and saint. Practitioners of the religion are called Lingayats, a term derived from their distinctive practice of wearing the lingam (phallus) of Shiva around their neck. Basava called for the abolition of caste and gender distinctions as well as Brahmanical ritual and preached a devotional religion focused on Shiva. No longer a radical social experiment, Virashaivism has become an institutionalized religion with ten million followers. Dwelling mostly in the state of Karnataka, Lingayats are major landholders and brokers of political power considered to constitute their own high caste. For ethnographic treatments of Lingayats, see McCormack 1963; Bradford 1976.

27 For histories of this appropriation and the revival of dance as an aestheticized form, see Srinivasan 1988; Gaston 1996. For a regionally specific account of salon dance in Madras and coastal Andhra Pradesh, see Soneji 2012.

28 On child marriage, see M. Sinha 1998, the introduction to the new edition of *Mother India*. On the sati debates, see especially Mani 1998. For nuanced considerations of the woman question in relation to the nationalist dilemma, see Sangari and Vaid 1989; Chakravarti 1989; Sarkar and Sarkar 2008.

29 In his widely read and influential study of South Indian religion, Reverend Henry

Whitehead wrote: "The Asadi girls, however, never marry, but are made *basavis*, i.e., are consecrated to the goddess, and become prostitutes. Certainly the degradation of religion in India is seen only too plainly in the degradation of the priesthood" ([1921] 1999, 45). In a text written at the end of the eighteenth century and dedicated to the East India Company, Abbé Jean-Antoine Dubois wrote: "Next to the Sacrificers, the most important persons about the temples are the dancing girls, who call themselves *Devadasi, servants or slaves of the gods*; but they are known to the public by the courser [*sic*] name of strumpets. . . . They perform their religious duties at the temple to which they belong twice a day, morning and evening. They are also obliged to assist at all the public ceremonies which they enliven with their dance and merry song. As soon as their public business is over, they open their cells of infamy, and frequently convert the temple itself into a stew" (quoted in Apffel-Marglin 1985, 3–4).

30 Janaki Nair writes: "The *agamiks* (scholars well versed in the *agamashastras* [Hindu text or scripture]) entrusted with the task masterfully demonstrated, through citation of a group of texts dealing with temple rituals—*Shaiva, Panchartra, Vykhanasagamasatras*—that devadasis did indeed have specific services to render in the temple. From the moment they woke up, bathed, put on fresh clothes, and adorned themselves with flowers, they spent the day participating in temple rituals that included waking up the deity with song and dance rituals, lighting the lamps in the evenings, and performing prescribed musical and dance oblations at set times. In addition, the agamiks said, the scriptures required them to perform a series of special rituals on specific days throughout the year. In turn, devadasis were entitled to a share of the offerings as a temple honor and to payments from temple revenues. Indeed, the nonperformance of these duties by the devadasis were deemed so grievous a violation of the temple code that the priests were required to perform rituals of atonement (*pryaschitta*)" (2011, 210–11).

31 In issuing its decision, the government specified that whatever the original (that is, shastric) purpose of the institution was, the current immorality of devadasis fully justified their exclusion (Nair 2011, 208–15; Vijaisri 2004, 155–58). In the words of the Maharaja of Mysore in 1910, "whatever may be the euphemism by which the *true nature* of the ceremony is concealed, *Gajje Puja* [temple dance] has an intimate connection to the profession of a prostitute dancing girl" (quoted in Vijaisri 2004, 157 [my emphasis]).

32 Although the bureaucrats banned the devadasis from temple service on the basis of their putative immorality the officials' motivation was more material than moral (Nair 2011, 212). I will elaborate on the dispossession of devadasi property rights in chapter 1.

33 In her work on debates in Madras, Kalpana Kannabiran (1995:165) writes: "Contemporary polygamous relationships among the devadasis . . . were aberrations which did not reflect the glory and sacredness of the Hindu nation. . . . and the narrowly redefined boundaries of the monogamous family: an adult female has to be either a wife or a prostitute."

34 For discussions of the midcentury legislative debates in the Madras presidency, see K. Kannabiran 1995. For more recent debates in the state of Karnataka, see Jordan 1993.

35 Indeed, some scholars have argued that their social and regional marginality placed them outside the concerns of the social purity activists—mostly members of the caste or class elite—whose campaigns focused on the dedicated women in Muzrai temples (Vijaisri 2004, 171). Priyadarshini Vijaisri's point that the difference between outcaste *jogatis* and *basavis* and low- and middle-caste women associated with more elite temples is salient both historically and sociologically is well taken. Like her, and unlike Soneji (2012), however, I situate all of these temple women in one category, that of dedication (for Vijaisri, the category is sacred prostitution). Unlike Vijaisri, I do not situate the failure of upper-caste reform campaigns to draw outcaste women into their ambit as a form of neglect—a characterization that remains in a reformist paradigm of 'rescue' and protection.

36 As Vijaisri (2004, 178) has noted, a range of styles and standards for women's comportment in the precolonial period was replaced by a single model of femininity across caste differences. Anupama Rao (2009), however, has argued that anti-caste radicals' calls for feminine respectability constitute repetition with a difference formed more in the terrain of political modernity and Dalit assertion than in that of anticolonial nationalism.

37 On the work of the Durbar Mahila Samanwaya Committee in Bengal, with 35,000 members, see Nag 2005. See also the statement by SANGRAM/VAMP Team 2011 for a report on the work of Veshya Anyay Mukti Parishad (VAMP), a "collective of women in prostitution and sex work" in Maharastra whose name translates from Marathi as The Whores Council for Freedom from Injustice and its nongovernmental affiliate Sampada Grameen Mahila Sanstha (SANGRAM).

38 On sex worker rights organizing, see Kotiswaran 2001, 2011. On the possible changes in the status of prostitution under Indian law, see Tandon and Grover 2006.

39 I am referring to "India's Shame: Sexual Slavery and Political Corruption Are Leading to an AIDS Catastrophe," the title of an article by Robert Friedman (1996).

40 For instance, in their discussion of Muthulakshimi Reddy, a prominent leader of the movement for devadasi reform in Madras, Kalpana and Vasanth Kannabiran note Reddy's belief that devadasis had been chaste temple servants in a Hindu golden age whose fallen state was inimical to the future of the Hindu nation. Quoting Reddy on the subject from a court case, they write: "Muthulakshmi's aim was to rescue Hindu society from the clutches of blind superstition and obscurantism, which, she believed, could only spell its doom: '(Prostitution) is a question that vitally concerns the dignity and status of every woman in India, inasmuch as it is a stigma on the whole womanhood, and a blot on Hindu civilization'" (2003, 24).

41 In a rich and detailed history of devadasis from Madras, Soneji (2012) offers a re-

cent example of an aesthetic reading of devadasis as performers who make their primary contribution to Indian modernity through their dance.

42 Shankar writes that the "devadasi system is a deliberately created custom in order to exploit lower caste people in India by upper castes and classes as: (a) The upper castes have influenced the establishment of an order of prostitutes who are licensed to carry on their profession under the protective shield of religion. (b) The establishment of such system facilitates [for] them that access to low caste women to fulfill their carnal desire. (c) The setting up of such a system can destroy the lower caste's sense of self-respect in a society" (1994, 65).

43 Nair (2011) shifts her figuration of the devadasi, bringing more attention to regional histories and caste critique.

44 Here I am suggesting that we abandon evolutionary and functionalist secular and social-scientific explanations of gods and spirits and the attribution of backwardness to forms of unenlightened religion that such explanations produce. As Dipesh Chakrabarty has put it, "we need to move away from two of the ontological assumptions entailed in secular conceptions of the political and the social. [The first is secular historical time. . . .] The second assumption [is] . . . that the human is ontologically singular, that gods and spirits are in the end 'social facts,' that the social somehow exists prior to them. I try, on the other hand, to think without the assumption of even a logical priority of the social. One empirically knows of no society in which humans have existed without gods and spirits accompanying them. Although the God of monotheism may have taken a few knocks—if not actually 'died'—in the nineteenth-century European story of 'the disenchantment of the world,' the gods and other agents inhabiting practices of so-called 'superstition' have never died anywhere" (2000, 16).

Chapter 1. Yellamma and Her Sisters

1 *Harijan* means people of God (Hari is a name for the god Vishnu). Gandhi coined the term as an alternative to, and atonement for, "untouchable." Many members of communities so designated still use this term, as did Durgabai in this telling. Others reject it as condescending and prefer the term Dalit. *Keri* means lane or quarter.

2 Matanga (the word means elephant in Sanskrit) is the ninth of the ten Mahavidyas, each a manifestation of the transformative power and anger of Sati, wife of Siva (Kinsley 1988, 162). She is "the incarnation of emotional frenzy. Her complexion is dark, her red eyes roll in her head; drunken and reeling with desire she stumbles like a furious elephant. For she is the phase where the world falls under the intoxication of mantra, Tantra and the longing for unity with Shiva" (Rawson [1973] 1995, 130). Sometimes called Mathamma, she appears in W. T. Elmore's ([1913] 1984) classic study as one of the seven sisters of Dravidian goddesses, of which Yellamma is the eldest.

3 In some versions of this devotional tale, the landlord cuts off Matangi's breast.

The sense of sexual violation is more explicit in this version, but it is evident even in the other. Wearing a nose ring—along with toe rings, bangles, and a marriage necklace (*mangalasutra*)—marks the marital status and active sexuality of women. To cut off Matangi's nose is to violate the integrity of her fertile body.

4 Sathianathan Clarke (1998) published a version of this tale as it was told to him by a Paraiyar (a Dalit from Tamil Nadu) *pujari*. Tales with some overlapping elements are referenced in Priyadarshini Vijaisri's history of devadasi reform (2004, 85).

5 *Jati* is generally understood to refer to occupationally specialized and endogamous social groups, of which there are thousands in the Indian subcontinent. It is often translated as "subcaste." However, for an important critical reappraisal of the historical links between supposedly polluted occupations such as leather working and low or outcaste status, see Rawat 2011.

6 Morgan's terms—"consanguinity" and "affinity"—and the premise they set out have been interrogated in several ways in the history of anthropological studies of kinship, which I take up in chapter 5. My point here that the kin making under discussion is not readily accommodated into either of the structure of blood and lineage or that of alliance and marriage.

7 Those dedicated to Matangi are exclusively members of the Madura (Madiga in some areas) *jati*. Those dedicated to Yellamma may come from any caste, though they are overwhelmingly from outcaste communities such as the Holeyar and Samagar communities. Throughout northern Karnataka, southern Maharastra, and western Andhra Pradesh, girls and boys are given to Yellamma, Matangi, Khandoba, Hulligamma, and Hanuman, among others. Dedications are generally made to the most powerful deity in the region where the dedication takes place. For a historical account of this variety of dedication practices in Kannada- and Telugu-speaking regions, see Vijaisri 2004. For recent ethnographic accounts of *jogini* as dedicated women in Andhra Pradesh are called, see Betlem 2012 and Flueckiger 2013.

8 On the turn from semiotic readings of language toward a consideration of speech acts as modes of social action, see J. L. Austin 1962. As Richard Bauman and Charles L. Briggs (1990, 65) point out, this is similar to Bronislaw Malinowski's understanding of language as a "mode of action" (1935, 59) rather than simply a "countersign of thought" (1923, 296). Focusing on ritual performances in Orissa, Frédérique Apffel-Marglin makes a similar point when she writes that rituals "precipitate reality" (2011, 15). In her ethnography about Dalit women who learn to accommodate the goddess in possession states, Kalpana Ram argues that mediums "bring the goddess alive" and "make her present" in ways that transform spectators into devotees, new kinds of subjects (2013, 169). Like those of Apfell-Marglin and Ram, my analysis moves away from the long-standing scholarly preoccupation with the semiotics of ritual action and toward its ontological force.

9 In a typology from Tamil Sangam poetry, which A. K. Ramanujan (1986) finds pertinent to the interpretation of Kannada folklore, tales are either *akam* (inner,

domestic) or *puram* (outer, public). *Akam* tales are told in the space of the home by women—they are called grandmother's tales—to an audience of kin. *Puram* tales are elaborately performed by bards, almost exclusively men, whose occupation it is to tell tales in the streets and temples for a public audience. The devotional performance of *jogatis* confounds this split between *akam* and *puram* and their correspondences, in that *jogatis* are feminine persons (whether sexed male or female) who sing and tell tales in the streets and temples for people outside their kin group or caste.

10 For a nuanced consideration of the position of sons of devadasis and their role in Dalit politics and reform, see Epp 1997.

11 On caste, see Desrochers and Veliyannoor 2004. On gender, see Agarwal 1994, 1998. The following all-India data for 1987–88 illustrate this point and show that poverty is concentrated among overlapping groups: rural laborers, scheduled castes and tribes (Dalits), and female-headed households: 35 percent of all rural households were dependent on labor, but they made up 46 percent of all rural poor since three-fifths of the group was in poverty; scheduled castes and tribes were 29 percent of households but 37 percent of the poor; and nearly half of all rural female-headed households ranked below poverty level (Patnaik 1998). According to a 2005–6 report from the government of Karnataka, Dalits make up 16 percent of the population but hold just 9 percent of the land, of which only 11 percent is irrigated (Sudarshan 2006, 214–15). A study of changes in rural poverty between 1993 and 2005 found that ownership of land significantly reduced a person's chances of falling into poverty and that those who stayed out of poverty owned twice as much land on average as those who remained poor (Krishna and Shariff 2011, 536).

12 Mark Elmore (2005) has argued that through changes in land relations and administration during the colonial period in Himachal Pradesh—where, in at least some documented areas, lands were held by the gods themselves until they were legally designated minors and dispossessed of their holdings—both the state and religion were reconceived in ways that situated the state as the prime arbiter of land relations, and religion as something that stands outside of economics and statecraft.

13 I am drawing here on the work of Bina Agarwal: "Rights are defined here as claims that are legally and socially recognized and enforceable by an external legitimized authority, be it a village-level institution or some higher-level judicial or executive body of the State. Rights in land can be in the form of ownership or usufruct, associated with differing degrees of freedom to lease out, mortgage, bequeath, or sell. Land rights can stem from inheritance, community membership, transfers by the State, or tenancy arrangements, purchase, and so on. Rights in land also have a temporal and sometimes locational dimension: they may be hereditary, or accrue only for a lifetime, or for a lesser period; and they may be conditional on residing where the land is located. As distinct from rights, a person may, in theory, have 'access' to land, say through informal concessions

granted by kin or friends. But these cannot be claimed as a right and their enforcement sought. 'Rights' thus provide a measure of security that other forms of access typically do not" (1998, 3).

14 In their analysis of the legacy of colonial land tenure systems, Abhijit Banerjee and Lakshmi Iyer (2003) write that the *ryotwari* system was attempted and failed in the Bombay Presidency in the 1820s, just after the Maratha territories fell to the British in 1818. Surveys were conducted under British officials in 1935, but in some areas landlords remained in place. On this point see also Tim Hanstad, Robin Nielson and Jennifer Brown (2004).

15 The reservation system means that a percentage of central and state government posts and university seats are reserved for members of listed scheduled castes—as noted above, the bureaucratic term for Dalits—but access to these posts and seats is almost always negotiated through cash payments to various officials.

16 On the politics of water, see J. Nair 2005.

17 Rahul Rao cites an estimate that three thousand farmers in Karnataka took their lives between 2000 and 2003 (2005, 2). See also Guttal 2003. Across India two hundred thousand farmers committed suicide between 1997 and 2008; there were 12,493 farmers' suicides in Maharastra alone between 2006 and 2008, according to the journalist P. Sainath (2010).

18 See also Mahale 1986; Vijaisri 2004.

19 Precolonial conceptions of territory, deity, and temple worked through identificatory relations. The temple was the house of the god, whose presence and power was felt across a territory, and who was usually allied with the force of the sovereign (Dirks 1993; M. Elmore 2005). Colonial regimes of property and taxation introduced new distinctions between (1) religious administration—as a matter of the conduct of ritual and the management of property or the economy as a matter of a temple trust, overseen by a government that existed to protect public interests—and (2) religious essence—as a question to be settled by recourse to the *shastras*, as interpreted by Brahman pandits. According to precolonial arrangements, devadasis were married to the deity, who granted them rights to land in recognition of their service or devotion (*seve*). Within modern conceptions, this kind of relationship between sexuality and property has been constrained to heterosexual matrimony.

20 For a discussion of Ambedkar within the context of anticaste social movements, see Omvedt 1994; A. Rao 2009. Gail Omvedt takes issue with histories that depict the anti-caste movement, which sometimes forged political alliances with the British, as a diversion in the anti-imperial nationalist struggle. She argues that the movement—as a part of a broader democratic revolution based on the values of freedom, equality, and autonomy—was "a crucial expression of the democratic revolution in India, more consistently democratic—and in the end more consistently 'nationalistic'—than the elite-controlled Indian National Congress" (1994, 16).

21 As the BSP party rose to national prominence in the early 1990s, it came to dominate Dalit politics in the region. In the 2009 general election, the party captured

twenty-one seats in the Lok Sabha or lower house of the Parliament of India, making it the fourth largest party in the country. Then led by Mayawati, who had been chief minister of Uttar Pradesh, the party was founded by Kanshi Ram in 1984 to represent *bahujans* or people in the majority. The Bahujan Samaraj Party succeeded other Dalit political movements in Karnataka—namely, the Dalit Panthers and the Dalit Sangharsh Samiti. Dalit movements in Karnataka have derived their inspiration from the Maharastran movement and its founders, Ambedkar and Phule. Lacking the kind of charismatic political activism that Ambedkar had brought to Maharastra and Periyar to Tamil Nadu beginning in the 1920s, Dalit political organizing in the region that is now Karnataka State has been fractured. Without the direct legacy of a charismatic leader, Dalits in Karnataka did not seek to establish a Dalit political party. Rather, they set up something of an umbrella organization for the various Dalit groups in the state. In the 1970s and 1980s chapters of the Dalit Sangharsh Samiti dedicated themselves to raising the consciousness of Dalit adults and children and to staging agitations and demonstrations about caste atrocities, including devadasi dedication. As in Maharashtra, in Karnataka the Dalit movement has been primarily an urban phenomenon. But whereas in Maharastra organization among Dalit women has been very strong, in Karnataka, Dalit women continue to struggle for recognition in feminist organizations and Dalit groups as activists in their own right, rather than simply as figures of victimhood deployed by caste feminists or Dalit men to their own political ends. For an account of Dalit political leadership and movements across India, see Mendelsohn 1998. For treatments of the gendered politics of caste reform in the region, see Epp 1997; Omvedt 1980; A. Rao 2009.

22 The district *panchayat* (governing council) has eighteen seats, of which three are held by members of scheduled castes or scheduled tribes. Of the remaining fifteen, eleven were held by Lingayats in 2001, the time of this conversation.

23 Rajeev Kamble's faithfulness to Ambedkar's view of devadasis was truer than I realized at the time. In her history of the anti-Brahman campaign for the reform of *joginis, murlis* and other Dalit dedicated women in Maharastra, Vijaisri describes a speech Ambedkar gave to a group of five hundred *murlis* from Kamatipura, the brothel district in Bombay, in 1936. The women had decided to convert to Buddhism in order to take refuge from the exploitation of caste Hinduism. Vijaisri writes: "But Ambedkar put a pre-condition on the *Murlis* converting: they would have to first give up their 'rotten habits and practices,' and purify themselves in body, language and heart. But he did not stop there. In phraseology strikingly reminiscent of caste Hindu discourse on femininity, he told the *Murlis*: 'women are jewels of society. Every society endows [communities with] immense credit for the chastity of [their] women and that our wives must be from cultured families is the desire of most of the community. The status of the family depends on the wives' behavior'" (Vijaisri 2005, 409).

24 Marking the brow with colored powder or sacred ash is a rite practiced by devotees of Hindu gods and goddesses all over India. Devotees of Yellamma offer turmeric—or its less costly synthetic substitute, bhandara—to her and take it from

her as a blessing. Turmeric has cooling properties and is often associated with hot goddesses like Yellamma. It also has medicinal properties as an antiseptic, anti-oxidant, and anti-inflammatory.

25 Here I am gesturing to the legacy of Louis Dumont's (1970) understanding of caste as an arrangement and logic of social order based on a hierarchy of purity and pollution. For a summary of critiques of Dumont, see Dirks 2001. My point here is that although upper-caste reckonings of purity and pollution and caste hierarchy structured the social and spatial relations of encounters between *jogatis* and landholding farmers, they did not determine the consciousness of the *jogatis*.

26 Her meaning was "we are feeding them." This narrative emphasizes the contrast between the perspective of the *jogatis* and that of young Dalit men somewhat at the expense of the variability within each group. I talked to *jogatis* who felt that going on rounds and asking for grain was a humiliating occupation and who had stopped, in favor of agricultural day labor. I also knew sons who would never have criticized their mothers this way and who honored them for the sacrifices their mothers had made to raise them well. This variability will emerge over the course of the book; here my aim is to bring out a general contrast that I found to hold true overall.

27 Mariakamba, or Mariyamman, who is found in the Malnad region of Karnataka and in the Tamil country, is one of the best known other examples of a goddess whose presence extends across an entire region. See Kinsley 1988; Bhattacharyya 1999, 55–56.

28 A. K. Ramanujan offers the following contrasts between (married) breast mothers and (autonomous) tooth mothers: "Breast mothers are married and subordinate to their consorts; related to auspiciousness and life cycle rituals; either house-hold or village deities within temples; represented in sculpted and anthropomor-phic form; benevolent unless offended; vegetarian and kept by Brahman or Brah-manized priests. Tooth mothers are independent or murderous towards consorts; crisis deities associated with the presence of affliction; manifest in rough or iconic form, often pots; lustful, angry, liable to possess those they want; identified with a village; demanding of blood sacrifices; kept by non-Brahman, often 'untouchable officiants'" (1986, 63).

29 But see also Babb 1988, for his delineation of an "indigenous feminism."

30 I consider the manifestations of these *jade* and the campaigns against them in more detail in chapter 2.

31 *Darshan* (auspicious sight of the divine) is perhaps the most basic form of en-counter between deities and devotees; to take *darshan* is to see and be seen by the deity. This encounter bestows a powerful form of blessing on the devotee. See Eck 1996, 59–62; Fuller 1992.

32 Under the provisions of the Renuka Yellamma Devastana (Administration) Act of 1974, the temple or *devastana* at Saundatti is administered by a board of trustees appointed by the state, generally referred to as the temple trust. For a brief overview of the history and authority of temple trusts, see note 23, chapter 2.

For a history of this temple under the modern state, see Assayag 1992, 412–81; Gurumurthy 1996.

33 In this version, the curse of impotence given by Jamadagni to his disobedient sons is omitted. *Jogappas* place themselves in the lineage of these sons for whom mother love trumps father rule.

34 For an elaboration of the theory of "spousification," see Gatwood 1985.

35 For an interesting interpretation of Parashurama as a heroic figure for Dalit religion, whose actions produce an anti-Brahman goddess and an "iconic symbol" of Dalit resistance, see Clarke 1998. For an account of the reversal of heads and the creation of Yellamma and Matangi, see W. Elmore [1913] 1984, 101.

36 For a fascinating account of the ways material (false) and spiritual (true) grounds for conversion came to inform colonial discourses about pariahs (outcastes) more broadly, see Viswanath 2010.

37 For a critique of Gimbutas as an overly inventive—and thus poor—historical scholar, see K. Young 1991. For a critique of her analysis of the archeological record, see Conkey and Tringham 1995.

38 Universalizing assumptions that Young critiques include the association between women and peace and the idea that men contribute nothing to the nurture of children. Her own attachment to and lack of ambivalence about a (benevolent) father god seem to pose their own problematic universalism, however.

39 Unlike Yellamma, who is beheaded by her son for her lack of chastity and then becomes a goddess, Gangamma is a goddess who marries an unsuspecting man with a reputation for sexual predation. She reveals herself to him in her fierce manifestation and he flees from the marriage scene, but she chases him down and beheads him. See Flueckiger 2013.

40 Joan Scott (2009b) makes this point about the antinomies that secure secularism in the context of Western Europe.

Chapter 2. Yellamma, Her Wives, and the Question of Religion

1 This is not to say that the distinction between true and false religion was first made in the modern period. Rather, what has come to count as religion in India under modernity was shaped by this Christian theological distinction, a distinction with decidedly different effects than the historical Brahmanical differentiation between high and low forms of Hinduism. See King 1999; Flood 1998.

2 Christian missionary projects focused especially on Dalits and their conversion (Kent 2004; Viswanathan 2003).

3 I am using "recognition" here in two different but overlapping senses. The terms of liberal recognition in the face of forms of life deemed morally repugnant, as Elizabeth Povinelli (2002a) has elaborated them, produce an impossible subject position in which those forms of life felt to be repugnant are asked to be different enough to be distinguishable from liberal forms of life, but not so different that liberals are forced to annihilate them, thereby undermining the liberal principle

of government by reason. This is the kind of recognition that devadasis are subject to in relation to projects of reform. They are also subject to the recognition of the devi. For Kalpana Ram, recognition also describes the relationship between the goddess and those she calls or speaks to: "The woman is transformed from a person who is insignificant into a privileged addressee. She is a subject who henceforth *matters*, because she matters to the goddess" (2013, 169).

4 In other versions and interpretations of this story, Durga's wrath is directed at her consort or husband, who has hidden in the body of a buffalo. See Brubaker 1978; Flood 1998; Kinsley 1988.

5 The rite is not mentioned in any of the three book-length ethnographic studies focusing on Karnataka devadasis (Assayag 1993; Shankar 1994; Tarachand 1992).

6 My use of "prestation" here is in keeping with that of Gloria Raheja who has insisted that the patterns of giving and receiving described by the word are significant not only in economic terms as so called payments, but also in ritual and symbolic terms. See Raheja 1988a for a discussion of the relationship between prestations and reproduction of caste distinction and interdependence and Raheja 1988b for a summary of scholarly debates about the meaning of prestations.

7 Mahanawami *phere* song no. 1. Thanks to Chandra Shekhar Balachandran, Ambuja Kowlgi, and Jyoti Hiremath for their assistance with the translation of this and other excerpted Mahanawami songs. Mahanawami is celebrated on the ninth night of Navaratri, in the Fall.

8 I am translating *pawana* here as "transformative." To say the devi is *pawana* means that to touch her, take her *darshan*, or otherwise encounter her is to be transformed by her. This term is usually translated as "sacred" or "pure," which places the emphasis on an essence or quality of the devi in language that is difficult to extract from Christian (sacred) or Brahmanical (pure) genealogies. In my translation I am emphasizing what transpires between the devotee and the devi, whose *shakti* is so strong it can change you.

9 Mahanawami *phere* song no. 4.

10 I never saw a Brahman or Jain devotee come to the Yellamma temple, which was located in a Dalit lane, an area considered to be polluting by upper-caste villagers. However, they did receive Yellamma, Matangi and their *pujaris* in an outer room of their homes.

11 Yellamma is not the deity most identified with the body of the village in Nandipur—Margoawwa, another *amma* devi, is. Unlike Yellamma, Margoawwa remains a meat-eating goddess and, village resources permitting, a large buffalo is sacrificed at her biannual festival. Both are boundary goddesses: they are kept in temples or houses outside the traditional boundaries of the village, in the Dalit quarter.

12 For the history of devadasi reform during the early and midtwentieth century in the region, see Vijaisri 2004, 141–62; Epp 1997, 136–66.

13 The importance of this study, though amply emphasized in the report itself, was

also recognized in the *Karnataka State Gazetteer: Belgaum District* (Kamath 1983, 965).

14 As of 2009, a total of forty-five cases had been registered by the police under the antidedication legislation. Of these forty-five, only one resulted in the conviction of three people, two of whom were sentenced to two years in prison, in addition to fines (Kumar 2009).

15 According to Laxshmi, a devadasi reformer interviewed by Linda Epp in the early 1990s, Gilada organized a fake dedication. He enrolled Laxshmi to play a brothel keeper, pressed turmeric on the forehead of young girl playing the person to be dedicated, convinced a *pujari* to conduct the ceremony, and then reported him to the police. They showed no interest in arresting anybody. Once back in Mumbai, Gilada mounted a major publicity campaign exposing the lack of local enforcement of the ban. The district commissioner in Belgaum characterized Gilada as an outsider corrupted by foreign funding and called on people "not to believe in scandalous and false propaganda" (1990). For a detailed discussion of these events, see Epp (1997, 224–31).

16 On the colonial histories of such a pedagogy of reform, see Pierce and Rao 2006.

17 In 2009, MASS reported cutting a total of 6,843 locks between 1997 and October 2009 (MASS 2009, 17). These numbers represent only the cutting work organized by MASS; cutting campaigns have been carried out by a variety of groups over the past three decades across the region.

18 Flier on file with the author.

19 Ganneth Obeyesekere notes that *pativrata* is the term used by many female ecstatics to refer their vow of celibacy. The word translates literally as "vow of devotion to the lord" and is most commonly used to refer to the Brahmanical ideal of a wife's conduct toward her husband, whom she treats as a god. Obeyesekere explains the use of the term to mean sexual renunciation: "The woman renounces sex with her husband. She then transfers her allegiance to a god . . . the etymological meaning of *pativrata* is maintained" (1981, 65).

20 For a more extended discussion of hair symbols through anthropological and psychoanalytic theory, see Ramberg 2009.

21 For an extended discussion of Obeyesekere's extraordinary work on ecstatic women and magical hair in relation to this material, see Das 1989.

22 On the social body, see Scheper-Hughes and Lock 1987. On the need to purify it, see Douglas 2002.

23 These improvements are but the latest chapter in over a century of state-administered temple management and reform in the subcontinent. Under British rule, elected Indian representatives were given authority over temples through the Hindu Religious Endowments Board, formed in 1926. The Hindu Religious and Charitable Endowments Administration Act was passed in 1952, after independence. It empowers temple trusts to oversee the authority of priests and other temple servants and to regulate temple landholding, land use, and ritual conduct. As Frank Presler (1987) has pointed out, this history offers an example of the ways

modern states penetrate religion, despite policies of noninterference (under the British) or constitutional secularism (after independence). This penetration was facilitated in large part through the redefinition of deities as minors who could not hold land (as they did in precolonial times) and the attendant secularization of land as alienable property (rather than the deity's territory) (M. Elmore 2005). The constitutionality of the later Endowments Act was upheld by the Supreme Court on the grounds that temples are public trusts, rightly administered by the state for the good of the people. The temple trust for the Yellamma temple at Saundatti is directed by the deputy commissioner for the Belgaum District, a political appointee made by the ruling party in the capital, Bangalore. For a description of the politics of the temple trust in the 1980s, when the contemporary wave of devadasi reform in the region began, see Assayag 1992.

24 See, for example, Ramesh 1992 for the findings of an evaluation study.

25 The collective of sex workers who act as HIV peer educators, Veshya Anyay Mukti Parishad or VAMP—working with the NGO that published this commentary, Sangram—has protested extensively and brilliantly in Maharastra and northern Karnataka against the state rehabilitation of sex workers as a violation of their right to work and as a form of state violence.

26 *Hijras* are seen, and see themselves as, persons who are "neither men nor women" in the words of anthropologist Serena Nanda (1990). Though some are intersexed, most are sexed male at birth but come to adopt feminine modes of comportment and dress. Nirvan (reborn) *hijras* have self-castrated as an aspect of their gender and source of ritual power in the world. Their bawdy performance of song and dance is sought as a form of blessing at births and weddings across the Indian subcontinent. On the complexity of the category *hijra* and the communities it names, see Lawrence Cohen (1995) and Gayatri Reddy (2005).

27 The temple official was drawing on a conception of the nature of deities and their relationship to the dramas of humanity that is widely held across South Asia. Consider William Sax's description of the meaning of the Sanskrit term *liila* (the play or dance of the gods): "*Līlā*, then, is God's play: it refers not only to the supreme being's playful actions but also to the dramatic 'plays' staged by human beings in memory of those actions. Thus *līlā* appears to mark a delightful difference between European and South Asian traditions, embodying a ludic dimension of Indian religious life that is muted or even absent in the dominant religious traditions of the West" (1995, 3).

Chapter 3. Tantra, Shakta, Yellamma

1 These are the two poles that Cohen defines: "In the case of transplantation debates, *terror* is the claim that there is a universal practice of trafficking in the bodies of the weak and the vulnerable and that all other registers of commitment must be rendered equivalent to the uncanny taking of the organ. Such traffics in kidneys abound, and their scale varies from scant kilometers between hospital and slum to multinational circuits of patients, vulnerable and needy suppliers,

clinicians, and operating sites. But many poor donors and sellers refuse to consider their decision to give up a kidney as motivated solely or even primarily by poverty or coercion. Many that do see both force and need as part of their coming to the operation still insist upon other forms of commitment—sacrifice, love, honor, submission to divine will—that are not yet assimilated to the hunger of the market. . . . The possibility of inassimilable commitments we might call *ethics*. There may be terrains of force to which the body is insistently given over. Other modes of giving over that may happen despite or in the face of these constitute a work on the self and the world that cannot be reduced to a response to coercive norms" (2005, 20–21).

2 I offer two examples. The first comes from the leader of the organization of ex-devadasis, Mahila Abhivruddhi Matthu Samrakshana Samsthe (MASS), in the context of an article by the British journalist Sarah Harris, who went on to make a sensationalist documentary titled *Prostitutes of God*. Note the interpretive frame that she gives to Shobha Dasti's account of her own dedication: "We met 31-year-old, former Devadasi Shobha Dasti, who was pimped by her parents and systematically raped in the guise of religious devotion until she finally managed to escape. This is her story. 'One night, when I was about 11, the Hindu goddess Yellamma came to my mother in a dream. When she told the local priest about her vision, he insisted that it was a sign from the goddess that she must devote me as a Devadasi in return for my sister, who left the system a few years earlier after marrying one of her 'patrons.' He warned her that if I wasn't initiated then my brother would be punished by the goddess. So it was decided that I would be *sacrificed* in her place" (Harris n.d. [my emphasis]). The second example comes from a book by Kevin Bales, cofounder of a U.S.-based antislavery organization: "The sheer volume of bonded labor in India means that many variations of both old and new slavery exist side by side. Some types use custom and superstition to control the enslaved person. Consider the case of the *devadasi*, a young woman who is married to a god, which is not as pleasant as it might sound. Poor families, in an effort to appease local gods and guarantee a happy future, will *sacrifice* a daughter by 'marrying' her to one [of the gods]" (1999, 199 [my emphasis]).

3 For an example of a contemporary invocation of dedication as a reason why Indians need Christian missionaries, consider the daily prayer suggested by the Christian Right organization U.S. Center for World Mission, September 11, 2009: "Pray for the efforts of Christian ministries to stem the spiritual corruption in India as they minister to the Devadasi prostitutes" (U.S. Center for World Mission, 2010).

4 On the desecration of Ambedkar statues, see Nicolas Jaoul 2006 for Uttar Pradesh and A. Rao 2009 for Maharastra. V. Geetha and S.V. Rajadurai (1998) have written about the political use of garlanding (with leather sandals) and other forms of desecration of Hindu idols by the leader of the non-Brahman movement in Tamil Nadu, E. V. Ramasamy Periyar.

5 The others are at Athani, Near Manvi, and Badami. As a part of my research, I conducted site visits, observations, and interviews at all of these temples.

6 For a detailed account of the perspective of the Dalit activists and the government response to the "Chandragutti Incident," see Epp 1992.

7 For a compelling account of the breast cloth controversy of 1858 and the broader politics of sartorial garb in missionary ambitions, Indian Christian aspirations, and nonconvert resistance in South India, see Kent 2004, 199–234.

8 The spirit of this retort found expression in a seminaked protest staged by devadasis in Mumbai who were demanding pensions from the state of Maharastra on independence day, August 15, 2010 (Kakade 2010). Accessed July 26, 2013, http://photogallery.outlookindia.com/default.aspx?pt=2&ptv=103029&photono=6&pn=1&pgid=27192#TopImage.

9 Epp interviewed a Brahman family in the early 1990s for whom the wife's *mane devaru* (family deity) was Yellamma. Described by her husband as "exhibiting the utmost decorum" in everyday life, the woman nonetheless annually participated in *bettale seve* at Chandragutti (1997, 133, note 8).

10 Drawing on Foucault's theory of sexuality and modern forms of power, Hugh Urban has argued against the repressive narrative that characterizes work by scholars of Tantra and New Age enthusiasts alike, which suggests that the strain that originated in the Indian subcontinent and is identified as Tantra has been neglected by historians of religion and subject to censure by Victorian Puritanism. On the contrary, Urban suggests, Tantra has proliferated in colonial and contemporary imaginings and emerged in an encounter between the East and the West. The Indian sacred prostitute is surely one site of such imagining.

11 Scholarship on Tantra can be characterized as either "popular celebration[s] of Tantric freedom, healthy sensuality and this worldly affirmation" (Urban 2003, 271) or apologia for Tantric philosophy, metaphysics, and mysticism as Tantra's true essence (M. Elmore 2007). In his genealogy of Tantra, Urban identifies two corresponding origin stories produced by contemporary scholars: the aboriginal (pre-Aryan) and the Vedic (see introduction, note 18).

12 *Tantrika* is sometimes opposed to *vaidika*, as in Kulluka Bhatta's commentary on the Laws of Manu, where the distinction refers to the twofold nature of revelation. But, as Urban notes, this broad distinction between non-Vedic (*tantrika*) and Vedic (*vaidika*) implies a much more inclusive notion of Tantra than the antinomian practices usually identified with it. The broad and indeterminate nature of Tantra as a set of practices and propositions, Urban insists, does not mean that its association with transgressive rites is unwarranted: "Many *tantras* do indeed contain explicit descriptions of sexual rituals, the manipulation of sexual fluids, consumption of wine and meat, and other transgressive practices, such as the infamous five M's, or five forbidden substances" (2003, 40).

13 My account of *jogatis* is considerably different than White's. Based on Jackie Assayag's work on Yellamma *seve* and in keeping with the narrative of decline that informs his writing on Tantra, White offers the following characterization: "Jogammas, are, like Yellamma, sterile fertility goddesses, who offer their fertility and sexuality without reproduction: Jogammas never become mothers. This is of a piece with their role in Karnataka society, where they are prostitutes. Thus, out-

side of festival times and life-cycle rites, far from being considered embodiments of the Goddess, the divine *sakti*—as the *devadasis* once were—Jogammas are treated as simple whores, 'public property,' by their generally well-heeled male clients" (2003, 270). In the course of my research I did encounter *jogatis* who were renouncers—who gave up an active sexuality and family life in order to serve Yellamma—but the vast majority of *jogatis* bear children. This finding is consistent with other studies of Karnataka *jogatis* (Epp 1997; Shankar 1994; Tarachand 1992).

14 For a review and critical reconsideration of the sacred whore complex, see Beard and Henderson (1997).

15 Reconstructions of original Tantric rites, for some scholars (White 2003), debunk neo-Tantric practices. Such practices conceptualize the achievement of intense orgasm as a yogic practice of altered consciousness (Sprinkle 1998). In contrast, the purpose of the reconstructed original rites was the shedding and consumption of bodily fluids in transactions of power and kinship. I am, after Foucault and like Urban (2003), deeply skeptical of the authenticating (or disauthenticating, in this case) search for true origins. Foucault (1984) poses the genealogical method, which attends to questions of emergence and descent, as an alternative to the search for origins. He is concerned about the Platonic assumptions—of essences and ideal forms across time and space—entailed in the quest for origins. He is also troubled by the truth effects of origin tales, which produce coherent and linear accounts of history and obscure questions about why certain discursive formations emerge at particular moments.

16 White focuses especially on a text attributed to a guru later celebrated as the founder of *Kaula*, which he dates to the ninth or tenth century. White takes the practices delineated in this text to be original, and later manifestations to be revivals.

17 In order to explain this logic, White quotes from Frederique Apffel-Marglin's work on 1970s Orissa: "the wives—who also belong to the clan—come from different lines (*kulas*) and are incorporated into the husband's line by the marriage ritual, and at the same time are severed from their father's line. . . . The fertility of women in the shape of sons preserves the *kula*" (Apffel-Marglin 1985, 57).

18 See Kalpana Ram (2013) for nuanced ethnographic readings of devi possession in South India and their implications for social theory. As she is in her writing, I am careful here not to fall into the usual invocation of possession as an occupation by the deity of a passive person, conceived of as a vessel for the active goddess. To borrow Ram's conceptual language, over time Kamlabai cultivated the capacity to accommodate and incorporate Yellamma in states of possession.

19 Hubert and Mauss describe agricultural sacrifice cycles, found in a range of mythical and historical contexts, in which the slaying of the god or monster is followed by a sacred marriage representing the renewing of the cycle of life and fecundity of the world. This type of sacrifice has three stages—the death of the victim, the communion through shared consumption, and the victim's resurrection into new life: "Just as personal sacrifice ensured the life of the person, so the

objective sacrifice in general and the agrarian sacrifice in particular ensured the real and healthful life of things" ([1964] 1981, 75).

Chapter 4. The Giving of Daughters

1 Writing about the conventions governing the distinction between auspicious marital status and inauspicious widowhood, Uma Chakravarti offers a useful analysis of the symbolism of the colors red and white: "The colour codes of red and white are systematically sustained in the wife/widow opposition. Whereas red symbolizes fertility and sexuality, white symbolizes asexuality. In the place of the red kumkuma [vermillion] banned for widows it is customary for them to use 'vibhuti' or ash instead to mark their foreheads. The white or ochre sari symbolizes purity, coolness and the sexuality of the non-bride, more pertinently the renouncers. White is also the colour of death; the 'vibhuti' or white ash is associated with the funeral pyre, and the exclusive use of this colour by widows among women indicates their continued association with asexuality and death" (1995, 2251–252). Following this logic, I would suggest that the alternating white and red beads worn by *jogatis* mark their alternating status: now a *muttaide*, now a *randi*.

2 Sometimes the male and dominant caste priests at Saundatti conduct these dedication rites, which has led to charges that these priests sexually exploit the girls whose dedication rites they officiate. It is by no means out of the question that these charges are true, but my research did not substantiate them, and in any case they seem dubious on practical grounds. Eight to ten years pass between the time of dedication and the onset of maturity, when devadasis become sexually active, and ongoing ties are tenuous at best between the Lingayat priests active at the main temple and the women whose ritual of dedication they conduct or have conducted in the past.

3 For an extended discussion of this "redistributive" economy of food, as Arjun Appadurai has termed it (1981, 18; 505–6), and *prasada* in the context of South Indian temples, see his *Worship and Conflict under Colonial Rule*.

4 Yamuna offered a delightful mix of caste categories in this list. Samagar and Holeyar are considered to be untouchable *jatis*. Harijan is Gandhi's designation for those formerly referred to as untouchable, a designation unrecognized in the Indian constitution. Wada is the Marathi term for a fortification, and here it designates the Brahman family who lived beyond the old Maratha gate. Lingayats are the dominant caste in the region. Vokkaligar is the dominant *jati* in southern Karnataka, but the name is used in Nandipur by Dalits to refer to members of upper castes in general. Sahukar and Gowda, terms for landlord, were used similarly. Inamdar refers to the Muslim community, Jain to the Jain. Koruba are the middle *jati* shepherding caste.

5 For an extended discussion of intercaste prestations and the difference between the axes of auspiciousness/inauspiciousness and purity/pollution in relation to

the constitution of hierarchies, as well as forms of interdependence, among caste communities in rural Uttar Pradesh, see Raheja 1988.

6 Unlike most village-based devadasis, brothel-based devadasis in towns or cities are not monogamous: they find cash for sex transactions to be more lucrative than patronage relations. For the purpose of my argument here, however, it is the similarities among dedicated women—whether village-based or brothel-based, that are most salient: marriage to the devi, lack of respectability, and economic responsibility for their natal family.

7 In Kerala in the nineteenth century Namboodiri Brahman families allowed only their eldest sons to marry within caste. Younger sons were expected to be "visiting husbands," a relationship contracted with a Nayar woman and consecrated by a rite called a *sambandham* that did not involve paternity or property rights. Among Nayars, matriliny combined with matrilocality and maternal uncles functioned as social fathers for the children of their sisters. See Janaki Abraham (2011) for an especially useful consideration of this form of marriage.

8 Working from Lévi-Strauss's *Elementary Structures of Kinship* (1969), Rubin theorizes compulsory heterosexuality as an effect of the division of labor by sex, which creates sexual difference and complementarity, and the incest taboo, which implies a prior unstated taboo against homosexuality. If the incest taboo works to divide the marriageable from the unmarriageable—categories whose definitions vary widely across cultures but are universally concerned exclusively with heterosexual possibilities—then, Rubin suggests, we can deduce a prior unspoken and unspeakable taboo on same-sex union. She writes: "The suppression of the homosexual component of human sexuality, and by corollary, the oppression of homosexuals, is therefore a product of the same system whose rules and relations oppress women" (1975, 180).

9 If same-sex desire, or homosexuality, is the constitutive outside to heterosexuality; cross-caste desire is the constitutive outside to caste endogamy, as Anupama Rao (2009, 235) points out. Liaisons across castes, therefore, have the potential to disturb the regulatory sexual economy of caste. In the early part of the twentieth century, anticaste radicals such as Jotirao Phule and E.V. Ramaswamy Naicker—or Periyar as he is more commonly called—critiqued both sexual purity and caste endogamy as fundamentally implicated in the reproduction of Brahmanical hegemony and called for intercaste marriages (Hodges 2005; A. Rao 2009, 50). However, as I have shown, sexual respectability has become central to projects of Dalit self-reform. One of the reasons for this, as Rao demonstrates in her work on the sexual politics of caste, is that the structural inequity of caste has produced an asymmetry among men, in which upper-caste men enjoy forms of extramarital sexual access to Dalit women while Dalit men are constrained from approaching upper-caste women (on this point, see also Kent 2004). The intersection of economies of caste and sexuality create a system in which upper-caste women are the most highly regulated (and thus the least circulating) and Dalit women are the least regulated (and most circulating). As I am arguing in this chapter, circu-

lation has its possibilities. At the same time, it is understandable that Dalit activists, both men and women, seek to bring symmetry to this system.

10 This form of cross-cousin marriage is ideal among caste Hindus in northern Karnataka. Here I frame it from the vantage point of a female ego. From the point of view of a male ego, as it is represented in most literature on alliance theory and classificatory kinship, it is referred to as elder sister's daughter marriage.

11 For a further ethnographic elaboration of the first client ceremony and its relationship to the onset of menses, see Orchard (2004, 213–18).

12 The owner of the house I rented.

13 See also Prabha Kotiswaran's (2012) feminist materialist analysis of sexual labor in India. She argues persuasively for the labor paradigm and against abolition through a nuanced consideration of legal frameworks and legislative effects in the everyday lives of female sex workers in Andhra Pradesh and Kolkata (formerly, Calcutta).

Chapter 5. Kinship Trouble

1 In a compelling structuralist analysis of this phenomenon, Nicholas Bradford writes: "Indeed, it is considered to be part of Yellamma's power and character to change a person's sex ('ganda hoogi henna maadataala, henna hoogi ganda maadataala')" (1983, 310).

2 Inga Hutter, an anthropologist who has been studying reproductive health since 1980 in the region where Yellamma is especially powerful, has also been told about these dreams and their effects. Young women told her about discontinuing sexual relations after having Yellamma come to them in a dream (personal communication, December 18, 2001).

3 This is the third person singular honorific pronoun. I use the Kannada pronoun here throughout because it allows me to remain closer to the speaker's utterance, in which the pronoun is gender neutral—a possibility English grammar does not permit. In order to avoid confusion, when the case is possessive, I follow English grammar, "avaru's" rather than using the Kannada, "avara."

4 Here I am referring to the claim made within the sociology of India that persons are substantialized through exchanges through others. For the relationship between the substantialization of persons and the embodiment of sex or gender, see especially Lamb 2000 and Busby 2000. The classic work on caste as a substance is the now much criticized Louis Dumont's Homo Hierarchicus (1970). For an especially powerful critical analysis of anthropological accounts of caste as a substantial form of relatedness, see Williams 1995.

5 The phrase "gender trouble" comes from Judith Butler, who has written: "There is no gender identity behind the expressions of gender; . . . identity is performatively constituted by the very 'expressions' that are said to be its results" (1990, 25). Butler has called for gender trouble—subversive confusion and promiscuous proliferation of genders—and therefore identity, beyond the binary.

6 For an interesting discussion of this iconography, see Evans 1998.

7 It also bears some resemblance to cultural feminist accounts of the origins of the oppression of women and its remedy in the reestablishment of gynocentric and matrifocal cultures. See, for instance, Gimbutas 1989. For a feminist critique of the recuperative project of cultural feminism, see K. Young 1991.

8 Friedrich Engels (1985) famously went on to develop this link between the advent of private property, family form, and the state.

9 It is no doubt evident to the reader that the public policy implications of such evaluations are tremendous. For critiques of Daniel Patrick Moynihan's famous report (1965), which interpreted the large proportion of female-headed households among African Americans as a negative sign of the group's general condition, see Davis 1971; Hooks 2003. For a discussion of U.S. family policy in the context of overhauls of welfare policy and the myth of the welfare mother, see Quadagno 1994. For considerations of the politics of same-sex parenting in the context of U.S. debates over marriage equality, see Cole, Avery, Dodson, and Goodman 2012 and Joslin 2011.

10 This kind of structuralist inquiry, based on the model of comparative linguistics, has been pursued most recently in the Dravidian context by Thomas Trautmann. He draws on historical and ethnographic data to reconstruct "Proto Dravidian" kinship (1995, 229–37). His study exemplifies what is useful about the structural analysis of kinship as a system governed by rules, norms, and taboos. Because Trautmann discusses both historical change and geographic variation in Dravidian kinship, he demonstrates the way kinship functions as a regulative field without ignoring the ways it is also produced through human actions.

11 "Kinship burns" is Kapadia's translation of the Tamil expression, "*sondam sudum*" (1996, 44). On the differences between Brahman and non-Brahman women in a South Indian village, see Ullrich 1977.

12 For an important exception and consideration of a marriage that cannot quite count as a marriage, see S. Pinto 2012.

13 On kinship among *hijras*, see G. Reddy 2005. On female renunciates, see Khandelwal 2004; Khandelwal et al. 2006. For a consideration of the kin making practices of peripatetic performers stigmatized as public women, see Seizer 2005.

14 Oldenburg undertook this study when her review of tax records for 1858–77 indicated that "the dancing and singing girls" (260) were in the highest tax bracket and had the largest individual incomes in the city. This research also demonstrated their support for the rebellion against colonial rule in 1857 (1990, 259).

15 For a study of the cultural production of female offspring as sons in Albania, see A. Young 2000.

16 For historical accounts of this process in the areas currently comprising the states of Maharastra and Karnataka, see A. Rao 2009; Sturman 2001.

17 To briefly explain these kinship terms: A parallel cousin is a cousin from a father's brother or a mother's sister, while a cross-cousin is from a father's sister or a mother's brother. A cross-cousin marriage takes place between a daughter and one of her cross-cousins (father's sister's son or mother's brother's son) or a son and one of his cross-cousins (mother's brother's daughter or father's sister's daughter) whereas

a parallel-cousin marriage takes place between a daughter and her mother's sister's son or father's brother's son and so forth. This reckoning of kin extends across generations and beyond first cousins. For instance, a mother's mother's brother's daughter's daughter would be a permissible cross-cousin match for a son. In the Dravidian region, matrilateral cross-cousin marriage is preferred and includes alliances between daughter's and their mother's brother (maternal uncle marriage).

18 Variations on this pattern are common. For instance, the mother's brother's son, or mother's male cousin's son, and so forth. From the perspective of a man, the elder sister's daughter is the ideal marriage partner.

19 For other work on *jogappas*, see Bradford 1983; Gayatri Reddy 2005. Reddy's wonderful ethnography of *jogins* dedicated to Yellamma in Andhra Pradesh, like her work more broadly on *hijras*, frames her subjects within multiple registers of identity—kinship, race, class, caste, and religion—rather than just the axis of sexual difference. This framing, which I follow in my discussion of *jogappas*, is also evident in the work of Lawrence Cohen (1995).

20 One *tola* is equivalent to approximately twelve grams.

21 For an elaboration of kin making as a technology of the human, see Ramberg (2013, 671).

Chapter 6. Troubling Kinship

1 Two important recent exceptions are found in Kalpana Ram's (2013) work on possession in South India and Frédérique Apffel-Marglin's (2011) work on ritual in the Andes and East India.

2 I am grateful to Chris Roebuck for this phrasing.

3 On this point, see also Fernando 2010; Mahmood 2004; Ram 2013; Scott 2004.

4 See also Marcella Althaus-Reid's (2000, 2003) readings of Latin American Catholic rites as scenes enacting dominant orders of sexuality and gender.

GLOSSARY

aarthi An offering of fire, usually a camphor flame, to an ancestor, god or person; the waving of a lamp before another, generally in a clockwise direction.

aata Game, play, sport.

akkatangi Sisters (literally, elder sister younger sister).

ambli Buttermilk fortified with millet flour.

amma Mother.

ammawase The new moon.

avaru The third person neutral pronoun, plural or singular honorific.

basavi A woman dedicated to a deity in Karnataka (literally, a female bull).

bettale seve Naked worship.

bhajan A devotional song.

bhaktaru Devotee.

bhakti Devotion.

bhandara Yellamma's turmeric.

cakka Paternal uncle.

chela Disciple.

chowdiki A one-stringed instrument typically played only by those dedicated to Yellamma.

darshan Sight or vision, to see and be seen by the deity.

devaru The god, the goddess, the gods.

dhandewali A woman in business, sex worker.

dhandha Business, occupation, a common euphemism for prostitution.

dhandha maaduvudu A common expression for sex work; literally, to do business.

ganda Husband, man.

ganda udugi A masculine woman (literally, wrapped or dressed as a man).

gandharva Otherworldly beings (literally, fragrance eaters).

gandullavalu Women with living husbands (see note 2 in the introduction).

gellate Commotion, riot.

gotra Patrilineal clan.

grammadevata South Indian village gods and goddesses.

guddha Hill.

harake Vow or promise by a devotee to make offerings to a deity or perform bodily sacrifices in exchange for a boon; also a blessing from or invocation of the deity.

helikke Oracle (literally, speaking or telling).

holige A pastry made with flour and jaggery.

hunnime The full moon.

hotte Stomach.

inam Land grants or usufruct rights in land.

inamdar A person holding an *inam*.

ittukondaru A patron, one who keeps a woman.

jade Matted locks of hair.

jaga Basket, world.

janma Family life.

jati Community, subcaste.

jatra Fair, festival, pilgrimage.

joga Alms; usually parched grain.

jogamma Someone who asks for *joga*, or alms; a wandering mendicant; one of the terms referring to women dedicated to Yellamma.

jogappa A male woman dedicated to Yellamma who asks for *joga*, or alms; a wandering mendicant.

jogati A female woman dedicated to Yellamma who asks for *joga*, or alms; a wandering mendicant.

jogini A woman dedicated to a deity in Andhra Pradesh.

kaadaata Trouble from the gods, distinct from everyday difficulty (*kashta*).

kettada keilasa Sex work (literally, bad work).

kumkuma Vermillion powder used for blessing, especially to mark auspiciousness; what married women press into the part in their hair or in a dot on their forehead; figuratively: marital status.

liila The play or dance of the gods.

maduve Marriage.

mahalwari Village collective system of cultivation.

mahar vatan A form of untaxed heritable land grant attached to caste-specific labors.

mahima Miraculous power, mystery.

mailige A contaminated or contaminating state, spoiled or spoiling, impure.

maji devadasi Ex-devadasi.

malak (Marathi) Patron, lover, husband, boss.

mane devaru Family deity, literally god of the house.

mangalasutra A necklace tied around a woman's neck at the time of marriage.

murti The form of the deity, usually composed of wood, stone or metal (literally, embodiment).

muttaide A wife; a married woman whose husband is alive; also, the auspicious status of such a woman.

muttu Beads, pearls; specifically those that are strung into a necklace and tied around the neck at the time of dedication.

nambikke Belief.

navedya Freshly cooked food offered to a deity.

nedaru The evil eye.

nityasumangali An ever married (to a diety) thus always auspicious woman.

paapa Sin.

paddati Tradition, custom.

pallu The loose end of a sari.

panchayat Governing council, traditionally composed of five (*panch*) members.

pativrata A celibate ecstatic, the term used by many female ecstatics to refer their vow of celibacy (literally, vow of devotion to the lord).

phere Rounds.

prasada Food offered to, tasted by, and thus blessed by the deity.

puja Worship, ritual, rite.

pujari Priest, caretaker of the deity, one who conducts *puja*

randi Widow, whore.

randi hunnime The festival marking the widowhood of Yellamma observed every year at the time of the full moon in the winter month of Pousha, which falls in December or January of the Roman calendar.

ryotwari Individual cultivator system of land cultivation.

sangha Community; traditionally a monastic order or community, often used to refer to self-help groups and community based organizations in contemporary parlance.

seve Service, worship.

shakti Female or feminine energy or power.

shanti Peace.

shastras Hindu text or scripture.

shruti A one-stringed instrument typically played only by those dedicated to Yellamma.

sudras Agriculturalists, laborers; the fourth Varna as prescribed in the Hindu text, the *Rig Veda*.

sukha Happiness.

sule Prostitute.

tali Marriage necklace.

tilak A religious or sectarian mark made with paste or powder on the body.

udaya Spontaneous stone, miraculous self-manifestation of a god in the physical landscape.

udi Lap or womb.

udi tumbuwudu A rite of fertility (literally, filling the lap or womb).

veshya Prostitute.

yogini A female mystic or tantrika; a renunciate who embodies the devi.

zamindari A system of landholding and revenue collection by zamindars; the land held or administered by a zamindar.

BIBLIOGRAPHY

Abeysekara, Ananda. 2008. *The Politics of Postsecular Religion: Mourning Secular Futures*. New York: Columbia University Press.

Abraham, Janaki. 2011. "'Why did you send me like this?': Marriage, Matriliny and the 'Providing Husband' in North Kerala, India." *Asian Journal of Women's Studies* 17 (2): 32–64.

Abu-Lughod, Lila. 2002. "Do Muslim Women Really Need Saving? Anthropological Reflections on Cultural Relativism and Its Others." *American Anthropologist* 104 (3): 783–90.

Agarwal, Bina. 1994. *A Field of One's Own: Gender and Land Rights in South Asia*. New Delhi, India: Cambridge University Press.

Agarwal, Bina. 1998. "Widows versus Daughters or Widows as Daughters? Property, Land and Economic Security in Rural India." *Modern Asian Studies* 32 (1): 1–48.

Agustín, Laura. 2005. "At Home in the Street: Questioning the Desire to Help and Save." In *Regulating Sex: The Politics of Intimacy and Identity*, edited by E. Bernstein and L. Schaffner, 67–82. New York: Routledge.

Althaus-Reid, Marcella. 2000. *Indecent Theology: Theological Perversions in Sex, Gender, and Politics*. London: Routledge.

Althaus-Reid, Marcella. 2003. *The Queer God*. London: Routledge.

Apffel-Marglin, Frédérique. 1985. *Wives of the God-King: The Rituals of the Devadasis of Puri*. New York: Oxford University Press.

Apffel-Marglin, Frédérique. 2008. *Rhythms of Life: Enacting the World with the Goddesses of Orissa*. New Delhi, India: Oxford University Press.

Apffel-Marglin, Frédérique. 2011. *Subversive Spiritualities: How Rituals Enact the World*. New York: Oxford University Press.

Appadurai, Arjun. 1981. *Worship and Conflict under Colonial Rule: A South Indian Case*. Cambridge: Cambridge University Press.

Appu, P. S. 1966. *Land Reforms in India*. New Delhi, India: Vikas.

Arondekar, Anjali. 2012. "Subject to Sex: A Small History of the Gomantak Maratha Samaj." In *South Asian Feminisms*, edited by A. Loomba and R. A. Lukose, 244–66. Durham, NC: Duke University Press.

Asad, Talal. 1993. *Genealogies of Religion: Discipline and Reasons of Power in Christianity and Islam*. Baltimore, MD: Johns Hopkins University Press.

Asad, Talal. 2003. *Formations of the Secular: Christianity, Islam, Modernity*. Stanford, CA: Stanford University Press.

Assayag, Jackie. 1992. *La colère de la déesse décapitée: Traditions, cultes et pouvoir dans le sud de L'Inde*. Paris: Centre National de la Recherche Scientifique.

Austin, J. L. 1962. *How to Do Things with Words*. Cambridge, MA: Harvard University Press.

Babb, Lawrence. 1970. "Marriage and Malevolence: The Uses of Sexual Opposition in a Hindu Pantheon." *Ethnology* 9 (2): 137–48.

Babb, Lawrence. 1988. "Indigenous Feminism in a Modern Hindu Sect." In *Women in Indian Society: A Reader*, edited by Rehana Ghadially, 270–87. New Delhi, India: Sage.

Babb, Lawrence. 2002. "Parasuram's Sacrifice: A Myth and Its Local Travels." In *Culture, Communities and Change*, edited by Varsha Joshi, 133–53. Jaipur, India: Rawat.

Bacchetta, Paola. 2004. *Gender in the Hindu Nation: RSS Women as Ideologues*. New Delhi, India: Women Unlimited.

Bachofen, Johan Jakob. 1861. *Das Mutterrecht*. Stuttgart, Germany: Krais and Hoffman.

Bailey, Michael D. 2007. *Magic and Superstition in Europe: A Concise History from Antiquity to the Present*. Lanham, MD: Rowman and Littlefield.

Banerjee, Abhijit, and Laxshmi Iyer. 2005. "History, Institutions and Economic Performance: The Legacy of Colonial Land Tenure Systems in India." *The American Economic Review*, 95 (4): 1190–213.

Banerjee, Sumata. 2000. *Dangerous Outcaste: The Prostitute in Nineteenth-Century Bengal*. Calcutta, India: Seagull.

Barrett, Michele, and Mary McIntosh. 1982. *The Anti-Social Family*. London: New Left Books.

Barry, Kathleen. 1995. *The Prostitution of Sexuality*. New York: New York University Press.

Basu, Srimati. 1999. *She Comes to Take Her Rights: Indian Women, Property, and Propriety*. Albany: State University of New York Press.

Beard, Mary, and John Henderson. 1997. "With This Body I Thee Worship: Sacred Prostitution in Antiquity." *Gender and History* 9 (3): 480–503.

Beck, Brenda. 1969. "Colour and Heat in South Indian Ritual." *Man* 4 (4): 553–72.

Bhattacharyya, Narendra Natha. [1977] 1999. *The Indian Mother Goddess*. New Delhi: Manohar.

Bhattacharyya, Narendra Natha. 1982. *History of the Tantric Religion: A Historical, Ritualistic, and Philosophical Study*. New Delhi, India: Manohar.

Blackburn, Stuart H., and A. K. Ramanujan. 1986. Introduction to *Another Harmony: New Essays on the Folklore of India*. Berkeley: University of California Press.

Borneman, John. 1977. "Caring and Being Cared For: Displacing Marriage, Kinship, Gender and Sexuality." *International Social Science Journal* 49 (154): 573–84.

Borneman, John. 1996. "Until Death Do Us Part: Marriage/Death in Anthropological Discourse." *American Ethnologist* 23 (2): 215–38.

Bradford, Nicholas J. 1976. "Affine and Devotee: A Study of the Lingayat Sect of North Karnataka." PhD diss., University of Sussex, UK.

Bradford, Nicholas J. 1983. "Transgenderism and the Cult of Yellamma: Heat, Sex and Sickness in South Indian Ritual." *Journal of Anthropological Research* 39 (1): 307–22.

Breckenridge, Carol Appadurai, and Peter van der Veer, eds. 1993. *Orientalism and the Postcolonial Predicament: Perspectives on South Asia*. Philadelphia: University of Pennsylvania Press.

Briggs, Charles, and Richard Bauman. 1990. "Poetics and Performance as Critical Perspectives on Language and Social Life." *Annual Review of Anthropology* 19:59–88.

Brown, Jennifer, Kripa Ananthpur, and Renee Giovarelli. 2002. *Women's Access and Rights to Land in Karnataka*. Seattle, WA: Rural Development Institute.

Brubaker, Richard L. 1978. *The Ambivalent Mistress: A Study of South Indian Village Goddesses and Their Religious Meaning*. PhD diss., University of Chicago.

Busby, Cecilia. 2000. *The Performance of Gender: An Anthropology of Everyday Life in a South Indian Fishing Village*. London: Athlone.

Butler, Judith. 1990. *Gender Trouble: Feminism and the Subversion of Identity*. New York: Routledge.

Butler, Judith. 1993. "The Lesbian Phallus and the Morphological Imaginary." In *Bodies That Matter: On the Discursive Limits of "Sex,"* 57–91. New York: Routledge.

Butler, Judith. 2000. *Antigone's Claim: Kinship between Life and Death*. New York: Columbia University Press.

Butler, Judith. 2004. *Precarious Life: The Powers of Violence and Mourning*. London: Verso.

Caldwell, Sarah. 1999. *Oh Terrifying Mother: Sexuality, Violence, and Worship of the Goddess Kali*. New York: Oxford University Press.

Cannell, Fenella. 2005. "The Christianity of Anthropology." *Journal of the Royal Anthropological Institute* 11 (2): 335–56.

Carsten, Janet. 2000. *Cultures of Relatedness: New Approaches to the Study of Kinship*. New York: Cambridge University Press.

Chakrabarty, Dipesh. 2000. *Provincializing Europe: Postcolonial Thought and Historical Difference*. Princeton, NJ: Princeton University Press.

Chakravarti, Uma. 1989. "Whatever Happened to the Vedic Dasi? Orientalism, Nationalism and a Script for the Past." In *Recasting Women: Essays in Indian Colonial History*, edited by Kumkum Sangari and Sudesh Vaid, 27–87. New Delhi: Kali for Women.

Chakravarti, Uma. 1995. "Gender, caste and labour: ideological and material structure of widowhood." *Economic and Political Weekly* 30 (36), 2248–256.

Clarke, Sathianathan. 1998. "Paraiyars Ellaiyamman as an Iconic Symbol of Collective Resistance and Emancipatory Mythography." In *Religions of the Marginalized: Towards a Phenomenology and the Methodology of Study*, edited by Gnana Robinson, 35–53. Bangalore, India: Indian Society for Promoting Christian Knowledge for United Theological College.

Cohen, Lawrence. 1995. "The Pleasures of Castration: The Postoperative Status of Hijras, Jankhas and Academics." In *Sexual Nature, Sexual Culture*, edited by Paul R. Abramson and Steven D. Pinkerton, 276–304. Chicago: University of Chicago Press.

Cohen, Lawrence. 1998. *No Aging in India: Alzheimer's, the Bad Family, and Other Modern Things*. Berkeley: University of California Press.

Cohen, Lawrence. 2003. "Transplants and the Problem of Operability." Paper presented at the conference Rotten Trade: Traffic in Humans, Whole and in Parts, Berkeley, California, April 24.

Cohen, Lawrence. 2004. "Operability: Surgery at the Margin of the State." In *Anthropology in the Margins of the State*, edited by Veena Das and Deborah Poole, 165–90. Sante Fe, NM: School of American Research Press.

Cohen, Lawrence. 2005. "Commitment." Paper presented at the conference Practicing Theory, Theorizing Practice: Physician Scholars in the Social Sciences and Humanities, San Francisco, California, May 14.

Cohen, Lawrence. 2013. "Given Over to Demand: Excorporation as Commitment." *Contemporary South Asia* 21 (3): 318–32.

Cole, Elizabeth R., Lanice R. Avery, Catherine Dodson, and Kevin D. Goodman. 2012. "Against Nature: How Arguments About the Naturalness of Marriage Privilege Heterosexuality." *Journal of Social Issues* 68 (1): 46–62.

Collier, Jane Fishburne, and Sylvia Junko Yanagisako, eds. 1987. *Gender and Kinship: Essays toward a Unified Analysis*. Stanford, CA: Stanford University Press.

Comaroff, John L., and Jean Comaroff. 1980. *The Meaning of Marriage Payments*. London: Academic.

Committee for Study on Farmers' Suicides. 2002. "Farmers' Suicides in Karnataka: A Scientific Analysis." Bangalore, India: Government of Karnataka.

Conkey, Margaret, and Ruth Tringham. 1995. "Archaeology and the Goddess: Exploring the Contours of Feminist Archaeology." In *Feminisms in the Academy*, edited by Domna C. Stanton and Abigail J. Stewart, 199–247. Ann Arbor: University of Michigan Press.

Dalmia, Vasudha. 1995. "'The Only Real Religion of the Hindus': Vaisnava Self-representation in the Late Nineteenth Century." In *Representing Hinduism: the Construction of Religious Traditions and National Identity*, edited by Vasudha Dalmia and Heinrich von Stietencron, 176–210. New Delhi, India: Sage.

Dalmia, Vasudha, and Heinrich Von Steitencron. 1995a. Introduction to *Representing Hinduism: The Construction of Religious Traditions and National Identity*, edited by Vasudha Dalmia and Heinrich Von Steitencron, 17–32. New Delhi: Sage.

Dalmia, Vasudha, and Heinrich Von Steitencron, eds. 1995b. *Representing Hinduism: The Construction of Religious Traditions and National Identity*. New Delhi: Sage.

Daly, Mary. [1973] 1985. *Beyond God the Father: Toward a Philosophy of Women's Liberation*. Boston: Beacon.

Daniel, E. Valentine. 1984. *Fluid Signs: Being a Person the Tamil Way*. Berkeley: University of California Press.

Das, Veena. 1983. "Language of Sacrifice." *Man*, n.s., 18 (3): 445–62.

Das, Veena. 1989. "Subaltern as Perspective." In *Subaltern Studies VI: Writings on South Asian History and Society*, edited by Ranajit Guha, 310–24. Delhi: Oxford University Press.

Das, Veena. 2007. *Life and Words: Violence and the Descent into the Ordinary*. Berkeley: University of California Press.

Datar, Chaya. 1992. "Reform or a New Form of Patriarchy? Devadasis in the Border Region of Maharashtra and Karnataka." *Indian Journal of Social Work* 53 (1): 81–91.

Davis, Angela Y. 1971. "Reflections on the Black Woman's Role in the Community of Slaves." *Black Scholar* 3 (4): 2–15.

Dempsey, Corinne. 2005. "Double Take: Through the Eyes of Yaksis, Yaksas, and Yoginis." *Journal of the American Academy of Religion* 73 (1): 3–7.

Denton, Lynn Teskey. 2004. *Female Ascetics in Hinduism*. Albany: State University of New York Press.

Deshpande, R. S., and D. V. Gopalappa. 2004. "Economic Poverty and Inequalities." In *Poverty, Marginalization and Empowerment in Karnataka*, edited by John Desrochers and Paulson V. Veliyannoor. Bangalore, India: Karnataka Regional Conference of Religious Justice and Peace Cell.

Desrochers, John, and Paulson V. Veliyannoor, eds. 2004. *Poverty, Marginalization and Empowerment in Karnataka*. Bangalore: Karnataka Regional Conference of Religious Justice and Peace Cell.

Dirks, Nicholas B. 1988. *The Hollow Crown: Ethnohistory of an Indian Kingdom*. New York: Cambridge University Press.

Dirks, Nicholas B. 1993. *The Hollow Crown: Ethnohistory of an Indian Kingdom*. Ann Arbor, MI: University of Michigan Press.

Dirks, Nicholas B. 1997. "The Policing of Tradition: Colonialism and Anthropology in Southern India." *Comparative Studies in Society and History* 39 (1): 182–212.

Dirks, Nicholas B. 2001. *Castes of Mind: Colonialism and the Making of Modern India*. New Delhi: Permanent Black.

Douglas, Mary. 1990. "Introduction." In *The Gift: The Form and Reason for Exchange in Archaic Societies*, Marcel Mauss. Translated by W. D. Halls. New York: W. W. Norton.

Douglas, Mary. 2002. *Purity and Danger: An Analysis of the Concepts of Pollution and Taboo*. 2nd ed. London: Routledge.

Dube, Leela. 1997. *Women and Kinship: Comparative Perspectives on Gender in South and South-East Asia*. New Delhi, India: Vistaar.

Dumont, Louis. 1970. *Homo Hierarchicus: The Caste System and Its Implications*, translated by Nature of Human Societies Series. Chicago: University of Chicago Press.

Dumont, Louis. 1983. *Affinity as a Value: Marriage Alliance in South India, with Comparative Essays on Australia*. Chicago: University of Chicago Press.

Eck, Diana L. 1996. *Darsán: Seeing the Divine Image in India*. 3rd ed. New York: Columbia University Press.

Elmore, Mark. 2005. "States of Religion: Postcolonialism, Power and the Formation of Himachal Pradesh." PhD diss., University of California, Santa Barbara.

Elmore, Mark. 2007. "Definitional Transgression, or the Revenge of the Vernacular in Hindu Tantric Studies." *Religion Compass* 1 (6): 752–67.

Elmore, Mark. 2011. *Bloody Boundaries: Animal Sacrifice and the Labor of Religion.* In Secularism and Religion-Making, edited by Markus Dressler and Arvind Mandair, 209–25. New York: Oxford University Press.

Elmore, Wilber Theodore. [1913] 1984. *Dravidian Gods in Modern Hinduism.* New Delhi: Asian Educational Services.

Engels, Friedrich. 1985. *The Origin of the Family, Private Property, and the State.* Harmondsworth, UK: Penguin.

Epp, Linda. 1992. "Dalit Struggle, Nude Worship, and the 'Chandragutti Incident.'" *Sociological Bulletin* 41 (1–2): 145–66.

Epp, Linda. 1997. "Violating the Sacred? The Social Reforms of Devadasis among Dalits in Karnataka, India." PhD diss., York University.

Erndl, Kathleen M. 1993. *Victory to the Mother: The Hindu Goddess of Northwest India in Myth, Ritual, and Symbol.* New York: Oxford University Press.

Evans, Kirsti. 1998. "Contemporary Devadasis: Empowered Auspicious Women or Exploited Prostitutes?" *Bulletin of the John Rylands University Library of Manchester* 80 (3): 23–38.

Faier, Lieba. 2009. *Intimate Encounters: Filipina Women and the Remaking of Rural Japan.* Berkeley: University of California Press.

Favret-Saada, Jeanne. 1980. *Deadly Words: Witchcraft in the Bocage.* Cambridge: Cambridge University Press.

Favret-Saada, Jeanne. 1989. "Unbewitching as Therapy." *American Ethnologist* 16 (1): 40–56.

Favret-Saada, Jeanne. 1990. "About Participation." *Culture, Medicine and Psychiatry* 14 (2): 189–99.

Fernando, Mayanthi L. 2010. "Reconfiguring Freedom: Muslim Piety and the Limits of Secular Law and Public Discourse in France." *American Ethnologist* 37 (1): 19–35.

Fitzgerald, Timothy. 1999. "Politics and Ambedkar Buddhism in Maharashtra." In *Buddhism and Politics in Twentieth Century Asia,* edited by Ian Charles Harris, 79–104. London: Pinter.

Flood, Gavin. 1998. *An Introduction to Hinduism.* Cambridge: Cambridge University Press.

Flueckiger, Joyce Burkhalter. 2013. *When the World Becomes Female: Guises of a South Indian Goddess.* Bloomington: Indiana University Press.

Fortune, Reo Franklin, and Bronislaw Malinowski. 1932. *Sorcerers of Dobu: The Social Anthropology of the Dobu Islanders of the Western Pacific.* New York: E. P. Dutton.

Foucault, Michel. 1978. *The History of Sexuality.* Translated by Robert Hurley. New York: Pantheon.

Foucault, Michel. 1984. "Nietzsche, Genealogy, History." In *The Foucault Reader,* edited by Paul Rabinow, 76–100. New York: Pantheon.

Foulston, Lynn. 2002. *At the Feet of the Goddess: The Divine Feminine in Local Hindu Religion*. Portland, OR: Sussex Academic.

Franklin, Sarah, and Susan McKinnon. 2001. *Relative Values: Reconfiguring Kinship Studies*. Durham, NC: Duke University Press.

Friedman, Robert I. 1996. "India's Shame: Sexual Slavery and Political Corruption Are Leading to an AIDS Catastrophe." *Nation*, April 8: 11–18.

Fuller, C. J. 1992. *The Camphor Flame: Popular Hinduism and Society in India*. Princeton, NJ: Princeton University Press.

Galanter, Marc. 1971. "Hinduism, Secularism, and the Indian Judiciary." *Philosophy East and West* 21 (4): 467.

Ganguly, Debjani. 2005. *Caste, Colonialism and Counter-Modernity: Notes on a Postcolonial Hermeneutics of Caste*. New York: Routledge.

Gaston, Anne-Marie. 1996. *Bharata Natyam: From Temple to Theatre*. New Delhi: Manohar.

Gatwood, Lynn E. 1985. *Devi and the Spouse Goddess: Women, Sexuality, and Marriages in India*. Riverdale, MD: Riverdale Co.

Ghosh, Durba. 2006. *Sex and the Family in Colonial India: The Making of Empire*. New York: Cambridge University Press.

Gilada, Ishwarprasad S. 1993. *Child Prostitution: A Blot on Humanity*. Bombay: Indian Health Organization.

Gimbutas, Marija. 1989. *The Language of the Goddess*. San Francisco: Harper and Row.

Goldenberg, Naomi R. 1979. *Changing of the Gods: Feminism and the End of Traditional Religions*. Boston: Beacon.

Gough, Kathleen. 1959. "The Nayars and the Definition of Marriage." *Journal of the Royal Anthropological Institute of Great Britain and Ireland* 89 (1): 23–34.

Gupta, Akhil, and James Ferguson. 1997. "Discipline and Practice: 'The Field' as Site, Method, and Location in Anthropology." In *Anthropological Locations: Boundaries and Grounds of a Field Science*, edited by Akhil Gupta and James Ferguson, 1–46. Berkeley: University of California Press.

Guru, Gopal. 2001. "The Interface between Ambedkar and the Dalit Cultural Movement." In *Maharashtra Dalit Identity and Politics*, edited by Ghanshyam Shah, 160–94. New Delhi, India: Sage.

Gurumurthy, K. G. 1992. *Harakeya Hennu: Devadasi Sampradayada Bagege Samsodhita Lekhanagalu*. Athani, India: Vimochana Prakashana.

Gurumurthy, K. G. 1996. "Status of Women under Devadasi Custom." In *Cross Cultural Research and Other Anthropological Essays*, edited by K. G. Gurumurthy, 130–45. New Delhi, India: Reliance.

Guttal, Shalmali. 2003. "Farmers' Suicides in Karnataka State." In *Focus on the Global South*.

Hanstad, Tim, Robin Nielsen and Jennifer Brown. 2004. *Meeting the Goals of Land Reform: An Analysis of the Effectiveness of the Legal Framework Governing Rural Land Policy in India*. Paper prepared under contract with The World Bank. Rural Development Institute USA.

Haraway, Donna Jeanne. 1991. "'Gender' for a Marxist Dictionary: The Sexual Politics of a Word." In *Simians, Cyborgs, and Women: The Reinvention of Nature*, 127–48. New York: Routledge.

Hardiman, David. 1985. "From Custom to Crime: The Politics of Drinking in Colonial South Gujarat." In *Subaltern Studies IV: Writings on South Asian History and Society*, edited by Ranajit Guha, 165–228. Delhi, India: Oxford University Press.

Harman, William. 2012. "From Fierce to Domesticated: Mariyamman Joins the Middle Class." *Nidan: Journal for the Study of Hinduism* 24: 41–65.

Harris, Sarah. n.d. "India—Holy Whore Story." Vice. Accessed November 4, 2013. http://www.vice.com/en_se/read/india-holy-whore-story.

Hawley, John Stratton, and Donna Marie Wulff. 1998. *Devi: Goddesses of India*. Delhi: Motitlal Banasidass.

Hayden, Corinne P. 1995. "Gender, Genetics, and Generation: Reformulating Biology in Lesbian Kinship." *Cultural Anthropology* 10 (1): 41–63.

Heidegger, Martin. 1975. *Poetry, Language, Thought*. Translated by Albert Hofstadter. New York: Harper and Row.

Hirschkind, Charles. 2011. "Is There a Secular Body?" *Cultural Anthropology* 26 (4): 633–47.

Hodges, Sarah. 2005. "'Looting' the Lock Hospital in Colonial Madras during the Famine Years of the 1870s." *Social History of Medicine* 18 (3): 379–98.

hooks, bell. 2003. *Rock My Soul: Black People and Self-Esteem*. New York: Atria.

Hubert, Henri, and Marcel Mauss. [1964] 1981. *Sacrifice: Its Nature and Function*. Chicago: University of Chicago Press.

Hutter, Inge. 1994. *Being Pregnant in Rural South India: Nutrition of Women and Well-Being of Children*. Amsterdam: Thesis Publishers.

Ilaiah, Kancha. 2006. "Why I Am Not a Hindu." In *Gender and Caste*, edited by Anupama Rao, 80–85. New Delhi, India: Kali for Women.

Inden, Ronald B. 1990. *Imagining India*. Oxford: Basil Blackwell.

Inden, Ronald B., and R. W. Nicholas. 1977. *Kinship in Bengali Culture*. Chicago: University of Chicago Press.

Irigaray, Luce. 1985. *This Sex Which Is Not One*. Translated by Catherine Porter and Carolyn Burke. Ithaca, NY: Cornell University Press.

John, Mary E. 2000. "Globalization, Sexuality and the Visual Field." In *A Question of Silence? The Sexual Economies of Modern India*, edited by Mary E. John and Janaki Nair, 368–96. New Delhi, India: Kali for Women.

John, Mary E., and Janaki Nair. 2000a. Introduction to *A Question of Silence? The Sexual Economies of Modern India*, edited by Mary E. John and Janaki Nair, 1–51. New Delhi, India: Kali for Women.

John, Mary E., and Janaki Nair, eds. 2000b. *A Question of Silence?: The Sexual Economies of Modern India*. New Delhi: Kali for Women.

Joint Women's Programme. 1989. "Prostitution with Religious Sanction: The Devadasi Problem, Venkatasani/Jogini, and Basavi Cult." Banhi: An occasional journal. Calcutta: William Carey Study and Research Center.

Joint Women's Programme. 2001–2. *An Exploratory Study on Devadasi Rehabilitation*

Programme Initiated by Karnataka State Women's Development Corporation and SC/ST Corporation, Government of Karnataka in Northern Districts of Karnataka: Report Submitted to National Commission for Women, New Delhi. Bangalore: Joint Women's Programme.

Jordan, Kay. 1993. "Devadasi Reform: Driving the Priestesses or the Prostitutes out of Hindu Temples?" In *Religion and the Law in Independent India*, by Robert D. Baird, 257–78. New Delhi: Manohar.

Jordan, Kay. 2003. *From Sacred Servant to Profane Prostitute: A History of the Changing Legal Status of the Devadasis in India, 1857–1947*. New Delhi: Manohar.

Joslin, Courtney. 2011. "Searching for Harm: Same-Sex Marriage and the Well-being of Children." *Harvard Civil Rights-Civil Liberties Law Review (CR-CL)* 46 (81): 81–101.

Kamath, Suryanath U. 1983. *Karnataka State Gazetteer: Belgaum District*. Belgaum, India: Government of Karnataka.

Kannabiran, Kalpana. 1995. "Judiciary, Social Reform and Debate on 'Religious Prostitution' in Colonial India." *Economic and Political Weekly* 30 (43): 59–69.

Kannabiran, Vasanth, and Kalpana Kannabiran. 1991. "Caste and Gender: Understanding Dynamics of Power and Violence." *Economic and Political Weekly*, 26 (37): 2130–33.

Kannabiran, Kalpana, and Vasanth Kannabiran. 2003. "Framing the Web of Deceit." In *Muvalur Ramamirthammal's Web of Deceit: Devadasi Reform in Colonial India*. Edited by Kalpana Kannabiran, and Vasanth Kannabiran, 1–47. New Delhi, India: Zubaan.

Kapadia, Karin. 1996. *Siva and Her Sisters: Gender, Caste, and Class in Rural South India*. Delhi: Oxford University Press.

Kaplan, Caren, Norma Alarcón, and Minoo Moallem. 1999. *Between Woman and Nation: Nationalisms, Transnational Feminisms, and the State*. Durham, NC: Duke University Press.

Kapur, Ratna. 2001. "Post-Colonial Economies of Desire: Legal Representations of the Sexual Subaltern." *Denver University Law Review* 78 (4): 855–85.

Keane, Webb. 2002. "Sincerity, 'Modernity,' and the Protestants." *Cultural Anthropology* 17 (1): 65–92.

Kempadoo, Kamala, and Jo Doezema. 1998. *Global Sex Workers: Rights, Resistance, and Redefinition*. New York: Routledge.

Kent, Eliza F. 2004. *Converting Women: Gender and Protestant Christianity in Colonial South India*. Oxford: Oxford University Press.

Kersenboom-Story, Saskia C. 1987. *Nityasumangali: Devadasi Tradition in South India*. Delhi, India: Motilal Banarsidass.

Khandelwal, Meena. 2004. *Women in Ochre Robes: Gendering Hindu Renunciation*. Albany: State University of New York Press.

Khandelwal, Meena, Sondra L. Hausner, and Ann Grodzins Gold, eds. 2006. *Women's Renunciation in South Asia: Nuns, Yoginis, Saints, and Singers*. New York: Palgrave Macmillan.

King, Richard. 1999. *Orientalism and Religion: Postcolonial Theory, India and "the Mystic East."* Oxford: Oxford University Press.

Kinsley, David R. 1988. *Hindu Goddesses: Visions of the Divine Feminine in the Hindu Religious Tradition.* Berkeley: University of California Press.

Kishwar, Madhu. 2004. "The Power of Mother Sita in Modern India." *Hinduism Today* (October/November/December). Accessed December 18, 2013. http://www.hinduismtoday.com/modules/smartsection/item.php?itemid=1303.

Kittel, Ferdinand. [1894] 1994. *A Kannada-English Dictionary.* Mangalore, India: Basel Mission Book and Tract Depository.

Kodoth, Praveena. 2001. "Courting Legitimacy or Delegitimizing Custom? Sexuality, Sambandham, and Marriage Reform in Late Nineteenth-Century Malabar." *Modern Asian Studies* 35 (2): 349–84.

Kotiswaran, Prabha. 2001. "Preparing for Civil Disobedience: Indian Sex Workers and the Law." *Boston College Third World Law Journal* 21 (2): 161–242.

Kotiswaran, Prabha. 2012. *Dangerous Sex, Invisible Labor: Sex Work and the Law in India.* New Delhi: Oxford University Press.

Krishna, Anirudh and Abusaleh Shariff. 2011. "The Irrelevance of National Strategies? Rural Poverty Dynamics in States and Regions of India." *World Development* 39 (4): 533–49.

Kulick, Don. 1998. *Travesti: Sex, Gender, and Culture among Brazilian Transgendered Prostitutes.* Chicago: University of Chicago Press.

Kumar, Shiva. 2009. "Finally, an End to Devadasi System." *Times of India,* January 23.

Lamb, Sarah. 2000. *White Saris and Sweet Mangoes.* Berkeley: University of California Press.

Leach, Edmund. 1958. "Magical Hair." *Journal of the Royal Anthropological Institute of Great Britain and Ireland* 88 (2): 147–64.

Lévi-Strauss, Claude. 1969. *The Elementary Structures of Kinship.* Translated by James Harle Bell and John Richard von Sturmer. Boston: Beacon.

Levine, Philippa. 2000. "Orientalist Sociology and the Creation of Colonial Sexualities." *Feminist Review* 65: 5–21.

Madan, T. N. 1998. "Secularism in Its Place." In *Secularism and Its Critics,* edited by Rajeev Bhargava, 297–320. Delhi, India: Oxford University Press.

Mahale, Prabha. 1986. "Basavis of Karnatak: The Daughters Endowed with Masculine Privileges." *Eastern Anthropologist* 39 (2): 125–30.

Mahmood, Saba. 2001. "Feminist Theory, Embodiment and the Docile Agent: Reflections on the Egyptian Islamic Revival." *Cultural Anthropology* 16 (2): 202–36.

Mahmood, Saba. 2004. "Women's Agency Within Feminist Historiography." *The Journal of Religion* 84 (4): 573–79.

Mahmood, Saba. 2005. *Politics of Piety: The Islamic Revival and the Feminist Subject.* Princeton, NJ: Princeton University Press.

Mahmood, Saba. 2009. "Religious Reason and Secular Affect: An Incommensurable Divide?" *Critical Inquiry,* 35 (4): 836–62.

Mahmood, Saba. 2012. "Sexuality and Secularism: In Conversation with Joan Scott." Unpublished manuscript.

Malinowski, Bronislaw. 1922. *Argonauts of the Western Pacific: An Account of Native Enterprise and Adventure in the Archipelagos of Melanesian New Guinea.* London: G. Routledge and Sons.

Malinowski, Bronislaw. 1923. "The Problem of Meaning in Primitive Languages." In *The Meaning of Meaning,* edited by C. K. Ogden and I. A. Richards, 296–336. London: Routledge.

Malinowski, Bronislaw. 1930. "Kinship." *Man* 30 (2): 19–29.

Malinowski, Bronislaw. 1935. *Coral Gardens and Their Magic: A Study of the Methods of Tilling the Soil and of Agricultural Rites in the Trobriand Islands.* London: G. Allen and Unwin.

Mani, Lata. 1998. *Contentious Traditions: The Debate on Sati in Colonial India.* Berkeley: University of California Press.

Marriot, McKim. 1968. "Caste Ranking and Food Transactions: A Matrix Analysis." In *Structure and Change in Indian Society,* edited by Milton Singer and Bernard S. Cohn, 133–71. Chicago, IL: Aldine.

Marriot, McKim. 1976. "Hindu Transactions: Diversity without Dualism." In *Transaction and Meaning: Directions in the Anthropology of Exchange and Symbolic Behavior,* edited by Bruce Kapferer, 109–42. Philadelphia, PA: Institute for the Study of Human Issues.

Marriot, McKim, and Ronald B. Inden. 1977. "Toward an Ethnosociology of South Asian Caste Systems. In *The New Wind: Changing Identities in South Asia,* edited by Kenneth David, 227–38. The Hague: Mouton.

Marx, Karl. 2008 [1957]. "Marx to Engels, June 2, 1853." In *On Religion, Karl Marx and Friedrich Engels,* 121–23. Mineola, NY: Dover Publications.

MASS (Mahila Abhivruddhi Matthu Samrakshana Samsthe). 2002. *Progress Report, April 2001 to March 2002.* Ghataprabha, India: Mass.

MASS (Mahila Abhivruddhi Matthu Samrakshana Samsthe). 2009. *NOVIB 2006–2009 Project Progress Report, April 2009 to October 2009.* Ghataprabha, India: Mass.

Mauss, Marcel. 1990. *The Gift: The Form and Reason for Exchange in Archaic Societies.* Translated by W. D. Halls. New York: W. W. Norton.

McCormack, William. 1963. "Lingayats as a Sect." *Journal of the Royal Anthropological Institute of Great Britain and Ireland* 93 (1): 59–71.

McDermott, Rachel Fell, and Jeffrey John Kripal. 2003. *Encountering Kali: In the Margins, at the Center, in the West.* Berkeley: University of California Press.

Mendelsohn, Oliver, and Marika Vicziany. 1998. *The Untouchables Subordination, Poverty, and the State in Modern India.* Cambridge: Cambridge University Press.

Menon, Parvathi. 2003. "From Debt to Death." *Frontline,* 27 September–10 October. Accessed December 17, 2013. http://www.frontline.in/navigation/?type=static&page=archive.

Mohanty, Chandra Talpade. 1991. Introduction to *Third World Women and the Politics of Feminism,* edited by Chandra Talpade Mohanty, Ann Russo, and Lourdes Torres, 1–47. Bloomington: Indiana University Press.

Morgan, Lewis Henry. [1870] 1997. *Systems of Consanguinity and Affinity of the Human Family.* Lincoln: University of Nebraska Press.

Morgan, Lewis Henry. 1877. *Ancient Society or Researches into the Lines of Human Progress from Savagery through Barbarism to Civilization*. Chicago, IL: Charles H. Kerr.

Morris, Rosalind. 2002. "Theses on the Questions of War: History, Media, Terror." *Social Text* 20 (3): 149–75.

Murthy, U. R. Anantha. 1988. "Why Not Worship in the Nude? Reflections of a Novelist in His Time." In *Bahuvachan: An Occasional of the Arts and Ideas*, edited by Krishna Baldev Vaid, 95–117. Bhopal, India: Bharat Bhavan.

Nag, Mona. 2005. "Sex Workers in Sonagachi: Pioneers of a Revolution." *Economic and Political Weekly* 40 (49): 5151–55.

Nair, Janaki. 1994. "The Devadasi, Dharma and the State." *Economic and Political Weekly* 29 (50): 3157–67.

Nair, Janaki. 2000. *Women and Law in Colonial India: A Social History*. New Delhi: Kali for Women.

Nair, Janaki. 2005. *The Promise of the Metropolis: Bangalore's Twentieth Century*. New Delhi: Oxford University Press.

Nair, Janaki. 2011. *Mysore Modern: Rethinking the Region under Princely Rule*. Minneapolis: University of Minnesota Press.

Nair, P. M., and Sankar Sen. 2005. *Trafficking in Women and Children in India*. New Delhi: Orient Longman.

Nanda, Serena. 1990. *Neither Man Nor Woman: The Hijras of India*. Belmont, CA: Wadsworth Publishing.

Nandy, Ashis. 2001. *Time Warps: The Insistent Politics of Silent and Evasive Pasts*. Delhi, India: Permanent Black.

National Center for Advocacy Studies. 2001. "Campaign for Dalit Human Rights." *Advocacy Update* 15 (January-March).

Obeyesekere, Gananath. 1981. *Medusa's Hair: An Essay on Personal Symbols and Religious Experience*. Chicago: University of Chicago Press.

Oldenburg, Veena Talwar. 1990. "Lifestyle as Resistance: The Case of the Courtesans of Lucknow, India." *Feminist Studies* 16 (2): 259–87.

Omvedt, Gail. 1980. *We Will Smash this Prison!: Indian Women in Struggle*. London: Zed.

Omvedt, Gail. 1994. *Dalits and the Democratic Revolution: Dr. Ambedkar and the Dalit Movement in Colonial India*. New Delhi, India: Sage.

Ong, A. 2003. *Buddha Is Hiding: Refugees, Citizenship, the New America*. Berkeley: University of California Press.

Orchard, Treena. 2004. "A Painful Power: Coming of Age, Sexuality and Relationships, Social Reform, and HIV/AIDS among Devadasi Sex Workers in Rural Karnataka, India." PhD diss., University of Manitoba, Canada.

Orchard, Treena Rae. 2007. "Girl, Woman, Lover, Mother: Towards a New Understanding of Child Prostitution Among Young Devadasis in Rural Karnataka, India." *Social Science & Medicine* 64 (12): 2379–90.

Orr, Leslie C. 2000. *Donors, Devotees, and Daughters of God: Temple Women in Medieval Tamilnadu*. New York: Oxford University Press.

Pandey, Gyanendra. 2007. "The Secular State and the Limits of Dialogue." In *The Crisis of Secularism in India*, edited by Anuradha Dingwaney Needham and Rajeswari Sunder Rajan, 157–76. Durham, NC: Duke University Press.

Parasher, Aloka, and Usha Naik. 1986. "Temple Girls of Medieval Karnataka." *Indian Economic and Social History Review* 23 (1): 63–78.

Parker, Kunal M. 1998. "'A Corporation of Superior Prostitutes': Anglo-Indian Legal Conceptions of Temple Dancing Girls." *Modern Asian Studies* 32 (3): 559–33.

Patnaik, Utsa. 1998. "Globalization, Poverty and Food Security: Towards the New Millennium." In *Conference of the Indian Association of Women's Studies*. Pune, India: South Asia Documents.

Periyar, E. V. Ramasamy. 2003. "Social Reform or Social Resolution?" In *Social and Religious Reform: the Hindus of British India*, edited by Amiya P. Sen, 69–71. New Delhi, India: Oxford University Press.

"Persisting Evil." 2002. *Deccan Herald*, July 3.

Pierce, Steven, and Anupama Rao. 2006. *Discipline and the Other Body: Correction, Corporeality, Colonialism*. Durham, NC: Duke University Press.

Pinto, Ambrose. 2004. "Caste, Power, Globalisation and Communalism." In *Poverty, Marginalization and Empowerment in Karnataka*, edited by John Desrochers and Paulson V. Veliyannoor, 47–59. Bangalore: Karnataka Regional Conference of Religious Justice and Peace Cell.

Pinto, Sarah. 2008. *Where There Is No Midwife: Birth and Loss in Rural India*. New York: Berghahn.

Pinto, Sarah. 2012. "The Limits of Diagnosis: Sex, Law, and Psychiatry in a Case of Contested Marriage." *Ethos* 40 (2): 119–41.

Poethig, Kathryn. 1992. "Virgin Mothers and Their Daughters: Indian Christian Feminists vs. the Devadasis." Unpublished manuscript.

Povinelli, Elizabeth A. 2002a. *The Cunning of Recognition: Indigenous Alterities and the Making of Australian Multiculturalism*. Durham, NC: Duke University Press.

Povinelli, Elizabeth A. 2002b. "Notes on Gridlock: Genealogy, Intimacy, Sexuality." *Public Culture* 14 (1): 215–38.

Povinelli, Elizabeth A. 2006. *The Empire of Love: Toward a Theory of Intimacy, Genealogy, and Carnality*. Durham, NC: Duke University Press.

Presler, Franklin A. 1987. *Religion under Bureaucracy: Policy and Administration for Hindu Temples in South India*. Cambridge: Cambridge University Press.

Punekar, S. D., and Kamala Rao. 1962. *A Study of Prostitutes in Bombay, with Reference to Family Background*. Edited by Association for Moral and Social Hygiene. Bombay: Allied.

Purkayastha, Bandana, Mangala Subramaniam, Manisha Desai, and Sunita Bose. 2003. "The Study of Gender in India: A Partial Review." *Gender and Society* 17 (4): 503–24.

Quadagno, Jill S. 1994. *The Color of Welfare: How Racism Undermined the War on Poverty*. New York: Oxford University Press.

Raheja, Gloria Goodwin. 1988. *The Poison in the Gift: Ritual, Prestation, and the Dominant Caste in a North Indian Village*. Chicago: University of Chicago Press.

Raheja, Gloria Goodwin. 1988b. "India: Caste, Kingship, and Dominance Reconsidered." *Annual Review of Anthropology* 17 (1): 497–522.

Rajan, M. A. S. 1986. *The Land Reform Laws in Karnataka: A Descriptive Account.* Bangalore, India: Government of Karnataka.

Ram, Kalpana. 2013. *Fertile Disorder: Spirit Possession and Its Provocation of the Modern.* Honolulu: University of Hawai'i Press.

Ramanujan, A. K. 1986. "Two Realms of Kannada Folklore." In *Another Harmony: New Essays on the Folklore of India,* edited by Stuart H. Blackburn and A. K. Ramanujan, 41–75. Berkeley: University of California Press.

Ramberg, Lucinda. 2009. "Magical Hair as Dirt: Ecstatic Bodies and Postcolonial Reform in South India." *Culture, Medicine and Psychiatry* 33 (4): 501–22.

Ramberg, Lucinda. 2013. "Troubling Kinship: Sacred Marriage and Gender Configuration in South India." *American Ethnologist* 40 (4): 661–75.

Ramesh, Asha. 1992. *Impact of Legislative Prohibition of the Devadasi Practice in Karnataka: A Study.* New Delhi, India: Joint Women's Programme.

Rao, Anupama. 2003. *Gender and Caste: Issues in Contemporary Indian Feminism.* New Delhi, India: Kali for Women.

Rao, Anupama. 2009. *The Caste Question: Dalits and the Politics of Modern India.* Berkeley: University of California Press.

Rao, Rahul. 2005. Blenheim and Bangalore: A Tale of Subsidies in Two Communities. Global Policy Forum. Accessed January 3, 2014. http://www.globalpolicy .org/component/content/article/97/32131.html.

Rao, Y. Chinna. 2000. "Dalits and Tribals Are not Hindu." *Hindustani Times,* January 20.

Rawat, Ramnarayan S. 2011. Reconsidering Untouchability: Chamars and Dalit History in North India. Bloomington: Indiana University Press.

Rawson, Philip S. [1973] 1995. *The Art of Tantra.* London: Thames and Hudson.

Reddy, Gayatri. 2005. *With Respect to Sex: Negotiating Hijra Identity in South India.* Chicago: University of Chicago Press.

Reddy, K. Santhaa. 2002. Devadasis—Time to Review History. Accessed April 30, 2010. http://www.samarthbharat.com/devadasis.htm.

Rege, Sharmila. 1998. "Dalit Women Talk Differently: A Critique of 'Difference' and Towards a Dalit Feminist Standpoint Position." *Economic and Political Weekly* 33 (44): ws39–ws46.

Reiter, Rayna R. 1975. *Toward an Anthropology of Women.* New York: Monthly Review.

Robertson Smith, W. [1889] 2002. *Religion of the Semites.* New Brunswick, NJ: Transaction.

Rosaldo, Michelle Zimbalist, and Louise Lamphere. 1974. *Woman, Culture, and Society.* Stanford, CA: Stanford University Press.

Rozario, Sister Mary Rita. 2000. *Broken Lives: Dalit Women and Girls in Prostitution.* Karnataka, India: Ambedkar Resource Center.

Rubin, Gayle. 1975. "The Traffic in Women: Notes on the 'Political Economy' of Sex."

In *Toward an Anthropology of Women*, edited by Rayna R. Reiter, 157–210. New York: Monthly Review.

Rubin, Gayle. 1984. "Thinking Sex." In *Pleasure and Danger: Exploring Female Sexuality*, edited by Carole S. Vance, 267–319. Boston: Routledge.

Rubin, Gayle, with Judith Butler. 1997. "Sexual Traffic: Interview." In *Feminism Meets Queer Theory*, edited by Elizabeth Weed and Naomi Schor. Bloomington: Indiana University Press.

Said, Edward W. 1978. *Orientalism*. New York: Pantheon.

Sainath, P. 2010. "17,368 Farm Suicides in 2009." *The Hindu*, December 27. Accessed January 11, 2014. http://www.thehindu.com/opinion/columns/sainath/17368-farm-suicides-in-2009/article995824.ece.

Sanderson, Alexis. 1988. "Saivism and the Tantric Traditions." In *The World's Religions*, edited by Stuart R. Sutherland, Leslie Houlden, Peter Clarke, and Friedhelm Hardy, 660–704. London: Routledge.

Sangari, Kumkum, and Sudesh Vaid, eds. 1989. *Recasting Women: Essays in Indian Colonial History*. New Delhi: Kali for Women.

Sampada Gramin Mahila Sanstha (SANGRAM), Point of View, and Veshya Anyay Mukti Parishad (VAMP). 2002. "Rehabilitation: Against Their Will?" In *Of Veshyas, Vamps, Whores and Women: Challenging Preconceived Notions of Prostitution and Sex Work*, 1(2). Bombay: Point of View.

Sampada Gramin Mahila Sanstha (SANGRAM) and Veshya Anyay Mukti Parishad (VAMP) Team. 2011. "The VAMP/SANGRAM Sex Worker's Movement in India's Southwest." From *Changing Their World*, 2nd Edition, edited by Srilatha Batliwala, 1–16. Toronto: Association for Women's Rights in Development.

Sarkar, Sumit, and Tanika Sarkar. 2008. *Women and Social Reform in Modern India: A Reader*. Bloomington, IN: Indiana University Press.

Sarkar, Tanika. 2001. *Hindu Wife, Hindu Nation: Community, Religion, and Cultural Nationalism*. London: Hurst.

Sarkar, Tanika, and Urvashi Butalia, eds. 1995. *Women and the Hindu Right: A Collection of Essays*. New Delhi: Kali for Women.

Sax, William Sturman. 1995. *The Gods at Play: Lila in South Asia*. New York: Oxford University Press.

Scheper-Hughes, Nancy, and Margaret Lock. 1987. "The Mindful Body: A Prolegomenon to Future Work in Medical Anthropology." *Medical Anthropology Quarterly* 1 (1): 6–41.

Schneider, David Murray. 1984. *A Critique of the Study of Kinship*. Ann Arbor: University of Michigan Press.

Scott, Joan Wallach. 2009a. *The Politics of the Veil*. Princeton, NJ: Princeton University Press.

Scott, Joan Wallach. 2009b. "Sexularism." The Ursula Hirshmann Annual Lecture on Gender and Europe, European University Institute, Florence, Italy, April 23.

Seethalakshmi, S. 1998. "Devadasis Substitute One Evil for Another. *Times of India*, January 25.

Sehgal, Rashme. 1999. "Law Unable to Curb Devadasi System in Karnataka." *Times of India*, December 21.

Sen, Ronojoy. 2010. "The Indian Supreme Court and the Quest for a 'Rational' Hinduism." *South Asian History and Culture* 1 (1): 86–104.

Seth, Sanjay. 2004. "Reason or Reasoning? Clio or Siva?" *Social Text* 22 (1): 85–101.

Shah, Svati P. 2008. "South Asian Border Crossings and Sex Work: Revisiting the Question of Migration in Anti-Trafficking Interventions." *Sexuality Research and Social Policy* 5 (4): 19–30.

Shahrukh, Husain. 1997. *The Goddess: Creation, Fertility, Abundance*. Boston: Little, Brown.

Shankar, Jogan. 1994. *Devadasi Cult: A Sociological Analysis*. New Delhi, India: Ashish.

Sharma, Mohan Lal. 1968. "The Myth of the Sacred Cow." *Journal of Popular Culture* 2 (3): 457–67.

Shastri, Sandeep. 2009. "Legislators in Karnataka: Well-entrenched Dominant Castes." In *Rise of the Plebeians? The Changing Face of Indian Legislative Assemblies*, edited by Christophe Jaffrelot and Sanjay Kumar, 245–76. New York: Routledge.

Shiva, Vandana. 2004. "The Suicide Economy of Corporate Globalization." In ZNET. Accessed January 11, 2014. http://www.countercurrents.org/glo-shiva050404.htm.

Shreedhar, Jaya. 1995. "HIV Thrives in Ancient Traditions." *Harvard AIDS Review* (September), 10–11.

Singh, V. D. 2000. "NGO Lobbies for Welfare Scheme of Devadasis." *Times of India*, April 25.

Sinha, Indra. 2000. *Tantra: The Cult of Ecstasy*. London: Hamlyn.

Sinha, Mrinalini. 1998. "Introduction" to *Mother India: Selections from the Controversial 1927 Text by Katherine Mayo*, edited by Mrinalini Sinha, 1–68. New Delhi, India: Kali for Women.

Sinha, Mrinalini. 2006. *Specters of Mother India: The Global Restructuring of an Empire*. Durham: Duke University Press.

Soneji, Devesh. 2012. *Unfinished Gestures: Devadasis, Memory, and Modernity in South India*. Chicago; London: University of Chicago Press.

Spivak, Gayatri. 1990. "Criticism, Feminism, and the Institution." In *The Post-Colonial Critic: Interviews, Strategies, Dialogues*, edited by Sarah Harasym. New York: Routledge.

Spivak, Gayatri Chakravorty. 1996. "How to Teach a 'Culturally Different' Book." In *The Spivak Reader: Selected Works of Gayatri Chakravorty Spivak*, edited by Donna Landry and Gerald M. MacLean, 237–66. New York: Routledge.

Sprinkle, Annie. 1998. *Post-Porn Modernist: My 25 Years as a Multi-Media Whore*. San Francisco, CA: Cleis.

Sreenivas, Mytheli. 2008. *Wives, Widows, and Concubines: The Conjugal Family Ideal in Colonial India*. Bloomington: Indiana University Press.

Srinivas, M. N. 1955. "The Social System of a Mysore Village." In *Village India: Studies in the Little Community*. Edited by Mckim Marriot, 1–35. Chicago: University of Chicago Press.

Srinivasa, L., and Prasannakumar Shivasharanappa. 2012. "Devadasi Practice in Karnataka." *Golden Research Thoughts* 1 (9): 1–4.

Srinivasan, Amrit. 1984. "Temple 'Prostitution' and Community Reform: An Examination of the Ethnographic, Historical and Textual Context of the Devadasi of Tamil Nadu, South India." PhD diss., Cambridge University.

Srinivasan, Amrit. 1988. "Reform or Conformity? Temple 'Prostitution' and the Community in the Madras Presidency." In *Structures of Patriarchy*, edited by Bina Agarwal, 175–98. New Delhi: Sage.

Stabile, Carol A., and Deepa Kumar. 2005. "Unveiling Imperialism: Media, Gender and the War on Afghanistan." *Media, Culture & Society* 27 (5): 765–82.

Starhawk. 1979. *The Spiral Dance: A Rebirth of the Ancient Religion of the Great Goddess*. San Francisco: Harper and Row.

Stein, Burton. 1978. *South Indian Temples: An Analytical Reconsideration*. New Delhi: Vikas.

Strathern, Marilyn. 1990. *The Gender of the Gift: Problems with Women and Problems with Society in Melanesia*. Berkeley, CA: University of California Press.

Strathern, Marilyn. 2005. *Kinship, Law and the Unexpected: Relatives Are Always a Surprise*. New York: Cambridge University Press.

Sturman, Rachel. 2001. "Family Values: Refashioning Property and Family in Colonial Bombay Presidency, 1818–1937." PhD diss., University of California, Davis.

Sturman, Rachel. 2012. *The Government of Social Life in Colonial India: Liberalism, Religious Law, and Women's Rights*. Cambridge: Cambridge University Press.

Sudarshan, H. 2006. "Status of Scheduled Tribes in Karnataka." Karnataka Human Development Report 2005. Bangalore, India: Planning and Statistics Department, Government of Karnataka.

Sunder Rajan, Rajeswari. 2000. "Real and Imagined Goddesses: A Debate." In *Is the Goddess a Feminist? The Politics of South Asian Goddesses*, edited by Alf Hiltebeitel and Kathleen M. Erndl, 269–84. New York: New York University Press.

Tambe, Ashwini. 2009. *Codes of Misconduct: Regulating Prostitution in Late Colonial Bombay*. Minneapolis: University of Minnesota Press.

Tandon, Tripti, and Anand Grover. 2006. "(W)Rec(T)ifying ITPA: Proposed Amendments to the Immoral Trafficking Prevention Act." *Lawyers Collective* 21 (3): 7–16.

Tarachand, K. C. 1992. *Devadasi Custom: Rural Social Structure and Flesh Markets*. New Delhi, India: Reliance.

Tharu, Susie. 2001. "Problems in Theorizing Feminism." Paper presented at the Academic Staff Conference, Pune University, Pune.

Trautmann, Thomas. R. 1995. *Dravidian Kinship*. New Delhi: Vistaar.

Tylor, Edward Burnett. 1874. *Primitive Culture: Researches into the Development of Mythology, Philosophy, Religion, Language, Art and Custom*. 1st American ed., from the 2nd English ed. 2 vols. Boston: Estes and Lauriat.

U.S. Department of Labor, Office of Policy Planning and Research. 1965. *The Negro Family: The Case for National Action.* By Daniel Patrick Moynihan. Washington, DC.

Uberoi, Patricia. 1993. *Family, Kinship and Marriage in India.* Delhi: Oxford University Press.

Ullrich, Helen E. 1977. "Caste Differences between Brahmin and Non-Brahmin Women in a South Indian Village." In *Sexual Stratification: A Cross-Cultural View,* edited by Alice Schlegel, 94–108. New York: Columbia University Press.

Urban, Hugh B. 2003. *Tantra: Sex, Secrecy Politics, and Power in the Study of Religions.* Berkeley: University of California Press.

Vijaisri, Priyadarshini. 2004. *Recasting the Devadasi: Patterns of Sacred Prostitution in Colonial South India.* New Delhi: Kanikshka.

Vijaisri, Priyadarshini. 2005. "Contending Identities: Sacred Prostitution and Reform in Colonial South India." *South Asia* 28 (3): 387–411.

Viswanath, Rupa. 2010. "Spiritual Slavery, Material Malaise: 'Untouchables' and Religious Neutrality in Colonial South India." *Historical Research* 83 (219): 124–45.

Viswanathan, Gauri. 1998. *Outside the Fold: Conversion, Modernity, and Belief.* Princeton, NJ: Princeton University Press.

Viswanathan, Gauri. 2003. "Colonialism and the Construction of Hinduism." In *The Blackwell Companion to Religion,* edited by Gavin Flood, 23–44. London: Blackwell.

Walkowitz, Judith R. 1980. *Prostitution and Victorian Society: Women, Class and the State.* Cambridge: Cambridge University Press.

Wardlow, Holly. 2004. "Anger, Economy, and Female Agency: Problematizing 'Prostitution' and 'Sex Work' among the Huli of Papua New Guinea." *Signs* 29 (4): 1017–40.

Wardlow, Holly. 2006. *Wayward Women: Sexuality and Agency in a New Guinea Society.* Berkeley, CA: University of California Press.

Warner, Michael. 1993. "Tongues Untied: Memoirs of a Pentecostal Boyhood." *Voice Literary Supplement* 112 (February), 13–5.

Warner, Michael. 2000. *The Trouble with Normal: Sex, Politics, and the Ethics of Queer Life.* Cambridge, MA: Harvard University Press.

Warner, Michael. 2009. "Sex and Secularity." Society for Cultural Anthropology Culture@Large Session presented at the American Anthropological Association Annual Meeting, December 5, Philadelphia, PA.

Weston, Kath. 1997. *Families We Choose: Lesbians, Gays, Kinship.* Rev. ed. New York: Columbia University Press.

White, David Gordon. 2003. *Kiss of the Yogini: "Tantric Sex" in Its South Asian Context.* Chicago: University of Chicago Press.

Whitehead, Henry. [1921] 1999. *The Village Gods of South India.* 2nd ed. New Delhi, India: J. Jetly.

Williams, Brackette. 1995. "Classification Systems Revisited: Kinship, Caste, Race, and Nationality as the Flow of Blood and the Spread of Rights." In *Naturalizing*

Power: Essays in Feminist Cultural Analysis, edited by Sylvia Junko Yanagisako and Carol Lowery Delaney, 201–36. New York: Routledge.

Yadav, Manohar. 2004. "Caste and Untouchability." In *Poverty, Marginalization and Empowerment in Karnataka*, edited by John Desrochers and Paulson V. Veliyannoor, 87–110. Bangalore, India: Karnataka Regional Conference of Religious-Justice and Peace Cell.

Young, Antonia. 2000. *Women Who Become Men: Albanian Sworn Virgins*. Oxford: Oxford International.

Young, Katherine K. 1991. "Goddesses, Feminists, and Scholars." *Annual Review of Women in World Religions*. Vol. 1, 105–79.

Zelizer, Viviana. 2005. *The Purchase of Intimacy*. Princeton, NJ: Princeton University Press.

Zimmermann, Francis. 1979. "Remarks on the Body in Ayurvedic Medicine." *South Asia Digest of Regional Writing* 18: 10–26.

INDEX

Note: Italics indicate figures; n indicates a note

affliction, 7, 32–35, 60–61, 70, 84–86, 97, 100–101, 109, 142, 151, 187, 214–15, 217, 234n28

agency: political, 26, 49, 68, 194; religious, 42, 67, 70, 218; sexual, 27, 108, 140–41, 164, 173, 175–77

Ambedkar, B. R.: and Dalit conversion to Buddhism, 17, 53–54, 86–87; and Dalit liberation, 52–54, 124–25, 232–33n20–21, 233n23; desecration of statutes of, 116–17, 239n4. *See* caste distinction; Dalit activists; reformers

Apfell-Marglin, Frederique, 27, 32, 230n8

Asad, Talal 16, 219, 225n16

auspiciousness: *darshan*, 94, 145, 234n31; devadasis as bearers of, 6, 27–28, 75, 87–88, 92, 97, 101, 145, 149–51, 155, 160, 170–71, 210; and devotees, 56–57, 78, 80, 83, 106; for *gandulla-valu* (women with husbands) 165–66; and gift offerings, 84, 165, 170–72; inauspiciousness, 83, 148, 152, 153, 160, 242n1; and marriage and fertility, 83, 128, 146; occasions that manifest, 1, 7, 75, 79; *prasada*, 151–52; signs of, 83, 148, 152, 242n1; vs. purity and pollution, 27, 133, 242–43n5; Yellamma's arrival as an event of, 81, 170

avaru (third person gender neutral pronoun), 182, 201–3, 205–6, 208, 244n3

bettale seve (naked worship): banning of, 119–20, 122; at Chandragutti, 116–22, 125, 240n9; and Dalit activism, 34, 117, 119, 122–26, 140; as a rite, 119, 122, 154, 240n9

body, the: bodily commitment, 34, 101, 114, 121, 129, 133, 140–41, 177, 215, 238–39n1; and castration, 100–101, 141, 202, 238n26; embodying the devi, 3, 66, 75, 85–88, 97, 100, 101, 105, 128, 142–43, 145, 160, 187, 203, 217, 219–21; of the devi, 2, 65, 80, 87–88, 101, 137, 139; as ecstatic medium, 34, 101, 134–37; epistemologies of, 101–2, 116, 124, 126, 127, 138, 140, 185, 210–11, 214–15, medicalization of, 90, 97, 99, 101–2, 220; as site of reform, 13, 16, 23, 101, 125; as symbol, 24, 34, 98–99, 101, 108, 137, 159, 219–20, 229–30n3

Brahmanism: Ambedkar's campaign against, 52–54, 124–25, 232–33n20–21, 233n23; as compared to Buddhism, 54; as compared to non-Sanskritic Hinduism, 15–16, 42, 63, 72, 234n28, 236n8; and conjugal monogamy, 22, 25, 158–59, 194–95; as Hinduism,

15–17, 72, 102, 115–16, 221; the logic of
purity and pollution, 56, 126, 152, 184,
234n25, 243–44n9; and nationalist
self-assertion, 14–17, 102, 115–16, 221.
See also Hinduism
British colonial government: and devadasi reform 20–23, 72; and Indian
nationalists, 15–17, 21–23, 51–52, 157–
60; and land administration, 45–46,
51–52, 231n12, 232n14; and prostitution, 157–59; and the remaking
of Hinduism, 16–17, 108–9, 139–40,
232n19, 237–38n23
brothels: under British colonialism,
157; devadasis based in, 6–7, 55, 169,
172–73, 224n7–8, 243n6
Buddhism, 17, 53–55, 66, 86–87, 115, 126
Butler, Judith, 5, 13, 100, 175, 184–86,
213, 217, 225, 244

caste distinction: Ambedkar's efforts
to end, 17, 52–54, 86–87, 124–25,
232–33n20–21, 233n23; anti-casteism,
16–17, 23–24, 26–27, 53–55, 123–24,
232n20, 235n35, 243n9; and *bettale
seve*, 123–26; Brahmans, 23, 45–46,
54–55, 72, 125, 243n7; categories of,
223n5, 242n4; and devadasi patronage, 23–24, 26, 66; and gender, 23–24,
27, 50–51, 54, 62–63, 163, 243–44n9;
and Hinduism, 127, 131, 133; Holeyars, 23, 150, 230n7, 242n4; and interdependence, 57, 59, 172–73, 236n6,
242–43n5; and land relations, 45–47,
51–54, 158; Lingayats, 46, 54–56, 125,
146, 226n26, 242n4; and livelihood,
17, 23, 52–53, 225n21; Mahars, 52–53;
marginalization of Dalit females
through, 26–27, 44; persistence of
43, 54, 56–57, 236n10; and purity and
pollution, 56, 152, 184, 234n25, 243–
44n9; and relatedness, 162, 244n4;
scheduled castes and tribes, 46–47,
71, 231n11, 232n15, 233n22; taboos

and practices that maintain, 163, 184,
243–44n9; untouchability, 23, 40–43,
53, 55–56
categories: in crisis 4, 19, 35, 218; as
normalizing 5, 13–14; religion 13–17;
sexuality 13, 18–19, 114, 156–59
celibacy, 98, 99, 156, 237n19
Chandragutti: archaeological significance of, 120–22; and *bettale seve*,
116–26
Chandrawwataayi (saint), 136, 182
chastity. *See* female sexual chastity
Chatterjee, Jyotsna, 89–90
Christian missionaries: and concept
of true and false religion, 16, 72–73,
115–16; and Indian social reform, 16,
22, 88, 108–9; and devadasis as prostitutes, 21–22, 25–26, 226–27n29,
239n3; and perceptions of Hindu
practices, 4, 15, 16, 19, 22, 33, 72–73,
108–9, 115, 139–40; and public nakedness, 124–25, 240n7; and sexual
mores, 116, 124–25, 156
Cohen, Lawrence: on commitment,
34, 114, 133, 140–41, 176–77; on operability and biological citizenship, 101,
215, 238–39n1
conjugal matrimony: as ideal, 23, 25,
50–51, 114; as just one means of kin
making, 3, 12–13, 40–41; as kinship,
12, 22–23, 25–26, 114, 116, 174; and
socioeconomic status, 157–61, 192. *See
also* female sexual chastity
cure, 34, 79, 83, 85–86, 91, 94, 96, 100,
189

Dalit activists: and *bettale seve*, 117–19,
122–24, 140; incorporation of democratic ideals by, 13, 54, 57, 123, 232n20;
and devadasi reform, 3–4, 23, 44,
49–51, 54–55, 57, 59–60, 71–72, 88–89,
92, 119, 124–25, 163–64, 228n36;
emancipation projects, 17–18, 69, 90,
124, 140, 141; and Hinduism, 15–17,

Dalit activists (*continued*)
50–51, 87; politicization of female
sexual purity by, 24, 50–51, 54, 59,
123–24, 228n36; shared interests with
nationalists and feminist reformers,
16–17, 26, 88–89, 92, 94, 220; and
untouchability, 17, 57, 124. *See also*
reformers
Dalit(s): and conversion to Buddhism,
17, 53–55, 66, 86–87, 115, 126; definition of, 223n5; and land relations,
45–60; liberation theology, 226n22;
sexual politics of caste, 6, 23–24, 163–
64, 184, 243–44n9; socioeconomic
plight of young men, 47, 57–58
dance. *See* rites
darshan: dedication and, 145; definition of, 94, 234n31, 236n8; practice of
taking, 64, 74, 103, 109, 119; preparations for giving or taking, 64, 82, 209.
See also Hinduism; Yellamma
dedication: criminalization of, 3, 24,
161, 217; account of Durgabai, 143–44;
Karnataka Devadasis (Prohibition of
Dedication) Bill, (1982), 6, 24, 74, 88,
90, 160–61; as inaugurating a distinct
mode of being in the world, 2, 9, 25,
31–32, 72–73, 218; as a means of earning 151, 167–70, 196–200, 202, 206; as
a means of familial transformation,
184–85, 196–201, 205, 210–11; account
of Pratima, 143; as a means of preserving familial wealth, 34–35, 146, 167–70,
172–73, 199–200, 210–11; as a rite of
marriage to a devi, 2–3, 9, 28, 155, 175–
76; as sacrifice, 113–16, 141, 143–44,
187; secular view of, 3, 54–55, 89, 105,
115, 160–62, 239n2; account of Shantamma, 167–69; tying *muttu* ("tying
the beads"), 6, 103, 144–45, 155, 208–9
devadasis: *agamashastras* regarding the
temple duties of, 22, 227n30; as auspicious, 6, 27–28, 75, 92, 145, 149–51,
160, 165–66, 170–71, 190, 210; as *ba-*

savi (female bulls), 21, 69, 154, 187,
247; as both liberated and sacrificed,
113–15, 141; as a challenge to patrilineality, 101, 172–73, 196–97, 213, 215;
critiques of reform by, 69–73, 97–98,
107, 125; and death rites, 204–5, 209;
Devaki (brothel-based ex-devadasi),
182, 184; *dhandewallis* (brothel-
based), 6–7, 24, 55, 169, 182, 201, 206,
224n8, 243n6; eradication of, 24–26,
54–55, 88–89, 91–106, 156–57, 160;
framed as nonmodern, 3–4, 13–15,
54–55, 107–8, 125–26; framed as prostitutes, 24, 71, 89, 145, 160, 214; Gangawwa (brothel-based devadasi),
169–70; as heads of households, 7,
169–70, 198–200; historic roles and
rights of, 20–23, 51–52, 232n19; and
jogatis defined, 3, 9, 223n4; Kamala
(brothel-based devadasi), 144–45;
Kamalabi (rural devadasi), 1–2, 29,
82–83, 152, 209; Karnataka Devadasis (Prohibition of Dedication)
Bill (1982), 6, 24, 74, 88, 90, 160–61;
key features of, 3, 7, 243n6; and kin
making with Yellamma, 4–5, 11–13,
184, 209, 214–16; land and property
ownership by, 47, 59, 168–70, 196–98,
200; marginal status of, 16, 25, 26,
44, 218; modernist disbelief in the
religiosity of, 25–26, 72–73, 125–26,
221–22; as both *muttaide* and *randi*
(wife and nonwife), 153–54, 160;
nonconjugal sexuality of, 3, 13, 23,
25–27, 101; and patronage, 6–7, 29, 55,
172–74; Pratima (rural devadasi), 143;
reformers' portrayals of, 155–61, 175,
214, 227n31, 228n40, 229n42; and relatedness to the devi, 73, 115, 217–18;
ritual responsibilities of, 1, 7, 75–77,
79; sex worker HIV peer educators,
7, 63, 144, 167, 169–70, 182; Shakti
Sangha, 63; Shantamma (brothel-
based devadasi), 167–69, 181; world-

making capacity of, 26, 69–70, 73–74, 182–83, 218, 236n8; as Yellamma, 1–2, 56–57, 83, 87–88, 94, 203–4. *See also* Durgabai; ex-devadasis; *jogatis*; Kamlabai; Mahadevi; *pujaris*; Yamuna devi. *See* goddesses and Yellamma

devotees: interaction of with dedicated women, 7, 56–57, 75, 171–73, 200–201, 210; and propitiation of the devi, 1, 61, 80, 136, 148, 150; regard of for Yellamma and Matangi, 80–84, 115, 117, 147–52, 155

devotion. *See* religiosity

Douglas, Mary, 96, 99, 162, 237n22

Dravidian culture: deities of, 54, 65, 190, 229n2; kinship practices in, 184, 193, 245n10, 245–46n17

Durgabai (rural devadasi): as a bearer of auspiciousness, 170–71; duties as a rural devadasi, 1–2, 29, 79, 147; economic hardship of, 44–45, 47, 48–49, 69–70; on her existence as a devadasi, 59–60, 69–70, 113–16, 141, 154, 171, 187; on familial trouble and dedication, 143–44; as niece of a *jogappa*, 39; as a *pujari*, 76, 77; ritual observation of *randi hunnime* by, 147–49; and story of Yellamma and the landlord's wife, 63; and story of Yellamma and Matangi, 39–40, 229n1. *See also* devadasis

ecstatic embodiment: continuation of, 115–16, 139; *jade* as a mark of, 34, 94, 98, 99, 101, 136–37, 237n21; reform of, 25, 69, 100–102, 115, 116, 129, 221; and relatedness to deities 1, 16, 102, 129, 137; and renunciation 102, 115, 128, 202–3

education: and antidedication reform, 16, 71–72, 89, 97–103, 221; apprenticeship as 6, 87; devadasis' abilities to provide for relatives', 6, 169–70, 198; general unavailability of to young

Dalit men, 47, 48, 58; HIV peer programs among sex workers, 7, 63, 144, 170, 182

endogamy 40, 114, 163, 243. *See also* conjugal matrimony

Epp, Linda, 91, 123, 125–26, 196, 237n15, 240n9

exchange and alliance: analytical models of, 133, 146, 161–65, 193–94; as basis for distinguishing marriage from prostitution, 155–59, 161–62, 174; as the logic underlying both marriage and dedication, 34–35, 165–67. *See also* gift transactions

ex-devadasis (*maji devadasis*): 2002 MASS annual meeting of, 102–6; accounts of and by 14, 103–6, 182, 184, 218, 237n13; effects on of the MASS *jade*-cutting campaign, 96, 100; policing functions of, 92, 94, 102–6; and rehabilitation schemes, 92, 103–4, 106–7; retention of Yellamma's *muttu* among, 85–86, 103; self-concepts of, 14, 92–94, 218. *See also* devadasis

family. *See* kinship

farmer suicides, 48, 232n17

female sexual chastity: Christian missionary concepts of, 15, 21–22, 124, 240n7; as compared to auspiciousness, 27, 170–71; politicization of, 14, 23, 44, 50–51, 59, 159; symbols of, 233n23, 242n1; Yellamma's distraction as a loss of, 11, 65, 102, 189–90. *See also* conjugal matrimony

feminist(s): on the agency of Asian women, 176, 233n21, 244n13; anti-caste, 26–27, 50–51, 60; critique of dedication, 3–4, 15, 24, 27, 88–89, 164–65, 175–77; emancipation projects, 17–18, 69, 90, 124, 140, 141; and goddesses, 66–69; on marriage as a gift relation, 163–64, 175–76; on reli-

feminist(s) (*continued*)
  gion as constraint, 17–18, 66, 69, 220;
  secular, 68–69, 220–21; studies of
  kinship by, 192–95, 214; woman question, 19–20, 26–27, 50–51. *See also*
  reformers
festivals: *bettale seve* rites at Chandragutti, 119, 120, 121–22; celebrants at,
  136–37, 206; Mahawanami *phere*,
  79–80; propitiation activities during,
  136, 139, 151; *randi hunnime* and *muttaide hunnime*, 146–53; ritual responsibilities of devadasis, *jogatis*, and
  jogappas, 6–9, 87, 200; of the river
  devi, 1–2, 29; seasonal, 7, 41, 75, 85,
  90, 236n11
Foucault, Michel, 16, 19, 27, 240n10,
  241n15
freedom: as emancipation from custom,
  17–18, 69, 123; nationalist configuration of religious, 14–15, 88; politics of,
  16, 220, 232n20

gandullavalu (women with living husbands); familial constraints on, 114,
  116, 153–56, 166, 223n2; land owner-
  ships rights of, 49, 217. *See also* marriage
gender: as an activity, 175–77, 185, 195–
  96, 199–200, 210–11; and agency, 27,
  141, 154; dedication as a disruption
  of, 35, 99, 145–46, 181–82, 185–86,
  196–201, 210–11, 213–16; hierarchy in
  modernity, 99, 124, 134, 192; as product of kinship, 163–64, 173, 184; and
  property rights, 45, 49–50, 52, 158. *See
  also* kinship; relatedness
gift transactions: as kinship, 129, 131–32,
  155, 158, 161–66, 174–77, 244n4; Mauss
  on 138, 162–63; and production of
  gender 162–66, 175, 185, 210–11; and
  propitiation of the gods, 2–3, 4, 61, 82,
  86, 113, 131, 133, 142–43, 149–50. *See
  also* exchange and alliance; kinship

Gilada, Ishwarprasad S., 90–91, 224n8,
  237n15
goddess worship: and feminine phallic power, 63, 100–101; and fertility, 6,
  61, 63, 82, 83–84, 151; goddess Durga,
  67, 79, 182; goddess Kali, 67, 130, 135;
  goddess Mariyamman, 63, 234n27;
  and matrilineal cultures, 67, 127, 134;
  shakti, 60–61, 83, 100, 131; and social
  order, 66–69; Tantric, 127–28, 135;
  tooth mothers vs. breast mothers,
  61, 234n28; Yellamma as autochthonous, 61–63, 127–28; Yellamma as the
  tamed spouse, 63–65. *See also* Kaula
  (Kula) practice; Shakta religion (goddess worship); yoginis
guru, 144–45, 201, 202
Gurumurthy, K. G., 65, 129, 189–90,
  191–92, 224n9

hair: grooming 96, 97, 99; reform,
  33–34, 64, 92–104, 221, 237n17; sexual
  symbolism of, 98–99. See also *jade*
harake: decision-making concerning
  form of, 86; definition of, 1–2, 248;
  ecstatic performance as a form of, 1,
  16, 102, 137; execution of, 75–77, 81,
  84, 122, 147, 200; *jogatis* and *jogappas*
  as given in fulfillment of, 2, 143–44;
  motivations for making, 84, 122, 143,
  215
heterosexuality: contravention of, 100,
  145, 192; as kinship 12, 134, 192; and
  patrimonial, patrilineal social order
  12, 145, 163–64, 192, 232n19, 243n8;
  obligatory and the reproduction
  of caste, 163; yogini rites as a kin-
  making alternative to, 129–30, 134
hijras, 107, 195, 201–2, 206, 238n26,
  245n19
Hinduism: autochthonous goddesses,
  61–62, 72, 115, 128–29; Gandhi's reform of, 17, 229n1, 242n4; goddesses
  and women, 44–45, 66–69; Kali (the

destroyer goddess), 67, 130, 135; Kaula practitioners and rites, 131–34, 140; and nationalism, 14–15, 88, 90, 108–9, 115–16, 125–26; powers of "hot" goddesses, 60–63, 86, 100, 137, 143, 234n28; practice of taking *darshan*, 74, 94, 103, 109, 119; reformers on non-Sanskritic, 15–17, 54–55, 71–72; saint Chandrawwataayi, 136, 182; Sanskritic vs. non-Sanskritic traditions of, 15–16, 22, 42, 61, 72; Sanskritization of vernacular traditions of, 65, 115, 127, 129, 189–90; *shastras* (scriptures, texts), 22, 108, 158, 227n30, 232n19; god Shiva, 63, 130, 229n2; Tantra strain of, 126–29, 240–41n10–13, 241n15; Tantric goddesses and yoginis, 131, 132, 134, 135; textual Brahmanism as the real, 15–17, 72, 102, 115–16; Vedas, 15, 115, 138, 223n5, 225n18; Vedic sacrifice, 138–39; Virashaivism, 102, 226n26; god Vishnu, 31, 60, 229n1. *See also* Brahmanism; *darshan*; Shaivism; Shakta religion (goddess worship); Tantra

Hindu oral traditions: concept of binary goddesses in, 61–62, 67; Dravidian (*amma*) mother goddesses in, 54, 60, 83, 229n2, 236n11; and Jamadagni, 235n33; hot goddesses in, 86, 100–101, 137, 143, 233–34n24; and marriage of Renuka Yellamma and Jamadagni, 9–11, 64–65, 102, 128, 146, 187–91; and Parashurama's matricide of Yellamma, 9–11, 43–44, 64–66, 121–22, 139, 191; and sisterhood of Matangi and Yellamma, 39–44; and triumph of Yellamma over buffalo demon Mahishasura, 79–80; and Yellamma and the landlord's wife, 63, 126; Sanskritization of Yellamma's power by modern, 64–65, 190; story of Gangamma and the sexual predator, 235n39; story of Shiva saving

Yellamma, 121–22; story underlying *randi hunnime*, 146; Vedic gods, 31, 54, 60, 65, 190

HIV/AIDS pandemic, 7, 24, 28, 63, 84, 90, 144, 167, 170, 197, 201, 238n25

Indian nationalists/nationalism: anticolonialism of, 17, 23, 159; and configuration of religious freedom, 14–15, 17–18, 69, 88, 91–92, 123; conformity of to Western mores, 13–14, 16–17, 25–26, 123–25; dismantling of historical devadasi functions by, 21–26, 160, 226n27; emphasis on female sexual purity by, 14, 23, 50–51, 159; and form of the family 11, 14, 25, 156–57, 159, 214; and Indian womanhood, 19–20, 23–26, 156–60, 220–22, 228n40; postcolonial, 14–15, 24–25, 108–9, 221–22; shared interests of with Dalit activists, 16–17, 23, 232–33n20–21; status of men as a priority of, 23–24, 161, 162, 197; and vernacular religion 16–17, 24, 108–9, 115–16. *See also* reformers

inheritance: colonial restructuring of rights, 52, 134, 157–58; among devadasis, 35, 145–46, 167, 196–200, 216; among men, 52, 134, 157–58, 197; among women, 48–49, 52. *See also* land rights

intimacy: as incompatible with material interest, 156, 161–62, 174; as the proper aim of sex, 19, 132,156,

jade (matted locks of hair): cutting campaigns, 33–34, 64, 92–93, 96–104, 221; as a manifestation of Yellamma, 34, 74, 86, 87, 94–101, 186–87, 217; medicalization of, 33–34, 96–97, 221. *See also* hair

Jainism, 115, 120, 125, 126, 203–5

Jamadagni: as avatar of Shiva, 61; boons to Parashurama, 11, 65; curse of his disobedient sons, 201, 235n33; lack of

Jamadagni (*continued*)
power of over Yellamma's devadasis, 145; sacrifice of in fertility rites honoring Yellamma, 128, 146; treatment of Renuka Yellamma, 9–11, 64–65, 102, 187–91

jogappas: attire of, 35, 182, 203, 206–7, 210; definition of, 3, 35, 182, 223n3, 246n19; as descendants of Yellamma's faithful sons, 190–91, 201, 235n33; divinations by, 84, 200; and *harake*, 84, 200; as HIV peer educators, 201; Kallappa, 201–2, 206; and kinship ties, 39, 182, 200–206, 210; Kishar, 182, 184, 206; Mihir, 203–5; performance of rites by, 35, 117, 137, 139, 147, 200, 206; and pronominal gender, 201–2; the proper death rites for, 204; the prosperity of some, 203, 206; as *pujaris*, 9, 122, 126, 128, 200–203; and *randi hunnime* and *muttaide hunnime*, 146–49; *sattipatti muttu*, 208–9

jogatis (*jogammas*): and *bhajans*, 42, 57, 75, 80, 83, 103; and caste, 59, 152, 234n25; as cultural producers, 5, 12, 30–32, 72–74, 87–88, 108–10; and devadasis defined, 3, 9, 223n4; divinations by, 75, 84–85, 87; framed as prostitutes, 3, 19, 27, 97, 156, 162; as keepers of vernacular Hinduism, 42; and kin making with Yellamma, 4–5, 11–13, 184, 209, 214–16; the landholding and inheritance rights of, 7, 48–49; married to the devi, 113–15, 156, 161–62, 192, 215–16; and patrilineality, 11, 99–102, 155–61, 196–97, 200, 210–11, 213–14; and performance of *harake*, 76–77, 84, 147–48; and *phere*, 7, 55, 79, 85, 171, 236n7; and procession of the devi, 2, 74, 117, 139, 147, 200; as *pujaris*, 9, 87–88, 122, 126, 128; and *randi hunnime* and *muttaide hunnime*, 146–49; rural vs. brothel-based, 7, 156–57, 169; sources of livelihood

of, 47, 156, 172–73, 234n26; possible Tantric Yogini ancestry of, 21, 127–9, 240–1n14. *See also* devadasis; *pujaris*

Joint Women's Programme, 4, 24, 89–90, 155, 160–61

Kallappa (*jogappa*), 78, 201–2, 206
Kamlabai (rural devadasi), 1–2, 29, 79, 82–83, 152, 209. *See also* devadasis
Karnataka (Prohibition of Dedication) Act, (1982), 24, 74, 88, 160
Kaula (Kula) practice, 131–35, 241n17. *See also* goddess worship; yoginis
kin making: human reproduction as just one motive for, 12, 101, 114, 127, 130, 132–34; between humans and deities, 28, 129–30, 133; *jogati* practices of, 4–5, 11–13, 184, 209, 214–16; Kaula rites as a form of, 133–35; between Matangi and Yellamma, 40, 42–43; material, transactional character of, 129–30, 161–66; spectrum of contexts for, 40–41, 67, 193, 230n6; and value, 161, 206, 210–11
kinship: anthropology of, 12–13, 192–96, 213–14, 245n10; and Antigone, 185–86, 221n15; and bodily commitment, 34, 133, 177; "consanguinity" and "affinity", 41, 230n6; dedication as a means of gender transformation, 184–85, 196–201, 205, 210–11; dedication as a means of preserving the natal family, 167–70, 172–73; father lack, 24, 44, 193; as gift relation, 163–64, 173, 193–94; "kinship trouble" as a product of dedication, 11–12, 35, 145, 184, 209–10, 214–18; "kinship trouble" as experienced by Yellamma, 11, 187–91; marginalizing effects of divine, 11, 44–45, 182, 195–96; marriage taboos, 194, 197–99, 216, 245–46n17; matrilineal relationships, 67, 131, 134, 157–58, 192–93, 245–46n17–18; patrilineal and matrilineal, 14, 52, 67, 159,

192–93; patrilineal and the status of women, 65, 101, 134, 166–67, 190; and production of gender, 163–64, 173, 185, 243n8; as sacrifice, 138, 140–41, 177; stigma of illegitimacy, 43–44, 55, 193; as variable, 12–13, 194–95, 245n13; as a wound, 5, 113–16, 124, 141, 177, 194–95, 215, 245n11; between Yellamma and Matangi, 39–44; with Yellamma, 9, 45, 161–62, 182, 192. *See also* gender; relatedness

Kishar (*jogappa* in southern Maharastra), 206

land rights: as basis for sustainable livelihood, 48–50, 69–70; and colonial reform, 7, 45–47, 51–52, 231n12, 232n14; dedication as a means of protecting familial, 146, 167–69, 213–14; definition of, 231–32n13; devadasis' historic, 20–21, 51–52, 232n19; land ownership among devadasis and *jogatis*, 7, 35, 47–49, 59, 168, 198; and personhood, 49, 51–53, 56, 158; as unevenly distributed, 26, 43–55, 59, 69–70, 105–6, 231n11; women's, 48–49, 52, 59, 196–97

Laxshmi (devadasi reformer), 90–91, 237n15

Lévi-Strauss, Claude: on gift exchange and kinship, 162–64, 243n8; on sexual economy, 34–35; the structuralist methodology of, 11–12, 193

Lingayats: as devotees of Yellamma, 125, 150; as *pujaris* at Yellamma's temples, 42, 61, 64, 102–3, 128, 146; the sociopolitical prominence of, 46, 54, 55, 226n26, 233n22, 242n4

Mahadevi (rural devadasi): as a devadasi, 1–2, 8, 29, 58, 76, 81, 85, 171–72; and *randi hunnime*, 147–49; on Yellamma's future, 109. *See also* devadasis

Maharastra (State of): anti-caste activism in, 51, 232–33n21, 233n23; brothels in Mumbai (Bombay), 3–4, 90, 167; conflicts of with the State of Karnataka, 88, 224n7; devotees to Yellamma in, 46, 107, 125, 201, 206, 230n7; poverty-related suicides in, 48, 232n17; migration to urban, 47; and sex worker rights organizing, 228n37, 238n25, 240n8; Yellamma temples in, 5, 7, 144, 206

Malinowski, Bronislaw, 162, 216, 230n8

Mahmood, Saba, xi, 16, 18, 213, 217, 222, 246

marriage: cross-cousin and the children of devadasis, 197–99; dedication to a devi as, 2–3, 9, 28, 113–16, 155, 175–76; devadasis vs. *gandullavalu*, 114, 116, 153–56, 166–67, 175; and female respectability, 22, 23, 50, 104–5, 155; and human relatedness, 12–13, 145, 163–64, 192; *kanyadan* vs. *asura*, 158; and legitimacy of children, 146, 158, 161, 167, 184; *pativrata*, 237n19; precolonial nonwife categories, 157; and the production of gender, 184–85, 191, 196–201, 205, 210–11; property and personhood, 158, 174, 192–93, 217; as a relation of obligation, 141, 165–69, 176–77, 192; and rights in labor, 146, 167, 196; shortcomings of conjugal, 83, 128, 174, 194; and the status of women, 13, 114, 158, 175–76; and the value of women, 164–69, 214. *See also gandullavalu*

Matangi: dedications to, 9, 42, 49, 119, 230n7; her sacrifice for Yellamma, 39–44, 65, 121–22, 139, 229–30n3; shrines and temples dedicated to, 105–6, 119–20; worship of with Yellamma, 4, 41–43, 55–57, 78–81, 147–48; as Yellamma's younger sister, 2, 33, 139

matrilineality: Kaula practice, 131–35; marriage practices in systems of, 194,

matrilineality (*continued*)
197, 216, 243n7, 245–46n17; shifts to
patrilineality from, 67, 157–58, 192–
93; and yoginis, 133–34
Mauss, Marcel: on the gift, 12, 34, 162–
63; on sacrifice, 138–39, 241–42n19
modernity: aesthetization of temple
dance, 24, 160, 226n27, 228–29n41;
as against 'backward' tradition, 3–4,
13–17, 21–22, 108–9, 123–25, 226n22;
and construction of Hinduism, 15–16,
115, 129, 235n1; and Dalit impover-
ishment, 45–50, 169, 231n11, 232n17,
238–39n1; and epistemology of truth,
13–14, 16, 69–70, 71–72, 108–9, 221–
22; as erasure, 17–18, 24–25, 69–70,
74–75; and personhood, 13, 27, 51–52,
159, 217, 221–22; the "postcolonial
predicament", 14–15, 94; as progress,
13–14, 115–16, 192–93, 218–20, 228n36;
and reform, 32, 88–89, 92–97, 101–2,
221–22; and the remaking of lifeworlds, 87, 93–94, 219, 225n16; and
social change, 51–52, 68–69, 96, 156,
161, 194. *See also* reformers
moral economy: affliction and the neglect of Yellamma, 73–74, 143; of
prosperity and affliction, 81–84,
150–51; prosperity and devotion to
Yellamma, 81–82, 168–70
Morgan, Lewis Henry, 41, 174, 192–93,
230n6
muttaide hunnime, 128, 146, 150, 153

Nair, Janaki 20, 25, 27, 51–52, 159, 195,
226n23, 227n30, 229n43, 232n16,
nakedness: as ritual, 124, 140; as scandal, 117–18, 123–26
NGOS: and devadasi dedication, 3, 14,
89; Indian Health Organization, 90;
Joint Women's Programme, 89–90,
155; MASS, 93, 96, 98, 102–6; Myrada,
92, 93, 104, 105, 106; SANGRAM/VAMP,
197, 228n37

offering. *See harake*
oracular states, 34, 94, 102, 149, 203

Parashurama: story as told by Dalit *pujaris*, 43–44; beheading of Renuka
Yellamma, 9–11, 64–66, 121–22, 139, 191
patrilineal family: and conjugal matrimony, 22, 114, 159, 166–67; and fall of
autochthonous goddesses, 61, 65, 67,
109, 189–90; as a marker of civilization, 67, 192–93; and land and inheritance rights, 52, 134, 166–67, 196–97,
215; as the norm, 11, 14, 44, 101, 133–34
patronage/patrons: and caste relations,
23–24, 66; of devadasis and *jogatis*, 6–7, 29, 55, 172–74; *jogappas* and,
201–2, 205; and monogamy, 29, 55,
104–6, 156, 167, 239n2; and temple
economies, 20–23, 51–52; on the
wane, 7, 51–52
Periyar, Ramasami, 17, 51, 232–33n21,
239n4, 243–44n9
personhood: and caste and gender
18–19, 23, 26; "dividual", 132–33, 165;
and dedication, 9, 58–59, 70, 198–99,
210–11, 216; and *jade*-cutting, 97–102;
modern, 13, 53, 217, 221–22; in nonwives vs. wives, 156–59, 177; and obligation 58–60, 133, 172–73; and property relations, 42–43, 49–53, 59–60;
and sexuality, 18–19, 27, 114, 116,
158–59, 163; transactional character
of, 129, 133, 164
pollution: and caste hierarchy, 56,
234n25, 242–43n5; livelihoods associated with, 17, 230n5; places of, 42,
56, 23610; sacrifice, birth, and death
as, 139, 144, 150; substances of, 99,
126; *See also* purity; purity and pollution
poverty: and devadasi dedication, 3,
173; of some devadasis, 26, 47, 224n8,
234n26; and farmer suicide, 47- 48,
232n17; intensification of among

Dalits, 48, 169, 231n11, 238–39n1; and land relations, 45, 46, 48–50; as sign of Yellamma's trouble, 142–43, 209; and urban migration, 7, 24, 47

prasada, 84, 87, 119, 150–52

Pre-colonial Indian culture, 20–21, 25, 51–52, 157, 232n19

processions: *bettale seve*, 117–18, 123; death, 204, 209; as rites performed by devotees, 2, 78, 117, 123, 139, 147, 200, 206. *See also* rites

property. *See* inheritance; land rights; women

prostitution: and colonial regulation, 157; and current law, 25; definitions of, 18–19, 22; devadasi dedication as, 3–4, 24, 55, 90, 98, 105, 155–57, 159–60, 175; *dhanda* and *dhandewalis*, 7, 168–70, 201–2; as labor, 106–8, 176, 238n25, 243n13; modern dichotomy between marriage and, 145, 155–61, 174, 227n33; and *randis* (untethered women) 43, 146, 160–61; "sacred prostitution", 127–28, 226–27n29, 240n10, 240–41n13. *See also* sexual economy

puja (rite, worship): local of Yellamma, 5, 61, 84, 209; performed by *jogappas*, 202–4; performed by Lingayat pujaris, 42; preparation of the devi for, 2, 41; for Yellamma at Chandragutti, 117–18. *See also* rites

pujaris: Yellamma's, 170–71, 181–84, 186–87, 190–91; dedication as initiation, 3–4, 73, 202–3, 223n3; duties performed by, 75, 81, 205–6; at Yellamma's temples, 42, 61, 119, 128, 146–47; religious duties of, 7, 9, 79, 81, 85, 148. *See also* devadasis; *jogappas*; *jogatis*

purity: caste, 11, 42, 163, 184, 242–43n5; and modern categories, 22, 161, 193–94, 228n35; and reform, 23, 243n9; and sexual chastity, 11, 14, 43–44,

50–51, 59, 242n1. *See also* pollution; purity and pollution dichotomy

purity and pollution: and caste hierarchy, 56, 152, 184, 234n25, 243–44n9; and discourses of hygiene, 96–99; vs. auspiciousness, 27, 133, 242–43n5. *See also* pollution; purity

randi hunnime: definitions of *randi*, 146, 153; exegesis on, 149–53; and gift relations, 151–52; and reform, 148, 149; and Yellamma's widowhood, 146–49, 150–51

reform/reformers: anti-caste and critique of Hinduism 17, 54, 123; anti-caste and status of women, 23–24, 221–22, 228n36; biomedicalization of religion by, 90, 96, 97, 99, 101–2, 220, 221; Brahmanism as Hinduism, 15–17, 72, 102, 115–16, 129; Christian missionary, 22, 97, 103–4; colonial and modern Western, 16, 21–22, 24–25, 88, 108–9; dairy buffalo project, 106–7; devadasi critiques of, 69–70, 73, 106–7, 125, 170; and devadasis as prostitutes, 24–26, 54–55, 88–89, 156–57, 159–60; use of economic incentives by, 91–93, 103, 106; emancipation projects, 17–18, 69, 90, 124, 140, 141; as erasure, 16–18, 69–70, 74–75; logic of devadasi, 8, 9, 92–94, 99, 100, 105, 156–57, 160–62; programs of the NGO MASS, 70, 93, 96, 98, 102–6, 237n17; use of physical violence by, 92, 98, 122; programs of the NGO Myrada, 92, 93, 104, 105, 106; secular character of, 68–69, 71–74, 225n16, 229n44; self-respect movement, 17, 51, 87, 229n42; and true-false dichotomies, 13–14, 69–73, 108–9, 115–16, 221, 235n1; of Yellamma, 91–92, 96, 102, 104. *See also* Dalit activists; feminists; Indian nationalists; modernity

relatedness: caste and, 244n4; dedication as, 115, 191–92, 210–11, 218;
heterosexuality as real, 12, 145, 163–
64, 192, 232n19, 243n8; human-divine,
66, 115, 132, 140–41, 215; and kinship,
161, 184–85, 195–96, 211; as productive of gender, 12, 195, 210–11. *See also*
gender; kinship
religion: category of, 13–17, 71–74; false
13, 16, 19, 54, 71, 88, 224n6, 235n1;
Hinduism as a modern 15, 72, 104, 115
religiosity: calling the gods, 115, 139–40;
costs of lack of devotion to the devi,
74–75, 150–51, 186, 238n27; devadasi
as world-making, 5, 31–32, 70, 74, 218;
gifts to gods, 34, 83, 115, 136, 138, 143;
gods as present, 66–68, 73, 77–78,
213–14, 217, 219; intermediaries with
gods, 32–33, 59–60; patriarchal gods,
66–67, 189–90; as private devotion,
15, 102, 109, 221–22; propitiating
the gods, 2–3, 4, 61, 82, 86, 149–50;
rewards of devotion to the devi, 73,
81–84, 203–4; true gods and false
gods, 5, 15–17, 108–9, 225n17, 229n44
renunciation: of ordinary family life,
9, 100–101, 102, 202–3; *pativrata*,
98, 237n19; renunciates, 25, 100, 191,
194–95; story of Yellamma's, 190–91.
See also yoginis
rites: the banning of *bettale seve*, 117,
119–20, 122, 123–24; banning of *randi
hunnime*, 148–49; *bettale seve*, 117–18,
122–23, 125, 140, 240n9; to celebrate
auspicious occasions, 79; continuation of banned, 2–3, 115, 148–50,
225n19; dance, 20, 22, 23, 35, 74, 149,
163, 182–84, 200, 226–27n29–31,
238n26; of divination, 84, 85, 87, 143;
Kaula, 130–32; of marriage, 6, 28, 60,
142, 144–45, 155, 181, 243n7; *randi
hunnime* and *muttaide hunnime*, 146–
49; seasonal *phere*, 55; sexuality as an
element of all, 222; as world making,

218. *See also* processions; *puja* (rite,
worship)
Rubin, Gayle: on gender, 185, 226n23;
on sexual economy, 12, 34, 162–66,
243n8

sacrifice: in Christian theology, 138–39;
dedication as, 113–16, 141, 143–44, 187;
kinship as, 34, 114, 133, 140–41, 176–
77; Matangi's bodily as the basis for
kin making, 43, 121–22; as mode of
bodily commitment, 34, 113–14, 116,
122, 139–41; modern Hindu ceremo-
nial, 115, 139–40, 148, 149; Tantric sacrificial practices, 116, 126–28, 134–36,
139
Sanskrit, Sanskritization. *See* Hinduism
Saundatti: K. G. Gurumurthy on, 129;
pilgrimage activities at, 41, 44, 74–75,
86, 128, 146; portrayals of Yellamma
at, 10, 43, 44, 61, 128, 188; Tantric
shakti rites, 128–29, 137, 242n2; and
reform, 44, 64, 74, 91, 93, 109–10,
149; temple trust for, 234–35n32,
237–38n23
secularism/secularity: and configuration of religion, 14–16, 68–69, 101–2,
229n44; and Dalit emancipation,
17–18, 123–24, 140, 226n22; devadasis as unintelligible within, 5, 18, 32,
71–73, 115, 214; and feminist emancipation, 32, 68–69; within Indian
modernity, 13, 21, 26, 51, 59–60,
225n16
sexual citizenship, 9, 11, 12, 13, 176, 215
sexual economy: as an analytic, 18–19,
34–35, 146, 162, 226n23, 243–44n9;
and the caste system, 129, 152, 243–
44n9; of devadasis and dedication,
34–35, 146, 175–77; and sexual agency,
173–77. *See also* prostitution
sexuality: conjugal as regulative, 19, 22,
25, 44, 50–51, 114, 116, 174, 221–22; of
Dalit women politicized, 24, 26–27,

44, 50, 54, 66, 88, 123–26; deployment of, 19, 100, 172–73; of devadasis as illicit, 3–4, 21–26, 51–52, 156, 160–61; and gendered agency, 141, 163–64, 173; and hair symbolism, 33–34, 97–101; heterosexuality and the gendered division of labor, 166–67, 232n19, 243n8; homosexuality, 159, 220, 243n8–9; as inherent to all rites and religions, 22, 35, 222; and materiality, 174–77; purposes of, 12, 15, 19, 114, 184, 219–21; as secret of the self, 18–19, 27, 114, 116, 159, 163; and secularity, 156, 159–61, 214, 218–22; and Tantric tradition, 128–35; uncontained female, 26–27, 62–66, 86, 190–91

sex work/sex workers: on the agency of, 176–77, 238n25, 243n6, 243n13; devadasis as HIV peer educators and urban, 7, 63, 144, 167, 170; estimates of dedicated women working in brothels, 224n8; MSM categories of male, 201; rights, 24–25, 176, 197, 228n37–38

Shaivism: and Shakta religious practices, 21, 42, 99, 127–28; and Tantra, 129–30; Virashaivism, 60, 102, 226n26; Yellamma as the spouse of Shiva, 61. See also Hinduism

Shakta religion (goddess worship): Adishakti, 61, 63, 83, 128; epistemologies of the body within, 34, 75, 86–88, 94, 97, 101–02, 128–29, 137, 139–41, 215, 217; as major strand of Hindu practice, 60–65, 67, 130–31; reform of, 67, 99, 108; shakti, 60, 100, 128, 131, 137, 236n8; as successor to Kaula religious practice, 131; and sisterhood, 39–45, 66–70, 131. See also goddess worship; Hinduism; Tantra; yoginis

Spivak, Gayatri, 32, 176

Sunder Rajan, Rajeswari, 68–69

superstition: as ignorance, 71–74, 90,

96, 101–2, 115–16; and devadasi reform, 3–4, 13–14, 19, 54–55, 96, 98, 109–10, 162, 224n6; as not religion 14, 16–17, 71–72, 88, 90, 108–9, 226n22

symbols: hair rituals as, 98–100; hibiscus flowers as, 119, 120, 137, 203; of *randi hunnime*, 153; sexual symbolism, 27–28, 62–63, 67, 129, 135

Tantra: antinomian qualities of, 126, 240n12; and goddess Kali, 130, 135; influence of on Hinduism, Jainism, and Buddhism, 34, 126–29; Kaula practitioners and rites of, 131–32; scholarly assessments of, 240n10–13; and Shaivism, 130–31; temple at Saundatti, 128; yoginis, 21, 127–28, 129–35. See also Hinduism

temple trusts, 64–65, 102–3, 109–10, 232n19, 234–35n32, 237–38n23

true-false dichotomy: and critique of dedication, 19, 73, 91–92, 221, 224n6; and logic of reform, 13–14, 54, 72–73, 88, 115–16, 221, 235n1, 235n36; as move of power, 16, 73, 108–9, 225n17; and secular nationalism, 69–70, 71–72

turmeric: *bhandara* (Yellamma's), 78–79, 118–19, 126, 143, 153, 204; the distribution of as Yellamma's blessing and cure, 57, 83, 87, 106, 181; as mark of a devi's presence, 64, 85, 94, 187; as offering by devotees to the devi, 80, 81–82; ritual uses of, 118, 143–44, 148, 152, 204, 233–34n24

undress. See *bettale seve*

untouchability. See caste distinction

value: and dedication, 145–46, 158–59, 167–69, 185, 210–11, 235–36n3; of devadasis, 149–52, 173, 176–77, 185, 210, 213–14; of *gandullavalu* vs. devadasis, 50–51, 165–66, 176–77; kinship and exchange as means of conferring,

value (*continued*)
9, 162–66, 175–76; of men in patrilineal societies, 210; transformation
of *navedya* into *prasada*, 84, 150–51;
Vijaisri, Priyadarshini, 228n35–36,
230n4&7, 233n23
violence: as coercive transformation, 92;
marriage and dedication as forms of,
176–77, 191; of reform, 34, 92, 98, 122,
238n25; sex work as, 24, 50, 175–77

women: agency of, 49–52, 68, 108, 141,
164, 173–77, 218; exchanged between
men, 163–67; and kinship as burden, 141, 194–95, 245n11; precolonial
Indian nonwife categories, 157; property rights of, 49–50, 52, 105–6, 158,
174; prostitute vs. wife, 145, 155–61;
as victims, 26, 70, 140–41, 164, 173;
"woman question", 19–20, 26–27,
50–51
world making: devadasi rites as, 5,
31–32, 70, 74, 218; reform as, 18,
69–70, 221

Yamuna (rural devadasi); on being a
devadasi, 57–59, 73–74, 156, 200; on
casteism, 56–57; duties as rural devadasi, 1–2, 29, 77, 83, 209; as head of
household, 58, 170, 196–97; land and
property ownership by, 47, 87, 106–7,
196–97; on marriage to Yellamma,
149–53; and *randi hunnime*, 147–49;
on reform and reformers, 59, 73,
170–71; on *sattipatti muttu* status by,
208–9; on Yellamma's widowhood,
149–51. *See also* devadasis
Yellamma: as Adishakti, 61, 63, 83, 128;
as *amma* devi, 54, 60–61, 83, 85,

191, 236n11; *bhandara* (turmeric) of,
78–79, 119, 126, 143, 153, 204; as consort of Shiva, 63, 68, 128, 191; dioramas and depictions of, 10, 43, 60–62,
187–89, 190–91, 234n28; as embodiment of disruptive power, 42–43,
55–57, 65–66; *harake* by devotees to,
1–2, 75–77, 86, 122, 143, 200; as husband 9, 61–65, 121–22, 190–91; and
jade, 98–101, 186–87, 217; and *jaga*
(basket, world), 7, 32, 39, 56–57, 75,
84; and *kaadaata* (trouble), 74–75,
85–86, 109–10, 142–44, 150–51, 186–
87, 207–8, 214–18; "keeping" her, 4,
32, 73, 75, 82, 87–88; musical instruments of, 2, 74, 75, 87, 92–93, 224n11;
and Parashurama's matricide, 9–11,
43–44, 64–66, 121–22, 139, 191; propitiation of, 2–3, 82, 85–86, 136, 143,
148–51; as *randi* (widow or untethered woman), 146; reform of, 91–92,
96, 102, 104; Renukamba temple at
Chandragutti, 117–22, 125; Sanskritic
vs. vernacular, 60–65, 67, 99, 127–28,
190–91; sisterhood with Matangi,
39–44, 65, 121–22; triumph over buffalo demon Mahishasura, 79–80; and
welfare of households and villages,
60–61, 85, 171–72. *See also darshan*,
goddesses, Shakta
yoginis: as possible precursors to *jogatis*, 21,127–9, 240–41n14; *Kaula*
rites involving, 130–35; kin making
among, 130–31,134; Tantric origins
of, 21, 128. *See also* goddess worship;
Kaula (Kula) practice; renunciation
Young, Katherine, 67, 235n37–38

Zelizer, Viviana, 161–62, 175